THE ABSOLUTE VALUE
OF HUMAN ACTION
IN THE THEOLOGY OF
JUAN LUIS SEGUNDO

Frances Stefano
Seton Hill College
Greensburg, Pennsylvania

UNIVERSITY
PRESS OF
AMERICA

Lanham • New York • London

BX
4705
.S523
S74
1992

Copyright © 1992 by
University Press of America®, Inc.
4720 Boston Way
Lanham, Maryland 20706

3 Henrietta Street
London WC2E 8LU England

Library of Congress Cataloging-in-Publication Data

Stefano, Frances, 1945-
The Absolute Value of Human Action in the Theology
of Juan Luis Segundo / by Frances Stefano.
p. cm.
Includes bibliographical references and index.
1. Segundo, Juan Luis. 2. Praxeology—History—20th century.
I. Title.
BX4705.S523S74 1992 230'.2' 092—dc20 91-36877 CIP

ISBN 0-8191-8511-6 (cloth : alk. paper)

To Man and Jean

Acknowledgments

Grateful acknowledgment is made to the following publishers for permission to reprint material from books by Juan Luis Segundo: Orbis Books, Maryknoll, New York, for permission to reprint material from *Grace and the Human Condition,* trans. John Drury, copyright © 1973; *The Historical Jesus of the Synoptics,* trans. John Drury, copyright © 1985; *The Humanist Christology of Paul,* trans. John Drury, copyright © 1986; *An Evolutionary Approach to Jesus of Nazareth,* trans. John Drury, copyright © 1988 (*The Historical Jesus of the Synoptics* and *The Humanist Christology of Paul* were originally published as *Historía y actualidad: Synópticos y Pablo,* Volume II/1 of *El hombre de hoy ante Jesús de Nazaret,* copyright © 1982 by Ediciones Cristiandad, S.L., Huesca 30-32, Madrid, Spain; *An Evolutionary Approach to Jesus of Nazareth* was originally published as *Lineas actuales de interpretación de Jesús de Nazaret,* Part 4 in Volume II/2 of *El hombre de hoy ante Jesús de Nazaret,* copyright © 1982 by Ediciones Cristiandad, S.L., Huesca 30-32, Madrid, Spain); Sheed and Ward, London, England, for permission to reprint material from *The Historical Jesus of the Synoptics,* trans. John Drury, copyright © 1985; *The Humanist Christology of Paul,* trans. John Drury, copyright © 1986; *An Evolutionary Approach to Jesus of Nazareth,* trans. John Drury, copyright © 1988; CollinsDove*Publishers,* Melbourne, Australia, for permission to reprint material from *The Historical Jesus of the Synoptics,* trans. John Drury, copyright © 1985; Ediciones Carlos Lohlé, Buenos Aires, Argentina, for permission to reprint material from *Grace and the Human Condition,* trans. John Drury (Orbis Books, Maryknoll, New York, copyright © 1973), originally published as *Gracia y condición humana,* copyright © 1968 by Ediciones Carlos Lohlé.

Grateful acknowledgment is made to Juan Luis Segundo for permission to translate into English and reprint brief passages from *Infierno: ¿Futuro o presente?,* unpublished transcript of a parish course (version not edited by the author), 1983.

Parts of Chapters I and II of this book appeared as "The Evolutionary Categories of Juan Luis Segundo's Little-known Theology of Grace" in *Horizons* 19 (1992). Reprinted by permission of the publisher.

TABLE OF CONTENTS

Good News

In the beginning was the Kingdom
Insofar as anything may be said to begin
although it didn't get that name
 to name is to make something real, to bestow,
    to recognize, to bless,
 to inaugurate
until it was given it by Jesus.
 something new.
And the Kingdom was with God.
 It was that for which God's Jesus died.

In the beginning God made love
Insofar as anything may be said of God
although it doesn't get that name
 to make is to do something with someone else,
    to build with others, to create a world,
until it is realized by lovers.
 something to do that never dies.
And the love was with God and was God.
 Nothing is lost that is love that is tried.

The world that never ends
 Is it not the case, my friends, that love evokes a world?
and opens up our eyes
 —those who have ears to hear, let them hear—
is here at hand, you poor!
 let us wake up, arise, rejoice!
Grasp only this.
 The world that's built on love
   comes back to life
 and lives with God forever.

Introductory Remarks

Perhaps to some it might seem backwards, or at least a bit unusual, to address the question of the value of human action with a proclamation of the good news. Yet Jesus did just that. When he was confronted with the problems of people of his time, it was the gratuitous gift of the reign of God and not the necessity of human striving that he preached.[1]

Yet as the gospels show, Jesus did not merely preach. He also acted. His preaching was grounded in *praxis,* commitment to a project in which his disciples were expected to share and for which he tried to prepare them.[2] That project, of course, was the placing at hand of the kingdom of God, to which Jesus gave the best of his energies and on which he spent the whole of his love. For its sake he finally handed over his life. From those who were to be recipients of the kingdom, however, from the poor and from "sinners" with whom he ate, from those whom his parables liberated and his miracles set free, Jesus asked nothing but that they accept the gift of God: "Go and tell John what you have seen and heard: the blind receive their sight, the lame walk, lepers are cleansed, and the deaf hear, the dead are raised up, the poor have good news preached to them" (Lk. 7:22).[3]

Exegetes have shown that Jesus' message and action concerning the reign of God were grounded in an utterly positive and unique relationship of intimacy with God, what Schillebeeckx has called Jesus' Abba-experience.[4] For Segundo, this is a matter of showing that vis-à-vis the synoptic writers at least, Jesus' religious significance is accessible through a look at what Segundo calls the "political key" of Jesus' message and action, for it is the key most faithful to the synoptic data and closest to Jesus' own understanding of his mission.[5] As such it is the key most capable of transmitting what Segundo calls Jesus' revelation of the values of God's heart, i.e., the very content of the gospel revelation concerning God.[6] This means that what Jesus called the kingdom of God must serve as preferred starting point for any theologically reliable interpretation of God.[7] Jesus' experience, in other words, remains a secondary consideration vis-à-vis the primary concern of theology, which must be to interpret what Jesus' kingdom *praxis* has to say about the values dearest to the heart of God.[8]

So far as Segundo is concerned, Jesus' kingdom *praxis* reflects a faith in and experience of God centered on God's priorities, which are concern with what is lost and happiness over its recuperation.[9] Knowledge of the values of God's heart is thus a matter of Jesus' revelation of what God wills for human social persons and their *praxes* on earth. It is a matter of accepting "God's bold preference for those who are suffering," and recognizing "God's joy. . .in rescuing sinners and the poor from the misfortune and marginalization in which they find themselves and in restoring their humanity to them."[10] For Segundo, this is equivalent to saying that the instances of liberation Jesus effected for "sinners" and the poor give sociopolitical concreteness to the religious content of the gospels. In other words, the transcendent referent of religious affirmations, which state that Jesus is definitive revelation of God, neither excludes nor obliterates the particular and relative character of Jesus' down-to-earth kingdom *praxis*. Scandalously, Segundo shows, the fact that the nature of that *praxis* was conflictual and political means that God is partisan. According to Jesus, God is on the side of the marginalized and poor.[11] For Segundo, this means that theological affirmations actually *require* prior recognition of the historical particularities of Jesus' kingdom *praxis* as condition for grounding the reliability of their religious truth. Moreover, it can not be denied that those particularities were clearly political, as in the case, for example, of Jesus' preaching of a 'kingdom' of God which promised happiness to the poor and required the destruction of oppressive religious ideologies by which the powerful interpreted the law against the destitute.[12]

Obviously we people today, disciples of Jesus or not, theists or atheists, are far away in culture and time from the experience that was Jesus'. We are even farther away from the problems of the first-century poor and "sinners" which gave rise to his kingdom *praxis*. Some of us may certainly be followers of Jesus, disciples and friends who believe in his project, share in its work and pray daily for the coming of God's reign. Others of us may be disinterested onlookers, pursuing other projects and following different goals. Still others may be interested questioners, asking what Jesus' message and action about the reign of God has to do with the complexity of social, political and ecological problems to which people of good will must respond at the level of action. For all of us, to whatever category we belong, the significant question is not what the kingdom of God reveals about the experience of Jesus but how its historically relative, culturally conditioned, politically tinged content can matter in the global situation of here and now, with its ambiguities, set-backs and failures, especially given the sense of urgency many people of good will feel today about the need for ameliorative action.[13]

In light of the paralyzing dimensions of evil in our time—what Segundo calls "the whole panorama of human suffering"[14] and what as early as 1917 Walter Rauschenbusch was calling "the bulk of unjust suffering in sight of the modern mind"[15]—the relevance of action and the need to back theological interpretation with a *praxis* of liberation emerge as central concerns. They form the starting point for virtually all theologies of liberation, among them particularly that of Segundo.[16] He moves from the need for action in the face of such problems toward an interpretation of Jesus' news of God's kingdom which makes use of a liberative logic internal to action itself.[17]

In these chapters I will try to follow Segundo's cue. I will ask what action has to do with the values of Jesus' kingdom *praxis* and how disciples' living of life and doing and suffering of love in this world are linked to the coming of God's reign. To what extent does what human beings do and suffer really count? Does action matter not only to the shape of history, society and the ecospheres but to the realization of an eschatological salvation that is said to be "coming down out of heaven from God" (Rev. 21:2)?

Before it will be possible to address these questions, it is necessary to acknowledge the relevance of two important issues. The first has to do with the difficulty of raising such questions in a North American context.[18] Because the importance of context has to do precisely with the shaping of content, it is inseparably bound to the second issue, the need to justify a Jesus-derived eschatological hope. Such justification demands a theological interpretation of what Jesus called the kingdom of God which is capable of coming to persons and groups of good will as a promise from God that is secularly liberative, in other words, as news that is good.

Considering the second of these issues first, we see that it has become a matter of political urgency as well as theological realism to address with hope—based in the message and action of Jesus about the kingdom of God—the growing sense of powerlessness and frustration facing many persons and groups committed to social and ecological justice in North America today. Although written about the situation in Latin America, the following description might easily apply to situations in the North as well:

> We find that we face the task of reconstructing a society from the foundations up, but at a point in time when there seems to be room only for despairing passivity....*Our impression is that we can no longer build anything,* anything of social significance in any case.[19]

What is needed, in other words, is a means—in the case of North America a politically and ecologically relevant one—of justifying a Jesus-derived hope in the definitive value of constructive action for change, precisely in the face of contradictory appearances, particularly when *prima facie* such appearances communicate a sense of the impotence of action against the forces of evil and confront disciples with a sense of seemingly total failure.

Attention to context makes the theological concern to justify hope a good deal more specific. It requires that, unlike Segundo, I raise the question of the worthwhileness of ameliorative action within a North American, so-called "first world" situation. It remains, to be sure, a context marked by the same international structures of domination and dependency, the same social, political and economic patterns of injustice which function to keep Latin American and other so-called "third-world" countries at an impoverished and peripheral level, but it must take its decisive features from a specifically North American experience.[20] For persons and groups who find themselves struggling to come to terms with the complexity of that experience, attention to context means a painful awareness of being located near the center, at the heart of patterns of domination and exploitation which release their most destructive consequences on the poor and marginalized.

Such experience suggests two things. First, insofar as the term *poor* refers concretely to individuals and groups whose victimization is caused by deformed social relations—e.g., classism, racism, nationalism, speciesism, sexism—and insofar as religious legitimations of established structures are in danger of supporting those deformations, solidarity with the poor and marginalized must be made into a hermeneutical category with reference to what Jesus called God's kingdom. No interpretation of the kingdom of God will be valid which permits the marginalized to remain marginalized or to suffer even further deprivation. Second, theologians and other disciples must affirm the positive value of constructive action and the effort to seek liberative solutions to secular problems in spite of the increasing awareness of their own (unavoidable) participation in the same oppressive structures against which the poor and marginalized and all in solidarity with them are struggling.[21]

Faced, for example, with the leveling effects of mass communication and media manipulation, North American theologians and other disciples of liberation must learn to employ kingdom strategies of differentiation in a culture in which distinctions have been blotted out.[22] Similarly, they must learn to speak kingdom dialects of concreteness in a language in which words have been emptied of their meanings.[23] This means that theologians and other disciples must shoulder the task—which is really a never completely solvable dilemma—of interpreting Jesus' kingdom values in categories conditioned by a language and culture aligned more visibly with the causes of injustice than with action against its consequences.[24] In the face of worn-out ideologies of freedom, e.g., conceptions of democracy and human rights which no longer serve to liberate but add to enslavement, theologians must find ways to retrieve liberty and justice as meaningful kingdom values and release their liberative power for political and ecological change.[25] That tasks like these need to be done is part of the rationale of these reflections.[26] In the following chapters I want to suggest that Segundo's insistence on the secular relevance of what Jesus called the kingdom of God provides a contextually relevant lever for moving aside some of the North American obstacles to making a theological interpretation of the values of God's heart that is hope-giving and prophetic—i.e., capable of coming to North Americans of good will as news that is good from God.

A first obstacle is the astonishing lack of attention by many political and liberationist theologians to the subject of ecology.[27] Attempts to overcome this gap of course already exist, but by comparison with Segundo's work many of them seem incomplete from the point of view of an adequately developed anthropological-ontological-hermeneutical base.[28] Such a base must deal with the constructive dimensions of human freedom from the point of view not only of its sociopolitical relevance but of its ecological responsibilities. It will succeed only to the extent that, thanks to its categories and the capacity they have for addressing the complexity of reality, disciples of Jesus become aware of having to speak and act on behalf of Jesus' kingdom values in a culture large segments of which have been placed at the service of high-speed, high-efficiency technologies with increasingly short-term benefits.[29] The questions raised by these technologies and their hidden values bring new demands to a constructive theological interpretation of human action and challenge the meaningfulness of the doctrine of grace.[30] They face North American theologians with the task of showing that freedom is not only personal and social but ecological, and that theological interpretation of the values of God must have something directly to do with the quality of life not only of oppressed human beings but of all living beings on earth.

　　Yet because the gospels show that Jesus proclaimed the kingdom of God as sheer gift, a North American liberationist theology must also overcome a second, more traditional obstacle. It must speak about the gratuitous character of God's eschatological salvation, but it must interpret it in a way that neither collapses eschatology into history and nature nor makes it superfluous to the problems of the world. On the one hand, eschatological salvation must not be reduced to intramundane liberation, but on the other, neither must it threaten to co-opt secular existence by depriving the earthly realm of what many people of good will today consider to be its own inherent value. Like its Latin American counterpart, a North American theology of liberation must determine whether a "secular" starting point like the logic of action does not conflict with the transcendence of God and the gratuitous nature of salvation implied, for example, by the prayer of Jesus which sets the tone for chapter one of these reflections: "Your kingdom come." Is not the realization of the eschaton the work properly of God? According to the message and action of Jesus, is it not the case that the kingdom of God occurs gratuitously as gift? Does not the notion of gratuitous salvation rule out talk of liberative efficacy and human causality on earth? As will be seen, I believe it does not. Although seemingly opposed, the two are actually one. What is first of all God's gift is ultimately a human task.[31] That is because, theologically speaking, the nexus of gift and task is the doctrine of cooperative grace.[32] According to that doctrine, human achievement and divine gratuity must never be placed in competition; the freedom of God and the freedom of human social persons must never be permitted to appear in theology as mutually exclusive or opposed.[33] On the contrary, precisely at their point of closest communication—action that is graced—the two freedoms must be permitted to remain autonomous and distinct.

　　That last point, of course, has become a fairly elementary component of a doctrine of cooperative grace.[34] Yet as Rahner has pointed out, it is only a first step. A second is to show how it is anthropologically, ontologically and hermeneutically appropriate that the gift of God be understood as task.[35] Because grace takes place in the social and public realm, it is necessary to show how God's offer of eschatological salvation affects the structures and institutions of history and society with all the complexities and ambiguities they entail.[36] Similarly, it is necessary to show how grace relates God's eschatological promise of definitive victory over evil to actual evils afflicting history, society and nature now, for theological consciousness in North America today is marked not only by post-Enlightenment epistemological problems like cultural relativity and modern historical consciousness but by looming ethical dilemmas and large-scale social and ecological ills. The theology of grace thus demands a coming to grips with the value of action aimed at the overcoming of evils here on earth.[37] As the following chapters will attempt to show, such a theology of grace demands a new philosophical base. It requires an anthropology, ontology and hermeneutics that are constitutively eschatological—i.e., a story of the relation between God and the world that is capable of making the definitive eschatological completion promised by God an integral but gratuitous element of creative action in the universe of the present.[38]

Already in the gospels, the link between the definitiveness of God's salvation and liberation from earthly evils shows up with dramatic force. In those narratives it seems that Jesus' project of effecting the kingdom of God, of making it actively present and placing it operationally at hand, is a profoundly social and historical one. As was mentioned above, Segundo argues that Jesus' life and mission, and even the meaning attributed to his death, can be adequately interpreted only by taking into account the "political key" employed by the historical Jesus of the synoptics.[39] In these gospels we learn that Jesus understood both his mission and the meaning of God's salvation in terms of actual liberations from concretely observable ills. Jesus healed the sick and delivered people from demons. He sat at table with outcasts and sinners and conversed with them seriously about God. In the beatitudes and parables and in much of his own and his disciples' activity Jesus overturned not merely the tables of the moneychangers but also the world of established religious values. He proclaimed that the sabbath was made for us humans and not we for the sabbath,[40] that religious observance without love of neighbor is flatter than savorless salt, that a theology that credits itself with possessing signs from heaven while ignoring the signs of the times on earth is a theology that supports the privileges of the powerful, blasphemes the grace of God and diverts God's power to ideologically self-serving ends.

Scandalously, Jesus was considered a drunkard and glutton by many of his peers and thought to be mad by members of his family. His following included not only a motley crew of fishermen, tax collectors and ex-Zealots but also a considerable band of women, some of whom were numbered among his dearest friends and most significant disciples (and were often denounced by the dominant ideologies as "sinners").[41] He announced God's year of favor to the poor and proclaimed a jubilee by which in the eyes of God all accumulated privilege was reduced to nothing, any thought of religious credit was wiped out and all persons of good will were granted equal access to, and could drink their fill from, the springs of God's salvation. Jesus even took time to converse with children and pay attention to their needs. As scandalous as it might appear to those seeking to make the kingdom of God an other-worldly, purely religious affair, Jesus immersed God in the everyday business of this world and made salvation a matter of release from secular evils.[42] It cannot be denied that in every liberation of "sinners" and the poor, there occurs what Jesus calls salvation, the gratuitous effect in the here and now of God's eschatological victory over evil.[43]

INTERPRETING THE GOOD NEWS OF WHAT JESUS CALLED GOD'S KINGDOM IN LIGHT OF A LOGIC OF ACTION

Given what the gospel data reveal, it is clear that the goal of these reflections can be met only by situating the question of human action within the broader context of a theology of history and nature. To do that, I will assume with Segundo and the historical Jesus that earth and the eschaton are not discontinuous but radically connected, and I will ask what it is that connects them. On what does the intersection of salvation and liberation hinge, and how can it be described? In the context of Segundo's liberationist-evolutionary ontology and against the background of the social and ecological complexities of our time, I will attempt to answer this question by showing that the substance of the intersection is action.

I will try to do this by pointing out first that an anthropological, ontological and hermeneutical map of the logic of action is a helpful key for opening up the significance of what Jesus called the kingdom of God and theologians call grace. The charting of these theologically inseparable "presuppositional zones" will be the subject matter of chapters one, two and three, respectively. Second, I want to show that the value of action when it embodies self-transcending love is synonymous with what poets and prophets from the biblical traditions both preceding and following Jesus have called the glory of God. The understanding of that symbol as gratuitous, definitive and conjoint realization of the impassioned love that is grace will be the topic of chapter four.

To accomplish these tasks in a way that makes use of the originality of Segundo's contribution implies taking several preliminary steps. First, it will be necessary to map Segundo's account of the logic of human action.[44] That means laying out the coordinates of its anthropological structure in light of grace (chapter one), seeing how they overlap with the ontological complexity and ecological density of freedom in light of evil and guilt (chapter two) and addressing the ethical question of their truth-criterion in light of action's intrinsically hermeneutical task (chapter three). Discussion of these points will try to show that, like Blondel, Segundo believes it is the complexity involved in our willing which makes us human and articulates the structure of reality.[45] For Segundo, the key to action lies in the destiny freedom receives from its own *modus operandi,* and it is that destiny which he believes both sheds light upon and is illuminated by the logic of action itself. At an underlying level, the guiding questions of this first part of the discussion will therefore be: what is human freedom for? How is it put together and what is it trying to accomplish? Above all, what does it mean, not only for disciples' destinies and that of the world, but for the meaning of history and nature as a whole and for the relation of the cosmos to God?

Second, it will be necessary to consider the logic of action in relation to the traditional religious doctrines of creation and redemption. The first points to the transcendence and sovereignty of God, and the second to the gratuitous character of eschatological salvation. Dealing with these means addressing the fundamental question of the efficacy of grace. On the one hand, given the difference which must remain between God and creatures, what is the point of the impassioned, gratuitous and evil-abhorring love that is the essence of God's grace? What, in other words, does grace do for us creatures, and what does it say about God who wills to love us absolutely and unalterably even before we are born? On the other hand, given what the message and action of Jesus reveal about the gratuity of God's kingdom liberation, to whom does the task of salvation belong? To whom pertains definitive liberation and to whom the creation of the eschatologically new? Does salvation refer solely to an eschatological reality in heaven or is it equally a matter of historical, societal and ecological accomplishment on earth? Does it depend more on the freedom of God or on the freedom of human social persons? Can it not depend entirely on both? Can our historically relative thoughts and deeds, the strivings of our earthly projects, produce for God something of lasting value? Can one remain a theist and yet insist that human action has definitive eschatological efficacy and absolute value in the eyes of God?

As will be seen, these questions articulate the sociopolitical and ecological dimensions of a theology of cooperative grace. They take the discussion not only back to the cluster of early controversies over the divine and human freedoms but into the thicket of philosophical and cosmological issues surrounding the question of the relation of God to the world.[46] They go to the heart of the Reformation disputes and make it necessary to reconsider seemingly peripheral questions like the value of Trent's doctrine of merit and the implications of Luther's *sola Dei gloria*. Finally, they make it necessary to ask whether the eschatological efficacy of grace, essentially a matter of God's promise of definitive salvation, must be considered not in relation to the overcoming of creaturely finitude—an outcome neither necessary nor desirable—but with respect to the everlasting value of constructive projects in history and nature now.

Only after addressing these preliminary issues will it be possible in the final chapter to make a theological interpretation of what Jesus called God's kingdom that is capable of coming to North American disciples of good will, and by extension to people of good will everywhere, as truly good news. This will be attempted in light of what I believe constitutes Segundo's major contribution to the theology of grace:

the notion that in relation to the eschaton, graced human action exercises an ontologically creative causality.[47] Not only do we human social persons depend on God, but God depends on us. We need grace in order that freedom be liberated to act in a way that is eschatologically valid, but God needs human freedom—in the form of liberated and liberative action—if grace is to be made at all efficacious in a universe subjected to the apparent futility of evil, sin and death.

As will be seen in the course of these reflections, the attempt to make such a down-to-earth theological interpretation of grace—which is really an effort to articulate the theological implications of Segundo's evolutionary ontology—makes it necessary to speak of grace as a project. This entails developing two basic assumptions: that grace is a reciprocally gratuitous companionship in love, and that it is a conjoint, productive making. It is not a state but an action. As theological reflection on the relation between God and creatures, the doctrine of grace is not a statement about human beings as objects of God's love but an affirmation of the gratuitous bond God forms with them as co-equal participants in a world-creative task, emphasis falling not on the nature of the lovers but on the mutually shared objective of their loving.

By speaking of grace this way, I want to build on Segundo's anthropology, ontology and hermeneutics of freedom to show not only *that* it is possible to make a project-centered interpretation of grace but also *how* such an interpretation can situate the logic of human action, already valid on earth, within the gratuitous setting of the action of God in heaven.[48] In other words, I want to show how Segundo's approach affirms the absolute value of human action without devaluing the transcendent and sovereign character of the action of God. At the same time, I want to direct the action of both God and human beings outward toward the world, insofar as in the end it is the objective value of the finished product—a conjointly fashioned world— and not the fact of the God-human relation which supplies grace with a fitting and worthwhile objective.[49]

Emphasis on the objective of grace will have the effect of directing these chapters as a whole toward the question of rationale: *why* is a shift in the language of grace of practical theological interest today? In attempting to address this question, I will draw out the eschatological relevance of Segundo's claim that freedom, whether of God or creatures, can make sense only in the context of a universe in which the definitive completion of creation is a task still needing to be done. In this way I will attend to the cosmic referent the doctrine of grace must have today if a Jesus-normed eschatology is to attribute meaning and value not only to the secularity of culture and the sociopolitical problems of human beings in history but to the ecological density and evolutionary complexity of the cosmos, or nature, as a whole.[50]

In attempting to map the coordinates of action in grace, I will suggest that in a universe in which the creation of the world is a project still suffering to be realized, an accomplishment still groaning to be made complete, a work still needing in each generation to be done painstakingly "by hand," it is necessary to translate the language of grace into a language of eschatology, and it is necessary to give the resulting idiom an explicitly "cosmocentric" accent.[51] That is because God's impassioned love involves human freedom in a love-building project aimed not at the attainment of a distant happiness pertaining to God and human beings alone but at the creation of a finally completed world that, in the end, both God and creatures will be able to pronounce definitively good and find everlastingly worthwhile and inhabitable.[52]

AN INITIAL CLARIFICATION ABOUT THE MEANING OF THE WORD *ACTION*

As the argument of the following chapters unfolds, it will become apparent that action is not synonymous with activity alone but includes the whole spectrum of thinking and willing, knowing and acting, being and doing. It involves negativity, passivity, suffering and endurance as well as positivity, activity and accomplishment. At one and the same time it is a doing and an undergoing, a making and a being made, an individual yet sociopolitical affair. Most importantly, it can be adequately understood only in connection with the objective givenness of reality, to which the projective character of action must ultimately conform, by which it is conditioned and facilitated, and in relation to which it has a creative responsibility.[53]

Action is thus extremely complex, yet it remains the most familiar and immediately accessible datum of experience by which to assess the meaning and value of life. It is the key to making sense of the human condition, the medium of the realization of knowledge and values and the source of worthwhileness in a seemingly futile universe. For the purposes of this discussion, action is thus a viable theological synonym for the structure of human existence. It is the expression of a limited yet not predetermined freedom which keeps us faithful to what we are, allows us to go after what we value, and manifests the path of *praxis,* with its actual objective content, by which we attempt to join what is and what ought to be in the living of our lives.

A FEW REMARKS CONCERNING METHOD

Although the structure of these reflections consists in these introductory remarks plus four main chapters, the logic of the chapters themselves creates an ascending schema of only three distinguishable "moves." More in the fashion of multiplication than addition, each of these is intended to incorporate the previous ones in a way that does not follow a lineal progression but rather increases the significance of what went before by placing it in a clarifying context.

The first of these "moves" comprises chapters one and two, which, taken together, form the two sides of a single theoretical analysis of the logic of human action. The task of that analysis is to come to grips with the anthroplogical logic and ontological complexity of action in a universe subjected to the apparent futility of evil and sin and yet graced with the love of God.

The second "move" occurs in chapter three. It is concerned with determining action's criterion for the making and doing of truth. The objective is to make a practical response to the question posed by the analyses which preceded, namely, given the nature of human action—its anthropological logic and ontological structure in light of the data of grace and sin—what are we human social persons to do? The point is to show that by its own intrinsic logic, which tends to address this question at the ethical level of everyday *praxis,* action poses for itself a constitutively hermeneutical task.

The third and final "move" is made in chapter four, which is intended to recapitulate the three preceding chapters and raise them to the level of conclusion. Given the anthropological logic of action and the ontological complexity of its structure, and given the fact that, in light of those, action poses for itself a constitutively hermeneutical task, what can be said, from a theological point of view, about action's definitive value? The posing of this question in light of the logic which precedes it (and not just "on its own") has the effect, almost, of creating a reversal of direction: where the previous "moves" are concerned with saying a theologically intelligible *human* word about what makes the good news good, the final move is concerned with saying an anthropologically intelligible word *from God* about what makes the good news news. It is the making of such a logical "reversal" which I believe permits the final chapter to articulate a reasoned cause for hope.[54]

In the course of these reflections, I will be treating the entire corpus of Segundo's published work from 1948 to 1988 as well as a selection of unpublished manuscripts. Since I will be dealing with his work as a whole, I will attempt to focus on key ideas rather than the making of textual analyses. In this way I will try to maintain a creative fidelity to the spirit of Segundo's work.

Such an approach can be justified by the high degree of internal consistency in Segundo's theology. His originary insight—embodied, I believe in the title of these reflections—has remained constant from the days of the *Berdiaeff* study until the present. Yet while the major theses have remained unchanged, the expressions of them have become more concrete and the categories have been elaborated in increasingly refined fashion over the course of time. Thus although I will be treating his theology as a whole, I will indicate where and in what manner various elements have undergone deepening or change. Finally, an attempt to situate Segundo's project in a critically constructive way within the relevant theological traditions will be made throughout rather than being located in a single place.

NOTES

[1] As Segundo points out, Jesus placed no conditions or prerequisites on the salvation he offered to those whose sufferings he cured (*HJS,* pp. 136-140).

[2] *HJS,* pp. 134-149. Segundo argues that "Jesus. . .associates his disciples with the religio-political task of unmasking the mechanisms of ideological oppression, giving them an assignment as hazardous as his own" (*ibid.,* p. 139). See also *RC,* pp. 103-109 and p. 128.

[3] Segundo believes that in the gospels, the kingdom of God can be accepted as gift only by those who have nothing to lose by accepting it. These are the poor and marginalized. They appear in the gospels as "sinners," i.e., public failures and social outcasts, persons and groups located at the bottom of a hierarchy constructed and maintained in the name of "God" by religio-political ideologies of the time. To groups who stood to gain by religious legitimations of established social structures, Jesus' announcement of the reign of God was surrounded by ambiguity. It could either be welcomed as opportunity for conversion or *metanoia,* or else be rejected as a curse (*HJS,* pp. 119-133).

[4] *Jesus: An Experiment in Christology* (New York: Seabury, 1979), pp. 256-259. Although Segundo does not explicitly discuss Jesus' experience of God, his interpretation of Jesus' message and action does not rule out the relevance of such discussion. It does, however, make Jesus' secular relevance—what Segundo calls Jesus' significance for human beings—of primary importance in Segundo's work (*HJS,* pp. 16-17; p. 21, and p. 32).

[5] *HJS,* p. 104; see also pp. 71-85 and pp. 178-188. As will be seen in the following chapters, Segundo maintains that the political key is one key among others. If it is to be helpful in unlocking Jesus' significance for people struggling against the powers of evil today (and against discouragement at evil's success), the political key must be completed and balanced by the anthropological key of Paul (which Segundo derives from an analysis of Romans 1-8) and by interpretive keys coming from the signs of our own times.

[6] *HJS,* p. 102, pp. 109-110, p. 123 and pp. 130-133.

[7] *RC,* pp. 60-61 and 70-72.

xxii THE ABSOLUTE VALUE OF HUMAN ACTION

[8] As will be seen in chapter three, the effect of Segundo's approach is to make God (God's love and values vis-à-vis the problems and sufferings of creatures on earth) and not the person of Jesus *per se* the center of theological concern. See, for example, *HJS*, pp. 130-133.

[9] See *RC*, p. 86. As will be seen in chapter three, Segundo shows that the heart of God is accessible particularly through Jesus' parables and beatitudes (*HJS*, pp. 104-133).

[10] *HJS*, p. 124.

[11] *Ibid.*, pp. 91 and 107.

[12] See *RC*, p. 61. What Segundo is getting at is that particularity is not a negation of transcendent truth but, under the conditions of refractedness and relativity in nature and history, provides truth's only mode of access and expression. See *EAJN*, pp. 91-92 and preceding. This principle is fundamental to Segundo's theology. As will be seen in the first three chapters, it is especially relevant to the logic of faiths and ideologies.

[13] This is not to suggest that the question of Jesus' identity is irrelevant to people and problems today. It is simply to remind those of us who want to be disciples that in our time such a question no longer constitutes the optimal starting-point for theological interpretation of his significance. This change of focus can be justified by appealing to the universal character of salvation and the gratuitous character of grace. Thanks to grace's being everywhere, any and every action done in self-transcending love, regardless of its connection or lack of connection with religious affirmations about Jesus, is action serving the interests of salvation; yet from the perspective of the utter gratuitousness of God's love, this is true only "negatively" or "indirectly," by reason of the fact that self-transcending love, whatever its intramundane source, does not work *against* the values of God's heart: "The one who is not against you is for you" (Mk. 9: 40; Lk. 9: 50). Non-religious persons and groups whose action is self-transcending love are thus viewed theologically as living utterly valid lives in their own right, without having to be linked to God either explicitly or implicitly by a relation of religious faith. In other words, persons and groups who are not disciples and who practice self-transcending love are neither opposed to the liberative interests of God nor required to accept a word of revelation about God. They are simply free to be themselves.

[14] *HCP*, p. 149.

[15] *A Theology for the Social Gospel* (Nashville: Abingdon, 1979), p. 181. Rauschenbusch was convinced of the relevance of using the kingdom of God as hermeneutical key to unlock the social meaning of the gospel message. In creating a theology for the social gospel, he anticipated the spirit of Segundo's interest in the liberative significance of action: "No theories about...the Kingdom of God are likely to be valuable or true which paralyze or postpone redemptive action [i.e., action that is liberative] on our part" (Rauschenbusch, p. 141).

[16] From the beginning, action has been central to Segundo's theology. His earliest theological work, *Función de la Iglesia en la realidad rioplatense* (Montevideo: Barreiro y Ramos, 1962), is an analysis of the conflicting pastoral practices in the Plate River area and the differing theologies which ground them. The main argument in this book is that the theology most faithful to the message and action of the historical Jesus is concerned not with religious attitudes but with love—i.e., effective action in history for the liberation of the neighbor from evils (pp. 30-35). For Segundo, love of neighbor is constitutively social and political, hence the importance of the term *realidad* in the book's title.

[17] Here I write "a" rather than "the" because it seems that there might be a variety of ways to conceptualize the logic of action. A viable alternative to Segundo's approach occurs, for example, in the notion of negative contrast experience in the work of Edward Schillebeeckx. See *Christ: The Experience of Jesus as Lord* (New York: Crossroad, 1980), pp. 817-821.

[18] Essential to the notion of context is the attempt to specify the problems the situation poses, since they provide the living framework of questions, both religious and ethical, within which theologians and other disciples of Jesus must try to articulate a reasoned and morally justifiable response of Jesus-normed faith. On the need to liberate theological interpretation from an a-contextuality that is ideologically oppressive and ethically problematic vis-à-vis the common human struggle to find liberative solutions to problems of the world, see *LT*, pp. 7-38 and pp. 97-124.

[19] *FI*, p. 305 (italics mine).

[20] Actually, of course, there exists no "North American experience." One is a citizen of either Canada or the United States. Within each country are countless varieties of experience depending in part on factors such as geographic location, socioeconomic status, ethnic origins, color, sex, creed, background, education, political affiliation and so on. But precisely because culture is not a monolithic entity but a complex mixture of strands and trends, some of the strands that are countervailing with respect to other dominating ones can be placed in mutually productive contact with the liberative significance of Jesus' kingdom values. This can be accomplished through the *praxis* of disciples and, as chapter three will show, is a major benefit of attending to the specificity of context.

[21] As will be seen in the following chapters, this second observation has a methodological significance: in a world in which sin is social and ecological rather than simply individual, there can be no monopoly on either goodness or truth.

[22] Although Segundo believes that Jesus' fundamental kingdom strategy was political and conflictive (*RC*, pp. 110-114; *HJS*, pp. 91-95), he refrains from advocating either simplistic separatism or manichæan opposition-making as norms for disciples' *praxis* (*HCP*, pp. 170-171). Rather, he shows that what Jesus aimed at, for example in the beatitudes, was the making of theological differentiations, i.e., the drawing of distinctions between liberative and oppressive relationships and structures,

precisely in order to bring to light the values at their roots. Segundo shows that the oppressive values Jesus unmasked (and named abhorrent to God's heart) were precisely those which the dominant ideologies of the time claimed were sanctioned on earth by "God." What Jesus denounced was the injustice which resulted from such ideologies, for it served to hide from "sinners" and the poor the good news of the true—and liberative—character of God's salvific love, especially God's impassioned commitment to those excluded, peripheralized, martyred and despised in the name of an alleged will of "God." As will be seen in n. 25 below, the theological urgency connected with the unmasking of oppressive ideologies is prophetic. It directly corresponds to the need to work at rehabilitating originary cultural and religious symbols, so as to release the liberative power of founding values that have been co-opted in the service of unjust structures. The aversion of dominant ideologies to the conflictual character of prophetic *praxis* is of course an argument for its theological necessity, and the legitimation of that aversion by dominant ideologies' continual co-opting of originary symbols, precisely for the purposes of obliterating prophetic critique, can be illustrated by an example from our times. On July 4, 1986, Americans celebrated "Liberty Weekend," the unveiling of the renovated Statue of Liberty and observance of the national holiday. In a speech at this event, President Ronald Reagan managed not to find it incongruous with the values of the nation's founders to condemn what he called "conflictive politics"—specifically of a kind that would oppose his days-earlier campaign to secure 100 million dollars in aid to *Contras* fighting the Nicaraguan government. Calling for a "national harmony" aimed at blotting out political differences, he presented as paradigm a (sentimentalized) account of how, in the name of "friendship," John Adams was allegedly able to rise above political differences with Thomas Jefferson (ABC, live coverage, New York Harbor, July 4, 1986).

23 For an account by an American linguistics scholar of systematic attempts by the U.S. government to empty words of their meanings, see Noam Chomsky, *Turning the Tide: The U.S. and Latin America* (Montreal: Black Rose Books, 1986). See also Penny Lernoux, *Cry of the People* (New York: Penguin Books, 1982), especially pp. 471-473, where Lernoux presents an outline of a Pentagon course entitled "Utilization and Containment of Rumors." Given the situation of contradiction, confusion and, ultimately, meaninglessness which accompanies the emptying of language, it is clear that, as Segundo points out, "the effort to transform language is a political act. . . .[For example], giving full, coherent expression to Paul's statement about oneness in Jesus Christ is such a political act: 'There is no longer Jew nor Greek, slave nor free, male nor female, for you are all one in Christ Jesus' (Gal. 3: 28)" (*HCP*, p. 180).

24 By no means is this to suggest that North Americans may be regarded in a simplistic way as the sole cause of social and ecological sin. Nor is it to say that it is not possible within a Northern context either to suffer oppression or, in face of the

apparently definitive power of evil and sin over cultural instruments like language and social structures, to find new ways of speaking and acting vis-à-vis the definitive efficacy of a Jesus-derived eschatological hope. On the contrary, it is only to point out the complexity of the tasks with which North American liberationists must increasingly learn to deal.

[25] In the United States, for example, in the face of an originally liberative impulse—the ideal of liberty and justice for all—betrayed by political ideologies of national supremacy, economic self-interest or self-righteous patriotism, it has become imperative for American liberationist theologians to retrieve the liberative potential of the founding rhetoric of freedom through strategies like those described in nn. 22 and 23 above. On the importance of this task for American theologians, see "Letter of Rosemary Ruether," in *Theology in the Americas,* Sergio Torres and John Eagleson, eds. (Maryknoll, N.Y.: Orbis, 1976), p. 85.

[26] Learning to make exactly such a liberative-hermeneutical prophetic theology is ultimately the point of Segundo's creative attempt in *JNYT* to study the trajectory of interpretive keys—from the synoptics', through Paul's, to Chalcedon's and Ignatius', to an ecological-evolutionary liberationist preunderstanding that is operative in the dominant culture today—by which theologians have continued to make successive contextual "renditions" of Jesus' significance. As Segundo shows in these volumes, each of those keys derives in one way or another from the originality of Jesus' own religio-political interpretation of the "at-handness" of the kingdom of God to "sinners" and the poor (Jesus' preferred theological symbol). From Segundo's point of view, such learning is equivalent to the liberation of theology. It is effected not for its own sake, but for the sake of allowing Jesus' good news of God's eschatological promise of definitive salvation to reach the poor and marginalized of the earth. This is the point of *LT* in its entirety, spelled out in capsule form on pp. 7-38 and made concrete in the volumes of *JNYT.*

[27] Segundo is unique among Latin American liberation theologians inasmuch as he attempts to incorporate the findings of ecological science into the anthropological base of a liberationist theology and links ecological principles with the sociopolitical context of the Latin American continent. See, for example, *FI,* chapters 10, 11 and 12. For Segundo, ecological problems are the result of the invasion of nature by an overdose of human purposiveness, to the exclusion of values like wisdom, love and humility. The latter establish relations of respect for and gratitude to natural processes (*EAJN,* p. 40 and p. 129, n. 64). They result in the use of appropriately scaled means and lead to sensitivity and flexibility in the effort to elicit change. While the more helpful dimensions of Segundo's ecological anthropology will be examined in chapters one and two, it must be admitted at the outset that Segundo's interest in ecology remains centered on the application of ecological wisdom and flexibility to the spheres of politics and society in a way almost exclusively concerned with the interests of human liberation (see *EAJN,* pp. 10-14 and *HCP,* pp. 161-182). While

he does not rule out explicitly ecological concerns but constructs an evolutionary ontology capable of supporting them, he does not address ecological issues as such. And he does not hesitate to suggest that insofar as North American motives for doing so often stem from economic and political self-interest, ecological concerns are secondary to the struggle for human liberation (*FI*, p. 260; *EAJN*, p. 14).

28 Four notable examples of ecologically conscientized theologies are James Gustafson's *Ethics from a Theocentric Perspective* (Chicago: University of Chicago Press, 1981); Charles Birch's and John B. Cobb's *The Liberation of Life from the Cell to the Community* (Cambridge: Cambridge University Press, 1984); Rosemary Radford Ruether's *Sexism and God-Talk* (Boston: Beacon Press, 1983); and Jürgen Moltmann's *God in Creation* (San Francisco: Harper and Row, 1985). A less theological example may be found in "Thomas Berry: A Special Section," *Cross Currents* 37 (Summer/Fall, 1987), pp. 179-239.

29 What makes such technologies objectionable, of course, is not that they are technologies but that they surrender long-term benefits to short-term efficiencies which deal out profit to a few but death and destruction to the many.

30 For a point of view which points to the ease with which religious symbols can be co-opted for socially divisive, ecologically destructive purposes, see Farley Mowat, *A Whale for the Killing*, (Toronto: Bantam/Seal Books, 1972). Describing human beings as "the planet's most accomplished killers" (p. 36), Mowat records the words of a 76 year-old Newfoundlander: "Dey [technologists, industrialists and modern people in general] got to tinker wit' *every* goddam t'ing dere is. . .and everyt'ing dey tinkers wit' goes wrong! . . .Dey says dey's makin' a heaven on dis eart' for we. But de troot onto it is, dey's headin' dereselves and all of we for hell, in a hoopin hurry-all. Smart? Oh yiss, dey do believe dey's de smartest t'ings God put on dis old eart' . . . dem politicians and dem scientists, and all dem fine, big-moneyed fellows. But I'm tellin' ye, byes, de codfish and de caribou, dey's ten t'ousan' times smarter in de head. *Dey* got de sense to lave well enough be. *Dey'll* niver blow up de world; no, nor pizzin us all to deat' . . . Bejasus, byes, I t'ink de healt's gone right out of we!" (p. 21; italics Mowat's).

31 This principle is fundamental to an understanding of cooperative grace from the point of view of modern historical consciousness. See Karl Rahner, "The Order of Redemption within the Order of Creation" in *The Christian Commitment* (New York: Sheed and Ward, 1963), pp. 38-74: "The unity of the world of nature and of grace. . .has its history. It is a unity which is to be realized; its achievement is a task entrusted to [human beings]" (p. 53; inclusive language substituted).

32 For Segundo, this principle conveys the underlying meaning of the teaching of Trent that grace involves two dimensions, namely the gift of the Spirit and the cooperative response of the recipient. This makes the work of grace depend totally on the initiative of God and totally on the human response (*RC*, p. 246).

[33] As Segundo illustrated early in his career (*Berdiaeff*, pp. 95-128), neither ought they to be opposed at the level of the philosophical presuppositions which provide theology with categories for the communication of revealed data.

[34] The fundamental importance of this doctrine, developed at length in Catholic theology by Rahner, is set forth with clarity in a contemporary liberationist context by Roger Haight, *The Experience and Language of Grace* (New York: Paulist Press, 1979). See especially the recapitulative summary statement on p. 183.

[35] Rahner, "Redemption within Creation," pp. 53-57.

[36] For a constructive discussion of the public dimension of grace and its implications in a liberationist context, see Roger Haight, "Grace and Liberation: An Interpretation of History," *The Thomist* 42 (October, 1978) pp. 539-581. (This essay forms chapter eight and part of chapter seven of the work cited in n. 34 above.)

[37] This demand involves a corollary central to Segundo's work. Just as grace rules out competition between the freedom of God and the freedom of human social persons, so the salvation announced and effected in Jesus' kingdom *praxis* rules out competition between "temporal," "earthly" or "secular" concerns and "eternal," "heavenly" or "sacred" ones (*TC*, p. 71). Action aimed at religious or "spiritual" effectiveness must never be placed in opposition to action aimed at temporal or "material" efficacy. Action pertaining to eschatological salvation can not be placed in competition with action pertaining to history and nature as if dedication to one sphere somehow obliterates the validity of the other.

[38] The categories for accomplishing such a task, virtually synonymous for Segundo with a critically defined philosophy of freedom, were already developed in preliminary form as early as 1963 in his doctoral thesis on the philosophy of Berdyaev. Unlike Berdyaev, whose latent Gnosticism (and a view of objective reality as enslaving) tends to sever the philosophy of freedom from the philosophy of being (*Berdiaeff*, pp. 402-403), Segundo attempts to construct a philosophy of freedom that in light of the data of revelation can act as a humanly liberative corrective to the rational categories of a philosophy of being. He shows that a philosophy of freedom can do this not by cutting itself off from the philosophy of being but by placing itself in a relationship of critical continuity with it. In developing this thesis, Segundo demonstrates that human freedom is not only personal and social but inseparable from the objective givenness of reality. Because freedom is fundamentally a (graced) orientation toward the realization of values, it is experienced existentially as (a potentially religious) faith. For this reason, freedom manifests itself in creative dialectic with the objective givenness of being, which serves both to condition and facilitate the expression of values and allows to emerge the objectively tangible creation of new reality. For Segundo, the latter is nothing less than the ontological manifestation of freedom's gratuitous efficacy. The following chapters will try show that this gratuitous manifestation constitutes the definitive eschatological value not

xxviii THE ABSOLUTE VALUE OF HUMAN ACTION

only of freedom but of reality as a whole (of which freedom is anyhow already only a part).

[39] *HJS*, esp. pp. 87-102. As will be seen in chapter three, what Segundo means by the political key is not the same as viewing Jesus as an activist or revolutionary. Nor does it constitute the only nor even the best key for unlocking the significance of Jesus' message and action. Rather, it forms the key most faithful to the trajectory of Jesus' life and most in tune with his own interpretation of his mission, to the extent that knowledge of either of those is available through critical study of the synoptic gospels. In this context the word *political* refers to Jesus' single-minded concern for delivering people from the evils which kept their humanity in check.

[40] For Segundo, this affirmation condenses the meaning and substance of Jesus' entire message and life (*RC*, p. 35).

[41] In *HJS*, Segundo tends to overlook the liberative significance of the *kinds* of disciples Jesus had. Their characteristics are documented in Elisabeth Schüssler Fiorenza, *In Memory of Her: A Feminist Theological Reconstruction of Christian Origins* (New York: Crossroad, 1983), especially pp. 97-241.

[42] Of course, Segundo does not claim that Jesus limits salvation exclusively to instances of earthly liberation. This point is basic to these reflections as a whole and will become especially evident in the discussion in chapter four.

[43] In a recent study entitled *Eschatology in the Old Testament* (Philadelphia: Fortress, 1986), Donald E. Gowan demonstrates that for the religious mentality of the Jewish scriptures—a mentality theologians may presume was shared by Jesus—the question to which eschatology responds is not the question of the end of history, time or the world but the question of the (definitive) end of evil (Gowan, p. 2). It seems appropriate to apply such an understanding to the gospel data, seeing in the kingdom *praxis* of Jesus (and, subsequently, in the work of Spirit) God's trustworthy downpayment on the definitive end of evil. What is eschatologically relevant about what Jesus called the "at-handness" of God's kingdom is that, when it comes, every tear will be wiped away and injustice, deprivation, suffering and death will be no more.

[44] By *logic* is meant the essential constitution of action as distinct from its content, the fundamental laws and inner coherence underlying its operation, the way it is put together and actually works.

[45] In spite of evidence that Segundo is familiar with the thought of Blondel (*Berdiaeff*, p. 385), this is not to suggest that Segundo's theology is influenced by Blondel's philosophy of action in any direct manner. On the contrary, it is far more influenced by the theology of grace of Leopold Malevez (*TC*, pp. 73-85) and is conducted in the spirit of a highly creative—almost eclectic—and critically interpretive liberative conversation with the philosophy of Nicholas Berdyaev (see n. 38 above) and, more recently, the ecological science of Gregory Bateson. (In the pages of *FI* alone, there are over thirty references to Bateson's work.) In addition, Segundo engages in productive conversation with many others, including Marx and Freud,

Darwin and Wallace, Ricœur and Gadamer, Rahner and Teilhard de Chardin, Bultmann and Niebuhr, Lukács and Machovec, the synoptics and John, and, above all, Paul. Reference to Blondel is made here only to underscore the profound importance in Segundo's anthropology of the priority of the will in human knowledge of God, a priority Blondel shared and which helped to shape the course of Catholic theology in this century. On the subject of "influence," I think it is significant that in a March 7, 1985 conversation with me at Regis College, Toronto School of Theology, Toronto, Segundo pointed out that early in his studies—during the third year of philosophy, to be exact—and because of a longstanding interest in the notion of the union of wills in the writings of Teresa of Avila, he moved from a philosophy of being to a philosophy of love and freedom, the latter constituting what he called his own kind of existentialism. This change in perspective was to determine the focus of all his works, explicitly announcing itself in his Ph.D. dissertation on Berdyaev in 1963 as a Christian interpretation of the human person. Because of this priority, the reflective functions of the intellect are incorporated into the essential structure of human willing, a fact which, as Blondel was intent on demonstrating, shows up existentially and epistemologically in life and *praxis* as the priority of action over consciousness and cognition. For a concise account of this priority in Blondel's thought, see his letter to André Lalande, ed., in *Vocabulaire technique et critique de la philosophie,* fifth edition (Paris: Presses Universitaires, 1947), pp. 4-5.

[46] On the need for a theological solution to the problem of the God-world relation which takes account of its social and political dimensions, see Anne Carr, "The God Who Is Involved," *Theology Today* 38 (1981), pp 314-328. A succinct articulation of the problem itself occurs in John Courtney Murray, *The Problem of God Yesterday and Today* (New Haven and London: Yale University Press), p. 92: "The central problem of Christian philosophy [is] the problem of the coexistence and coagency of the infinite and the finite, the necessary and the contingent, the eternal and the temporal, the absolute and the relative." For a clarifying account of the same problem from a process theological point of view, see Shubert Ogden, *The Reality of God and Other Essays* (New York: Harper and Row, 1977), chapter one.

[47] The notion of the causality of human action vis-à-vis realization of what Jesus called the kingdom of God sums up Segundo's entire theological project. It reiterates the principle referred to in n. 12 above and appears consistently throughout his writings. See, for example, *LT,* pp. 143 and ff. and "Capitalism—Socialism: A Theological Crux," in *The Mystical and Political Dimensions of the Christian Faith,* Claude Geffré and Gustavo Gutiérrez, eds., *Concilium* 96 (New York: Herder and Herder, 1974), p. 113. Its most explicit expression occurs in *HJS,* pp. 158-161.

[48] As will be emphasized in chapter four, the word *heaven* is a technical theological category for talking about the transcendence of God.

[49] This is not to say that the relation between God and human beings is therefore meaningless or insignificant. On the contrary, that relation defines the

structure of grace *qua* Faith and forms the basis for the mystical dimension of love with its indispensible emphasis on the interior transformation of the individual. It seems to me that the effort to keep the (religious) dimension of individual transformation in sight is one of the benefits of Segundo's insistence on complementing the political relevance of Jesus' kingdom message with the anthropological relevance of Paul's reinterpretation of it (*HCP*, pp. 161-182). Yet the structure of grace must not be confused with its *objective*. In the absence of something definitive and worthwhile to *do*, transformation of the individual, even if it be the gratuitous effect of the unmerited love of God, is unable to make that love an objectively efficacious reality. It is unable to make the reciprocity of that love an experience that can be realized and celebrated (*CIE*, p. 91). Love tends toward consummation, and grace tends toward completion. As chapter four will show, the consummation of grace in glory involves the definitive completion and gratuitous manifestation of love's creative efficacy.

50 That nature and history are inseparable is a major presupposition of Segundo's theology (*EAJN*, p. 64). Its effect is to make it impossible to speak about human social persons and their relation to God in history without at the same time speaking about the ecological complexity of their immersion in, indebtedness to and responsibility for nature. In a recent issue of *Concilium* entitled *Cosmology and Theology* (New York: Seabury, 1983), David Tracy and Nicholas Lash make a case for reuniting history and nature in contemporary theology, but in the context of the assumption that the corrective for anthropocentrism is theocentrism (see p. vii and pp. 87-92). It seems to me that such an assumption contributes to rather than solves "the problem of the coexistence and coagency of. . .the absolute and the relative" referred to in n. 46 above. A major contribution of Segundo's approach is its capacity to solve exactly that problem, through a healthy refocusing of the God-human relation on the objective toward which the logic of grace points, namely the definitive creation of a world, with all the eschatological overtones such an objective carries. The appropriateness of Segundo's approach is that it resolves the problem at the level of action. It addresses the problem of *coexistence* between the absolute and the relative (a doctrine of creation) in conjunction with the problem of *coagency* between them (a doctrine of grace). It does not address the God-world relation at the level of being/ coexistence—i.e., a doctrine of creation—alone. Even should the traditional doctrine of creation be filtered through a contemporary ecological consciousness (Tracy and Lash, pp. 89-90) and structured to incorporate eschatological hope (*ibid.*, p. 91), outside the context of a doctrine of cooperative grace it risks remaining tied to abstract categories like the omnipotence and sovereignty of "God," possibly at the expense of concrete realities like the manifest and impassioned love of God for creatures in a universe subjected to apparent futility by evil.

51 Unlike the traditionally either theocentric or anthropocentric accents arising out of the Reformation and Enlightenment, the effort to translate the language of grace into a "cosmocentric" idiom is an effort to focus on the significance of God's

gratuitous love not just for human beings but for all creatures. On the one hand, it is an attempt to move theological categories away from excessive preoccupation with human interiority and subjectivity, especially where the latter result in Faith's being understood (possibly in the absence of sociopolitical relevance) as a "change of state" (from unsaved to saved or from natural to supernatural), a change said to be effected either by the action of God alone (the theocentric accent) or through some form of implicit or explicit knowledge of God thought to constitute a human religious faith (the anthropocentric accent). On the other hand, it is an effort to interpret the doctrine of grace by means of evolutionary categories that are ecologically conscious, situating the God-human and God-world relations in the context of an eschatology pertaining to both the experience of creaturely suffering in history and nature and the dense complexity of evolving reality in an ambiguous and, thanks to seemingly definitive negativities like evil and death, apparently futile universe.

[52] In a world ravaged by ecological destruction and the exploitation of species, the notion that creation and grace are linked by God's manifest eschatological will that the earth be *inhabitable* (and not a futile waste) seems deserving of theological attention: "For thus says the LORD, who created the heavens (who is God!) who formed the earth and made it (God established it; God did not create it a chaos, but formed it to be *inhabited!*): 'I am the LORD and there is no other'" (Is. 45:18; RSV translation; inclusive language substituted; italics mine). The point seems to be that God, whose creative will as "LORD" in heaven is that the earth be inhabitable, expects a like response from creatures on earth, i.e., creative action aimed at making it so.

[53] As will be pointed out in the discussions ahead, in the context of Segundo's categories the notion of creative responsibility, like the action itself of creating, does not have to do with Marx's well-known notion of transformation of the world. Creative responsibility does not involve changing reality (by imposing on it a determinative, purposive aim) but has to do with the efficacy—i.e., the new-making, free-making, appropriately scaled power—accompanying self-transcending love. In the human sphere, creative responsibility is thus a matter of freedom's allowing reality to change according to a logic of gratuitousness already at work at the heart of reality itself (of which freedom is a minoritarian but not merely negligible part).

[54] That does not mean that it is intended to *furnish* a cause for hope, e.g., in relation to persons and groups who are not disciples of Jesus. On the contrary, it is intended to articulate a cause that has already been accepted in faith by disciples of Jesus today. As the discussion in chapter four will suggest, what is being attempted is not an apologetical or foundational argument but a theological interpretation.

I

THE LOGIC OF ACTION AND THE THEOLOGY OF GRACE: FAITH AS HUMAN PARTICIPATION IN THE CREATION OF THE WORLD

Your kingdom come.

In this initial chapter I will begin with the assumption that the logic of action can best be understood from the point of view of Segundo's ruling theological presuppositions about the meaning and value of human freedom. I will take as starting point his conception of the logic and complexity of freedom in a universe in which the world is not yet finished being created and is marked in the interim by a tragic susceptibility to suffering.[1] After a brief consideration of these preliminary issues, I will move to the more central topic of Segundo's phenomenological analysis of the essential structure of human freedom. Key to his grasp of the complexity of the latter is the notion that under the "dense" conditions of history and nature in an evolving world, freedom is oriented toward the realization of efficacious results and yet is radically limited by the objective givenness of reality, of which, paradoxically, it is already part. For Segundo, this paradox culminates in the positing of faith and ideologies as fundamental anthropological dimensions. By focusing the first stage of the discussion on them as key elements of Segundo's philosophical base, I will highlight the pivotal role an evolutionary ontology of freedom plays in the attempt to develop an anthropological map of the logic of action.

Then, building in the second section on the foundation provided by Segundo's analysis of freedom, I will present an interpretive account of what I regard as his original contribution to the making of a theology of cooperative grace. The aim of this part of the discussion will be to summarize Segundo's understanding of Faith as the ontologically creative, secularly liberative appropriation by human freedom of God's gratuitous and impassioned love. Although the interpretation presented here will be grounded in Segundo's analysis of the theological significance of Jesus' God-revealing kingdom *praxis*, it will be developed in light of Segundo's reliance on the anthropological categories of Paul.[2]

The third and final section will be an effort to make a constructive hermeneutical transposition of Segundo's theology of cooperative grace. By crossing the anthropological categories of his evolutionary ontology with the task-oriented language of the biblical notion of *charism*, I will try to validate Segundo's claim that in a universe in which creation is not yet complete, grace begins for human beings in God's liberation of freedom for the task of constructing works of love in nature and history and ends in freedom's gratuitous capacity to contribute together with the freedom of God to the definitive creation of a world.[3] The point is to come up with a language of grace that rings true to its character as action.

The Logic of Human Action

The logic of action does not appear as a discrete topic in Segundo's theology but must be inferred from his conception of freedom. Insofar as the latter is not limited to the analysis of human freedom but includes anything analogous to it in other spheres, it is necessary to consider freedom as a technical evolutionary category before turning to the central task of addressing Segundo's phenomenological analysis of human freedom and its relevance to the logic of action.

THE EVOLUTIONARY LOGIC AND ONTOLOGICAL COMPLEXITY OF FREEDOM

In a world that from the perspective of human experience is evolving and from the perspective of revelation is graced with the gratuitous love of God, Segundo focuses his attention on the complexity of human freedom as it appears vis-à-vis two theological referents at once: the data of revelation about the sovereign freedom of God and the data of human experience about the tragic character of an evolving world in an incomplete and apparently futile universe.[4]

Factoring into one another the data of science and revelation, Segundo assumes that a phenomenon as complex as human freedom can be experienced as meaningful only if it is acknowledged at the outset that the world is not a finished product.[5] In fact, he believes, freedom can be given theological value only if it is admitted that the creation of the world has not yet been completed. In the interim, neither is it capable of being pronounced good.[6]

According to revelation, Segundo believes, the making of a world capable of being pronounced good will be accomplished only by the participation of human freedom with the freedom of God in a project of co-creative love. Such love is constitutive for Segundo of what theology means by grace. As will be discussed in greater detail in subsequent sections of this chapter, the project-like character of such love corresponds to the basic theological datum that, for human beings at least, the structure of grace comprises a dynamic reciprocity of freedoms: it involves a gratuitous initiative of God toward creatures as well as a free response of creatures to God. In fact, Segundo's evolutionary categories suggest, the reciprocity of freedoms embodied in grace is the condition for the actuality of God's creating a world at all, let alone a world that is good, although to pursue the implications of such a statement so early in the discussion is to get a little ahead of the story.[7]

At the present stage of the discussion, it must suffice to say that if the creation of a world capable of being pronounced good will be manifest in the end as worth every ounce of trouble it took to create it, the reason has to do with the constructive character of a created, finite and limited freedom in the eyes of God and creatures. More specifically, it has to do with the ontologically creative value of such freedom under the tragic conditions of a universe that is unfinished, and thus not only fraught with the abstract possibility of suffering but also marked by suffering's ever present actuality, which looms in the face of creatures as a continual disruption and affront.[8] For Segundo, the capacity of both God and creatures to look in the end on the world they have created and be moved to pronounce it good depends on whether or not they can say in the meantime that freedom itself is worth what it costs in the actual price of suffering. For Segundo, the answer to that question has got to be yes, since, not only for creatures but apparently for God, there is no other way to make a world. There simply is no easy, inexpensive and painless way to create.[9]

From Segundo's point of view, the truth of this statement can be measured only by the testimony of experience, in particular by reflecting on the costly phenomenon of self-transcending love, which, in the sphere of human experience at least, seems to accompany the manifestation of freedom in the evolutionary project as we know it. To do this in a way that relies not only on the personal testimony of witnesses but finds empirical backing at the systematic level in contemporary human science, it is helpful to approach the topic of self-transcending love by taking a closer look at the apparently futile but ultimately creative logic Segundo finds at work in the universe itself, i.e., the project-mindedness reality seems to display at its roots according to data from current theories of evolution.[10]

The Project-Minded Logic of History and Nature in an Evolving World. In a universe in which the world is as yet neither good nor finished being created, Segundo believes that both history and nature find themselves participating in a constructive task, an evolutionary "project-mindedness" which impels them toward the continual manifestation of freedom.[11] In this context, freedom is a generic term, a technical evolutionary category. It refers not only to human freedom but to anything analogous to it in other spheres.[12] In this sense, freedom of any sort, but certainly human freedom, is capable of functioning as a "homeostatic mechanism" at the heart of the evolutionary project.[13] It represents the happy resilience reality seems to display at its roots, the indefatigable tendency to start all over again in the face of seemingly overwhelming odds. Ultimately, freedom in this sense is the indomitable, positive, novelty-carrying vector of the evolving world which makes history and nature capable of "learning something new through [the] experience of error and its correction."[14]

Potentially at least, freedom is thus a constructive factor contributing to the emergence of the new.[15] It is the tendency toward flexibility at the heart of reality, the capacity innate in history and nature by which the world remains capable in this or that atomic structure, this or that chemical reaction, this or that species or individual, of continually experimenting with the complex task of dealing constructively with ever changing situations and conditions.[16] Thanks to the resilience that comes to light in the evolving cosmos as freedom, history and nature are continually at work to learn a self-regulatory wisdom which places the cosmos as a whole at the service of efficacious change. This seemingly inexhaustible capacity for "learning to learn" makes freedom the qualitative factor of an evolutionary economy aimed at the wise investment of gathered up energies, the efficacious expenditure of resources in the face of quantitative factors like randomness and time.[17] For the sake of the emergence of new and worthwhile syntheses—qualitative creative change—the flexible continuity between the qualitative and quantitative dimensions of evolving reality guides freedom through a course of learning to learn which constitutes its proper *charism*.[18]

In this sense, the manifestation of freedom is very costly. It takes large amounts of energy and obliges freedom to follow an evolutionary discipline: freedom must save energy in one area where this can be done without unnecessary danger in order to invest energy in another area where it might produce better and more lasting results.[19] Freedom is thus "not creative, strictly speaking."[20] Efficacious change, the creation of something new, results not from the purposive character of freedom but from the capacity of this or that atom, molecule, organism or species to learn a wisdom and flexibility in the face of constant demands from two equally dynamic evolutionary factors: the tendency toward the conservation of energy on the one hand and the tendency toward the expenditure of energy on the other. In the face of continual flux, freedom is not the cause of change but rather that which is made manifest within it. Freedom is released anywhere there occurs an optimal economy of energy. It comes to light wherever there occurs a graceful flexibility, a wise energy calculus, an efficacious way of conserving and expending energy.[21] In this sense, the manifestation of freedom represents what Segundo, using the categories of Gregory Bateson, calls "communication," i.e., the making of "a difference that makes a difference."[22] Wherever it comes to light in the evolutionary project, the manifestation of freedom is a sign of the efficacious transmission, in the face of incalculable odds, of qualitative change.[23]

Ultimately, Segundo believes, freedom is made manifest in history and nature anywhere there is evident not just any change whatsoever, but a "difference that makes a difference" which serves precisely to counter entropy.[24] The latter is the seemingly disintegratory vector of the evolutionary project which can make it appear, to human eyes at least, that the project itself is futile, headed toward eventual run down and decay.[25] Yet paradoxically, entropy supplies the necessary complement to the projective dimension of evolutionary change by placing at the disposal of freedom the quantitative richness of the realm of givenness, the sheer multiplicity of chance.[26] Freedom cannot be creative in a vacuum; it requires the timely incorporation of random elements made possible in the first place only by the quantitative massiveness of chance.

In this sense, the surfacing of freedom represents the gratuitous realization of negentropic breakthroughs that actually depend for their efficacy on entropy, specifically, on entropy's constructive capacity to "prepare the way," by making random contributions to the creation of something new. In other words, in the evolutionary project as we know it, change can be efficacious only thanks to chance. The structure of freedom thus displays a complexity that is intrinsically bound up with what might be called the "happy fault syndrome" at the heart of reality: freedom is made manifest only when its projective energies graciously accept the laws and requirements of entropic determinisms, i.e., only when freedom learns to integrate the negative aspects of reality into new, more efficacious syntheses. Freedom does not make change happen; rather, it allows entropic energies to prepare the moment of newness and appropriateness in which change can actually occur.

Insofar as freedom depends for its manifestation on the incorporation of entropic elements such as enormous quantities of chance and time, its efficacy is gratuitous.[27] It is the unsolicited gift to freedom of chance. In an evolutionary context, in other words, freedom is able to be made manifest at all only thanks to the gratuitously efficacious character of (sometimes seemingly, sometimes really) negative elements like time and chance, each of which in its own way makes constructive contributions to the emergence of the new.[28] In the words of Segundo, "There is a surrender to entropy, a place given to chance, that is *positive,* salutary, and necessary."[29] In the context of an old joke which asks what is necessary for the lighting of a lamp (answer: that it be out), he observes: "If we want to use the innovative mechanisms [i.e., in order to create something new] the first and foremost requirement is that they be turned off [i.e., that a period of entropy intervene]."[30]

The idea that freedom is guided by randomness, time and chance toward learning to allow continual realizations of efficacious change analogous to the creation of whole new worlds, unprecedented breakthroughs that the evolutionary project had hitherto not yet "learned"—this idea Segundo factors into the data of revelation about grace. The result is that, for Segundo, human freedom is directed conjointly with the freedom of God toward the creative negation—or positive integration—of entropy, a project of learning the "knack" of creating the new, what Segundo calls an "adventure in gratuitous living."[31] The "new thing" being learned, of course, is the effective realization of rich syntheses of entropic forces, an accomplishment which, as Jesus' life-story makes clear in light of God's having raised him from the dead, is gratuitously creative of self-transcending love.[32] Out of the gradually learned implementation of the project of gratuitous living will emerge in the end the creation of a world definitively capable of being pronounced good because built negentropically of love.

The Ontological Complexity of Feedom. In the sphere of human action, the factoring into one another of these scientific and revealed pieces of data is not a simple matter. It creates a need to come up with appropriate sets of categories on which to base theological affirmations about the value of self-transcending love. Segundo addresses this need by taking a radically anthropocentric starting point. He begins with the apparent futility, in the universe as it appears to human beings, of suffering.[33]

Considering suffering in light of data from contemporary science about the complexity of entropy and the resilient tendency of reality to continue manifesting freedom even in the face of seemingly overwhelming odds, Segundo tries to make a rationally coherent theological response (not the same as an explanation) to what earlier in his career, relying on Berdyaev, he had regarded as the irrationality of evil.[34] This leads him to take a view of human freedom which situates it within the objective reality of an unfinished universe, with all the complexity that entails.

Insofar as the givenness of reality includes (but is not simply co-extensive with) the random phenomenon of actual occurrences of evil, the continual surfacing of evil as the apparent negation of efficacious change is the salient characteristic of the universe. As was seen in the previous section, it gives the universe an intrinsically tragic character.[35] As a glaring contradiction at the heart of reality, evil strikes human beings as a fundamental disjointedness.[36] It drains the energy of the evolutionary project and frustrates the efficacy of action. It is an index within reality itself of the constant experience, which at the biological level finds voice in creatures' anguished cries of grief and suffering, of how difficult, costly and seemingly exorbitant it is to create.

Evidence of such evil, which seems to become increasingly obvious and devastating the "longer" the evolutionary project perdures, means that the world can not have been pronounced good from the beginning, even if someone should suppose that the one making such a pronouncement should or would be God. How could God pronounce creatures' cries of grief and suffering good? Rather, the world will be pronounced good—by both God and creatures—only after it has been finished, only after every tear will have been wiped away, only after a world has been definitively created and judged to be inhabitable and good.[37]

In the context of this perspective, Segundo finds the *raison d'être* of human freedom in the struggle to incorporate the quantitative forces of chance and time, including the random occurrences of evil and suffering a universe of chance and time entails, into the construction of something good. This view he finds compatible with the datum of revelation about the impassioned character of God's gratuitous love. In the negative context of a universe that from time immemorial has displayed empirical evidence of being not only incomplete and subjected to apparent futility but fraught with creaturely suffering, the datum of God's gratuitous love, which is the datum of grace, represents God's unswerving commitment—precisely in "empathy" with human objections to suffering and evil—to the creation of a world that is capable in the end of being pronounced good.[38]

Segundo observes that the creative sensitivity of God's gratuitous love manifests a project-mindedness analogous to that accompanying the manifestation of freedom in the evolutionary project: it is headed toward the negation of entropy and the manifestation of freedom. He then employs that analogy to come up with a cosmogony that can refer the freedom of both God and human beings to the creative integration of the entropic forces of evil in the universe by incorporating them into works of love that are creative of a world that is good. This is a cosmogony that can suit the interests not only of God and human beings but of all creatures, since it is capable of involving God and creatures alike in a project aimed at building a world no longer fraught with futility and suffering but embodying the values of community, companionship and friendship. Such a world will be all-inclusive and inhabitable. It will be the product of a conjoint struggle against evil that is capable in the end of being celebrated as good—i.e., worth the price that had to be paid in risk and suffering to achieve it:

> Only an unfinished world, entrusted to humanity in a way that entails suffering and death, can give irreplaceable and definitive value to human responsibility, to the human hands that are completing creation *as they fight against all the painful elements that affect God Godself.* Only thus can we all bear in our hands the destiny of all, including the destiny of God Godself who chose to [befriend] us.[39]

For Segundo, in other words, a world that has to be made good gradually and painstakingly by hand is a world that entails suffering not just for human beings but for God, a world in which both God and human beings must work together in the context of a shared destiny, as companions and co-workers along a common way, at a project in which the destiny of God is tied to that of every single creature.

From the perspective of the need to establish theologically intelligible relations between two seemingly incompatible things—an unfinished universe that is not already good and God whose will toward creatures in exactly such a universe manifests itself in revelation as committed to the creation of a world that is good—the incompleteness of the cosmos redounds on human freedom by offering it a worthwhile project, a constructive significance and goal. Attending to the negative dimension of reality thus has the effect of making the relevance of human freedom theologically apparent in view of the creative love-building character of God's own freedom in grace. It shows that responding to the demands of a world still to be created is the only way of insuring that both God and human beings will be involved in the most pressing of tasks, the definitive victory of impassioned action over pointlessness and futility. For Segundo, in fact, the very existence of human freedom, if it is to be taken seriously, presupposes a creation expressly left incomplete by God, in order to place the creative task in the hands of human beings.[40]

Such a schema is appropriate to the making of a theology of cooperative grace insofar as the only conception of creation against which action can make theological sense, whether for creatures or for God, is one in which a lasting evidence of meaning and value is not simply given from the start by the action of God alone, but is in need of being fashioned by the action of God and creatures working together in love. For Segundo, creation can happen only through the long route of impassioned action, the day-to-day evidence of God's and creatures' mutual willingness to continue suffering whatever it is going to take to "live gratuitously" in the face of evil, and thus through self-transcending love to arrive in the end at a shared realization of building a world that is good.

A universe in which freedom is the willingness to suffer the realization of self-transcending love only slowly, through a gradual discipline of learning to create, is a universe in which freedom is impassioned action. In such a universe, freedom is worthwhile only if it can accomplish something of creative value on behalf of creatures and of God.[41] That is the case not because of any value inherent in suffering but because of the entropic structure of freedom in an evolving world. Insofar as evolution is not a mechanistic process but a creative project in which freedom must learn to participate like an apprentice, the creation of something new requires a willingness to be gradual, a willingness to work at objectifying values through the expending of energies and the taking of concrete directions that is the long, laborious route of passion; and the name of that passion in the face of such continual trouble is self-transcending, evil-abhorring love.

What does such a conception of freedom mean? It means that in the evolutionary framework of a universe like Segundo's, in which the creation of a good world is a project still needing to be completed, neither God nor creatures can realize freedom, or suffer the realization of self-transcending love, in the abstract.[42] If love is to be directed outward toward the ultimate creation of a world, it can be realized only concretely, under ontological conditions genuinely conducive to the release of creaturely freedom. Yet by definition these are conditions of ontological incompleteness involving the continual randomization, through forces of breakdown and decay, of previously created syntheses.[43] Like the logic of the paschal mystery, Segundo's logic of creativity involves the whole of created reality in an apparently futile yet actually efficacious circuit of death and life, a circuit of impassioned action—i.e., gratuitousness—ever at work in the evolving cosmos for the sake of effecting new manifestations of self-transcending love.

The completion of creation is thus a conjoint labor of self-transcending love. It is a shared participation in the emergence of the new, an impassioned commitment to suffering the birth of gratuitousness—in the sense of allowing it to happen—and a work to which both God and creatures contribute. Insofar as their mutually shouldered responsibility of having to contend with evil is the only way God and creatures have at their disposal to realize the project to which they are both committed in love, human freedom must be willing to drink from the chalice of suffering a universe of entropy entails. And this is a passion God does not take away but in solidarity with creatures and in response to their cries, drinks with them to the dregs. Segundo thus suggests that in the love that is grace, God responds to suffering creatures with an impassioned action of God's own. God welcomes the creative efforts of human freedom and cherishes them as something infinitely valuable, capable of achieving worthwhile results that, in the end, will be manifested as having a value that is definitive.[44] Indeed, God's own action gratuitously manifests the definitive value of human action insofar as God's most characteristic action consists in God's manifest passion in the face of human action, God's expressed need to rely on the freedom of human beings for the creative integration of the entropic forces of evil and suffering into negentropic breakthroughs of self-transcending love.[45]

In an evolving cosmos still incomplete and only gradually coming to term, God suffers the risk of initiating a laborious creative work. God gratuitously invests God's action in the willingness to accept the constructive contributions of a finite and still maturing human freedom for the sake of realizing a love-building project creative of a world.[46] That impassioned project of creative love—the eschatological task of placing at hand what Jesus called the kingdom of God—is initiated on earth in grace but will not be completed until the coming of love's definitive manifestation in glory.[47] To be effective, it requires the participation of human freedom in the fashioning of the "raw materials" of the unfinished universe into the substance of a new creation.[48] In each generation, human social persons are invited to become companions with God in building out of the rudimentary materials of an incomplete universe a new heaven and new earth that will live with God forever.[49]

Segundo's creative integration of the data of revelation and the data of evolutionary science ultimately has the effect of showing that the freedom of God and the freedom of human social persons are pointed in the same direction. Attending to both sets of data means acknowledging that human freedom exists not for its own sake but for the sake of transforming a rudimentary universe in which evil seems definitively to reign into a mature cosmos that is ruled in the end by the gratuitous realization of self-transcending love. The use of evolutionary categories thus facilitates the effort to speak in a coherent way about the theological relations between the divine and human freedoms. The data of evolutionary science tend to keep theological reflection about the meaning and value of human freedom humble by placing it in touch with the limits and complexity of objective reality, and the data of revelation tend to keep that reflection bold enough to move human action in the direction of God-like self-transcending love.

SEGUNDO'S ANTHROPOLOGICAL MAP OF THE LOGIC OF ACTION

Segundo's analysis of the evolutionary logic and ontological complexity of freedom makes it clear that epistemologically prior to the need for a theological interpretation of graced human action is a need for an adequate anthropological foundation on which to construct it. The business of the latter would be to address the question of how freedom actually functions, assuming that to some extent we human social persons actually can, do and want to accomplish something efficacious with our freedom in an incomplete and tragic universe. How can it be demonstrated that in fact at least some of the time persons and groups of good will can and do strive to make "a difference which makes a difference" to the objective shape of society, history and ecology in an evolving world? In other words, leaving aside for the moment what Jesus' kingdom *praxis* and resurrection reveal about God's initiation of a creative project in grace, it is necessary to ask whether action has a logic of its own which is visible anywhere to anyone, strictly on its own terms.[50]

For Segundo, the answer to that question is yes, and it takes the form of what he calls faiths and ideologies.[51] They describe the structure of freedom and define the logic of action. In them he sees two universal tendencies. These he defines as anthropological dimensions, and he makes them constitutive elements of every human existence. The anthropological version of the ontological tension between freedom and being, faiths and ideologies are names for the exercise of freedom every human being is capable of, regardless of the objective content they actually receive in the course of people's actions. Always operating simultaneously, faiths and ideologies show that freedom is a matter of attempting to realize projects. To a greater or lesser extent this means that freedom tends toward expressing itself in work.[52] It tends to find itself "at work" on projects amid the objective givenness of reality.

Segundo believes that a careful look at faiths and ideologies provides convincing evidence that freedom not only wants something (which refers it *qua* faith to the sphere of meaning and values) but also strives to see things through and get things done (which refers it *qua* ideologies to the sphere of efficacy). The coexistence of these referents in one and the same phenomenon of action suggests that freedom is structured in such a way as to be inclined to accomplish what it originally desires. This makes freedom less a matter of choosing objects than of trying to accomplish objectives. It makes it a matter of the willing and doing of projects. By its very structure, freedom is oriented toward a task: achieving efficacy or completion in the sphere of objective reality.[53] For Segundo, in fact, the combination of factors at work in the givenness of reality and resulting in the human sphere from the influx of a profusion of freedoms, i.e., a quantum leap of chance thanks to the coming on the scene of a multitude of individual personal freedoms, furnishes a vast array of possible objectives for human freedom.[54] The melding of these factors in the human sphere suggests that the objective realization of values is freedom's inherently given project in the universe.

Yet the givenness of reality is always prior to the working of freedom. Although the latter occurs for the sake of realizing an objective result or goal, a specific value, it can take place in an evolving world only by means of the objective givenness of mechanisms and capacities already operative in the structure of reality. Given the objective character of that structure, freedom must work according to reality's limits and under its conditions, within the contours of its laws. Not only is freedom radically conditioned by mechanisms already at work in the sphere of objective reality, but it is made possible and facilitated by them. For that reason it is exceedingly complex.

The Constructive Logic of Anthropological Faith. The complexity begins to appear when Segundo considers in more datail the first essential dimension of freedom, anthropological faith. Not to be confused with religious faith, which is one of its possible manifestations, anthropological faith constitutes a wager which we human social persons cannot avoid making and which is necessitated by the social structure of our freedom. What is that wager? At bottom, it is a bet made in advance, before all the data are in, that when all is said and done, living life in a certain way will turn out to have been definitively worthwhile. Yet because we are not isolated individuals but constitutively social beings, we are unable to verify—or even make— the wager of freedom by ourselves. No one can "test-drive" a variety of lives in advance in order to determine which one will end up being worth the effort. Instead, we must rely for data on a particular community of witnesses, an already existing tradition of testimony, a line of significant others, none of whom need have any connection with what is commonly understood as religion, from whom to pick up the values we eventually assemble more or less explicitly into a faith. Segundo refers to the data on which the values of faith are based as "transcendent data," because they are not able to be empirically verified. Their validity can be demonstrated only from "outside," by means of experiences entirely "other" than our own which must be communicated to us by others.

What is more, it is according to the values communicated by these data that we are already going about living our lives, for the epistemological premises which lead us to accept the testimony of certain witnesses rather than others also lead us to "punctuate" the events of life and history according to one particular set of presuppositions rather than another. In fact, the tendency to punctuate events is what prepares a pre-existing readiness—what Segundo calls a set of partially self-validating premises—by which we begin to incorporate the data of such witnesses. It makes us susceptible of picking up the values of others who have gone before us or surround us in the present. Usually, the process involves reliance on a combination of both.

In this sense, anthropological faith is a socially transmitted way of seeing and understanding reality. It is something people learn from others. Segundo describes it as a learning how to learn, a gradually developed "knack" of making sense of our existence in the world. Ultimately, it is the way we human social persons learn to relate to others and respond to the world as a whole, the way we go about "reading" the meaning of life. Anthropologically speaking, the tendency of freedom to learn and live values in an anthropological faith means that the logic of action is constitutively social (without, of course, thereby ceasing to be individual) yet capable of being adequately understood only as an orientation that is conditioned and facilitated by the objectively given structure of reality in an evolving world.

With that initial assertion, Segundo attempts to map a universal fact of experience. He shows that it pertains to the inmost structure of action that the meaning toward which it points and the destiny toward which it tends are gradually picked up—however inchoately—in the course of action itself. They arise from the working of freedom in reality. Like Blondel, Segundo posits the existence of a kind of knowledge built into the logic of action itself. The name he gives it is faith—a basic stance, largely unthematized yet no less operative and real, about our preferred way of seeing and relating to the world. It funds our everyday modes of thinking and acting and is the ground of *praxis*. It furnishes action with epistemological premises and provides it existentially with concrete motives and hopes. In this way anthropological faith actually functions as a cognitive principle: it "enables us to see certain things rather than other equally obvious things."[55] Because it is based not on our own experience but on experiences that are socially communicable, it must rely for effective transmission on the "iconic" power of symbols. These express the experiences of others in stories, images and metaphors capable of involving freedom and committing it *qua* faith to the values being communicated. In this way, Segundo argues, anthropological faith "saves energy" for people. Insofar as it does not require their having to start off every line of deliberation "from scratch," it is a social form of knowledge which allows them to rely for the meaning of their action on the living symbols of already existing traditions.[56]

Yet Segundo's analysis does not rest with the assertion that the logic of action is faith. The existence of cultural traditions shows that freedom also attempts to preserve and hand on the values toward which it points. Freedom tends to "implant" the perceptions of faiths in the objective givenness of reality, so as to see what kind of world will come of them. It tries to institutionalize faiths' characteristic modes of relating to others and fashion them into a reality. This it does not only through the linguistic and cultural symbols of faiths themselves, but by means of historical-ecological embodiments aimed at either the preservation of established values or the efficacious realization of change. This means that freedom tends to engage in a continual effort to incarnate the values of faiths in practical things like explanations, tools and sociopolitical structures, concrete expressions of people's preferred modes of relating to other beings and to objective reality as a whole. These Segundo sums up under the term *ideologies*. They comprise the systems of theoretical and practical means by which freedom turns the values of a given anthropological faith into objective *praxes*.[57]

The Efficacious Logic of Ideologies. As *praxes*, ideologies are inseparable from faiths but not identical with them, complementary and yet distinct. Faiths without ideologies are ahistorical and empty, and ideologies without faiths are as problematic and deadly as a corpse. Faiths give meaning to ideologies, and ideologies give historical and ecological substance to faiths. Ideologies are the objective substantiations of faiths. They constitute the cultural traces and historical-ecological markers of humanly held premises, and they manifest the values which fund human personal and corporate action. Ideologies give faiths a discernible human face in history and nature. They make faiths operative in the realm of action. By constructive contact with the objective givenness of reality, they can also counteract the ossifying tendency latent in every human faith to preserve its values and hand them on unexamined from the past. In this sense, ideologies help to move faiths toward maturity. They allow faiths to live and function with a thread of continuity amid the changing conditions of the world. In other words, they permit faiths to take into account and attempt to deal with the phenomenon of constant change amid the givenness of objective reality. By putting faiths' premises into historically and ecologically discernible form as practice, they reveal faiths' values for everyone to see.

The phenomenon of ideologies thus suggests that action is aimed at giving objective continuity to a particular human faith under the conditions of historical-ecological flux. Ideologies show that from the point of view of action, to talk about reality is to speak about something that evolves. That is because a human faith can continue to realize its values and make the power of its perceptions felt only by means of ever changing objective incarnations. Unless in one way or another new *praxes* are letting the ideological impact of faiths be felt, the values which ground them can not be communicated. They can be neither meaningful nor efficacious under the entropic and ever changing conditions of chance and time. And unless such ideological incarnations are in some way still embodying the faiths that gave them birth, still in continuity with their values, they end up "full of sound and fury, signifying nothing."[58] Although that implies, of course, that ideologies are a constitutively relative affair, they remain absolutely essential to the faiths they embody. Faith inevitably tends to objectivize its values through work.[59] The logic of action is faith at work in the sphere of objective reality through ideological works.

Paradoxically, however, once such ideological "works" are created, they are capable of distancing themselves from the faiths which ground them and begin to take on a life of their own. As systems of means to more or less immediate and purposive ends, ideologies are fragile creations. They are only as good as the faiths which fund them and the degree of efficacy they achieve. Yet they are capable of becoming very strong, with either positive or negative results. That is because ideologies do not simply express faiths. More importantly, they provide concrete means by which to back faiths, criticize the premises by which they work and keep them honest and humble.

Yet insofar as ideologies are capable of taking on a life of their own, they are susceptible of failure, miscarriage, and even outright contradiction vis-à-vis the faiths they are meant to serve. Ideologies can conceal values as well as reveal them. They can become cut off from the faiths which ground them, alienated from the intentions of freedom which gave them birth.[60] In that case, ideologies cease being expressions of faith and begin being faith's enslavers. They may permit anthropological faith to become hardened of heart and insensitive to truth, gradually turning it into "bad faith." This means that ideologies must continually be subjected to radical critique by both the values they are meant to serve and the effects they actually create in the sphere of objective reality. While it is the task of ideologies to strive toward efficacious expression and transmission of the values of faiths, it is the task of faiths to judge the appropriateness and worthwhileness of that efficacy.

This reciprocal dynamic suggests that ultimately faiths and ideologies make freedom a matter of truth.[61] The significance of human faiths is precisely that they direct ideologies, and thus freedom itself, toward the concrete *praxis* of truth.[62] The significance of ideologies, on the other hand, is that they embody the objective means of substantiating and testing that truth. In short, ideologies make faiths answerable to the demands and limitations imposed by the objective structures of the evolving world, and faiths make ideologies answerable to the criteria and demands of truth.[63]

THE ECOLOGICAL DENSITY OF FAITHS AND IDEOLOGIES

By mapping the logic of faiths and ideologies in terms of freedom's intrinsic reference to the structure of an objectively given universe, Segundo succeeds in creating an evolutionary interpretation of human freedom which responds not merely to anthropological, social and historical demands but to ecological ones as well. He understands by faiths and ideologies the ecological density of social existence itself. He shows that because human faiths are implicated in ideological works or *praxes,* the logic of action includes the lifelong process of testing the values of any given faith against the objective givenness and inevitable resistance of an already existing reality.[64] In this way Segundo makes action answerable to the limits and conditions imposed on it by the mechanisms of evolutionary change and the objectivity of its laws. In fact, he admits those conditions and mechanisms into the logic of action itself. He makes action capable not only of effecting changes *in* nature but also, and far more importantly in the context of ecological concerns today, of receiving genuine contributions *from* nature.[65]

THE LOGIC OF ACTION

For Segundo, the randomness in nature and the slow, patient tempo of efficacious change are internal to the logic of action. This opens up a route by which to arrive at an appropriately modest estimate of the status of human freedom with regard to the objective givenness of the rest of the universe, especially in comparison with the resilience analogous to human freedom in other beings, living or not, including the structures and mechanisms of objective reality itself.[66] Such an approach liberates human freedom to take its rightful place neither outside nor above the objective givenness of nature but within its essential structure. From Segundo's point of view, this means that the spheres of both nature and "second nature," or culture, can be freed to take their rightful place as well. Nature and history are thus freed to regain their original ontological continuity as constitutive dimensions of the manifestation of freedom in an evolving world.

The complexity of the relations between human freedom and the objective givenness of nature and culture contributes to what Segundo early in his career had considered a dialectic at work internally in freedom. [67] Far from making freedom a purely subjective affair, Segundo recognizes in the structure of human freedom itself both an orientation toward the objectification of freedom's projectivity and a conditioning of it by the objective givenness of reality—a capacity, in other words, to be constructive of history but only in nature and by means of nature's laws. As constitutive poles of a single evolving reality, freedom and objective nature are reciprocally dependent.[68] Alienated from one another, they produce evolutionary dead ends. Working together, they are capable of producing something truly new, "a difference which makes a difference," within the contours of objective reality in an already given evolving world.

What is such new material? Segundo answers that it is the substance of history and nature. It is the construction of a world through the conjoint work of freedom and objective givenness, the work of the evolutionary project itself, of which not only freedom but also objective givenness, is a constructive part. For Segundo, the creation of a world is an outgrowth of the internal dialectic of freedom. It is human freeedom at work in objective reality through the constructive tendency of anthropological faith and yet radically limited by objective reality in the givenness of nature— a dialectic embodying faith's at least potentially creative tension with ideologies. Under the conditions of evolutionary change, the logic of action has a constitutively ecological structure. The efficacy of ideologies depends on the contributions of nature and second nature that are made available to anthropological faith only insofar as it recognizes its interconnectedness with, and recognizes its reliance on, the determinisms and mechanisms of an already given, independently working objective reality of which it is already a part. Whether people will it or not, the logic of action is implicated in a creative dialectic involving both projectivity and givenness

How the ecological density of faiths and ideologies connects with the efficacy of grace is the proper subject matter of chapter two, but its pertinence to the making of a language of grace will appear in the following sections. To set the tone for those discussions, perhaps a small example will serve. Imagine a woman working in a field, sowing seeds. She plants the seeds one by one, but she herself is unable to make them grow. She must dig and fertilize and water the ground. She must tend the shoots, but the harvest depends on rain and sunshine and the chemical-biological processes of the earth. The woman is action. The seeds are the values planted by human faith. The digging, watering and tending are ideologies. The harvest, however, is the gratuitous product of nature. The fruits of human action—what Jesus creatively referred to as the good news of a gratuitous kingdom construction coming from the heart of God— these fruits grow "in secret" like the seed within the ground. What they will look like in the end cannot be verified in advance but must be labored for, and, when reaped, accepted gratuitously as gift.

The Logic of Action and the Goodness of the News of Grace

In spite of the fact that Segundo begins the series *Theology for Artisans of a New Humanity* with a volume explicitly devoted to the subject of grace, his most constructive contribution to a Jesus-normed theology of cooperative grace occurs in *Jesus of Nazareth Yesterday and Today*.[69] In the five volumes of that work, after introducing the anthropological foundation of faith and ideologies on which to build, Segundo constructs a liberative interpretation of Jesus' kingdom *praxis* and life-story and then "multiplies"[70] its effectiveness with a theological exegesis of Paul's account in Romans 1-8 of the seemingly inefficacious (but ultimately efficacious) character of human action in an incomplete and tragic universe.[71]

As that mammoth effort shows, grace makes sense for Segundo only if it is presupposed that the interests of God under the conditions of nature and history in an incomplete universe center on the liberation of human freedom for the work of realizing a world-creative project with God. In the creative realization of a liberative project consists God's definitive values, which Jesus manifested as the will of God and Paul describes as the work of Faith in a yet to be created world.[72] Segundo shows that the will of God was Jesus' food and drink on earth, and in Jesus' God-revealing kingdom *praxis* and Paul's interpretation of it we learn that God abhors the sufferings of "sinners" and the poor and takes the side of the release of historical existence and the cosmos as a whole from meaninglessness, futility and fear.[73] From God's raising of Jesus from the dead we learn that God unconditionally values the creative participation of persons and groups of good will in the release of a Jesus-like kingdom freedom and the construction of a Jesus-normed kingdom love on earth.

Segundo thus views Paul's analysis of Faith in Romans 1-8 as a reinterpretation in an "anthropological key" of Jesus' original kingdom message and *praxis*, carried out in light of the clarifying datum of Jesus' resurrection and aimed at a universal audience. In other words, even though Paul transposes Jesus' kingdom gospel into a different key, Paul remains faithful to Jesus' original revelation of God's project and its values by showing the anthropological relevance of the intramundane liberations which Jesus called salvation, i.e., their relevance to the logic of human action.[74] While discussion of the historical-ecological, hermeneutical and eschatological significance of Segundo's original exegeses of Jesus' kingdom *praxis* and Paul's anthropological reinterpretation of it must be reserved for chapters two, three and four, it is necessary to bring out the anthropological significance of both exegeses here in order to focus on the project-centered character of Segundo's theology of grace. From his point of view, both Jesus' kingdom *praxis* and Paul's anthropology, although in different ways, succeed in showing that grace is a project made efficacious and real through the logic of human action.[75]

In this section I will look at the significance human action has in the eyes of God in light of Segundo's key theological affirmation that grace is a project. I will consider the anthropological schema of faiths and ideologies from the point of view of what a language derived from Jesus' God-revealing kingdom *praxis* calls the *good news*.

GOOD NEWS FOR FAITHS AND IDEOLOGIES

As has been seen, the "anthropological logic" of faiths and ideologies suggests that universally we human social persons tend to go on acting in the world as if our actions were ultimately worth the effort, even in the absence of empirical guarantees. We continue to act on the basis of suppositions and premises supplied for us by our anthropological faiths, even when the data of everyday experience seem to contradict those suppositions and premises. This tendency, which Segundo regards as a constant of human existence, is the answer provided by the logic of action itself to the question action poses: in the end, is the living of life in this—my, our, your— particular way and no other, e.g., in keeping with the values of persons and groups of good will who act constructively for the solution of problems in the world, is this way of living worth the long-term effort required in spite of the fact that we act always knowing that not only the efficacy of our actions but also our very lives will end?

For each person, as for every group and institution unified to a greater or lesser extent by the evocative power of symbols and traditions, the answer to that question appears concretely in action at the visible, and constitutively social and ecological, level of ideologies. The *praxes* we employ, the ideologies in which we and our faith traditions participate, serve either to substantiate the wager of faith, which responds to the question of the worthwhileness of action with an underlying fundamental yes, or else to keep on questioning that wager and perhaps even radically bely it, by providing evidence of a sort which cannot be reconciled with the premises of such a faith. The resulting discrepancy requires either a change of faith—an almost impossible phenomenon for adults[76]—or a revision of ideologies. It demands either a new wager and a different set of premises, ones more capable of taking into account the contradictory evidence and data of experience, or a readjustment of customary ideologies.[77]

For disciples of Jesus, however, the search for an answer does not end there, with the lifelong project of action's self-critique. Instead, it must take the step (perhaps the giant one of *metanoia*) of looking toward Jesus, taking into account what he said and did about the news of the kingdom of God. A disciple's faith must present to Jesus the same question every human faith presents to the witnesses on whom it is based: in the end, when all is said and done, is there any guarantee that living and acting in keeping with the values of God's heart manifested in the kingdom *praxis* of Jesus will actually turn out to have been as worth the effort as an anthropological faith in those values led one to believe? In other words, disciples must ask themselves, is anthropological faith in the values of Jesus worth it? Assuming, as always, the need for good will, an answer to that question could only be arrived at if there were some means of reliable verification, a definitive pledge or guarantee, capable of coming to disciples not only from outside the realm of their own experience—as in the case of transcendent data supplied for anthropological faith by the witness of others—but directly from the realm of the transcendent itself. *Is* there such a guarantee? *Has* the transcendent "spoken?"

According to the gospels (and the experience of disciples of Jesus), the answer is a joyous yes. The guarantee consists in God's having raised Jesus from the dead.[78] In the resurrection of Jesus, God demonstrated with the certainty of a guarantee that action in keeping with what Jesus revealed in his kingdom *praxis* to be the values of God's heart, i.e., action lived according to an anthropological faith in the kingdom values witnessed by Jesus, will, precisely in the end, show itself to have been definitively worth the effort. The resurrection is the gratuitous and yet "redundant"[79] yes of God in heaven to the question posed—and already being answered—by action on earth.

What makes the good news good, then, is its eschatological relevance for action. It is capable of answering the question about the final outcome of action which is posed by, already being answered in, but unable to be guaranteed through, the logic of action itself. In other words, what makes the good news good is precisely its appropriateness: that God *(qua* impassioned lover of suffering creatures in the gratuitous and concrete sphere of grace and not merely *qua* transcendent, sovereign "Lord" with respect to the abstract phenomenon of creatureliness as such) has shown that when action is modeled on the values of God's heart revealed in Jesus' kingdom *praxis,* its definitive worthwhileness is not an empty promise. Not only here and now, where the problems of the world call out for constructive solution and the evils of history and nature cry out for solidarity and resistance, but also in the end, when God will wipe away the tears from every eye, constructive action is guaranteed to have been worth the effort even if in the meantime it appears, like the life of Jesus and his death on the cross, to have been utterly ineffective or worthless. As Segundo is fond of saying, the good news in a nutshell—for people of good will—is that "in the history we share with God, no love is lost."[80] What is done in love will last with God forever. However small, it will show up in the eschaton as a definitive contribution to what Jesus called God's kingdom, that gratuitous yet appropriate project which manifests God's impassioned love for creatures and realizes God's commitment to the worthwhileness of their work.

GRACE FOR THE CREATION OF A WORLD

In order to make the goodness of this news from God—the eschatological relevance of action—accessible to people of good will, Segundo sets out to "reunite eternal life and the construction of history."[81] Such a task requires nothing less than a fresh interpretation of salvation. It is precisely that to which Segundo turns, through a theological revaluation of the logic of action in grace. In graced human action, he sees the moment where the freedom of God and the freedom of human social persons meet. In the structure of graced action, the realms of transcendence and immanence, absolute and relative, eschatological and historical—these two distinct but not incompatible spheres—are brought together and engage in a common work; for the freedom of God liberates human freedom, giving faith a God-like mission—creative love—and permitting human ideologies to contribute to the work of God in the single conjoint project of creation of the world.

For Segundo, the whole of Jesus' gospel is contained in the conjunction of the divine and human freedoms in grace. Their reciprocal relation means that graced action works at two different "logical levels," eschatological and historical, at once.[82] Viewed "from below," action that is graced appears as something wholly relative, a matter of tentative ideologies and incomplete *praxes* carried out by freedom under the ambiguous conditions of history and nature in an evolving world. Viewed "from above," the same action appears as something definitive and enduring, a matter of eschatological value directed toward definitive realization of the kingdom values of God. In this double significance, graced action condenses the deepest meaning of the doctrine of salvation: the liberation of human freedom is liberation coming from God, but it is liberation for the sake of creating with God a world.

When it comes to creating a theological understanding of salvation adequate to Jesus' kingdom message, Segundo believes, the importance of the liberation of freedom cannot be exaggerated:

> None of the great themes of Christianity can be understood without reference to liberty, that liberty which, like eternal life, comes from on high but is at the same time breakthrough and continuity, crisis and incarnation, life in the world and eschatology.[83]

Clearly, the liberty to which he is here referring is a freedom made capable of experiencing now, on earth, the eschatological relevance of salvation offered by God. The gratuitous liberation which grace effects is a liberation not from "matter," "nature," "finite being," "self" or "world," but precisely for the sake of them and capable of being effected at all only thanks to the capacity of each of those realms gratuitously to facilitate the projects of God's and creatures' love. Salvation, in short, is grace liberating freedom from timidity, immaturity, closed-circuitedness and every form of servile fear on behalf of the creation—in God-like love—of a world.[84]

The grace that brings salvation makes human freedom incredibly bold. By the free-making Spirit Who visits faith both in and as the gratuitous "news" of grace, disciples make bold to say to God, "Our Imma dear, our own beloved Abba!" In that boldness and in the capacity it gives human freedom to act for the construction of love on earth are contained the goodness of the news of grace and the fullest sense of its salvific logic so far as Segundo is concerned. The healing and liberation, elevation and reconciliation which according to a gospel-normed theology are what derive from grace—these have meaning in the audacious theology of Segundo insofar as they refer to the maturity, *qua* boldness, which results from human beings' being made co-workers with God and equal sharers in God's world-creative project.[85]

At the same time, however, it is equally true that the grace of salvation makes human freedom incredibly humble and meek. That is because freedom can not manipulate at will the laws of objective reality. Reaping eschatological results from intramundane action can not be had on demand. Efficacy is utterly gratuitous. It neither arises out of human purposiveness nor falls mysteriously out of heaven but arrives gratuitously during the tedious lifelong projects of love in which a meek and yet bold human Faith continues laboring in the realm of provisional ideologies. In such ideologies made gratuitously efficacious in Faith, creatures can learn to laugh for joy, but not at anyone's or anything's expense. Instead, efficacy arrives spontaneously like the naked affirmation of life which is the perfect body of a newborn child. It comes as news that is good. In the striking words of American novelist John Updike, one catches a glimpse of the overwhelming character of the experience of gratuitousness described in secular language: *"We are rewarded unexpectedly. The muddled and inconsequent surface of things now and then parts to yield us a gift. . . .[We get] the impression of being surrounded by an incoherent generosity."*[86]

In reflecting on such experience, particularly in the gospel idiom which must characterize the making of a Jesus-normed theology, theologians can speak about the apparent incoherence of that generosity in categories coherent enough to be translated into an intelligible theology. There it can be designated as grace-incited meekness, the anthropological appropriation by human Faith of the sheer generosity of God's impassioned love in a tragic and unfinished universe. It is the liberation of freedom by grace, the goodness of Jesus' news of God's gratuitous salvation. Because it comes to freedom as something redundant—a gratuitous and appropriate project which engages anthropological faith in love and includes it in a world-creative project—it is necessary to uncover what Jesus' gospel reveals about the grace that brings salvation. How is it with the exciting *raison d' être* of freedom which Segundo claims can make human beings both meek and bold, *raison d' être* that Jesus describes as God's good news of a liberative kingdom placed here at hand and, very soon afterward, Paul interprets with the anthropological notion of Spirit-guided Faith?

Grace Liberates Freedom for Creative Action in History. As was pointed out in the introductory chapter, central to the goodness of Jesus' news about God is the at-handness of a kingdom announced free of charge to "sinners" and the poor. What was so good about this announcement was that it was not just the promise of a future event but the inauguration of a whole new way of experiencing the present.[87] In other words, Jesus' news about God's kingdom was heard by "sinners" and the poor as news that is good thanks to the capacity of Jesus' kingdom *praxis* actually to convey tangible liberations from evils and ills suffered in history now. Jesus' *praxis* shows that concrete instances of liberation on earth are capable of being experienced with joy and welcomed as news that is good not only by the deprived themselves but by those who are sensitive to their sufferings and in solidarity with their struggle. Outstanding in compassion and fidelity among the latter, Jesus claims, is God.

According to Segundo, Paul's assertion in Galatians that "in Christ there is neither Gentile nor Jew, slave nor free, male nor female," shows that, like Jesus' kingdom *praxis,* what Paul calls Faith has an inherently liberative effect on human beings which occurs at the level of action: it results in the transformation of enslaving relationships, turning them into relationships of freedom, justice and love.[88] Segundo's treatment of the Galatians text thus provides an appropriate exegetical gloss on the meaning of Faith in Romans 1-8. There, Segundo points out, grace liberates freedom to engage in new ways of relating to other beings, both human and other-than-human, including God and the world as a whole. It replaces unfree relationships, flawed by the divisiveness of dichotomies like those enumerated in the Galatians text, with free and innovative relations modeled on the gratuitous love of God. In this way grace frees action for constructive God-like love.

What do these new social relations look like? On the one hand, grace replaces a cold, theologically deficient Creator-creature schema[89] by initiating a warm and reciprocally involving love relation of kinship or friendship with God, what Paul calls equality with God by adoption.[90] The gratuitous reciprocity of this love makes creatures capable of working with God as equals at a common interest or task. In the warmth of friendship, God is moved to a deep and everlasting kinship with creatures, welcoming them as partners and companions into the challenging prospect of participating conjointly in a worthwhile project of world-creative love. At the same time, and deriving from the logic of what Paul calls adoption, grace founds the building of a sororal and fraternal community with others in the world, what Paul calls disciples' becoming actual (as opposed to merely legal) sisters and brothers of Jesus.[91]

By linking the notions of adoption and community, Segundo underscores the prominence Paul gives to the social and historical dimensions of grace, in particular the centrality of Paul's assertion that Faith is not a religious privilege but a sociohistorical task.[92] Segundo believes that in a universe in which the definitive creation still has to be completed and made good, grace ignites an inextinguishable spark of creative power, a gratuitous coincidence between two distinct yet compatible logics: the logic of God's love in grace and the logic of human action at its inmost point of origins, i.e., the point at which freedom finds itself already situated in an objectively given universe and oriented toward the realization of values. In other words, grace initiates a friendship capable of realizing both the gratuitous love of God for creatures and the intrinsic meaning and value the world already strives to give itself in the phenomenon of action. Grace proposes and Faith realizes a gratuitous coincidence between the values dearest to God's heart and the values more or less being espoused by the hearts of individual human beings and social groups at the level of anthropological faith.

For Segundo, the coincidence of divine and human values in Faith is actually the realization, at the level of action, of a union of the divine and human wills in love, a divine-human communion which means not to be at one with God ontologically but to build together with God at the practical level of a sharing of faiths (and ideologies) in the world. Since community is a function of communion, Faith strives not so much to attain a static harmony with the being of others as to be engaged in a project of building together with them in love. Communal action with other creatures in Faith is thus as essential to the successful realization of God's creative project as is kinship between God and human beings in grace. As Segundo insists, love can be realized only at the level of action. It is a matter of the gratuitous meeting of mutually shared values. In the apt words of Segundo, "We cannot truly love someone unless we share a common *project* with that person, a project that is important both to that person and ourselves."[93]

Segundo thus begins his interpretation of Faith with a premise provided by his own anthropological faith in the Jesus-derived tradition: both the gospel preached by Jesus and the gospel transposed into a different, yet coherent key by Paul make it plain that God wills the maturity of human freedom.[94] God wills that human beings be neither slaves nor children but heirs to a gratuitously given promise, inheritors of a creative task, adult companions and friends, co-workers with God in God's creative project of love and liberation in history and nature.[95] Although "Jesus does not give a name to this crucial, decisive attitude," Segundo believes it is identical with what Paul calls Faith.[96]

Jesus' kingdom *praxis,* which freed those bound by social and religious rigidities in the alleged name of "God," shows that God considers salvation to consist in liberation from social and historical enslavements beginning here and now. Jesus' resurrection suggests that we may go even further and say that God wills that disciples be Spirit-guided participants in the same kind of liberative kingdom project which received its name and distinctive features from Jesus.[97] In making that project accessible and familiar to disciples, Jesus initiated for all human beings the possibility of a mature relationship with God, a daughterhood and sonship come of age. By this kinship disciples are freed from infantile fears and self-centered insecurities about their own salvation to inherit instead from God a full participation in Jesus' kingdom mission and an adult responsibility for its success. Like Jesus, disciples, too, may enter with full maturity into creative kingdom *praxis* with God.[98]

Taking a cue from Paul, Segundo argues that the maturity God wills for disciples is not a matter of child-like obedience to "God's Law" but of a new *raison d'être* for human freedom. It is identical with what Paul means by Faith. For Paul, Segundo says, Faith is the liberation of freedom from timidity and fear into full maturity for the sake of constructive, love-building action.[99] "Faith," he writes, "is something very different from a specific act. . . .We see it as *a way of being human,* as something which moves the human being from infantile timidity to maturity, from action based on petty calculation to action performed in a gratuitous and creative manner."[100] It thus points toward the same type of historical liberation that Jesus' kingdom *praxis* effected and that, according to Jesus, conveys the experience of salvation.[101]

Segundo insists that at one and the same time the Faith that brings salvation both defines the *raison d'être* of human action and provides the guarantee of its validity as something worthwhile here on earth. For Segundo, salvation is God's gratuitous subsidy, God's freely given "down-payment," on the eschatological validity of what nevertheless remains a fully this-worldly task: construction of Jesus-like kingdom love for the sake of creating a world. As such, it is a matter of the building of God-like love in this world, a task to which disciples must address the best efforts of their intelligence, for success at working at God's project depends as much upon how the intellect interprets the needs of others and the problems of the world as upon the willingness of freedom to act in love on their behalf.[102]

In this sense, Segundo defines salvation as a whole new grounding for action.[103] Because salvation involves participation in a project, the Faith that realizes it is a matter of disciples' learning to relate to God in an intimacy capable of being lived by adults, a matter of their embarking on a way of living by which, neither moving in too close nor drifting too far apart, they share God's goods, enjoy God's company and promote God's dearest values.[104] It is a matter of knowing that everything which is God's has been made available to disciples as their own, that as devoted friends and intimates of God they drink the same cup of suffering as Jesus, share the same history as Jesus' Spirit and work for the same eschatological goal as God whom Jesus called Abba.

Finally, Segundo believes, this new and trusting relation of kinship or friendship with God is what Paul means when he speaks of justification. It is the Faith by which God declares human beings just, the Faith that effects salvation.[105] At bottom, it is the Faith which makes human beings both meek enough and bold enough to love and be loved by God. Faith permits creatures to share in the creative efficacy of God's love. It turns creatures into friends,[106] engaging human freedom with the freedom of God for the sake of a project dear to the hearts of both. It allows human beings to take joy in that friendship and make it the matrix of constructive action. In short, it makes them adult kin and equals by "adoption" to God:

In order to understand Segundo's account of Paul's anthropological schema, it is important to note that what Paul means by Faith in the letter to the Romans is not equivalent to what Segundo means by faith as an anthropological dimension. Rather, Segundo points out that Faith for Paul is synonymous with what the latter calls living by the Spirit.[107]   In this sense, Faith is the life of God which, dwelling in anthropological faith, animates, directs and enlivens it with the good news that, limited though it be, it is charged with a creative task and possesses for the project of God's heart a genuinely constructive value. Faith requires as condition of its efficacy what Paul calls Flesh, a notion synonymous with the human condition.[108] Segundo's entire argument centers on the conviction that Paul's notion of Flesh is coterminous with the essential structure of human freedom. It is identical with the anthropological tension between faiths and ideologies that defines the logic of action.

When anthropological faith is liberated in grace to function as Faith, Flesh is liberated to function as Spirit. This transformation sums up for Segundo the logic of salvation Faith. Aimed at the creation of a world out of love, that logic is what Segundo believes defines the liberative dimension of the logic of grace. According to it, Faith is what Flesh gratuitously welcomes and Spirit is what Flesh gratuitously becomes when grace liberates anthropological faith for participation in God's creative project. "In Faith," Segundo writes, "the Spirit. . .lays down the initial foundation for a completely new existence, one opposed to the mechanisms of the Flesh. Only this new life is capable of the creative boldness proper to children of God, of achieving something new in the history of the universe, which is the Creator's heritage."[109]

Faith Is a Gratuitous Anthropological Dimension. The liberation of freedom in grace is thus a liberation with two dimensions. Objectively it is experienced as salvation and subjectively it is apprehended as Faith. Because it is a liberation of anthropological faith in no way earned or due to it but is entirely the result of grace, Segundo refers to Faith as a "gratuitous anthropological dimension."[110] It is the gratuitous human appropriation of the values of God's heart. Appropriating God's values creates an intimacy and kinship with God and not the other way around.[111] To appropriate God's values, however, i.e., to act gratuitously in self-transcending love, human faith must be liberated by the Spirit from the self-justifying and security-seeking tendencies of fear. In the language of the gospel of John, anthropological faith has to be able to know, and be sure, that God has first loved creatures if creatures are to be made free to love God in return. As that which makes effective a human confidence in God's initiative of love, Faith forms a constitutive—although gratuitous—element of graced human existence.[112] Paradoxically, it is constitutive because it manifests the *possibility* that without Faith, anthropological faith would be incapable of loving God with a truly human response, and it is gratuitous because it points to the prior *fact* that God has loved creatures first. Faith is the gratuitous dimension of anthropological faith which brings the good news to Flesh that it is capable of finding itself already liberated, already graced with Spirit and garlanded with love.

According to Segundo's interpretation of Romans 1-8, Faith is thus a new way of living made actual for Flesh by the Spirit. It is a new way of seeing, a new way of punctuating the events of everyday reality which results from the sheer gratuity of grace, the joy of experiencing from God God's irrevocable commitment to the creation of a world that is good and God's gratuitous option to share in its struggle and validate the work for its realization. In this sense the Faith that justifies and brings salvation is experienced as a deep trust and confidence in the freely initiated companionship and whole-hearted love of God for creatures.[113] Faith thus gives anthropological faith new epistemological premises on which to base a positive interpretation of even the most negative and futile experiences.[114]

In the end, Segundo's exegesis of Paul's analysis of Faith suggests that Faith involves an acceptance and affirmation by God of humans' fundamental anthropological structure with its already existing logic of faiths and ideologies, the structure Paul calls Flesh, the essential element of the human condition. Faith places Flesh in a context of gratuitous relationship with God for the sake of creative participation in the love-building project of God. In this sense, grace "recapitulates" the logic of human action.[115] It is redundant to that logic yet capable of being welcomed by it, giving action itself a teleological reorientation, a gratuitous vocation: co-creation with God of a world built of love. At the same time, grace gives anthropological faith the capacity to live this meaning and vocation. It "redounds upon" the anthropological logic of faiths and ideologies with a brand new *raison d' être*—the kingdom logic of grace—so as to make action itself a constitutive element of the creation of the new heaven and new earth promised by God. When that creative project is finally finished, there will be manifest in its light the definitive value of creative action: there will be visible at last a world that is good, a world in which ideologies of Faith, Flesh though they be, will have contributed an eschatologically enduring substance—love—to God's definitive work of Spirit in the eschaton.

The Theological Significance of the Liberation of Human Freedom. For Segundo, God's invitation to human beings to be included in grace in a project of eschatological creation clearly implies that the point of our being human at all is to learn in grace to open the wellsprings of freedom. His saying that, of course, can sound rather dangerous. For one thing, it may remind us of some of the existentialist philosophies of the first half of this century. Often they made human subjectivity the major concern, forgetting the objective givenness of the rest of reality, in particular, the complex realm of history and nature with its social and ecological dimensions. For another thing, Segundo's focus on freedom may strike us as backtracking to the Enlightenment and its interest—liberal rather than liberative—in the ideal of human autonomy. As the critique of Enlightenment shows, an abstract concept of human freedom can easily be translated into sociopolitical ideologies of individualism and nationalism and ecological technologies of exploitation: vis-à-vis objective realities like nature and the second nature of culture, the normative relation can become one of human conquest.

In trying to ground an ideal of freedom released from external constraints, for example, existentialism frequently ended up interpreting autonomy in a predominantly anthropocentric way.[116] Freedom was often made to oppose the objective realm in such a way as to cancel out the constructive value of limits. Merely to reduce freedom to "free will," on the other hand, represents its radical subjection to an extraneous order—the law—in such a way as to erase stray marks of human creativity and force freedom to choose between two apparently equal alternatives, good and evil.[117]

So far as Segundo is concerned, the resulting dilemma is one of the principal signs of the times. It shows that vis-à-vis the task of theological interpretation of Jesus' revelation of God, positions like these are ultimately retrogressive. Each leads to the same dead end: competition between the freedom of human social persons and the freedom of a seemingly arbitrary and ungracious Creator.[118] In a competitive schema, freedom can appear largely as a curse, a cruel joke inflicted by "God" in order to put human beings to a test. If, along with Sartre, for example, we rebel against such devaluation of the human, we must once and for all do away with the divine test-giver, even if it means setting out alone in the direction of an absurd and meaningless universe.[119] On the other hand, if, along with neoscholasticism, for example, we follow the rules and attempt to pass the test, we must shackle freedom in order to keep it within the orderly bounds of the law. One never matures into adulthood but remains the obedient child of an arbitrary and demanding parent. Given the healthiness of Sartre's atheism of protest against the latter, the theist faces a dilemma: Is it possible to affirm the definitive value of human freedom without having to negate the transcendent value of the sovereign freedom of God?

To escape such an impasse, Segundo follows the cue of those atheists who reject all alienating and enslaving images of "God" in favor of human responsibility and maturity.[120] Because he is a theist and a Christian, however, he puts forward a new cosmological base, a new set of philosophical presuppositions on which to found a concept of freedom capable of supporting not only responsible human maturity but also meaningful relations between God and the world. On this base he constructs a Jesus-normed concept of freedom which aims to be true to what experience points out about the logic of freedom and coherent with what Jesus' kingdom *praxis* reveals about God.

God whom Jesus' kingdom *praxis* revealed does not diminish human freedom or threaten it with extinction but welcomes and wills it, precisely for the sake of placing at hand what Jesus called the kingdom. God wills the maturity of human freedom because God wills the liberation of all who are enslaved, especially when that slavery is imposed—blasphemously—on the many by a few who claim to be acting in the name of "God." Because human social persons are ends in themselves, they may never be used as means, even by God. God stands at the door and knocks but does not manipulate or coerce. God frees. God liberates human freedom for creative action in history and nature.[121] By freeing action for constructive participation in the creation of a world, God frees anthropological faith to take up a vocation compatible with the logic of its own action: the realization of gratuitous, God-like love in a world being created painstakingly "by hand" on earth.

As was seen in the opening sections, a world not yet finished being created can not be originally and already good. Creation is open-ended and incomplete; anything can happen, depending on how things go, depending on who acts or does not act and on how action itself is carried on. Precisely as something that in such a situation God deliberately wills should *not* be tragic and futile but meaningful and good, God's project requires the contribution of human freedom if it is to be worthwhile from the point of view of *God*. Segundo is convinced that God cannot utter the word "good" about creation at all, unless creatures themselves work with God to build a world out of love. When all is said and done, the world that is thus created will be pronounced good not by God alone, but by God and creatures rejoicing together at the completion of a creation that resulted from the co-creative power of their conjoint work of love.

The creation of a world that is good is thus capable of being understood in an ontologically meaningful way as the definitive human vocation. It is a task to be carried out by action. Transposing the categories of such an ontology into a theological key results in an interpretation of grace capable of being understood in terms compatible with the impulse toward creative responsibility at the heart of the logic of action. In grace, God takes the first step at making the "suggestion" that the creation of a world that is good is a worthwhile human vocation. God does this by initiating a situation of loving reciprocity in which God and human social persons can gradually learn to work together as equals. To this gratuitous and novel project, Jesus, who was experienced by the poor as sheer grace and by the disciples first as task and then as grace of God risen from the dead and incarnate on earth in action—to this project, Jesus gave the name kingdom of God. To verify that name, he placed the project as a whole on an unshakeable foundation: the very kingdom *praxis* unto death which formed the logic and substance of his life.

In light of such a theology of grace, one must conclude that the shape of the eschaton is not definitively known, even by God. So far, thanks to the datum of the resurrection, we can be sure of the shape of its cornerstone, Jesus, God's oil of gladness anointing creatures with the redundant and yet appropriate goodness of the gratuitous news of grace. The ideologies Jesus created, the fruits of his life-work and death—these, like the the wounds which identify his risen body, are established in the eschaton as its basic and definitive structure. What will be the final dimensions of its architectural design, however, remains to be seen. That definitive work of art must leave room for contributions of love from every crack and crevice of the universe through which, by whatever struggle and in the face of however many tears, love was brought forth as something done gratuitously for others.

Grace Is Action's Love-building *Charism,* Creative of a World

As has been seen, Jesus inaugurates the kingdom of God as a project. It is a liberative project initiated by God in nature and history—a task to be accomplished on earth as it is in heaven—and it is revealed in the kingdom *praxis* of Jesus as good news for "sinners" and the poor. As good news, Jesus' inauguration of God's kingdom comes upon the world as grace. Through the down-to-earth action of Jesus, whose kingdom *praxis* in word and deed releases captives, gives sight to the blind, makes the lame walk, hands salvation to outcasts and sinners without attaching a price, brings good news, free, to the poor and restores the dead to life—through these concrete actions, grace arrives in flesh and blood, is broken and distributed, poured out in abundance as gift almost "too good to be true" from God.

When Jesus is put to death, however, it appears that the project of the kingdom is defeated. In the fiasco of the cross, Jesus dies hoping against hope that God has not abandoned him. For all practical purposes, that is the same as Jesus' hoping against appearances that God has not abandoned the kingdom project. As bringer of good news to the end, however, God does not leave Jesus' action at the mercy of appearances. Instead, God creates out of Jesus' kingdom *praxis* and death—i.e., allows gratuitously to emerge out of the entropic elements of Jesus' entire work and life—a resurrection.

By raising Jesus from the dead, God manifests that the seemingly defeated efficacy of Jesus' kingdom project has resulted in the eruption of a new and unprecedented efficacy in the form of a living, ongoing love: transmission of the values and logic of the kingdom project through disciples who carry the risen Jesus' news of the creative and liberative power of Jesus' unbounded Spirit.[122] In that good news, recorded in the texts of the gospels, Acts and letters of Paul, is embodied what might fittingly be called the first side of the news of grace, the sheer gratuitousness of the love of God for "sinners," among whom not only was Jesus numbered but with whom he was in solidarity unto death.[123] The gospels show that this is a love that, made manifest through God's love of "sinners" and the poor, is also an unshakeable love creative of an everlastingly valid world. What this first side of the story reveals is that vis-à-vis the liberative strivings of human faiths and the value of love-building projects, of which Jesus' kingdom project has been made by God into definitive prototype, the definitive validation of freedom in the invigorating atmosphere of grace is God's absolutely free and gratuitous gift.[124]

Yet the gospel of grace has a second side as well, a dimension that manifests itself historically and ecologically as task. The task dimension of grace derives from the intramundane orientation of grace itself, which is a matter of God's love for creatures and of the creation with them of a world. Because grace is a love in which God is caught up with creatures in a project creative not just of any world whatsoever but of a world that is inhabitable and good, it results in the innovative salvaging of all the worthwhile works that will ever have been accomplished or suffered in a tragic and unfinished universe and the weaving of them together into the fabric of a world built out of the only material strong enough to last, namely love. Grace is God's gratuitous love initiating a project of the making of love a reality in the world. It is a love that wants to be realized. Creation remains a divine *fiat* empty of substance unless creatures embody it in action.[125]

In order to be real, grace has to show up in objective reality at the level of action, for action is the medium in which freedom incarnates values. It is the means by which a love that is yearning to come to term may be objectified or put into concrete existence. Action is the medium through which the values of God, which have been made available in grace through God's impassioned solidarity with the logic of human action *qua* Faith, can be put into concrete social, historical and ecological form. Action that participates in this way in the creative action of God is capable of mediating the everlasting love of God. It is the realization in Faith of a love directed toward definitive creation. This occurs not only at the individual and sociohistorical levels but at the ecological level as well, through objectification of the values of Faith in *praxes* and institutions. All political and social structures, every societal order, all human patterns of interrelating with other persons and groups, all interrelationships with other creatures and with the spheres of living and non-living beings, all scientific theories and technologies, all the arts and every symbolic, cultural and linguistic form—all of these are institutions. They are what Segundo calls ideologies: objective traces of human action implicating the evolving continuum of history and nature in the values of human faiths.

Into these ideologies God's values seek entry by "knocking at the door" of anthropological faith, for it is only through anthropological faith's objectification of values in ideologies that God can effect the gratuitous realization of God's unbounded love, can make the effects of that love felt as unsolicited yet welcome gift of God. The news that Faith is constitutively social, historical and ecological is thus the second side of the story of grace, evidence of its continuous arrival in history and nature as a task. Anthropological faith experiences grace as a call to action, an invitation to shoulder responsibility for the quality and shape of human ideologies in nature and history. Grace arrives at the door of anthropological faith as a summons or mission, a calling upon freedom to gather its energies for the sake of realizing God's project of creation in an unfinished world; its appropriation in Faith manifests itself historically as a response to a vocation.

The positing of a task dimension in grace has a radical effect on what it means to speak about discipleship of Jesus, what in the categories of traditional theology pertains to the notion of *church*.[126] Because disciples inherit the task of translating Jesus' good news of the kingdom project into categories appropriate to the situation of differing times and places and must incarnate God's values in ideologies aimed at the solution of problems confronting creatures in history and nature, they give public witness to what theology has traditionally called God's universal will to save.[127] In every time and place they are charged with manifesting Jesus' revelation about God's love and making it historically and ecologically effective. The community which is founded on Jesus' God-revealing kingdom *praxis* must bear public witness to the news from God that grace is given precisely in order to be realized.[128]

Grace is thus the word of love initially spoken by God which needs objective ideologies—Faith at work—to become substantial and complete. This means that grace must be incarnated in flesh and blood, what, relying on the language of scripture, one might call an authority of word backed by deed, exactly as it was in the case of Jesus.[129] Something has to result from grace. It has to become historically and ecologically tangible on earth if God's love for the world is to become a reality.

ACTION'S *CHARISM* FOR THE GRATUITOUS REALIZATION OF SELF-TRANSCENDING LOVE

The inseparable dimensions of gift and task that appear in the structure of grace suggest that an appropriate language by which to communicate Jesus' news about God's initiative of a creative project is the language of gratuitousness and responsibility, i.e., *charism*. By initiating a project aimed at the creation of a world that is built on love and will last with God forever, God's love for creatures gratuitously funds action, already meaningful and valid in itself, with the God-like creative *charism*.[130]

Insofar as grace liberates anthropological faith for the work of God's project in Faith, it makes faith capable of mediating God's love for a world still suffering to be born. Precisely because it is a *charism,* the realization of such love is not static, like a "state of being," but actionable, like a project. It makes creatures not objects of God's love but rather responsible subjects co-equal with God in a love which shares a common objective. It points toward the making of a new and lasting creation that will be the single result of a conjoint work, the realization of a mutually committed love.

Conceptualizing Faith as Action's Charism. The language and experience of *charism* is appropriate to grace because, strictly speaking, a *charism* is a gift that is a task.[131] It does not alter the identity or value of recipients but recapitulates their intrinsic capabilities by placing them in a gratuitously new context. It multiplies the significance of their power. To speak of Faith as the *charism* of human action is to understand grace as God's initiative in love toward anthropological faith, a knock at the door that results in a reorientation of faith's possibly already existing love-building goals and aims. God's love does not change the status of creatures but involves them in a project they are already capable of valuing as something meaningful and worthwhile to do. It places in a new context—God's project—the intramundane logic of their own action but does not make itself necessary to that logic for either the validity or integrity of anthropological faith. With respect to the logic of action, in other words, grace is gratuitous yet appropriate. It is gratuitous insofar as it is not demanded by the evidence; i.e., for the validity of the logic of action, God's project is neither deserved nor required. It is appropriate insofar as it is fitting to the logic of action; i.e., it is a contribution capable of being welcomed by action's already existing logic of faiths and ideologies.[132]

Grace as action's *charism* is therefore not a latent dimension of anthropological faith. It is not a simple completion of action's logic. It relates to action as neither infinite horizon of finite being nor limit dimension of finite freedom but rather comes to both freedom and being at the point of their creative intersection in faith and ideologies. It arrives as an unsolicited piece of good news, purely and simply as gift. It is utterly gratuitous, like an invitation. It invites an anthropological faith already integral and meaningful in itself to embark upon a Spirit-inspired project that is suitable to faith but not necessary to its proper operation. This leaves a healthy amount of distance between God and the world. It "makes room" for the acceptance of risk on both the world's and God's parts, not only of the cosmos' being placed at the service of a project in which creatures participate equally with God but of the cosmos' being placed at the service of projects other than the one inspired and willed by God. The *charism* of grace leaves anthropological faith its proper "room to breathe." It responds to the integrity of action's own logic by respecting anthropological faith's capacity to realize through means that are fully its own an initiative that comes from God. Grace enables Faith to remain the proper achievement of a fully autonomous human faith.

The charismatic character of graced action comes to light in the orientation of faiths and ideologies toward the efficacious carrying out of projects. In other words, the appropriateness of God's creative initiative resides in action's already existing affinity for constructive action in history and nature.[133] As was suggested earlier, creativity is not self-expression. On the contrary, it is the drive of anthropological faith toward the objective realization of results. It refers to the incarnation of values, the building of ideologies in which the values of a particular anthropological faith attain a more or less efficacious degree of objective expression in reality. It is the objective dimension of the implementation of values that is expressed in creative action and not primarily the subjective dimension of the self. The difference between the two is that the expression of values is impossible without respect for and gratitude to the constructive contributions of objective reality. Expression of self, on the other hand, can be attempted without reference to the objective givenness of reality, and to the extent that it is, it can be carried on ungraciously, lacking in gratitude to contributions from objective nature and lacking in sensitivity to the ecological continuity nature and history share in an evolving world.

With regard to values, action is humanity's occupational hazard, its typifying trait. On the one hand, in the preoccupation of anthropological faith with creating ideologies out of values, action seems to have an inherent interest in being interested. Action represents the inalienable tendency of anthropological faith to commit itself to projects deemed to be worthwhile. On the other hand, in the phenomenon of ideologies action exhibits a dependence on and delimitation by the objective givenness of reality. The values it seeks to incarnate are not only radically conditioned by the objective reality that rises to the surface in ideologies but sometimes actually resisted or inhibited. It is at the heart of this logic that the charismatic quality of graced human action resides. Grace gains access to action at the level of anthropological faith, bringing news of a gratuitous and yet appropriate project to which Faith can deem it worthwhile to commit itself: the construction of works of love that, even should they die, are not going to stay dead forever. This is a project which is not at all alien to anthropological faith but rather highly compatible with its own inmost orientation: the incarnation of faith in ideologies.

The Causality of Human Action in Grace. Capable of signifying both gift and task, *charism* is thus a constructive theological category. It is especially appropriate for interpreting what Segundo regards as the causal relation between human action and efficacious realization of God's project. Realization of what Jesus called the kingdom of God, which, in the language of Paul is the love of God made Flesh in grace as fully human love, depends in a way definitively important for God on what we human social persons do and do not do in history.[134] It depends on what Segundo calls the "historical causality" of human freedom.[135] Just as in the case of Jesus' kingdom *praxis*, to which God gave definitive validation and eschatological value through the gratuitous action of raising Jesus and the kingdom project from the dead, so too will God "raise up" and validate the projects Faith does in love.[136] God will incorporate the fruits of such projects into the eschatological reality which endures forever.

What about the projects that we failed to carry out, the abortive ones, or those which miscarried before they were even conceived? The answer is that just as there could have been no resurrection without the prior, fully human and historical creativity of the kingdom *praxis* of Jesus, God will not make up for what we human social persons have failed or fail to do.[137] Segundo's reasons for this are ontological: without our action, God can not create a world that is good. In an incomplete universe, God can not act to remedy injustice or protest against the sufferings of creatures without the contribution of human action.[138] The power of God to eliminate suffering depends entirely on what we do (or refrain from doing). If we do not act with our freedom, there is no way for God to prevent suffering, to free our sisters and brothers from earthly hells.[139]

Whatever we do not accomplish will therefore simply not become an eschatological reality. It will not be able to be present in the eschatological "salvaging" of history which is the definitive realization of what Jesus called God's kingdom. God's capacity to resurrect the projects of human action in history and nature depends in a radical way on our first having objectified those projects in concrete institutions or ideological forms, however imperfect those objectifications might continue to be under the conditions of incompleteness in an evolving world. Because grace initiates not only a gift but a task, it depends on social, historical and ecological objectifications—human ideologies—for its eschatological effectiveness.

Paradoxically, to be making such statements is not only to be affirming the objective value of the secular world and human ideologies within it but to be acknowledging the restraint and sensitivity of the creative action that is God's gracious love. It is to be saying with Segundo that the "laborer par excellence"[140] who is God "does not invade our history. . . .The Absolute enters the world of [history and nature] in such a way that [God] does not take over possession of it; instead [God] places [Godself] at the disposal of every [woman, child and] man, and each [woman, child and] man becomes absolute in turn."[141] This conception of God's action means for Segundo that history (and, in an ecologically conscientized perspective one must add, nature as well) is the realm of the meeting of two absolutes, two equally determinative creative freedoms, that of God and that of human social persons.[142] Creation is a deed that must be done conjointly, the accomplishment of partners who are equal in love and freedom, each contributing to an action in which neither takes over the unique contribution of the other. Creation can not be the work of God alone. It represents a common project or cooperative labor between God and human beings which respects human freedom and recognizes its capacity to prevent, or at least alleviate, the suffering of creatures on earth.[143]

At bottom, to be making such theological assertions is to be saying that, in the face of human freedom, God's action is a passion, God's love is a suffering of human action. It is a willingness to keep on "putting up with" the evils creatures will and do inflict on one another, particularly in the human sphere, at the same time that it is a power strong enough to raise the dead to life. By such impassioned love God is committed to an everlasting solidarity with creatures in the face of evil and suffering. To be making such assertions is to be saying, in the spirit of Maurice Blondel, that God is *patient* before the action of creatures, that God does not "lord it over" creatures but, taking their ontological status *qua* creatures with absolute seriousness, suffers the risk of their acting in God's eyes as *equals,* relating to creatures as if their action has something as substantial and valuable to offer God as God has to offer them. Blondel's text on this subject is intriguing and deserves being quoted:

> But if things are active and truly real, if they subsist under their objective aspect, in short, if they are, it is because the divine eye sees them through the eye of the creature itself, no longer insofar as He creates them, but insofar as they are created and their author makes Himself passive of their proper action.[144]

In the gratuitously initiated friendship that is grace, God relies for the authentic realization of God's project as much on the contributions of creatures' action as on the contributions of God's own action. God thus realizes God's proper identity *qua* God by respecting an equally valid yet different identity proper to creatures *qua* creatures. In other words, God refuses to invade the integrity of creatures' freedom.

In the language of Segundo about the historical causality of human action, a similar image seems to be at work concerning the action of God. God stands at the door and knocks.[145] God's love is patient. It waits for the action of creatures to run its course, and it gives them room to breathe. God is not afraid to tolerate error and even welcomes the lifelong projects of gradual maturing and the learning through which anthropological faith must go.[146] God's love can suffer ideologies to run their course, even when they contradict the love-building rationale of the project of God and violate the logic of action.[147] And since God's principal concern is with the realization of a love that is gratuitous and centered on the creation of a world, God is unconcerned about whether God gets loved "sufficiently" in return or gets recognized as "God." God is patient of creatures' action because God's love for them is real. It will not be undone, even by the forces of evil, but remains forever faithful in solidarity.

When the two sides—gift and task—of the logic of grace are joined together, the good news of grace is complete. It may then be summed up in the form of a simple thesis: in a tragic and unfinished universe, God is interested in working with creatures at a project that both of them are capable of valuing: the creation of a world that is good, a world that will last forever because it is a conjoint work of art, a world that, when finally finished being created, will be able to be lived in and enjoyed, a world built not out of divine (or human) "genius" alone but out of the suffering patience and sustained commitment of a conjointly shared passion that is realized *qua* action in self-transcending love.

The Theological Significance of the Language and Experience of Love. It could be said that the notion of God's being patient in the face of human action represents a practical, objective dimension apparently missing from Schleiermacher's seminal notion of human beings' absolute dependence on God. It balances out what is often overlooked or at least passed over lightly since theology's decisive but still heavily Cartesian "turn to the subject."[148] What Segundo's notion of intramundane causality seems to restore is a healthy realism, a return to the importance of objective reality.[149] Since Segundo sees freedom as both oriented toward and conditioned by the objective givenness of reality, his theology is capable of bringing out the Blondelian insight about God's dependence on the action of creatures.[150] If grace is to achieve its end, which is the incarnation in a definitively completed world of God's love for those whose action has contributed substantially to its creation, then the love of God for creatures and the love of creatures for God must be realized not at the level of intersubjectivity or experience alone but in the sphere of objective reality.

That is because, when all is said and done, love *qua* experience is not only an intersubjective relationship but an objective held in common. It is a communication of values, something that can be realized only by God's and creatures' sharing in one another's interests and participating with one another in the responsible context of an equally shouldered project. The love of God for creatures stands in need of an ontologically solid response from creatures, a fleshing out of Faith through ideologies upon which God looks as utterly valid. In the unprecedented action of raising Jesus and his apparently defeated kingdom project from the dead, God has promised that at the dawning of the eschaton God will incorporate into the new heaven and the new earth not only historical subjects, i.e., persons and groups who love, but objective reality itself, the tangible fruits of the concrete ideologies those subjects' faiths have constructed, the fragile results of projects at which they have labored in love.

Thinking of grace as a project thus entails making some basic shifts of perspective. A first change involves shifting traditional theological understandings concerning God's sovereignty. In its classical formulations, traditional theology tended to regard the sovereignty of God in two closely related ways. On the one hand, due to the need to refrain from compromising the sovereign freedom of God, God was considered to be the true, inner subject of both the creation of the world and the gracing of human beings in history. History was understood in terms of what came in this century to be called "the history of salvation," a God-directed realization of a gradually unfolding revelation. According to this logic, creation exists for the sake of the historical realization of God's self-revelation. It is the first step of a "double *donum*," the second of which is grace. The point of grace is the realization in history of God's self-revelation, and the point of human existence is the either thematized or unthematized acceptance of it.[151]

At the same time, however, traditional theology tended to regard God's self-communication as the proper object of human freedom and love. This meant that human existence in this world was understood in terms of its last end or object, the ultimate goal of which was to possess God eternally (suprahistorically) as object of a *visio* which would fulfill in beatific glory a knowledge of God begun on earth by grace.[152] By the indwelling of the Holy Spirit (grace), human nature was said to be elevated in such a way as to be made capable of becoming the vessel in which God as subject takes possession of the human subject in so close a union as to permit the latter to experience God as fulfillment of its every desire and in such a way as to enable it to possess God fully as object. Graced human freedom, or Faith, was considered the "place" where God accepted God in a gratuitous outpouring of love for (sinful) humankind.[153] The history of each human individual as well as the collective history of the world came in this way to be understood as the history of salvation.[154]

By contrast, a theological interpretation of grace in terms of a divinely initiated project requires a shift from Faith as object of salvation to creation as Faith's God-given gratuitous objective. On the one hand, Faith is already the grace of salvation, yet on the other, Faith must strive to realize salvation objectively in constructions of love for the making of a world. The point of grace is not that there be something other than God which is capable of receiving and responding to God but that both God and creatures come to work as companions at something they both can value as worthwhile: communal participation in a common project, creation of a world built on love.[155]

To interpret grace as God's initiation of a love-building project is thus equivalent to restructuring the logic of its efficacy. It is to center grace on the value of human ideologies vis-à-vis the creative action of God. So far as traditional theology is concerned, action is capable of achieving efficacious results in two ways at once: in itself, on its own, so to speak, and as a result of grace. Such a distinction, however, is purely conceptual. It derives from a logical abstraction which makes it possible to separate what neoscholasticism calls action carried out at the "natural" level from action performed at the "supernatural" level, i.e., action flowing from God's grace. While it is possible to make such a distinction at the level of theory, it is impossible to do so at the level of practice or experience.[156] In the historical situation where action is lived, effects which are caused by grace are indistinguishable from those which are not.

That last point refers back to the scholastic axiom that grace can be experienced but it cannot be experienced as grace. The point of this axiom is that disciples of Jesus can never rest on a self-satisfied assurance of salvation. They can never lapse into certainty about what in the categories of neoscholasticism was called "being in the state of grace." Looked at from a positive point of view, it is clear that the intention of this distinction is to maintain the autonomy of God. To do this means indirectly positing the existence of some positive value in the world itself, apart from God's freely proffered self-donation in grace, i.e., understanding the world as the "good creation" originally made so by God. In other words, neoscholastic theologians traditionally believed that the only way to protect the gratuitousness of grace was to create a distinction: to separate the relative autonomy of the created realm from the "absolute" and "uncreated" autonomy of God. We human beings could have carried on in a "natural" way, they maintained, with our actions producing valid, although "purely natural," results in history, even if God had never offered us the gift of grace. Yet because we know from revelation that the offer has already been made, it is impossible in retrospect to sort out the complexities of our experience and determine which initiatives come from ourselves and which flow from the action of God.

While the axiom itself thus points to an important existential truth, the distinction on which it is based raises a serious problem. It creates a conceptual gap which is difficult to close. If each realm has its proper efficacy and autonomy which must somehow be respected, how in fact can the two be actually joined? How is grace to be saved from what Blondel called extrinsicism and Kant articulated as the problem of heteronomy, the superimposition on human freedom of an oppressive authority coming entirely from outside? That these two problems are inextricably related shows up with particular clarity during the debates of the modernist era. There they take the form of the relation between history and dogma. But as the work of Gabriel Daly has shown, the confrontation between dogma and history was actually only one dimension of the deeper problem of the reconciliation of transcendence and immanence.[157] That the latter persists throughout the twentieth century is documented by the work of theologians like John Courtney Murray and Schubert Ogden.[158] It transcends denominational lines and brings us back to our original question in a particularly ecumenically relevant way: with respect to God's initiative in grace, how is the relation between God and the world finally to be interpreted?

Segundo's solution is that the development of an appropriate theological language of grace can be accomplished only by making an analogy between the logic of grace and the logic of human love. As has been seen in the preceding discussions, the experience of love most appropriate to conveying the structural complexity of grace is human friendship. Only such an analogy can permit the divine and human freedoms to retain their proper autonomies because only such an analogy is capable of maintaining a distinction that does not deteriorate into a separation. In a language and experience of friendship, the theological phrase *the grace of God* represents the dimension of gratuitousness essential to God's freedom. It means that God is freely committed to including human social persons in the project to which Jesus gave a distinctive name and character by his liberative kingdom *praxis*. The phrase *the Faith of human social persons* means that God must stand at the door and knock. God does not barge in upon human freedom but respects its logic and permits anthropological faith and ideologies their proper this-worldly autonomy. That is, after all, the meaning of the love that is friendship: a gratuitous reciprocity of freedoms. The love God gratuitously offers creatures in grace rejoices only in an equally gratuitous response. And the objective content or actual substance of that response shows up at the level of human faiths and their concrete ideologies.

As was suggested above, the notion of divine-human reciprocity makes grace not a status but a project. As this discussion has attempted to show, such a radical redefinition flows from Segundo's choice of ontological base. Where a neoscholastic metaphysics talks about the efficacy of grace in terms of an elevation of human nature to participation in the nature of God, Segundo's evolutionary ontology conceives of an interpersonal participation of freedoms in a conjoint creative project. How do the two approaches differ? Both recognize that the problem of talking about grace is that it posits some sort of ontological change. It involves a real relation between God and human beings. Neoscholastic language describes that change as a change of state: grace transforms human nature into a nature informed by grace. The original nature is given a new supernature; it is added to from "inside" and made to exist in a wholly different state. Human *being* thus changes radically from what it was "before:" thanks to grace, it receives a new supernatural "habit of being." The divine being, however—what neoscholasticiam refers to as God's nature—undergoes no change.[159]

By contrast, Segundo describes the change in anthropological language as an ontologically creative communication of love between persons. If grace is not a change of state, it is not something that happens solely to human being. Instead, it is an action. It occurs at the dynamic level where freedom interacts with the objective givenness of reality. Grace therefore initiates a friendship that involves human freedom with the freedom of God for the sake of something that from an ontological point of view is objectively worthwhile: freedom's painstaking labor of bringing into being a world that is inhabitable and good. Segundo believes that grace is not a self-donation of God to human social persons (a communication of natures), but an impassioned love initiated by God and taking place between human social persons and God (a communication of values). Paradoxically, the strongly anthropological-anthropomorphic, interpersonal character of Segundo's approach keeps grace from pertaining exclusively to a relationship between God and human beings. By focusing on the love-constitutive dimension of a project, Segundo shows that grace points outward from God and human social persons toward the incarnation of conjointly shared values creative of a world. Grace is a category for neither something to have nor something to be but something important to do. It can be understood only in terms of action—the project of God's heart—and interpreted only by means of categories oriented to the communal sharing of a task.

Insofar as it is the initiation of a project, grace is God's fundamental creative act, the world-directed aspect of God's impassioned freedom. It is a matter of God's gratuitous willingness to make God's creative sort of love by accepting the characteristic sort of love that creatures are capable of making. To say this in a way meaningful to the logic of action, however, it is necessary to raise a question about God's and creatures ways of "making love." Would it be possible, let alone plausible, for God really to love creatures if God did not engage them in the project dearest to God's heart? Would grace, let alone the creation of a world, be credible apart from the possibility of creatures' making a constitutive contribution to God, their sharing with God in something interesting and worthwhile to do? For Segundo the answer is clearly no. Interpersonal love in the absence of a project remains locked in upon itself and bears no ontologically creative fruit. It is a vicious circle. What makes it vicious is neither that it is a circle nor that it is interpersonal but that it has no bearing on objective reality; it is creative of nothing new.

What all this boils down to is the importance for theology of an ontology not of being but of love, the need for philosophical categories complex enough to convey the density of a reality not simply and already given but both given and still outstanding, given and yet having to be built.[160] According to such an ontology, which is actually a philosophy of action, it is not enough merely to be in love, and when it comes to the theological understanding of grace, it is not enough to be encircled in grace as in a "state." Grace, like love, initiates a commitment; it is the initial step of a commitment from God which proposes something worthwhile to do, something that is worth the trouble it takes to do it.

Because grace involves the utterly gratuitous and yet inherently interesting phenomenon of God's manifest solidarity with creatures, it is appropriate to the logic of their own constructive action in the world. It is the beginning of God's and the world's becoming capable of sharing a common end or *telos*, the making actual of God's will to participate with creatures in a conjoint mission or task by validating the intrinsic finality of their freedom. Like love, which it is, grace must be directed endward, toward the accomplishment of something definitive for the world. It must be compatible with the givenness of the situation, arriving on the scene as a down-to-earth commitment from God to shoulder a relevant task. In the context of creation's manifest incompleteness, God does not create a world in order to show God's love for creatures. Rather, God shows God's love for creatures in order to create with them a world.

In effect, this means that in both reflection and practice, the theological doctrines of creation and eschatology must be reconfigured so as to make eschatological creation the impassioned *raison d'être* of grace rather than letting creation serve as the logical (and emotionally indifferent) condition for the possibility of grace and eschatology. As was pointed out at the beginning of this chapter, the clue to this reconfiguration is Segundo's notion of an incomplete and tragic universe, which requires the intrinsically eschatological notion that the "nothing" in the context of which God initiates a creative project is not a simple *nihilo*.[161] It is not a neutral "nothing," the naked opposite of "something," as if being were simply the negation of non-being (were that the case, then being would be "something" already definitively created; it would have nothing meaningful toward which to move, and there would be nothing important left to do).[162]

Even less ought creation to be conceived of as a simple *fiat*. Even for God, the creation of a world is not a flat and already final statement of origin, a static positing by freedom of being over non-being. Rather, it is a creative action or work. It is a gradually learned, long-suffering task for God and creatures together, a complex dialectic entered into for the sake of creating something worthwhile and lasting in the end. Ultimately, it is a project that takes place against the background of an incomplete universe which, lacking the creative tension of finality, would remain an inefficacious spinning of wheels, a tragic and futile recklessness, a descent into a hell more terrifying than the blank and simple emptiness of "nothing," for it would be the reign of a relentless rush of evil and suffering in which exists no hope.

 A Final Word about the Logic of This Chapter. By introducing into the discussion of grace the biblical notion of *charism*—i.e., a gift of love which constitutes a task—I have attempted to revitalize forgotten aspects of what theology can mean by grace today in a universe that is manifestly incomplete and burdened by the tragic lack of goodness. I have called on the task-oriented connotations of a largely forgotten first-century biblical category with a view to multiplying the theological validity of Segundo's twentieth-century ontological categories, and I have done this by giving the human appropriation of grace in Faith a relevance not only to the freedom of God and the freedom of human beings at work together in history but to the objective givenness of reality as a whole and thus to nature, or the cosmos, itself.

 The purpose of the chapter has been to argue that Segundo's evolutionary ontological base is highly compatible with the biblical content of revelation about God's commitment of love in a universe in which the attributes of completeness and goodness are still outstanding by their absence. As will be seen in the following chapters, this means that Segundo's categories are especially suited to conveying the content of Jesus-derived data about God's liberative commitment to suffering creatures in the divided, conflictual and unjust state of the evolving world here and now, since, more than the categories of mere being, Segundo's categories are capable of supporting a sociopolitically conscious theological conception of gratuitous love, i.e., a love that in the end will show itself to have been definitively constitutive, like God's own love of creatures, of a goodness creative of justice here on earth.

[1] Although the tragic character of reality forms the proper subject matter of chapter two, it is necessary to consider it in a preliminary way here in order to show that for Segundo, a sufficient grasp of the complexity of action can be arrived at only in the context of a universe in which negative, delimiting factors play a constitutive role. As Segundo admits, for such a context correspondingly complex evolutionary categories do not as yet exist (*EAJN*, pp. 109-110 and pp. 28-29; *RC*, p. 320).

[2] This reliance is developed at length in *HCP*, but appears throughout Segundo's writings, notably in *¿Utopia?* Part II, pp. 25-45; *GHC*, pp. 14-28, pp. 30-37 and pp. 78-79; and *EG*, pp. 41-47.

[3] As subsequent discussion will show, essential to such creative participation is that it is aimed at producing not just any world whatsoever but a world capable in the end of being pronounced good.

[4] This double focus originates with Segundo's analysis of freedom in *Berdiaeff*, pp. 95-128. The philosophical base developed in this early work remains the constant underpinning of Segundo's theology but undergoes considerable development and clarification, eventually surfacing as a full-blown anthropology in *FI*.

[5] This theme remains constant throughout Segundo's career. See *Berdiaeff*, pp. 111-113; *RC*, p. 265; *HCP*, p. 137, p. 160 and p. 215, nn. 202 and 203; *EAJN*, p. 24 and p. 116.

[6] *HCP*, p. 215, n. 202. In this important note, Segundo observes that "the idea of a creation that is incomplete and for the moment condemned to uselessness, not good *in itself*, seems to be original with Paul" (italics Segundo's). Segundo suggests that a world already good in itself localizes evil in human freedom and thus devalues freedom in the eyes of both human beings and God. For this reason, Segundo prefers Paul to Thomas Aquinas. The same logic appears in more detail in an unpublished transcript of a course on the doctrine of Hell: *Infierno: ¿futuro o presente?* (Pocitos: Parish of San Juan Bautisto, 1983), pp. 40-41. In this manuscript, Segundo points out that there are two basic alternatives concerning the doctrine of the good creation: either freedom breaks the established order of an already good universe in such a way that the uniqueness that remains to be contributed by freedom is equivalent to evil (order in this schema being equivalent to good), or else the world is not yet finished being created and thus is not already good, the task of human freedom being to create

a good that does not as yet exist. Segundo chooses the second option, in which God needs human action in order to redeem the suffering of creatures and turn the seemingly futile character of an incomplete universe toward the construction of a world that is good.

⁷ The full import of God's needing human action for creation of a world that is good can not be appreciated until its recapitulation in chapter four in an eschatological setting. There it will become apparent that the doctrine of grace is not a statement about creation as condition for the possibiltiy of God's self-communication, but rather the affirmation of God's impassioned love for creatures as condition for the actuality, or realization, of a definitively created world.

⁸ See *RC*, pp. 321-322. In these pages, Segundo describes the universe as a tragic creation in which the fate of each human being is linked to that of every other through the working of freedom. The incompleteness of the universe, experienced as suffering, points freedom toward the cosmic responsibility—creation of a world that is good—which the tragic character of the universe imposes on human action. In his later writings, Segundo specifies that the tragic character of the universe is not revelatory of God's values but results from the entropic elements of time and chance at the heart of the evolutionary project (*EAJN*, pp. 42-92).

⁹ For Segundo, creation, like all action in an evolutionary context, is a slow and demanding work (*EG*, p. 139). It occurs in the disconcerting context of seeming ineffectiveness, and, as many a student or artist will attest, is never painless. It can be effected only experientially, through the gradual maturation of freedom in actually attempted projects of greater or lesser objectively measurable success.

¹⁰ It is important to recall that the most important strands of evolutionary theory today have little in common with determinism or worn-out ideologies of progress and are moving away from anthropocentrism. See Stephen Toulmin, *The Return to Cosmology* (Berkeley: Cambridge University of California Press, 1982), pp. 271-272. As Segundo observes, thanks to the incorporation of categories from the ecological, genetic, cybernetic and physical sciences, much evolutionary science today is almost synonymous with an ecological consciousness (*EAJN*, pp. 12-13, p. 30 and pp. 59-60). The latter is marked by a recognition of the interconnectedness of all reality (*RC*, p. 324). It derives from the fact that "to speak of evolution is to recognize a basic *analogy* among the mechanisms operative in any of the realms we designate as nature or world" (*EAJN*, p. 30; italics Segundo's). This more nuanced understanding of evolution creates a new ontological-epistemological context which faces theologians not primarily with questions of historical subjectivity but with problems arising out of objective reality itself. As Segundo points out, this new context brings with it a new theological task: to make a theology that is not only political but ecological (see *ibid.*, p. 12).

¹¹ See *EAJN*, pp. 42-66, especially pp. 45-48 and pp. 51-52. Segundo believes that "every glance backward at the process of evolution must assume an active

intelligence and project from the very start" (*ibid.*, p. 51). Although he understands this projective dimension as "an invasion of mind," he means by that phrase only a constructive evolutionary dynamism capable of counteracting the complementary tendency toward disintegration and breakdown, and he notes that the evolutionary project comprises both such elements from the beginning (*ibid.*, pp. 47-51). Insofar as Segundo defines *mind* in Gregory Bateson's terms as "a natural or artificial apparatus capable of receiving and processing information" (*ibid.*, p. 130, n. 85), he makes it a generic evolutionary category by which to classify any projective action. It is thus an analogical concept pertaining to the nature of change and must not be hypostacized into a god or demon or absolutized into a process. It does not refer to anything like a "mind of 'God'" or an "Omega Point," which would posit the existence of a determining moment of either origins or climax. Rather, it describes a tendency in the evolutionary project *qua* project: efficacious movement toward the realization of change. Under human observation, the components of evolving reality behave *as if* they were engaged in projects, and this requires positing neither an ascent toward an overriding goal nor a descent from an originating god.

[12] Segundo points out that recognition of something like freedom in evolutionary spheres other than the human is contingent on our being able to use human freedom as the referent for an analogy between ourselves and other beings. He is careful to point out, however, that the making of an analogy at the epistemological level is not a license for drawing ontological conclusions. In other words, perceiving the evolutionary project through human eyes does not constitute a justification for either subjecting other beings to human purposes or measuring the value of other beings by the value of the human (see *EAJN*, pp. 35-38, p. 30 and p. 40).

[13] A homeostatic mechanism is any device, whether mechanical, electronic, organic or cosmic, for maintaining equilibrium or continuity in the face of continual change. Examples include mechanisms like thermostats, codes like DNA, organic regulators like glands and, in the moral realm, the conscientious capacity of sensitivity of heart.

[14] *FI*, p. 311.

[15] For an important preliminary discussion of this category, which in chapter four will appear as an essential element of Segundo's eschatology, see *GHC*, pp. 117-122. Segundo defines newness as "a discontinuous breakthrough or rupture within a framework of continuity" and goes on to add that in the occurrence of the new, "something begins or opens up to deeper levels of experience; but we can say that this 'new' something, which makes the previous situation 'old,' was possible thanks to the old even though the latter does not explain it. 'Newness,' then, is a category essential to the notion of history" (*GHC*, pp. 118-119). Ten years later, in an ecologically conscientized context, Segundo applies newness not only to history but to nature. In response to Monod's notion that chance alone is responsible for the creation of the truly new, he writes, "The 'innovation' detected by science is an

interruption in a constancy, the birth of a new and more complex constancy, the appearance of a redundancy (i.e., precisely that which escapes chance, which does not result from it)" (*EAJN*, p. 35). Newness as redundancy (as in the case of Jesus' resurrection) thus has a *clarifying effect* on the human experience of gratuitousness: "one has the unmistakable sensation that a *threshold* has been crossed. . . .[which] may be viewed. . .as an accentuation of gift, as *grace,* as an opening to meaning" (*HJS*, p. 177; italics Segundo's).

[16] I use the word *experimenting* deliberately here, in spite of what could turn out to be its misleading connotations. By doing so, I want to convey the sense of open-endedness and flexibility required for the manifestation of freedom. Essential to the latter is a generosity of spirit, a tolerance for error, a humble willingness to begin all over again, which has nothing to do with calculated purposiveness but much to do with "living gratuitously," i.e., being able to sense the appropriateness of means and the "rightness" of timing in relation to the efficacious realization of values (not the same as efficient, cost-effective or expedient).

[17] Of course the economy of energies needs a criterion—wise for whom? This question will be addressed in chapter three.

[18] Segundo regards the quantitative and qualitative dimensions of reality as complementary. They are equally valuable from the perspective of achieving efficacious change. In his earlier works, he often refers to them in terms of "mass" and "minority" (see *¿Utopia?* Part I, pp. 15-68; *EG*, p. 113 and pp. 128-131; *LT*, pp. 222-237). Although these terms (originally deriving from the categories of Ortega y Gasset) are potentially misleading, it seems to me that the positive value of quantitative, seemingly negative "mass" elements, the fact that they are a necessary element of the efficacious working of freedom, is the key insight of *EG*. Yet paradoxically, as Segundo observes, that volume, although the most original of the five-volume *Artisans* series, remains the least understood, in spite of its importance for completing the doctrine of grace with a rehabilitated doctrine of sin (*RC*, p. 271). Critics who would accuse Segundo of elitism, thinking he values only "minoritarian" and not "mass" elements, thus miss the complexity involved in the evolutionary perspective he first tentatively shapes in *EG* and then develops with important ecological refinements ten years later in *EAJN*.

[19] *FI.,* pp. 308-310.

[20] *Ibid.,* p. 8.

[21] See *ibid.,* pp. 309-310 and pp. 314-315.

[22] See *EAJN*, p. 33 and pp. 45-52. Segundo notes that a difference that makes a difference "is a difference serving a function or purpose, altering something in accordance with some plan or project" (p. 46). For Bateson's account of this phenomenon, see *Steps to an Ecology of Mind* (New York: Ballantine, 1972), pp. 448-466, especially p. 453. As will be seen in chapter three, a "difference that makes a difference" is, ontologically speaking, identical with self-transcending love.

23 As will be seen in chapter two, this achievement requires the investment of large amounts of time. It pertains to what Segundo variously describes as the slowness of stochastic processes (*EAJN*, p. 15) or "the slowness of complex evolutionary processes" (*EAJN*, p. 17). See n. 9 above.

24 As subsequent discussion will show, the manifestation of freedom, although real, may not be fully visible under the ambiguous conditions of nature and history on earth. In fact, ordinarily it is not. Freedom's projects seem to be headed for rundown and decay. People seldom see the results of their efforts, whether for good or evil, as genuinely representing—or even resembling—their intentions. This congenital inefficacy in freedom is the subject matter of chapter two. The discussion in chapter four will show that the invisible character of the manifestation of freedom on earth will be overcome in the eschaton, where the manifestation of freedom—its constructive results on earth in spite of appearances to the contrary—will be made permanently visible in the definitive completion of freedom's work which is called glory.

25 *EAJN*, p. 45 and p. 71.

26 The evolutionary project is not a matter of "mind" or projectivity alone, but is a complex duet between project-mindedness and chance. The two are equally significant, equally valuable elements of a single reality, to the extent that chance is utterly necessary for the realization of anything new (*EAJN*, pp. 44-47). Projectivity is thus the risk-taking mechanism that, conditioned by chance, allows emergence of the new.

27 *EAJN*, p. 64. It does not seem far-fetched to conclude that, in Segundo's sense, the gratuitousness connected with the manifestation of freedom is something like the "Eureka" experience of Archimedes in the bathtub—an ecstatic mixture of humility and joy.

28 Examples of the affinity of chance for gratuitousness include the indeterminacy of electron fields and the reproductive process of sexual beings. Examples of successful manifestations of freedom (or what is analogous to it) over long periods of time include the emergence of appropriately structured biological organs, the appearance of new individuals and species, the discovery of clean energy sources, the altruistic behavior of love, the advent of a reality as complicated and costly as a world, which is so risky and expensive that its value can be manifested only eschatologically— i.e., it can be pronounced good only in the end.

29 *EAJN*, p. 79 (italics Segundo's). Segundo believes that the most dramatic and challenging example of entropy is death (*EAJN*, pp. 71-74 and pp. 78-79; *RC*, p. 324). Even from the point of view of the data of revelation, death is utterly negative. Yet as God's action of raising Jesus from the dead reveals, gratuitous love is capable of incorporating even death into a new creation. Both death and entropy will be addressed in greater detail in chapter two.

30 *EAJN*, p. 72.

31 *EG*, p. 113. About gratuitous living, which he defines as gratuitous giving, Segundo observes: "Jesus' law is one that talks about deeds based on gratuitous giving, on *grace* (Luke 6: 32-34). Now attitudes centered around 'gratuitous' giving . . .are not *legal* exigencies. Blessing those who curse us, offering the other cheek to someone who hits us on one cheek, giving our coat to the one who takes our shirt, and lending to people who cannot repay us—all these things are examples, and only examples, of an adventure in gratuitous giving with which the whole doctrine of the gospel is bound up. These dicta were not existing laws. They pointed toward a love that was efficacious in its very gratuitousness. Jesus was the first to regard them, not as a static norm. . . but as the goal of a creative effort which is sensitive to those moments in the life of a group or a society when only this gratuitousness is capable of new and richer syntheses" (*ibid.*). Segundo goes on to add that living gratuitously is extraordinary, not because it is done by few people but because the love it brings to life is at the service of negentropy (*ibid.*). The significance of these observations will return in chapter three in the discussion of a morality of appropriateness.

32 *EAJN*, p. 64. Segundo believes that Jesus' life-story (which to be complete must include his kingdom *praxis*, death and resurrection) manifests the efficacy of self-transcending love even in the face of a failure as enormous as a violent and premature death (*EG*, p. 113). In a striking statement about what he calls "the law of evolution", Segundo comments that "all the mechanisms or laws of the universe . . .'aspire' to this same goal," namely love—and this is a law which holds in spite of the fact that "the universe seems condemned to uselessness" (*EAJN*, p. 104).

33 This theme runs throughout Segundo's writings, surfacing most explicitly in *Berdiaeff*, pp. 95-103 and *HCP*, p. 137 and pp. 265-275. For Segundo, suffering is the unavoidable result of creatures' existing in a tragic universe subjected to randomness and chance (see n. 8 above). His starting point, however, is not what Edward Schillebeeckx calls the "scandal" of suffering, the oppressive and over-whelming senselessness of its excess [*Christ: The Experience of Jesus as Lord* (New York: Seabury, 1980), p. 725]. As will become evident in chapter two, I believe this difference is a by-product of Segundo's evolutionary categories, which incorporate evil into a philosophical base more systematically coherent—and theoretical—than that presupposed by the practical starting point of Schillebeeckx. This raises the question whether evil can reach what scientists call a critical mass, a weight so oppressive as to exclude the possibility of its being creatively incorporated into works of self-transcending love. In fairness to Segundo, I think it must be admitted that the only answer possible in light of God's eschatological promise is no. Evil will not have the final say, no matter how massive it becomes, preisely because the resurrection of Jesus shows that, in the end, love is ontologically stronger. As Segundo emphasizes, "One single performance of the good means more than all the abhorrent 'alien' stuff that has accumulated" (*HCP*, p. 204, n. 127). This aspect of Segundo's theology will return as a crucial element of the discussion in chapter four.

THE LOGIC OF ACTION

34 *Berdiaeff,* p. 148. Although Segundo agrees with those who hold that evil can not be rationally explained, he does not allow that to serve as an excuse for theologians' abdicating their responsibility to reflect on evil intelligently, i.e., to interpret it through the use of scientific or philosophical categories appropriate to both the human experience of suffering and faith in the revelation of God's values.

35 For all we know, this tragic streak has perhaps run through the universe from before the recorded origins of reality as we know it. Possibly it is capable of continuing to run even after the accomplishment of what will appear later in this discussion to be God's and creatures' conjoint action of "saving" the fragile threads of whatever increments in reality their action will have made, creatively salvaging them and knitting them into the fabric of a new reality, a world that finally will be capable of being pronounced good.

36 Referring to the traditional biblical term for this disjointedness, namely, *hamartía,* or "missing the mark" (*HCP,* p. 216, n. 215), Segundo describes it as *"the gap or distance* that is always there between what a human being *intends* and what he or she *actually performs or accomplishes"* (*HCP,* pp 145-146; italics Segundo's).

37 In this context, in fact, one could say that the notion of a beginning becomes virtually irrelevant. What is important is not the point of origin but the attaining of ecologically appropriate (i.e., wise and flexible) proportions among already existing parts. If evolution is not an ascent but a project, its *telos* does not consist in someplace to go other than the present universe but in something valuable and worthwhile to do in the universe right now. It is not a chronological development set on a future goal but an "adventure in gratuitous living" in the present, a commitment to the efficacious use of entropy in the face of what Paul calls "the sufferings of the present moment" (Rom. 8:18; *HCP,* p. 137). What is significant about the eschaton is not that it is a "new beginning" but that it imparts a new and everlasting value to what is being done in the present.

38 How it actually comes about that a good world can be created in face of the accumulated evils and sufferings of the present and past will be explored in the following chapters from the historical-ecological, hermeneutical and eschatological points of view, respectively. Here it is possible only to introduce the main outlines of Segundo's ontological-anthropological grounding for the assertions of revelation.

39 *HCP,* p. 160 (italics mine; inclusive language substituted; the bracketed text originally read *fraternize*).

40 *RC,* p. 265; *HCP,* p. 137; *EAJN,* p. 24 and pp. 112-120. As these sources show, Segundo emphasizes that God deliberately creates an incomplete universe, for the sake of insuring human participation in a creative project of love. With this emphasis, Segundo suggests that God could have created a different kind of world but chose to make a tragic one. To the extent that such an emphasis places undue stress on the freedom of an all-powerful creator, it contradicts Segundo's more character-istic interest in the cooperative character of grace and represents an unfortunate discrepancy in his theology. Yet while Segundo's language raises questions on this point, his basic approach displays a fitting ambiguity. In an important note (because it is his only mention of the subject), he states: "Exegetes debate the identity of 'the one who subjected' creation to uselessness: God, Satan, Adam, or humanity. *It does not matter for our purposes here.* The point is that in any case God has left creation dependent on human decision" (*HCP,* p. 215, n. 203; italics mine). In other words, a rational interest in determining the origins of evil is less important than the practical urgency of asking what, given its reality and perdurance, God and creatures are going to do about it.

[41] Ultimately, I think one is forced to admit in the spirit of Thomas Aquinas that an incomplete universe is a universe in which freedom can make sense for the simple reason that it is the only kind of universe there is. It is the only kind of universe it is *conveniens* to consider. Although Segundo's language on this point is sometimes less *conveniens* (see previous note), one of the merits of his underlying approach (against the background of a theological tradition that tended to ignore it) is to retrieve the insight and experience of the saints. As Segundo notes, the *praxis* of saints, often in contrast to official theological formulations, tends to stress the *"reciprocity* that God Godself has established in God's relations with human beings" (*OIG,* p. 137; inclusive language substituted; italics mine). In other words, the *praxis* of saints shows that, according to the (practical) theology that is being lived every day as a spirituality, God *needs* human action. Segundo suggests that the *praxis* of saints embodies an image of God that is indispensible not only for the making of a responsible theology but for the making of a mature response to the affrontiveness of evil: "We do not claim that this [notion that God needs the action of human beings] resolves the problem of evil. But we do indeed feel that the Christian God offers elements that are critical to understanding its import and meaning: (a) evil is the price to be paid for a human liberty that is placed before the universe in all seriousness; (b) something absolute depends on the responsibility therein confided—even for God; (c) *in the meantime, God shares with human beings all the sorrow of this gestation"* (*OIG,* p. 139; inclusive language substituted; italics mine). It seems to me that in our time, the awareness of God's solidarity with the oppressed against suffering—God's sharing in the sorrow of the world's gestation—is more obvious than ever in the experience of saints, many of whom are neither Christians nor theists, and that their *praxis* constitutes a new *locus* of theological reflection. Segundo argues in exactly this direction in *RC,* pp. 124-128, and, from a different but complementary perspective, so does Charles Davis, "From Inwardness to Social Action: A Shift in the Locus of Religious Experience," *New Blackfriars* 67 (March, 1986), pp. 114-125.

[42] The notion that there is no abstract love, expressed explicitly as early as the *Berdiaeff* study (p. 209), amounts to a basic principle of Segundo's entire theology. See also *¿Utopia?* Part II, pp. 64-75.

[43] *EAJN,* pp. 73-74.

[44] *Berdiaeff*, p. 78, p. 112 and p. 377; "Intellecto y salvación," *De la sociedad a la teología* (Buenos Aires: Carlos Lohlé, 1970), p. 104; *EAJN*, pp. 104 and 116. The nature of this manifestation is the subject matter of chapter four.

[45] On God's need of human agency, see n. 41 above.

[46] According to this scheme of things, salvation is for the sake of creation, not creation for the sake of salvation. Creation is an ongoing project, a single, prolonged action the definitive shape of which will come to light only in the eschaton. The difference between these views is crucial and will be addressed in chapter four.

[47] Glory is a theological category by which to speak about the definitive manifestation of the true worth of action which God will bring to light in a gratuitous and yet appropriate setting in the eschaton. It forms the subject matter of chapter four.

[48] As has been seen, the "raw materials" of the universe do not consist for Segundo in "matter" or "nature." Action is aimed not at "transforming the world" but at integrating the negative energies of evil and suffering into a circuit gratuitously productive of negentropic realizations of love. This means that love is not a "victory over nature" but nature's own culmination in the creation of something new.

[49] As the next section will show, the efficacious completion of such a project depends for its success on freedom's gratuitous release from anxious efforts at self-justification in the eyes of God and preoccupation with one's self-importance in the eyes of others (*HCP*, p. 209, n. 161).

[50] Of course Maurice Blondel has already answered this question, beginning from exactly the opposite direction. When Blondel wrote *L'Action* (Paris: Alcan, 1893), he was writing strictly as a philosopher. His thesis was that action has a logic which concludes to an openness to the transcendent as a constitutive dimension of existence. Unlike Blondel, Segundo is not interested in finding a way to open up immanence to the possibility of transcendence; he wants to celebrate the transcendent value action already has.

[51] The discussion of faiths and ideologies in this and the following paragraphs is based on material in Parts I and II of *FI*. In order to avoid excessive footnoting, I shall provide references only when the data in question either do not proceed from that source or else directly quote it.

[52] For Segundo, the concept of *work* must be contrasted with *works* (*HCP*, p. 131), work being "the totality of a human being's activity" (*ibid.*, p. 130). In the eschaton, it is the work of the human being and not the human being as such who will be judged, or "tested by fire." Where "works" are quantitative, work is qualitative. While works are acts that can be counted up on the basis of the letter of the Law, work is "the free prolongation of the human being in reality through the only project that is truly free, i.e., . . .real, effective love of brother and sister humans" (*ibid.*, p. 131). Thus Faith is not opposed to work (as it is to "works") but is work's origin (ideologies being work's actualization in results). Finally, work under the conditions of history and nature is an ambiguous and "mixed" phenomenon: "The work of the human

being, done in conjunction with God, is a building made up of *a mixture of materials of diverse quality and resistance"* (*ibid.*, p. 131; italics Segundo's). As subsequent discussion will show, the "mixed" quality of human work is what shows up in the phenomenon of faith and ideologies, for between action's ideological results in the objective realm and the values of Faith from which they proceed, there is an inevitable "distance" or gap, what Segundo refers to as Paul's anthropological insight into the ontological complexity of "the divided human being" (*HCP*, pp. 114-116).

[53] As will be brought out in chapter two, recognizing this orientation is not the same as saying that action in fact succeeds in being efficacious. The phenomenon of the "divided human being"—the congenital inefficacy of action—is proof of that (*HCP*, pp. 114-116). Segundo's emphasis on efficacy is therefore not the same as a utilitarian emphasis on efficiency. Efficacy points toward the effecting of something not only worthwhile and new but also beneficial to others (in accordance with an other-directed criterion, as will be seen in chapter three). Efficiency refers to something cold and calculated, an immediate pay-off which may or may not be beneficial from the point of view of long-term effects and which has a purely self-interested criterion. The significance of faiths and ideologies is thus that a mature balance between them can produce something truly efficacious, while a one-sided emphasis on "quick fix" ideologies might produce efficient results in the short term but destructive and inefficacious ones in the end. This is a major thesis of *FI* and appears in summary fashion in *HCP*, pp. 181-182.

[54] *EAJN*, p. 100.

[55] *FI*, p. 14.

[56] Although Segundo seldom discusses symbols as such, it is precisely their link with efficacy which illumines why "dead" symbols (Tillich) are socially, politically, religiously or artistically ineffective.

[57] For Segundo, "praxis, and 'practice' as another term for it, specifically means practice grounded in a theory. In turn, theory is nurtured and revised by new elements discovered in experiential practice" (*HCP*, p. 223, n. 251). As chapter three will show, both the theoretical and practical elements of *praxis* are included in ideologies, which are grounded, in turn, by faith.

[58] For the practical purposes of human social persons acting in the world, it is of course neither necessary nor possible that the faith underlying an individual's ideologies be spelled out explicitly in advance. Because of the existential inseparability of thinking and doing, we human social persons are already "living by faith" before we attempt to explicitate its values either to ourselves or to others. Many human beings, in fact, probably never explicitly make that attempt, given that life for great numbers of persons provides neither the leisure, training nor modicum of sociopolitical security—not to mention basic necessities like food and livelihood—even to initiate such a task.

[59] The question to what extent faith in fact "works"—i.e., actually achieves the goals of its work under the historical and ecological conditions of existence in an evolving world—of course remains to be answered. It will be addressed from the historical-ecological, hermeneutical and eschatological points of view in chapters two, three and four respectively.

[60] Chapter two will attempt to deal with the disconcerting datum of experience that under the conditions of history and nature, such alienation is to a greater or lesser extent inevitable.

[61] The hermeneutical truth-making aspect of faiths and ideologies is the proper subject matter of chapter three. Although Segundo grounds the *praxis* of truth in sensitivity of heart to the needs of the deprived, he shows that such *praxis* pertains to the logic of faiths and ideologies itself, the greatest problem for which is the alienation of action's results from its original intentions. This alienation is what Segundo calls Sin, a congenital disjointedness which "lodges" in action and makes the *praxis* of truth a difficult and ambiguous task. "Liberty operates. . .in the realm of truth," writes Segundo. "It operates against bad faith and the deceitful tendencies whereby we pass off, as our own, things that are in fact imposed on us by the determinisms with which we work, think and feel. . . .Thus the struggle for truth— and liberty—is a struggle to *interpret* in all our end results that which truly comes from us; to separate it from that which is spuriously presented as ours, . . .to separate what is ours from that which 'lodges in us' (Paul)" (*GHC,* p. 33; italics Segundo's).

[62] As will be seen in chapter three, this implies that faith "works," i.e., succeeds in accomplishing the work it originally set out to do, only when the premises out of which it operates ring true.

[63] It will remain for chapter three to address the central question of the truth criterion by which a given *praxis* can attempt to put faith concretely to work in ideologies.

[64] Paradoxically, Segundo shows that if an anthropology of freedom is to be anything more than an anthropocentric trip into the subjective, it must take serious account of objective reality and give to the realm of nature, which includes what he refers to as the "second nature" of culture, its full weight and value. What he thus constructs is an ecology of human action which pays attention to its objective consequences in the interconnected realms of nature and culture. In this lies one of his most creative contributions to the liberation of theology from what in a similar spirit, although in a different context, Rauschenbusch called "senility," i.e., irrelevance to the problems of the world [*Theology for the Social Gospel* (Nashville: Abingdon, 1917/1981), pp. 12-17]. Where Rauschenbush sought to revitalize action on behalf of God's kingdom by creating a theology for the social gospel, Segundo seeks to revitalize it by creating a theology for a gospel which is not only social but political and ecological as well.

[65] It is important to recall that for Segundo, nature is not equivalent to the realm of plants and animals nor coterminous with matter. Rather, it is a synonym for objective givenness. It represents the entire scope of reality as given, with all its mechanisms and laws, including those of the "second nature" of culture. Those "laws" reflect the "make-up" of reality in whatever sphere, whether physical, biological, psychological, anthropological, ecological, or other, and thus nature as objective givenness operates independently of the values freedom wants. Nature serves either to facilitate or resist freedom's aims, depending on the situation. In this sense, nature has "a mind of its own" and can not simply be manipulated at will. In fact, freedom's proper relation to nature ought to be one of respect and love—a gratitude to objective givenness in face of its gifts (*EAJN*, p. 40).

[66] For Segundo, an ecological mentality is one which maintains an equilibrium between the intentionality of projects and the energy-giving mechanisms of the environment (*EAJN*, p. 99). This leads to "a certain *modesty*. . .in our human pretensions," what he regards as a healthiness in action by which we "reproduce in our mind the process by which nature obtains its objectives" (*ibid.*).

[67] *Berdiaeff*, p. 126. For Segundo, speaking of such a dialectic is an attempt to address the ontological complexity of the relation between freedom and givenness (being). The manifestation of freedom is effected only with reference to the objective givenness of reality, of which, paradoxically, it is already a part (*¿Utopia?* Part I, pp. 33-34). Freedom's capacity to realize qualitative change is simultaneously effected in and affected by the givenness of objective reality, which either facilitates or inhibits efficacy. When the result of this interaction embodies a "right" or fitting proportion between freedom and givenness, it is creative (*Berdiaeff*, p. 410; see also pp. 44 and ff. and pp. 204-214). The notion of fitting proportionality appears in Segundo's later works in an ecological context in the tension between energy-saving and energy-expending mechanisms (*FI*, pp. 309-310) and in an anthropological context in the tension between intention and performance (*HCP*, p. 124, p. 129 and pp. 131-132). As was pointed out in the preceding section, this method of creating new reality is both laborious and time-consuming. It is a long, slow process of learning to prepare for the gratuitous breakthrough of the moment of equilibrium between the projective character of freedom and the objective givenness of being. In its work for efficacious change, it requires love, the liberative "art" of sensing when to welcome the appropriate moment of the gratuitous emergence of the new.

[68] For Segundo, the dialectic between freedom and nature represents in the sphere of human action what the dialectic between freedom and givenness represents ontologically. Early in his career it is typified in the relations between personal freedom and the extrinsic character of the law (*Berdiaeff*, pp. 109 and ff.). Later it is categorized as the creative tension between interior freedom and what Paul calls either the "the law of the members" (*GHC*, pp. 30-35; *¿Utopia?* Part II, pp. 25-62; *HCP*, pp. 103-111) or Flesh and Spirit (*GHC*, pp. 77-81). Finally, it appears in fully

developed form as the fundamental structure of evolving reality, expressed as the creative tension between rigor and creativity, quantitative resistance and qualitative change (*EAJN*, e.g., pp. 74-75). As the present discussion shows, it is reflected in *FI* in the anthropological structure of freedom *qua* faith and ideologies (and in practical epistemological tensions like that between scientific and poetic languages). Ultimately, as will be seen in chapter two, it refers to the tension between Faith and Sin (*HCP*, pp. 145-154). In every case, the dialectical tension between freedom and objective givenness is creative of love and thus is ontologically constructive. As will be seen in chapter four, it is capable of producing the new heaven and new earth that God is going to make manifest in the eyes of all in the eschaton.

[69] Much of the material presented in this series appears in condensed form in *RC*, the volume of critical reflections Segundo appends to the *Artisans* series at its 1983 reprinting in Spanish. Most notably, see pp. 35-128 on Jesus and pp. 219-275 on freedom and grace.

[70] *HCP*, pp. 171-172 and *HJS*, p. 139. Segundo insists that the disparate christologies, not only of the gospels and letters but over the course of the tradition, may not simply be "added" to one another in the hope of coming up with a single comprehensive christology. Rather, they must be carefully distinguished so as to serve the ongoing hermeneutical project of learning to interpret the significance of Jesus' life-story anew in every generation. That project works not by the facile addition of one christology to another but by the comparison and contrast of disparate interpretations of Jesus' significance in a way that "multiplies" disciples' understanding and permits it to serve the needs of neighbors and the signs of the times (*EAJN*, p. 18).

[71] For Paul, what makes the universe tragic is the divided character of human action (Rom. 7:14-25). According to Segundo's reading of this passage, the phenomenon of the "divided human being" is Paul's anthropological description of the seeming futility of action in a world where results are congenitally alienated from intentions (*HCP*, pp. 113-125). In contrast to the visible inefficacy of action in history is the invisible (yet no less real) eschatological efficacy of Faith, Paul's anthropological category for the gratuitous and definitive efficacy of which action is capable when it realizes God's values in self-transcending love (*ibid.*, pp. 126-160).

[72] In order to distinguish what Segundo calls anthropological faith from what Paul calls Faith, from now on I shall use lower- and upper-case letters respectively.

[73] Segundo believes there is a genuine continuity between Jesus and Paul, and he argues that it shows up in the correspondence between their respective understandings of God's project (*HCP*, pp. 57-58). In both cases, the values of God's project are eschatological, i.e., God is concerned with the definitive liberation of creatures from intramundane evils and ills. Where for Jesus this liberation was expressed in a political key (the kingdom of God directed to the granting of salvation, absolutely free, here and now to "sinners" and the poor), for Paul it is expressed in

an anthropological key (Faith directed toward the liberation of human beings and the cosmos as a whole from infantilism and the enslaving power of Sin).

[74] A concrete picture of Segundo's understanding of Paul's fidelity to Jesus appears in *HCP*, p. 96.

[75] The essence of the continuity between Jesus' revelation of God's project and Paul's anthropological reinterpretation of it is summed up in what Segundo calls "the revaluation of the historical" (*HCP*, pp. 137-138) and "the dense fabric of historical causality" (*HJS*, p. 160). In other words, what binds them together is precisely the constructive value of human action vis-à-vis definitive realization of God's project. As subsequent discussion will show, that consists for Segundo in a definitive salvation, effected in history and nature by the action of God and human beings at work together in Faith at a conjoint project: the creation of a world. In the light of the eschaton, the latter will be made manifest at last as the new heaven and new earth promised to suffering creatures by God (*HCP*, pp. 154-160).

[76] According to Jesus, it is easier for a camel to pass through the eye of a needle than for a rich person to enter the kingdom of God. Yet because of grace, conversion *(metanoia)* is never an impossibility; all things are possible for God. (The sense of the latter is not that God is "omnipotent" but that the creative power of God's love is stronger than the impotence to which creatures are apparently reduced in face of the enslaving power of evil.)

[77] Although important, it is not germane to the question at issue in these paragraphs to pursue the implications of this line of thought. However, Segundo does so at length in *FI*. There, he shows, for persons and groups moving toward maturity, the discrepancy is handled by mutual critique between a given human faith and the traditional ideological expressions of it in symbols and institutions. Such critique keeps faith and its traditions alive and operative and prevents ideologies from ossifying completely. It provides ongoing criteria for deciding what type of action is called for in light of the values to which faith is committed and in view of the probable effectiveness of existing or newly devised ideologies.

[78] Experience of this guarantee is effected in historical periods other than Jesus' by the working of God's Spirit, who is God's "downpayment" on the eschatological worthwhileness of an anthropological faith in Jesus, and God's pledge of surety vis-à-vis the value of secular *praxes* of self-transcending love in Faith.

[79] That which is gratuitous is redundant insofar as the newness effected by the breakthrough of the gratuitous sheds a clarifying light on what already exists in its own right. Jesus' resurrection thus has a clarifying effect on the already existing premises of anthropological faith, yet at the same time gives it the gratuitous gift of a new Spirit-transmitted context, a pledge of surety. In Jesus' resurrection, Segundo observes, "one has the unmistakable sensation that a *threshold* has been crossed. . . [which] may be viewed. . .as an accentuation of gift, as *grace,* as an opening to meaning" (*HJS*, p. 177; italics Segundo's). See also n. 15 above.

[80] *OIG*, p. 46.

[81] *GHC*, p. 72.

[82] *HCP*, pp.122-125 and pp. 156-157.

[83] *GHC*, p. 81.

[84] It is significant that Segundo nowhere seems to regard human freedom as needing to be liberated from pride. As chapter two will show, sin as moral evil consists for Segundo in a fear that is a lack of creative boldness. It is a willing regression into immaturity and false securities. For Reinhold Niebuhr, sin also consists in the failure of freedom, but for him, pride is the principal sin. Segundo's view has important benefits. For example, it makes his theology more compatible with the criteria of a feminist theology of sin and grace than that of Niebuhr. [For a discussion of such criteria see Judith Plaskow's feminist critique of Niebuhr's doctrine of sin in *Sex, Sin and Grace: Women's Experience and the Theologies of Rienhold Niebuhr and Paul Tillich* (Boston: University Press, 1980), pp. 54-73]. But Segundo's view also presents a problem. What about willful wickedness? What about the wickedness, for example, of those who design and order large-scale, systematic torture? Does Segundo overlook the destructive effects sin has on victims in favor of an optimistic doctrine of human co-creativity with God? (See n. 33 above.)

[85] In *GHC*, Segundo describes these traditional aspects of grace as the dimensions of height, depth, breadth and length, the existential dimensions of the love of God for the world. According to Segundo, grace does not result in equality in an abstract ontological sense. Rather, he argues that human social persons and God become equal at the concrete level of action or projects. Equality with God, effected in grace, is neither scientific nor literal but analogous. It is the necessary—and humanly empowering—presupposition of a genuinely gratuitous love.

[86] *Olinger Stories: A Selection* (New York: Random House, 1964), p. vii (italics Updike's). Iris Murdoch, *The Sovereignty of Good* (London: Routledge and Kegan Paul, 1970), p. 43, points toward a similar experience when she writes: "We often receive an unforeseen reward for a fumbling half-hearted act: a place for the idea of grace."

[87] *HJS*, p. 158.

[88] *HCP*, p. 139.

[89] *Ibid.*, p. 108.

[90] *Ibid.*, pp. 135-138. For Segundo, adoption signifies God's manifest will to invite participation in God's project. It is God's unswerving commitment to the causality of human freedom, even though God thereby commits Godself to an everlasting kinship with creatures in which the success of God's project is ultimately dependent on what human freedom does or does not accomplish. God's personal love for human beings thus embodies a grace by which God considers the "riskiness and pain of the inconclusive and unfinished [universe] to be better" than a pre-fabricated world in which God alone has done everything in advance (*HCP*, p. 137).

[91] *HCP,* pp. 138-142. For Segundo, the essence of community consists in "the abolition of all more or less religious criteria that give some human beings an excuse to place themselves above other human beings" (p. 139). It involves the transformation of one-sided relations into non-competitive ones, the attempt to replace the perpetuation of injustice with the making of justice. Segundo recognizes, of course, that "it is no easy matter to see to it that in a divided world a particular community reflect universal brotherhood and sisterhood in a meaningful way" (*HCP,* p. 141). And he goes on to consider what it would involve, not only for communities of followers of Jesus (e.g., the churches) but for every human being, particularly the poor and marginalized.

[92] *HCP,* p. 139. As will emerge more clearly throughout these reflections, a major interest in exploring Segundo's theology of grace is to show (what Paul could not have shown) that Faith is also an ecological task. This is a dimension that Segundo does not fully emphasize, in spite of his creative appropriation of ecological categories in the exegesis of Romans 1-8.

[93] *CIE,* p. 91 (italics Segundo's). As Segundo observes, that is why no project can be merely individual.

[94] In his earlier works, written in the context of a Christian study group, this primarily meant the liberation of freedom from infantilism and fear vis-à-vis the doctrine of Hell and from moral enslavement to the law (*GHC,* pp. 43-46 and pp. 162-167). Looking back on *GHC* ten years later, however, Segundo admits that, in that same "in-house" context, a new problem has arisen which creates the need to change his earlier approach. Somewhere in the sixties, he observes, the concept of Hell slipped quietly out of the picture in catechesis, theology and preaching. As a result, the problem today is not that Christians are victims of constrictive fears about their own salvation—i.e., about Hell; rather, it is that they tend to have no theologically useful concept of Hell at all, and thus little notion of the seriousness of freedom, a seriousness Segundo derives precisely from a reinterpretation of the traditional doctrine of Hell. Because of this, modern Christians tend to have an immature notion of salvation (see *RC,* pp. 219-252, especially pp. 239 and 242; *Infierno* pp. 1-3).

[95] *HCP,* pp. 136 and ff.

[96] *Ibid.,* pp. 57-58.

[97] *RC,* p. 327; see also p. 170.

[98] This does not mean, of course, that only if disciples are first "fully mature" in a psychological sense can they enter into kingdom *praxis* with God. Maturity refers not to the subjective state of individuals, who will never be completely liberated from "hang-ups," but to the objective capacity to participate in the task to which the gracious love of God invites them. Focus on the communal and mission-oriented dimensions of kingdom building thus makes up for (but does not obliterate the significance of) whatever might still be lacking personally in the lives of individuals and communities. Could not Segundo's concept of maturity be the meaning of the

gospel saying: "Seek first the kingdom of God, and all these things shall be added unto you"? (Segundo seems to suggest exactly that in *HCP*, p. 73.)

99 On this point, Segundo's later work corrects and completes a misleading impression which is sometimes created by an isolated reading of the earlier and less developed logic of *GHC*, namely that grace is a matter of the liberation of freedom, understanding of the importance of objective reality for the efficacious functioning of freedom on the other, in other words, by a tempering of evolutionary categories with insights from ecological science. One notices this shift in Segundo's move from an abstract Teilhardian notion of grace as the "positive vector of evolution" *(EG)* to more concrete anthropological categories derived from categories of ecological science placed in conversation with a creative theological exegesis of Paul. That movement helps to make clear what was always the case, namely that the point of freedom in Segundo's theology is not freedom in and of itself but the historical realization of a Jesus-like self-transcending love.

100 *HCP*, p. 68 (italics mine). In this same passage, Segundo points out that the grounds for Faith are thus open to everyone who loves gratuitously. In Jesus' resurrection those grounds come to light in a clarifying way. As chapter three will indicate, this leads to the important conclusion that the good news of Jesus' resurrection is not the cause of Faith but rather its confirmation.

101 *HCP*, p. 90. On the same page Segundo writes: "The installation of the kingdom of God on earth (political key) is translated by Paul as the creation of a *reconciled, justified* and *saved* humanity (anthropologial key)" (italics Segundo's).

102 This is the main point of the early essay "Intellect y salvación," *De la sociedad a la teología* (Buenos Aires: Carlos Lohlé, 1970), pp. 63-106. Segundo argues that an enormous pastoral failure in the church consists in the fear of relating faith and salvation to the intellect, the everyday capacity people have for figuring out how to deal with life (p. 66, n. 3). For Segundo, the problem is that, thanks to poor catechesis and preaching, the average Christian thinks the annulment of the intellectual function is connected with the achievement of salvation or that the abdication of intellectual analysis of the secular situation is the surest route to reaching salvation *(ibid.,* p. 67). The result is that Christians are easily disoriented by the complexity of historical reality (p. 73), a phenomenon linked to the devaluation of the secular realm and of action within it. This leads to stress on an other-worldly conception of salvation and to the alleged need (in matters of doctrine and morality) for continual guidance from ecclesiastical authorities.

103 *HCP*, p. 104. See also the discussion of action in "Intellect y salvación," pp. 93-99. There, Segundo replaces the static notion of salvation as passive acceptance of something given by God (or the church) with Paul's dynamic notion of salvation as a way of acting based on the awareness that one is saved. In these pages, Segundo argues that salvation constitutes a historically constructive project aimed at efficacious love and construction of the new creation promised by God.

[104] As in all human relations, so it is by analogy in our relations with God: Segundo advocates the balance that proceeds from maturity. If the mature working of human freedom is to be preserved without destruction, then a theology of grace must make sure that God is neither too far away to make a difference nor too close to leave human freedom its autonomy to act (see *RC*, p. 325). The point is that grace frees freedom to participate with God in a project that is liberative not only with respect to the task (finding this-worldly solutions to evils afflicting creatures) but also of participants themselves. For disciples, this means on the one hand becoming an adult, taking mature responsibility and making one's own decisions about how to carry out the goals of the project (not having God be too close) and on the other hand being constantly in touch with the values of God's heart at the center of one's Faith (not having God be too far away). On the practical nature of this maturity, which includes (but is not simply coextensive with) the critical-analytical functioning of the intellect, see "Intellect y salvación," pp. 96-101.

[105] *HCP*, pp. 68-69 and pp. 72-75. Segundo gives an idea of what such Faith looks like in the following passage: "Who is a child of Abraham, 'the man of faith'? Every atheist, pagan, Jew or Christian who refuses to have a contractual relationship with the Absolute, who trusts in the promise inscribed in the human values offered by existence and fights for them as if death did not render that struggle futile" (p. 68). At bottom, in other words, Faith is a "hoping against hope" in the value of self-transcending love (*HCP*, p. 152). For Segundo, the anthropological faith which is capable of asserting that loving is worthwhile is not already "anonymous Faith." Rather, it is distinct from a Faith that is fully and voluntarily embraced while at the same time being a readiness for Faith (or at least not being incompatible with Faith's values). As Segundo puts it, "Love is faith that is beginning" (*CCC*, p. 56). Those who refuse "to have a contractual relationship with the Absolute" and those who "hope against hope" that "loving is worthwhile" are those whose Faith is "beginning." According to Segundo (and Paul), both an anthropological faith that is a readiness for Faith and an anthropological faith that fully embraces Faith equally result in justification. Moreover, it is not theologically necessary to think that the first type of Faith must move either consciously or unconsciously in the direction of the second one.

[106] *Infierno*, p. 12.

[107] *HCP*, pp. 108-109.

[108] *Ibid.*, pp. 155-156.

[109] *Ibid.*, p. 56.

[110] *Ibid.*, p. 117 and p. 211, n. 171.

[111] Traditionally, the relationship between loving God and doing God's will has been conceived of as working in the opposite direction. Segundo's reversal is an example of what happens when knowledge of God is considered as *praxis* (which pertains to the priority of action in knowledge) rather than as cognitive content (which

pertains to theory first and to practice or action as either subsequent application or product). The danger in the latter view is that what starts out being a logical priority (of theory over practice) often gets translated into everyday understanding as a chronological priority.

[112] Obviously, Segundo's interpretation of the gratuitous appropriation of salvation by Faith has something in common with Rahner's. There is a difference between the two, however, and it is striking. For Segundo, emphasis is placed not on knowledge of God, as it is for Rahner, but on action with God. This does not mean that Rahner leaves no room for action or that he ignores its significance for salvation. It only means that Segundo's emphasis on action is fundamental. It makes salvation a matter of a union of wills (anthropological faith functioning as salvation Faith) without requiring in addition to that a knowledge, however inchoate, of God's project. This is different from a notion of salvation in which a union of wills is conceived of as already including within it an implicit or "anonymous" cognitive appropriation of God's will in truth. The two interpretations are not completely dissimilar, however. For both Rahner and Segundo, salvation cannot be limited to only certain human beings and held to be excluded from others. It becomes operative and real whenever and wherever there is self-transcending love.

[113] *HCP*, pp. 56-57 and p. 67.

[114] See *ibid.*, pp. 127-142. As will be seen, Segundo sums these up under two main categories: failure and death.

[115] This is a key term for Segundo: "'To recapitulate' (to 'put a head on') is 'to give meaning' to something," not by summing it up in a unity but by bringing to light its definitive value—in other words, not by compression but by culmination (*EAJN*, p. 104). That from the beginning this term has been an element of Segundo's theology of grace is evident from its appearance in early works such as *¿Utopia?* (Part II, pp. 10-11 and ff.) and *EG* (p. 125, n. 15, and p. 126).

[116] Even in its more developed forms (e.g., the work of Bultmann) existentialist theology tends to approach freedom primarily as a matter of human subjectivity and historical self-consciousness. While the individualistic tone of the latter may of course be corrected to include the social and political dimensions of human subjectivity, for example, as Dorothee Sœlle does vis-à-vis Bultmann's work in *Political Theology* (Philadelphia: Fortress, 1974), existentialism remains emphatically subjective. Too facilely it can skip over the significance of objective reality. For example, in *Faith in History and Society* (New York: Crossroad, 1980), Johann B. Metz renames the subjective dimension by demonstrating that faith is "faith in history and society," and he uses this as a lever to distance his theology from Rahner's. In reality, however, Metz's theology is more subjective than Rahner's, for, unlike Rahner, Metz tends to overlook the significance of the objective realm of nature. In stressing the (subjective) categories of memory and narrative, for example, he takes a negative view of evolution (Metz, pp. 169-179).

[117] For Segundo, this is virtually equivalent to Manichæism (*EAJN*, pp. 69-70; *Berdiaeff*, p. 105).

[118] Segundo adverts to this problem in *RC*, p. 281. He observes that theological affirmation of the power of God does not oblige us to close our eyes to questions of value so as to permit ourselves to affirm as good something which would otherwise be considered unjust and inhuman—for example, the death of a child or the division of society into wealthy and wretched. See also *ibid.*, p. 295.

[119] Such is the depressing price Oerestes has to pay for freedom in Sartre's *The Flies*.

[120] For Segundo, atheism serves to critique the God language of the occidental tradition, attempting to correct the "theoretical deviations" and abstractions which obscure the reality of God as Jesus (and other prophets) reveal God in the concrete: "If our Christian existence is really authentic, then it must be a continuing journey from atheism to faith"(*OIG*, p. 179).

[121] As will be elaborated in more detail in chapter three, the criterion of the liberation of freedom is nothing other than the same self-sacrificing, generous and gratuitous love for creatures that God's Spirit definitively displayed in the kingdom *praxis* unto death of that irrepressible lover of "sinners" and the poor, Jesus.

[122] Elisabeth Schüssler Fiorenza (*In Memory of Her*, pp. 130-140) and, in a different context, Edward Schillebeeckx (*Jesus*, pp. 429-432), have both called attention to the wisdom traditions in which Jesus' Spirit is Sophia. It would be fruitful to explore the link between Sophia and Jesus' God-revealing kingdom *praxis* from the point of view of the project-centered theology of grace being elaborated in these chapters. The result could be a subversively feminine rendition of what Segundo calls a "project-christology" (*CIE*, pp. 102-103). Such a christology would be a Sophia-normed theological interpretation of the values of God. Its key would be the evil-abhorring exhuberance of Sophia—irresistibly wise and attractive Sophia, kindler of Faith, maker of justice, manifest lover of the marginalized and poor, Spirit of that stronger-than-death, irrepressible, joy-bringing "sinner"/wanderer/teacher/prophet Jesus, who, like Sophia, went about "rejoicing in the inhabited world" (Pr. 8: 31) and bringing forth from the wasteland a world that is inhabitable and good.

[123] The word "sinners" is used here in the gospel sense, as a technical term for the marginalized and poor. It pertains to those who were officially rejected and outcast by their religious peers and does not refer to an "offense" that is given to "God" (*HJS*, p. 94 and pp. 117-118). As marginalized of the marginalized, Jesus died a "sinner" *par excellence* in the sense of his having become the ultimate outcast, the poorest of the poor. He was condemned not only to the fringes of society but to death. Rejected by the powerful, betrayed and abandoned by followers and friends, and allegedly abandoned also by "God" because he, Jesus, had not followed the proper religious and political protocol regarding the values of "God," Jesus died a "sinner." In other words, Jesus was a heretic. According to the magisterial authorities of the

time, his theology was all wrong. It was a theology of the signs of the times, of the liberation of the deprived on earth, and not a theology concerned with interpreting "signs from heaven" (*HJS,* pp. 86-149).

124 As Segundo points out, God's eschatological action consists in bringing to life not only the dead but their projects; it is the kingdom, and not just Jesus, that God raises to life (*HCP,* pp. 74-75). This dimension of Segundo's eschatology will be a key element in the discussion of God's glory in chapter four.

125 In this respect it is important to remember that God's unprecedented creative act of raising Jesus from the dead did not occur in a vacuum. Gratuitousness is not the same as arbitrariness. Rather, as will be pointed out in detail in chapter three, the self-transcending love that Jesus realized in his kingdom *praxis* stands in causal relation to God's raising of Jesus from the dead. Had Jesus' love, embodied unto death in a *praxis* of fidelity to God's kingdom, not been actual and real, God could not have raised Jesus from the dead. And the same causality holds true anywhere and everywhere there is evidence of self-transcending love (see *HCP,* pp. 94-98).

126 This word does not refer to particular entities or institutions (e.g., the Catholic or Lutheran churches) but to the phenomenon of conscious, voluntary participation in God's project as it was made known in Jesus' kingdom *praxis* (*CCC,* p. 11). Disciples' knowledge of God's project requires a reflective way of living and acting in Faith—what Segundo calls the tasks of "prophetism and conscientization" associated with working on behalf of the coming of the kingdom (*HJS,* pp. 134-149). This is a way of living and acting that is actually a spirituality (*CIE,* pp. 125-126, n. 8). This constitutes a daily living out of the task-dimension of grace, a *praxis* of love grounded in the fact that "there is a *causal connection.* . . between the establishment of the kingdom and human activity directed toward it" (*HJS,* p. 158; italics mine).

127 *CCC,* pp. 31-32.

128 As Alfred Hennelly observes (borrowing an image from Jürgen Moltmann), Segundo's ecclesiology implies not that the church has a mission but that the mission has a church [*Theologies in Conflict* (Maryknoll, N.Y.: Orbis, 1979), pp. 69 and 83].

129 This line of thought also has implications for a theology of the eucharist. It would seem that the point of Jesus' saying "This is my body" is not that bread becomes Jesus' body, but that Jesus' body becomes bread. His entire life, the project of the kingdom and all its *praxes* are going to be broken down in the death in which they culminate in order to become nourishment for the building up of hope and the realization of love. This suggests that the point of disciples' existence is to be food for others, to be wine of solidarity and bread of life, salt for giving savor to the world. It indicates—and in Jesus' own experience of death and resurrection it gives grounds for the claim of Faith—that to be human is to be willing to surrender one's projects, and indeed, one's entire life, to the laws of entropy (*EAJN,* pp. 67-92). These laws surface in our action and in our lives in the shape of our own suffering and death. In dealing creatively with these forms of entropy, we succeed in freeing the results of

our projects, making them available to be picked up by the creativity of others. That enables the fragile and limited accomplishments of our freedom to come upon the scene of others' suffering in a neighborly and God-like way, i.e., to greet them not as a curse but as a blessing.

130 Although Segundo does not use this term, I believe his theology as a whole tends in the direction in which I am moving here.

131 See Gerhard Kittel and Gerhard Friedrich, eds., *The Theological Dictionary of the New Testament,* Vol. 9 (Grand Rapids: Eerdmans, 1974), pp 402-404. Of particular relevance is the observation that *charism* denotes "the result of *charis* viewed as an action" (p. 403). Also significant is what the authors call the "eschatological orientation" of the term as it appears in the Pauline corpus (p. 403). This indicates that "the gift is present but its possession is only provisional" (p. 404). To be realized, the *charism* must be appropriated at the level of action.

132 As was pointed out earlier, this makes grace "redundant." It serves to clarify a logic of action which already exists in its own right rather than replacing or transforming it with a different—and alien—logic.

133 The full theological import of this notion, its grounding in the ontological indestructibility of love, will appear in chapter four.

134 This does not mean that only doing is important. As was pointed out in the introductory remarks, action includes thinking as well as acting, knowing as well as doing, suffering and passion as well as accomplishment and activity.

135 It seems to me that the notion of historical causality is utterly basic to Segundo's theology of grace. It appears consistently in his writings, whether implied by the context or stated explicitly, as it is in "Theological Crux," p. 113, *LT,* pp. 143 and ff., *HJS,* p. 149 and *HCP,* p. 94 and pp.123-124. Its most explicit expression occurs in *HJS,* pp. 158-161.

136 Not all of our human projects, of course, will be capable of being validated by God in the eschaton. Or, putting it better, not every aspect or dimension of our projects will be able to be so validated, for, as will be explained in greater detail in chapters two and four, historical projects are by nature always profound mixtures of "heaven" and "hell," love and egoism, good and evil (*HCP,* p. 83; *Infierno,* p. 25 and p. 53). It is therefore necessary to have a criterion by which to determine which projects and which aspects of them will be made manifest as having eschatological validity, and that criterion the sensitive human heart attests—and God has also revealed—to be the needs of the deprived. The liberative implications of that criterion and its derivation from the kingdom *praxis* of Jesus form the topic of chapter three.

137 As will be seen in chapter two, Segundo believes that the greatest sin is omission. Not what we have done wrong, but what we ought to have done and failed to do constitute the greatest sins (*EG,* pp. 121-123).

138 *HCP,* p. 137; *RC,* p. 266.

¹³⁹ *Infierno*, p. 56.

¹⁴⁰ *OIG*, p. 25.

¹⁴¹ *Ibid.*, p. 27 (inclusive language substituted, and the original wording of Segundo's phrase "the world of man" replaced by "history and nature").

¹⁴² *Berdiaeff*, pp. 112 and ff.

¹⁴³ *Infierno*, p. 47. This understanding of creation was already at the heart of the *Berdiaeff* study (see n. 142 above), and sums up the logic of Segundo's entire subsequent work. "Creation. . . is destined to be prolonged through [human] labor," he writes (*OIG*, p. 22 ; inclusive language substituted).

¹⁴⁴ *Action* (University of Notre Dame Press, 1984), p. 419 (English translation by Oliva Blanchette). I am indebted to Roger Haight for bringing this passage to my attention during a conversation.

¹⁴⁵ Segundo first uses this phrase (taken from Rev. 3:20) in *Berdiaeff*, p. 78. Twenty years later, in *JNYT*, he refers to it in the context of the ontological category of the project, which runs through every volume of that work as the major hermeneutical key.

¹⁴⁶ See *RC*, pp. 214-215, n. 19; pp. 236-237; and p. 237, n. 15.

¹⁴⁷ Rather shockingly, Segundo believes that grace will dialectically integrate human sins into the creative destiny of human beings (*RC*, p. 275). The complex evolutionary logic of such dialectical integration, which is that of an ecological circuit rather than a dialectic strictly speaking, will be dealt with in chapter two.

¹⁴⁸ For a critique of the Cartesianism that still can be found even in sociopolitically conscious theologies, see Fergus Kerr, "The Need for Philosophy in Theology Today," *New Blackfriars* 65 (June, 1984), pp. 248-260.

¹⁴⁹ Segundo is interested in exploring such realism in *Berdiaeff*, Part II. There, he points out that, paradoxically, it is through recourse to forgotten philosophical achievements of Hegel and Kant that one can attempt to save Berdyaev's dialectic from the gnostic temptation to which it virtually succumbs in the denigration of being in favor of a spiritualized emphasis on freedom (see *Berdiaeff*, p. 387 and pp. 402-410).

¹⁵⁰ Paradoxically, what Gregory Baum has called a "Blondelian shift" to the subject thus seems to carry within it the seed for a second "shift," a turn toward the subject's link with the objective givenness of reality and the creation of a world.

¹⁵¹ See Karl Rahner, "History of the World and Salvation History," *Theological Investigations* 5 (Baltimore: Helicon, 1966), pp. 97-114.

¹⁵² Of course, it was considered essential to such knowledge that it be expressed in action as love. See Karl Rahner, "Reflections on the Unity of the Love of Neighbor and the Love of God," *Theological Investigations* 6 (Baltimore: Helicon, 1966), pp. 231-249. At the popular level, however, the relation between knowledge and love tended to be modeled more on the (chronological-cum-causal) logic of an application of knowledge in love than on the logic of action.

153 Hans Urs von Balthasar, *The Glory of the Lord,* Vol. I (New York: Cross-road, 1982), takes this conception of grace in an aesthetic direction, considering human action to be the art of allowing God alone to act. For von Balthasar, that art consists in "making self available as matter for divine action" with a "feminine and bridal plasticity" (p. 36) so as to become the creaturely "womb" which "God" as "Lord" fructifies (p. 116). He writes, "God's goal and purpose is absolutely contained in himself and *requires nothing external for its realization.* . . . God is his own father, mother and child, all in one" (p. 116; italics mine).

154 Largely neglected in this schema was the role of objective givenness, or nature. In an early article, "On the Theological Concept of *Concupiscentia,*" *Theological Investigations* 1 (Baltimore: Helicon, 1961), pp. 347-382, Rahner employs the concept, placing the impersonal givenness of nature in tension with the personalizing tendency of freedom, but Segundo criticizes him for not developing the implications of the concept in later writings (*Infierno,* p. 12).

155 The latter view gives a fitting value not only to the self-donation of God but to its concrete results in nature and history. The emphasis on results brings out the eschatological orientation of grace, for, as Segundo observes, whatever is given life in grace has to be given life in glory also (*Infierno,* p. 18). On the eschatological orientation of *charis* in the Christian scriptures, see n. 131 above.

156 That practical impossibility is part of what Rahner means by the supernatural existential: although grace is entirely gratuitous—i.e., in no way owed to human beings as an essential element of their anthropological structure—it nevertheless actually surrounds them as a constitutive dimension of existence. This makes nature (in the neoscholastic not the ecological sense) a "remainder concept," i.e., a logical abstraction ["Concerning the Relationship between Nature and Grace," *Theological Investigations* I (Baltimore: Helicon, 1961), p. 313].

157 *Transcendence and Immanence: A Study in Catholic Modernism and Integralism* (Oxford: Clarendon Press, 1980).

158 See John Courtney Murray, *The Problem of God Yesterday and Today* (New Haven and London: Yale University Press, 1964) and Shubert Ogden, *The Reality of God and Other Essays* (New York: Harper and Row, 1977).

159 Thomas Aquinas admits of a real relation between creatures and God but posits a notional relation between God and creatures. Segundo believes that if the doctrine of creation is to be meaningful today, a real relation must be shown to obtain in both directions. In this sense, Segundo's concern has something in common with Schubert Ogden's protest against a notional metaphysics of God's relation to creation (*The Reality of God,* Chapter One). However, Segundo's use of project-centered evolutionary categories distinguishes him from Ogden, who looks for a solution in the Whiteheadian categories of process philosophy.

160 At bottom, the theological reason such an ontology is so urgently needed has to do with the protest action itself instinctively raises against the thought—or

actuality—of its own and others' sufferings being rendered null. The very trouble that it takes to act unto good demands such a protest. As Segundo points out, if value and good proceeded only from God, we human beings would have lived and suffered for nothing, even if we were to be saved (see *Berdiaeff*, p. 106).

161 According to Segundo, to say that God made the world out of nothing is a way of stressing the fact (which is not the only theological fact about creation) that the definitive creation is going to be the kind of world that *God* wants it to be—i.e., a world in which will reign not evil and suffering but the ontological goodness of love (*HCP*, p. 154).

162 To conceive of being as the opposite of non-being is to think of being and non-being in digital terms, as if they were operations on a computer. In computer language, operations are either "off" or "on." There is no progression between "states," no possibility of anything new being learned or anything unexpected emerging "along the way." Between the "off-ness" of one state and the "on-ness" of the other, there is not a dialectical relation but a simple opposition. Although a dichotomous logic is efficient in computers, it is inadequate to the complexity of evolutionary realities. To model creation on it is to program out the creativity typified by God's impassioned style of action (indeed, it is to program out passion utterly). It is to leave no room for love, i.e., the willingness to suffer the risk of open-endedness and ambiguity, factors which derive from a radical openness to the random contributions of time and chance.

II

THE ONTOLOGICAL STRUCTURE OF HUMAN ACTION AND THE ECOLOGICAL DENSITY OF REALITY: SIN AS MEDIUM OF A LOVE-BUILDING PROJECT CREATIVE OF A WORLD

Give us this day our daily bread, and forgive us
our trespasses as we forgive those who trespass against us.
And lead us not into temptation but deliver us from evil.

On the basis of Segundo's evolutionary and anthropological categories, the previous chapter argued that in a tragic and incomplete universe, grace is God's gratuitous initiation of a project for the creation of a world that is inhabitable and good. Offered as invitation to kinship with God and experienced as salvation coming from God, grace is God's impassioned love, a love that liberates freedom for constructive participation in the creation of the world and makes God's relation to creatures real. Releasing freedom from insecurities and fears, grace introduces new epistemological and ontological premises to anthropological faith. It transforms faith into Faith, the freedom to use ideologies in a mature way—both meek and bold—for creative work in the building of a world out of self-transcending love. As has been seen, an understanding of Faith as creative appropriation of a *charism* centers on the causality of human freedom in grace. Knowledge of it derives from the datum of revelation that action is capable of mediating the love of God for suffering creatures, a love which comes to realization in ideologies or *praxes* that transmit the values of God's heart. So vital is action to realization of God's project that without the contributions of Faith, God would not and could not communicate God's love, and the eschaton—what Jesus called the kingdom of God—would not be able to come.

Yet for Segundo, this positive and enthusiastic vision tells only half the story. It describes the objective dimension of grace, the "news" that comes to anthropological faith as something able to be welcomed but not Faith's own, a word that is appropriate but not required, that occurs within the bounds of experience yet arrives gratuitously from outside, i.e., from God, and reveals in the logic of action God's love in a world still suffering and struggling to be born. This first half of the story tells that grace dawns in the horizon of anthropological faith as an objective fact: good news from God about the eschatological validity of action. Grace illumines the logic of action, reconfiguring the data of experience and providing for anthropological faith a gratuitous new context: Faith. Faith recapitulates the logic of action with the "news" that faiths and ideologies have lasting validity in the eyes of God. Paradoxically, that "news" is objective insofar as it forms a gratuitous yet able to be welcomed element of the structure of action, and it is good insofar as it validates exactly what the logic of action already suggests but cannot itself guarantee: that in the seeming futility of an incomplete universe the value of love is definitive, that vis-à-vis the heart of God there is lasting import to the work of human Faith.

For Segundo, the second half of the story is more subjective. It refers to something that, in every age, disciples of Jesus know not gratuitously in Faith but existentially in the depths of their experience. It pertains to the impression they and all persons and groups of good will every now and then get that the fundamental "Yes" of action, the affirmative response of anthropological faith to its own question— whether action itself is worthwhile—might actually be mistaken. Even if only an inkling, such an impression raises a question that the results of action, whether that of disciples or others, make it impossible to avoid: given the obvious limits, both ontological and moral, of the human condition, how can frail ideologies make Faith efficacious at the building of love on earth?[1] Given the seeming impotence of what people of good will do and suffer in face of the overwhelming load of problems weighing down the world, and given the apparent increase, with each new generation, in the kinds and degrees of evil afflicting history, society and the ecospheres, is not a positive valuation of the efficacy of ameliorative action overly optimistic? Even should we experience intermittent success in one or the other aspect of our individual or corporate lives in lessening the distance between intentions and results, the gap between the values implied by Faith and the ideologies that serve to structure the world seems to be as wide as ever, if not actually widening. Individuals and groups sometimes can and do improve, but the state of the world, we are tempted to think, is as bad as, if not worse than, ever. How, under such conditions, especially in the social and public spheres, can ideologies give definitive value to the work of individual and corporate human Faiths?

The pessimism behind this question suggests that the doubt raised by the experience of action as a limited and inefficacious phenomenon is really a cry of protest about the seeming inability of freedom to accomplish lasting good. It centers mainly on whether action can be efficacious on behalf of ameliorative change in history and nature, and to what extent, since at the level of consequences evil sooner or later seems to get the upper hand in every human project. Because this experience points to a discrepancy between intention and execution in every action, it embodies a fundamental complaint about the human condition: the inefficacious character of a love that is Flesh. Although the discrepancy may not be willed, it is always present. Often it is responsible for causing ourselves and others a great deal of suffering, even in action aimed explicitly at the building of love. This seems to contradict the logic of action and challenge the goodness of Jesus' revelation about grace. If grace liberates anthropological faith for constructive action in nature and history, what must be said about the negative return it gets from ideologies: the familiar and cumulative experiences persons and groups of good will have of failure, contradiction, miscarriage, frustration, the achievement of results that were not wanted and, what is worse, seem impossible to undo? Apart from the obvious difficulty of trying to overcome the inertia of structures and institutions vis-à-vis the requirements of change itself, persons and groups of good will know from experience that even when set on a course of love, action has mixed results: selflessness is inhibited by a need to preserve the self, generosity is checked by a certain incapacity, openness to the world is bounded by a more or less continual crashing against the shores of objective limits.

More problematic still is the question of guilt. In light of the ceaseless corruption, dissolution and co-optation of ideologies by things like egotism, self-interest, cowardice, short-sightedness, taking the easy way out, one might be tempted to ask whether Segundo's view of the constructive vocation of action is anthropologically realistic, in a Niebuhrian sense. For example, can optimism about the efficacy of freedom stand up to the fact that much of the suffering and meaninglessness in the world is recognized today as linked to injustice, thus humanly invented and possibly deliberately caused? Particularly from the perspective of the deprived, the problem with a high valuation of freedom is that in so many ways today, that same freedom seems to be channeled toward the creation and perpetuation of unjust structures and institutions. In the name of freedom itself, particular ideologies allow some human beings systematically to deny freedom to others and large numbers of human beings to deny freedom to other beings. Linked as it can be and often is with ideologies of privilege and aggressivity, freedom seems to display an anti-creative side, a potential for the production and perpetuation of ideologies more or less consciously bent on injustice, suffering and death.[2]

In the face of deliberate wickedness, the attempt to exploit ideologies by placing them at the service of death-dealing faiths or the outright doing of evil, some historical and experiential justification must be found, first, for taking an optimistic rather than a pessimistic view of the constructive value of human action and second, for making the release of freedom for creative action a value above every other.[3] In attempting to meet these requirements, it is not enough for Faith to rely on the affirmations of revelation about the value of action in grace and the constructive character of the fundamental human *charism*. Evidence that action can be efficacious even in the face of evil consequences proceeding from action itself (and possibly serving to inhibit further action of a new and liberative sort) must be brought to bear from the depths of human experience. It must be shown that there is something about the way we human social persons are put together that can be correlated with the affirmations of Faith, something about the structure of human action *qua* Flesh that is capable of supporting the news of grace or at least permitting it to ring true to the human experience of freedom in the face of its own ambiguity. The fact that grace requires from recipients a capacity and readiness to receive it as news that is good implies that it is necessary to explicate and clarify, in exactly such an ambiguous context and with philosophically coherent categories, how that news is capable of making liberative—or at least life-giving and hope-confirming—contact with the basic structure of the human condition.[4] In addition, this requirement must be met in light of freedom's negative and conflictual dimensions and not just its positive moments.[5]

In light of these requirements, the questions of evil and sin show themselves to be questions less for Segundo than for Faith. Is the optimism of a gospel Faith able to withstand the overwhelming experience of negativity induced by the failure of ideologies: not merely disciples' experience of the distance between what they actually end up accomplishing and what they originally intended to do but the experience of the obstacles they meet, both in themselves and others, in trying to bring about constructive change in the face of injustice, socio-ecological evil and individual and corporate moral failure? That Segundo's categories provide ontological and experiential justification for exactly such optimism and that the logic of that justification, particularly in his later writings, can stand up to experiences of negativity and failure, will form a major part of the content of this chapter.

More important, perhaps, than the coherence of categories that makes such justification anthropologically meaningful is the fact that Segundo's approach contributes to bolstering the hopes of persons and groups for whom the burden of injustice in the world today, with the increasingly violent and totalitarian tendencies it seems to display, spells a growing sense of urgency and discouragement and carries the threat of planetary disaster. According to Segundo's analysis, it *is* possible to act efficaciously on behalf of good, even in a world subjected to apparent futility, if not to the extent of overcoming the evils afflicting ourselves and the social and ecological environments, at least to the extent of resisting, obstructing or subverting their enslaving tendencies to a degree that can make a difference, and this not by any passive reliance on an intervention more efficacious than our own but by a steadfast commitment to the logic of our own action.

To accomplish the goals of the chapter in a way that takes into account the originality of Segundo's contribution, it will be necessary to take as a first consideration what is at issue in the effort to establish experiential grounds for such seemingly unrealistic optimism. I will do this by making a few observations in section one about the heightened consciousness of evil in our time, attempting to re-think the affrontive negativity of evil and sin within the methodological framework of Segundo's eschatological rendition of the doctrine of cooperative grace.

As will become immediately clear, the effort to come to grips with the negativity of evil makes it necessary to return to the theological preunderstanding or philosophical presuppositions of Segundo's theology,[6] particularly the most basic, the need to move from immobilist to evolutionary categories in the interpretation of reality.[7] Discussion of these in relation to what, relying on the terminology of Paul, Segundo calls Sin will form the topic of the second section.[8] There it will become apparent that, as was seen in chapter one, Segundo derives the categories of his evolutionary ontology from the complexity of reality itself. He believes that the use of such categories has been made necessary by increasing scientific evidence that the universe is engaged in an evolutionary project the *telos* of which is neither ascent nor progress but creative efficacy, i.e., the attaining of gratuitous breakthroughs into ecological equilibrium for the making of something new.[9] Insofar as actual instances of the latter involve the communication of significant difference in the face of quantitative and seemingly homogeneous elements like randomness and time, breakthroughs into ecological equilibrium surface in reality as efficacious attainments of qualitative change. In this sense, each realization of efficacious change is synonymous with the creation of something new, the accomplishment of something ontologically worthwhile, i.e., the gratuitous manifestation of freedom.

As chapter one showed, the tendency to achieve such gratuitous but down-to-earth moments of ecological equilibrium involves organisms in a project that is communal and eschatological. It is communal insofar as, learning to thrive together in what Segundo regards as a "synthesis of centers," organisms are implicated in a complex economy in which the ultimate value of the whole is dependent on the value of each of the parts and yet is greater than their collective sum.[10] And, as chapter one has already pointed out, the link that binds them together is self-transcending love. But the project as a whole is eschatological insofar as its *telos* is the creation of something worthwhile, good and new.[11]

Discussion in this chapter will thus build on the foundation laid in the preliminary sections of chapter one to show how, for Segundo, the observable effects of what Paul calls Sin give God's project as a whole, and self-transcending love within it, a profoundly ecological density.[12] Of central importance will be Segundo's account of the creative dialectic activated by grace in the working of Sin and Faith. Key to the logic of gratuitous breakthrough at the heart of Segundo's eschatology, the working of the Sin-Faith dialectic brings to light what in theological categories might be called the eschatological consistency of human action, its hidden yet no less real pertinence to the definitive character of the new creation promised in grace by God. The point of section two will therefore be to bring into view the ontological structure in which the "eschatological consistency" of action consists. It will do so by focusing on the ecological density of faiths and ideologies, which will in turn prepare the ground for attention in chapter four to the eschatological complexity of self-transcending love as manifest secret of the creative efficacy, or definitive power over Sin and death, God shares with creatures in Faith.

Looking at the density of the Sin-Faith dialectic under the conditions of time and entropy will make it necessary in the third section of this chapter to turn to the moral significance of human freedom insofar as action can be, and more or less actually is, marked by guilt or sin. Segundo's analysis will carry the discussion to the borders of an ethic that can be grounded in the kingdom *praxis* of Jesus and directed toward eschatological realization of God's project in grace and yet, for those very reasons (and not in spite of them), cannot be limited to being a merely "Christian ethic." Although it is not the topic of these reflections to examine the contours of that ethic, which would be human and this-worldly rather than "Christian" and "other-worldly" in scope, it will be helpful to observe what forms its most original element, namely Segundo's conception of sin. Neither the breaking of a divine or "natural" law nor the devaluing of "God" by a supposed overvaluation of human freedom and secular values in this world—something Segundo would perhaps regard as impossible, or at least not problematic from a gospel point of view—sin for Segundo consists in freedom's willed abdication of its native yet gratuitous *charism*, anthropological faith's anxious refusal in the face of Sin to live gratuitously in Faith. The nature of this abdication and the challenge it presents to Segundo's vision of Faith's eschatological responsibility will form the subject matter of section three.

Finally, the fourth and concluding section will provide a brief overview of the practical significance of the Sin-Faith dialectic in Segundo's work and give a preview of the remaining chapters. There, it will be seen how, when human freedom welcomes the evolutionary complexity and ecological density of its own structure, i.e., when Faith incorporates into the "circuit" of its ideological *praxes* the apparently futile yet ultimately creative logic of Sin, action is capable of realizing the creative project of God. It is capable of creating new reality in the definitive eschatological sense.

The Affrontive Face of Moral Evil and the Priority of Ontological Evil over Guilt

Before addressing Segundo's reasons for why such apparently unfoundable theological affirmations should find realistic grounds in a structural analysis of action, it would be useful to set the stage for the discussion as a whole by pointing out what is at issue in trying to establish grounds at all. A first issue is the need to face in a theologically coherent way the affront to human sensibilities presented by evil as a fact of experience. This affront is openly visible in the faces of the poor, in the bodies of the murdered, raped, tortured, oppressed and plundered of the earth, in the suffering of the outcast, forgotten and condemned. In our time, at least for a minority of liberationists, humanitarians and religious and secular activists, consideration of this affront has taken on a new complexity. In face of a heightened awareness of the cumulative and seemingly endless amounts of suffering, meaninglessness and injustice in the world, evil has ceased being a "problem of God" and has become a— perhaps *the*—question of the meaning of human freedom. It has moved from being a metaphysical question to becoming the ground and starting point of a liberative *praxis* aimed at ameliorative action in the world.[13] Distress over evil as a rational "problem," a theological "mystery" or metaphysical "flaw" has turned to outrage and horror at the massiveness and scope of suffering, and this response is accompanied by a new and troubling consciousness that the ills of history, society and the ecospheres are largely humanly caused.[14]

These signs of the times have taught many theologians that evil can no longer be regarded innocently as a cognitive problem.[15] No longer is it a metaphysical knot waiting to be untangled but an existential outrage demanding to be confronted and overcome.[16] Yet this new awareness is only a first step toward a constructive way of dealing with the issue. Viewed from an eschatological perspective—a Jesus-normed revelation of God's project of working conjointly with creatures to create a world that is good—evil must be understood as more than an affront; it must be recognized as *raison d'être* for the vocation disciples accept from God in grace. As disciples experience the destructiveness of evil and are caught in the nets of societal and ecological injustice, they can continue the effort to counter these negativities with the constructive ideologies of a human faith that stakes the worthwhileness of ameliorative action on the relevance of what Jesus called God's kingdom. They can respond to the affrontiveness of evil by working, like Jesus, toward the alleviation of suffering and injustice on earth, toward creation in the present of the kind of world that will be manifest in the end as meaningful, lasting and good. In the language of a gospel faith, this means that in spite of appearances to the contrary, disciples affirm the ontological validity and creative efficacy of ameliorative action. They affirm that on Faith's Spirit-like refusal to surrender its creative power, the Jesus-like refusal to abandon an alternative view of what faith in God's kingdom values ought to be effecting, depends the goodness of the world and the worthwhileness of life within it. Disciples assert that on human social persons and the consequences of their action rests full responsibility for the eschatological success—or failure—of the world-creative project of which God's steadfast and impassioned will, God's definitive commitment to creatures and solidarity with them in suffering, in short, God's irrepressibly creative love, has made itself a constitutive although gratuitous element.

In this sense, the new theological preunderstanding about the affrontive face of evil, at least vis-à-vis those who strive to counter its negativity on however small or great a scale, connects at several points with what the previous chapter had to say about Segundo's theology of cooperative grace and leads directly into what the present chapter has to say about the appropriateness of evolutionary categories.[17] First, the experience of evil as a glaring contradiction at the heart of reality provides a universal anthropological context for Segundo's conception of Faith as constructive freedom and creativity. This is because the news that grace gives freedom a *charism* to work with God to create a world that is good is capable of coming as news that is *good* to persons and groups struggling to counteract evil and injustice in this world.[18] Second, the experience of evil as an affront to the sensibilities of at least a minority of conscientious people suggests that questions of evil and sin impinge on a Jesus-normed theology as a challenge to the efficacy of grace.[19] Given the persistence of evil and sin in history and nature, how can God's project be expected to succeed?[20]

A way of combining these issues into a coherent theological approach is to note that from a secular point of view, the fact that evil can be experienced as an affront demands from theologians who are disciples of Jesus a reputable account of the historical and ecological relevance of the goodness of Jesus' "news" about God's love. If evil is not first of all an abstract metaphysical problem but a concrete matter of historically caused injustices crying out for historical-ecological solutions, then the dilemma of evil challenges precisely the meaningfulness of history and nature, and that poses a challenge to Jesus' gospel message *now*. It cries out for evidence of the truth of what Jesus called the "at-handness" of God's kingdom and its relevance to the elimination of injustice and deprivation in the present. If in grace God initiates a project, that is, wills the appropriation of salvation for the purpose of creating out of constructive contributions of human Faith a world that is lasting and good, then the theological challenge of evil and sin can be met only to the extent that history and nature are able to be given meaning and value not merely in the end (and even less by the action of God alone) but now. This means that theologians must attempt to ground two distinct yet inseparable affirmations about the relation of grace to historical and ecological evils: they must try to show *that* graced action is capable of prevailing over evil in the here and now on earth (and not only that "grace"—in the abstract—is capable of overcoming it eschatologically, *qua* "glory" or "God" in heaven), and they must try to show *how* such good, yet hard-to-believe news can ring true to experience in the face of contradictory appearances.

To ground these different yet closely related affirmations, Segundo places evil and guilt in a single teleological framework, the evolutionary context of God's project.[21] In an incomplete and tragic universe, Segundo situates evil and guilt within the project-mindedness of God's gratuitously manifest love: the desire to work together with creatures in the face of evil, entropy, suffering and inefficacy—the historical and ecological effects of what Paul calls Sin—at the creative making in the here and now of a world that will be good. As was indicated in chapter one, for all practical purposes this is equivalent to opting for a radical reversal in the traditional "order of continuity" between salvation and creation: it means subordinating to God's eschatological goal in grace the traditional notion of God's universal will to save.

And as was seen in chapter one, this means bringing salvation and creation together into a single eschatological action—God's gratuitous initiation of a project. This is an action of self-transcending love which in a universe subjected to the apparent rule of Sin will turn out in the end to have been definitively creative of a world that is lasting and good, but only thanks to the impassioned action of creatures working together with God in love at the building of a reality that is new and worthwhile now.

If the significance of grace centers on Faith's eschatological power (a significance which incorporates the notion of salvation into God's project of bringing to term conjointly with creatures what the scriptures call the new creation) and if grace is a gratuitous and impassioned love initiated by God precisely in the face of evil, it follows that evil can not be understood as the ruinous event of a distant and catastrophic past.[22] Nor can it be explained as a problem concerning the freedom of either God or human social persons alone. Even less can it be made a deadly matter of the divine and human freedoms in competition. In other words, evil can not be thought to result—in a fatalistic way—from a unilateral human "fall" that must be righted, equally unilaterally, by the justice and mercy of God. Rather, the effort to come to grips with evil must begin exactly where the most troublesome doubt appears about the value of earthly existence and the meaningfulness of history and nature now. For certain consciences at least, that doubt shows up at the heart of human action, where there is continually being raised an ontological question about the meaning and value of the universe itself. And such a question leads, potentially at least, to existential discouragement over the inefficacious character of human freedom in face of the affrontive power of moral evil and to a Niebuhrian sort of pessimism about the impotence of creaturely freedom in an apparently futile universe.[23]

In the logical order required by an evolutionary understanding of the universe, Segundo believes that the challenge created by pessimism and doubt can be met theologically, but only by admitting at the outset that ontological evil has priority over moral evil.[24] In the perspective of evolutionary categories, this means that the existence of evil is not the result of—much less a divine "punishment" for—a human "fall" into sin; rather, the actuality of sin is a result of the gratuitous advent of a definitively significant yet only relatively efficacious moral freedom that here and there in the evolving world begins to surface in living beings, surfaces clearly in the human sphere and finds itself implicated there in a complex ontology in which evil already plays a constitutive, constructive part.[25] This logical reversal suggests that the fact that freedom is capable of sin must not be made so enormous an issue in a theological anthropology as to constitute everything that can be said about freedom.[26] In meekness, theologians must recognize the magnitude of moral guilt as a challenge to the quality of all relations in which human social persons are involved; yet in boldness, they, like God, must make an anthropologically liberative choice: they must dare to think there must be more to grace than the forgiveness of sin.

As will be seen in the final section, the theological consequences of such a decision are scandalous. Like other liberationists, Segundo believes that evil demands creative action by human beings and God in history.[27] It is a threat that makes the deprived and those who, in solidarity with them, are responding to their cries attempt release. Unlike other liberationists, however, Segundo also believes that evil is a *sine qua non,* a crucial ontological requirement, for making human action meaningful and worthwhile, for giving it efficacious power, for enabling it to create. If not true of the action of God alone—a kind of action that anyhow (outside of data from revelation) lies beyond human ken—then certainly it is true of the action of human social persons working conjointly with God: evil is more than a deprivation and more than a matter of humanly caused injustice, although of course it is and obviously must be both of those. It is more, Segundo believes, because within the complicated contours of an evolving world, it is condition for the manifestation of creative freedom, condition for the realization of self-transcending love, condition for the mediation of gratuitous instances of earthly liberation, condition for the achievement in the here and now of a lasting good willed freely by God in grace and appropriated just as freely by human beings in Faith.[28] Just as evil conditions disciples' action of effecting God's values in Faith, so it conditions the ultimate actuality of there being any love in the eschatological creation. That is because, as Segundo notes, "Evolution is not a contest between two contradictory forces that would cancel each other out, unless one should partially or totally eliminate the other. Though they point in opposite directions, these two vectors—or tendencies, or forces [i.e., evil and love]—are indispensible and complementary, *each in its own way.*"[29]

In order to be able to make such a claim, it is necessary for Segundo to make, and keep, a careful distinction between ontological and moral evil at the same time that he notes their continuity.[30] In the context of evolutionary categories, he points out significant differences between the two in light of their common origins. While recognizing the disconcerting tendency of ontological and moral evil to appear in the anthropological complexity of action as ambiguous phenomena that somehow overlap, he distinguishes them from one other by means of the theological categories of *Sin* and *sin.* How do the two notions differ? As will be seen in the following sections, the answer lies in the nature of their respective relations to the evolutionary structure of reality. Where ontological evil, or Sin, is essential to the structure of freedom, moral evil, or sin, is not:

> Sin *dwells* in the human being in a total way. That is not true of *sins,* the specific acts that represent the visible fragments of Sin. Indeed sins as such, precisely because they are visible, can constitute a force opposed to Sin. The latter power, Sin, is not the innermost humanity of the person; but its mechanisms are not external either. Sin and its mechanisms are part of the human condition as such.[31]

A comparison of the two will show, in fact, that sin is anti-evolutionary while Sin is ultimately constructive.[32] In the context of evolutionary categories, in other words, what distinguishes Sin from sin is how each stands with respect to the efficacy of freedom.

The Entropic Economy of Sin and Faith and the Ecological Density of Reality

Segundo takes as a basic tenet a principle from the work of Teilhard: what is observable in more complex evolutionary spheres is observable by analogy in every other.[33] Evolution is not uniform, but it is uniformly dense, in the sense that to speak of one of its spheres is to speak by analogy of every other. This principle suggests two corollaries. First is one that Segundo, building on Teilhard's evolutionary foundation with more fully developed ecological categories from the work of Gregory Bateson, calls "the general *redundancy* of nature."[34] To state this corollary as a general rule, we might say that redundancy means one can "see the world in a grain of sand" (Blake), but one can never account for the world's complexity and diversity by attempting to reduce all entities in the world to sand. One obvious reason is the appearance on the "scene" of freedom, not only human freedom but also whatever is analogous to it in other evolutionary spheres. Because the advent of freedom (and its analogues) multiplies randomness and introduces new and unlimited occasions of novelty into already existing patterns of change, it challenges the tendency to make facile analogies, requiring instead the making of careful—and prior—differentiations. This tension between difference and likeness points to a balance which must always be maintained in evolutionary theory between what Segundo calls the "pinpoint" and "relational" axes of thought.[35] Although it is true that for the making of workable analogies relations are of primary concern and the terms being related are secondary, it is also true that the recognition of particular differences among persons, groups, species and entities is the only legitimate condition under which the phenomenon itself of diversity can be placed in a unifying context or generalized into a coherent analogical framework.[36]

The second corollary can be formulated as a basic principle about the distinction between epistemology and ontology. Being human, we human social persons must interpret all entities through human eyes, but we must resist the anthropocentric temptation to account for the value of those entities by reducing them to the common denominator of how useful they can be made vis-à-vis the interests of human purposiveness or the satisfaction of human needs. So far as Segundo is concerned, what is required of a theological appropriation of evolutionary categories is that it be ecologically conscientized, that it refuse to dichotomize reality into "human" and "non-human" segments. This means resisting what he calls the "Manichean tendency. . .to divide beings into *things* and *persons*."[37] Instead, theologians and all human beings must cultivate "an attitude of utmost respect for the complexity of nature as if it were 'an end-in-itself'"—in other words, "the capacity to absolutize, or better, almost absolutize, certain valid and sure things we are tempted to destroy by merely using them as our instruments."[38]

More than anything else, the capacity to "almost absolutize" things pertains to a respect for and cherishing of the processes of nature, which for Segundo always includes the "second nature" of culture.[39] Such an attitude implies a positive valuation of the complex mechanisms by which nature tends to achieve (what appear to be) its "projects." Seen through the eyes of analogy, the efficacy of projects continually being carried out in nature without any help from the purposiveness of human freedom allows us human beings vis-à-vis the logic of our own projects to recover our *"respect* for what we had downgraded as mere means."[40] Respect for, i.e., love, not of such processes as mechanisms in themselves but of the disciplined and ecologically appropriate ways such processes go about being efficacious, can give anthropological faith a moral sensitivity and humility. It can open up the ideological dimension of freedom—the orientation toward means that plays a part in every human action—to the new reality of trying to live gratuitously, i.e., according to the values of an anthropological faith that does not strive after efficacy on demand but is capable of welcoming it as gift. The gratitude to gratuitousness that results from such a faith can teach it a wisdom about ideologies. In this way, human projectivity can learn to commit itself to only those kinds of efficacy that are ecologically sensitive and appropriately scaled. Such efficacies are flexible in the evolutionary sense, i.e., beneficial not with a view to the expediency of immediate returns but in face of the random requirements of time and chance and the meandering character of change.

Segundo's development of these corollaries shows that he transposes Teilhard's evolutionary principle into an ecologically viable key. He makes the abstract character of analogical thinking self-consciously ecological and concrete. By affirming that analogies among the evolutionary spheres must certainly be made, he admits the existence of a genuine continuity among all beings in the world. Yet he makes it clear that the presupposition for making any analogy at all is the concrete fact of distinction, or discontinuity, among them. For Segundo, the recognition of ecological likeness and difference is indispensible to an adequate theological appropriation of evolutionary categories, since an understanding of evolution in the absence of concreteness not only is inaccurate from a scientific point of view but poses insoluble problems for theology.[41]

The theological relevance of ecological consciousness hinges not only on the notion that the spheres of evolving reality are interconnected and distinct but on the fact that each sphere has the creative capacity to "discover" efficacious means for the realization of appropriate change. The latter is achieved by the basic tension between strictness and laxness, rigor and creativity, at the heart of evolving reality. That is what makes it ecologically dense, a characteristic which shows up as key to the creation of new reality in every evolutionary sphere. In the sphere of physical reality, for example, under the rubric of the second law of thermodynamics, ecological density results from the tension between the continual dissipation of energy into ever less usable states on the one hand and creative syntheses which put that same energy back to work in new and more usable forms on the other. In the biological sphere, under the rubrics of genetics and homeostasis, an even greater density results from the multiplication of the tensions of the physical sphere by a whole new set of reproductive tensions such as genetic heredity and random difference or chance— e.g., the attempts of organisms and species to maintain an equilibrium between death and life, continuity and change or themselves and their environments.

Without losing any of the density already in evidence in the physical and biological spheres, the phenomenon of ecological density takes on increasing complexity in the sphere of human action. There, it comes to light in the working of Faith, where at both the individual and social levels it is visible in the more or less evident discrepancy between intentions and results. Basing his analysis on the categories of Paul in Romans, Segundo refers to this discrepancy by the biblical name of Sin; it is the apparent inefficacy of human ideologies which exists in creative tension with the eschatological efficacy of Faith.

Considering the discrepancy from the point of view of God's reliance on ideologies for the creation of a world that is good, Segundo demonstrates that in the sphere of human action, Sin is aptly characterized by Paul's description in Rom. 7: 14-25 of "the divided human being."[42] This is the familiar dilemma of the seeming inefficacy of ideologies aimed at good, the condition of apparent futility to which Flesh is subjected under the ambiguous conditions of entropy. Sin is Segundo's theological-biblical name for the universal anthropological experience—and complaint—that, in the exercise of freedom, execution never realizes intention. In every human action, an unbridgeable gap forever remains between what the inner "I" of Faith intends and what the objective results of ideologies achieve.[43]

Segundo views the phenomenon of dividedness as the anthropological version of the ontological structure of the universe. It is the benchmark of ecological density in the sphere of human action. At the historical, sociocultural and ecological levels at which Faith goes about working, the dividedness of action is epitomized by the seemingly futile situation of Faith's having to maintain a continuity of tradition, or stability of values, *via* ever changing ideological means that do not always work and never completely succeed. This tension is evolutionary insofar as it involves faiths' having to learn a delicate balance between rigor and creativity, strictness and laxness, continuity and discontinuity at the everyday level of *praxis*. But it is ecological insofar as it involves Faith's having to maintain a creative equilibrium—a lived and living continuity—between values and efficacy, or what Segundo calls the iconic and digital dimensions of *praxis*, much as a circuit "learns" how to work by sensing alternately when to break, and re-make, contact.[44]

Sin—what Paul calls "the law of the members" which resists the intentions of the "I" of Faith—is thus a technical evolutionary term. It refers to the phenomenon of resistance—morally neutral in itself—which is presented to Faith by the very instruments and means that it must try to use for the realization of its aims.[45] As such, it points to the paradoxical requirement to which Faith must respond at both the individual and corporate levels: in a universe subjected to the apparent reign of entropy, Faith has at its disposal for the achievement of its aims only the use of instruments and ideologies which have a "mind of their own." As a result, it must follow the circuitous and time-consuming route of incorporating into everyday *praxis* the seemingly futile but actually constructive periods of "off-ness" or inefficacy that the resistance of ideologies involves, and it is this situation of disjointedness and alienation which Paul describes as Sin. As the distance which separates the intentions of action from its output in results, Sin represents the entropic dimension of evolving reality within the seemingly futile context of which Faith must do its work.[46]

The analogies Segundo makes among the evolutionary spheres are thus intended to explain how Sin can refer to something not merely anthroplogical but structural and ontological as well, to the mystery of pre-moral or non-moral evil as it appears as an elemental dimension of every movement toward change and not only of human action. The making of these analogies helps to explain why in the human sphere Sin is experienced as inevitable and given, why in an anthropological context it faces, Janus-like, in two directions at once. Looked at objectively, Sin appears as evil. It represents a deprivation of efficacy, a disconcerting incompleteness built into the structure of reality and plaguing the efficacy of freedom. Looked at subjectively or existentially, however, Sin is neutral. In itself it is neither good nor bad but simply always there. As such, it is morally ambiguous. It has the disconcerting capacity to go either way.

On the one hand, Sin may function to facilitate the aims of the inner "I" by inducing anthropological faith to "face reality," as it were, urging it to employ ideologies that are humbly scaled and that fit the ecological laws and evolutionary mechanisms built into the structure of the universe. On the other hand, Sin may be exploited by an overdose of purposiveness: freedom may grasp at the entropic character of Sin as an easy way out of the difficulty of trying to elicit the sort of efficacy that, ecologically speaking, is appropriate, flexible and wise. Without directly being the cause of moral evil, Sin may permit sin to occur and even provide a convenient "groove" into which freedom can install ideologies and along which it can be carried by them (all the while pretending to carry itself), although in this way freedom succeeds only in delivering up the efficacious potential of ideologies to an increasing inefficacy by which they wane ever more pointlessly into the law of diminishing returns.

So far as Segundo is concerned, the ambiguity in Sin serves to highlight the paradox that the laws and mechanisms of objective reality operate independently of human freedom at the same time that they are constitutive elements of its structure. Because this is the case, those laws and mechanisms exact an inescapable price. They take their toll in entropy in every human action. In relation to the eschatological agenda introduced into action by grace, they show that, in order to be efficacious unto good, Faith must pay a constructive debt to Sin.[47] Faith must recognize that insofar as Sin is an essential element of reality's make-up, incorporation of its entropic aspects into the project-mindedness of action is the condition for efficacy.

Like the incompleteness of the universe of which it is a part, Sin imparts to the projects of freedom a tragic yet almost bizarrely comic character. It gives the creative tension between faith and ideologies a built-in pull toward inefficacy: things just appear to be continually breaking down. This readily seems to be the case at the level of everyday experience. There, Sin is recognized by what for lack of a better term might be called a *Tristram Shandy*-sort of homespun wisdom (*Tristram* meaning sad, *Shandy* meaning "crack-brained"); Sin's capacity to bring people up short with suffering and deprivation—and cut them down with death—makes persons of good will deeply conscious of the tragic dimension of life, yet the irrepressible phenomenon of hope keeps them a trifle "crack-brained" about the worthwhileness of it all. This paradox shows up at the popular (and trivializing) level in adages like *"C'est la vie,"* cartoon characters like "Charlie Brown" and "Ziggy" and sayings like "Things never turn out the way one plans."[48]

Even more paradoxically, however, things sometimes turn out *better* than one had planned. New things sometimes arrive on the scene, and here or there smaller or greater changes end up being made. Improvements occasionally find themselves being brought about, good things spontaneously happen, and people find themselves moved every now and then to wonder at the sheer abundance of gratuitous surprise.[49] This suggests that the Sin which appears to be the source of structural inefficacy is actually the facilitative condition under which Faith achieves its work. If in this or that instance action succeeds in producing at least temporarily efficacious results, creative syntheses of disparate energies that, even if they are not capable of keeping results alive forever, at least give birth to something new, it seems capable of doing so only thanks to, and by means of, Faith's seemingly futile service to the law of Sin.

This means that from the perspective of efficacy, the apparent victory of Sin must not be the final word. According to the evidence of reality itself, action seems capable of incorporating entropic energies into syntheses that are creative and efficacious by the continual appearance on the scene of things that are new—and, from the point of view of the entropic economy of break-down and decay, utterly gratuitous. New forms of organization emerge gratuitously out of the randomness of chance over the course of time, and qualitative syntheses follow the breakdown of previously exhausted energies into quantitative pieces, apparently useless bits and crumbs.[50] Entropy admittedly has a high level of visibility in the universe, but it is not all there is to see.

Segundo's understanding of the ambiguity of Sin makes it clear that in the human sphere, the evolutionary tension between entropy and negentropy is multiplied and recapitulated by Faith and Sin. The two are integral elements of every action. They form an ecological circuit. Unless disturbed by stupidity, simplistic forms of problem-solving or the ugliness of expediency and over-purposiveness— i.e., culpable forms of evil—their dialectical relations make action seemingly inefficacious but actually efficacious, capable of creating something new. When Faith respects the entropic requirements Sin imposes on the work for qualitative change—e.g., the need for large doses of quantitative energy and sizable periods of "off" time—it is capable of being efficacious on behalf of freedom's goals. Quality emerges every time Faith respects the ecological density of reality and works with, rather than against, the grain of Sin.

By making ontological evil—in the form of Sin—an essential and universal element of the structure of Faith's efficacy, Segundo prepares theological ground not only for continuing to believe in the worthwhileness of Faith in nature and history but also for the optimism—or Jesus-derived hope—that ideologies can and will be of definitive value to eschatological realization of the creative project of God.[51] Segundo shows that, in the gratuitous context of God's project, the ecological density of the Sin-Faith dialectic is capable of facilitating the creation of a world that is good. He begins with the fact that Faith and Sin are related to one another as origin and result.[52] Although they pertain to two different logical levels (invisible and visible), they are not incompatible.[53] The two are non-identical but not opposed, distinct yet not mutually exclusive. In the ecological idiom of Segundo's evolutionary categories, they form a single world-creative circuit—grace—in which they relate to one another as discontinuous yet radically continuous components of the structure of human action. From the point of view of the apparent victory of Sin in history and nature, their discontinuity is what shows up, yet from the point of view of eschatology, they are utterly continuous. What is capable of making the invisible visible in the midst of Sin is precisely the new way of seeing that proceeds from Faith.[54] The eyes of Faith confirm what experience suggests but cannot guarantee, namely, that the creative constructions that Faith has made, composed of nothing other than the entropic energies of Sin turned into works of human love, are going to last forever. In spite of the inefficacy ideologies display as a result of their subjection to the law of Sin, Faith can be efficacious.

One way to clarify what Segundo means by "subjection to Sin" is to contrast Sin with the traditional theological notion of concupiscence, showing in particular the link between Rahner's re-thinking of the latter term in the categories of existentialist philosophy and Segundo's transposition of it into an evolutionary framework utilizing the vocabulary of Paul. According to the manuals of neoscholastic theology, the salvific effect of the cross (in neoscholasticism an event ordinarily viewed apart from Jesus' *praxis* and resurrection) was to eliminate the guilt which the human species had "incurred" through the sin of Adam. According to this doctrine, redemption cancelled the guilt of sin but did not do away with its effects. These continued to make themselves felt through a lingering human tendency to keep "falling into" sin. Evil inclinations and desires, typically associated with "natural instincts" and often characterized as "unruly passions" or "snares of the flesh" betrayed that the (allegedly) orderly powers of reason had been weakened by the "sin of Adam" and made to suffer embarrassment and infirmity by what traditional theology called "the Fall."[55] The name given to the resulting tendency to continue to "fall" was concupiscence.[56]

Relying on what at the time of its publication was a revolutionary essay by Rahner entitled "The Theological Concept of *Concupiscentia*," Segundo sets out to retrieve the theological insight at the root of this notion in a way pertinent to both an ecological consciousness about the density of reality and an evolutionary understanding of Sin. For Segundo, as for Rahner, concupiscence is not a tendency to fall into sin but the impossibility of freedom's being able to accomplish any action—whether for good or evil—with an efficacy that is absolute.[57] Concupiscence represents the innate distance or lack of fit between the intentions which freedom sets out to achieve and the objective realizations it effects. In the thought-world of Rahner, which in the 'fifties was still a mixture of transcendental Thomism and Heideggerian existentialism, concupiscence pertains to the (healthy) system of checks and balances between personal freedom and impersonal nature, a notion Rahner applies to the ontological limitations of freedom under the ambiguous conditions of history.[58]

Segundo draws on Rahner's pioneering effort because of its capacity to show that concupiscence pertains essentially to what Segundo is calling Sin and not exclusively to sin. In the evolutionary idiom of Segundo, however, concupiscence is given an ecological rather than an existential accent. It becomes a theological synonym for entropy. It is a name for the morally neutral element of inefficacy in the universe, the alienating distance between faiths and ideologies, the unavoidable discrepancy between the dimension of meaning and values and the dimension of efficacy. If the experience of concupiscence is to be trusted, it leads to the disconcerting conclusion that ideologies—the very structures on which God and creatures have to depend for the eschatological efficacy of grace—appear congenitally inefficacious under the conditions of Sin.

In spite of the obviousness of this inherent limitation, however, God continues to need and rely on ideologies. Although they typically miscarry and even fall wide of the mark, they remain the necessary building blocks of the eschaton.[59] On that day, when human beings can see with eyes no longer overwhelmed by the high visibility of Sin, they will discover, as Jesus did, that what seemed under the conditions of concupiscence to be miscarriages and failures have in fact, in the eyes of God, produced eschatologically valid and definitively creative results. Human beings will see that God has taken those results and inserted them into the eschaton as part of its enduring structure. In the context of God's project to create with creatures a world that is good, it is apparently "all right" with God that action must include an unavoidable "dose" of inefficacy or Sin.

At the existential level, God's project thus manifests a concupiscent economy that is disconcerting and even scandalous. It is experienced as the apparent victory in history and nature—and, in the human sphere, in society and culture—of Sin. This is the victory of quantity over quality, homogenizing tendencies over creative differentiation, degenerative breakdown over constructive build-up, i.e., the apparent reign of entropy.[60] Yet for Segundo, the theological relevance of this economy is precisely that, like entropy, Sin is not something to be overcome—a scientific and theological impossibility—but something susceptible of being integrated into a constructive circuit from the point of view of Faith, something capable of being welcomed by the anthropological logic of faiths and ideologies and incorporated into action in a wise and flexible way. According to Segundo, Sin can be—but is not always—incorporated into the projects of human action by the creativity of anthropological Faith; and when it is, it gratuitously produces negentropic, i.e., efficacious and constructive, results.

Segundo's analysis of the ecological density of human action thus leads to a key theological conclusion: in an evolving universe, the efficacy of Faith is gratuitous. It can never be forced but is the gift to freedom of the objective—and "concupiscent"—givenness of reality. However, just as efficacy is not something that can simply be had on demand, neither is it something purely random. On the contrary, because it pertains to entropy's capacity to produce efficacious results in the course of what the scriptures call "the fullness of time," it must continually be prepared for by a "discipline"—a "learning to learn," a "Tao" or way of wisdom— that is the *praxis* of an ecologically sensitive Faith. Such Faith is humble and wise insofar as it displays a constant flexibility. It readies itself for the emergence of new reality by the patient action of "creative waiting." This characterizes a mode of human freedom conscientized by the conditioning demands of a Sin-full (but by no means simply evil) objective reality. Such "conscientized waiting" makes itself ready for the appropriate moment, the acceptable time, the "moment of salvation."[61] It is alert and practical, like the women in the gospel story who, having oil in their lamps, are prepared for whatever might be about to happen—or become important to do. Timing or flexibility—in the case of action, the flexibility which marks an ecologically conscientized anthropological faith—is thus the *sine qua non*, the trait *par excellence* of an efficacious Faith.[62] It is the Spirit-taught capacity to allow gratuitousness its place. In the context of a theological discussion about grace, flexibility is the responsiveness of the human heart to the ecological density of the Sin-Faith dialectic which readies the conditions for both the realization and recognition of gratuitous breakthroughs into efficacious love.[63]

Faith and Sin thus recapitulate the constructive logic of the evolutionary project. Faith provides a gratuitous eschatological *telos* for the entropic work of Sin. What is that *telos?* It is Faith's creative incorporation of action's unavoidable—and highly visible—"service to Sin" into an everlasting, although as yet still invisible, reality that is new and good. It is the definitive creation of a world, the efficacious realization of self-transcending love, the making of something new and the doing of something definitively worthwhile in the face of obstacles as seemingly insurmountable as evil, guilt and death. The constructive *telos* of Faith gives action a new "head" or meaning, a new eschatological logic, and that logic places Sin in a God-given context of grace, the creative love that comprises the project of God. Precisely as a project, the love that is grace incorporates both the values of God (appropriated in the as yet invisible substance of what Faith "sees" and hopes for) and the achievements of human social persons (appropriated through Faith's ideologies which are visibly "serving" the law of Sin) into a single circuit (efficacious love), which it gratuitously "activates" with definitively creative eschatological power.

As was pointed out in chapter one, if anything can be said about the eschatological efficacy of love, it is the gratuitous but also redundant news that God needs human action in order to create. Here, however, Segundo is showing that not only does God need Faith and ideologies, but Faith and ideologies need Sin. According to the way Faith is structured, Sin is what mediates the efficacy of love. In a world that must be made gradually and patiently by God and creatures working together in a project that is love, "Sin-full Flesh" is the only efficacy God and creatures have by which to mediate love and create a world that is good. Sin does this when anthropological faith is liberated by contact with God's Spirit and begins living as Faith.[64] The ontological structure of the universe is such that by its own ecological density, Faith is capable of being efficacious when it works with and not against the grain of Sin.

This means that the definitive eschatological creation is built on apparent inefficacy and, until the eschaton, will never be without it. Under the conditions of incompleteness in history and nature, reality will never be without ontological evil, or Sin:

> Only a world in which Sin can accumulate and become. . .as meaningless in itself as Death is, can prevent the accomplishments of one generation from diminishing the importance and decisive character of the next generation. If Sin were quantitatively overcome as humanity advanced in history, then human beings would become useless and wander in vain about the world. We need a world in which creation, love, and life triumph qualitatively, transforming reality irreversibly without ever escaping the quantitative victory of Sin. Only such a world can make human existence worthwhile, can put Faith

in the human heart as energy concentrated on its committed involvement in history, and all the power of God in its inner creativity as child of God.[65]

Quantitatively speaking, there will always be endlessly randomized amounts of Sin "at hand" for Faith to contend with in each generation—the ontological effect of the universe's having structured itself in such a way that efficacious change depends on the randomness of chance and the need to take enormous amounts of time. And the concupiscent elements of chance and time provide the "raw material" in every generation and in the life of every individual for the creation of something new, the making of a love that contributes good and worthwhile reality to the creation of the world.

Working under such conditions, action must pay the costly price demanded by both the laws of its ecological density and contact with God's Spirit.[66] That is, when disciples are willing to live according to the values of God's heart revealed in Jesus' kingdom *praxis*—when they are attempting to model their ideologies on the paschal significance of Jesus' death and resurrection (what Paul calls living by the Spirit in Faith)—then the works of Faith, which remain fully human works of Flesh under the concupiscent conditions of Sin, are gratuitously efficacious as works of God as well. Under the appearances of history and nature they may show up as inefficacious and failed, but in the light of the eschaton they will show up as genuine concretions of the creative love of God. Creative works of Faith gratuitously effected in an apparently inefficacious medium of Sin are God's eschatologically creative love for the world surfacing gratuitously and definitively in creatures. Besides being expressions of creatures' own love, they are gratuitous concretions of God's love, and because of this, the works of love such action builds will last with God forever. As will be seen in chapter four, they have an ontological value that is genuinely eschatological.

The Moral Density of the Sin-Faith Dialectic

As was suggested in the introductory section of this chapter, Segundo's notion of Sin as evolutionary vector both necessary and complementary to the vector of Faith—and thus necessary to the realization of God's eschatological project—remains inseparable from a central concern of this discussion: the dilemma of moral evil or guilt. Traditionally, theology has referred to the latter as *sin*, and Segundo continues to do so, but in a context of ecologically conscientized categories. He recognizes that because anthropological faith is not innocent with respect to the ecological density of reality, human freedom is not only subject to the laws of its own ontological structure but also capable of guilt. The advent of a specifically human form of freedom on the evolutionary scene thus introduces an ethical complexity into the working of entropy. It implicates Sin in the effects of moral decisions.[67] Insofar as freedom has the capacity either to incorporate Sin into the logic of action or else to incur guilt by forcing Sin to serve the purposes of sin, Sin takes on an ethical complexion in the phenomenon of ideologies and a moral density in the working of Faith. This makes it possible for human social persons and their action to transform Sin into sin, to thwart the *telos* of God's project—in which Sin but not sin is a necessary part—and to a greater or lesser extent reduce what ought to be the self-validating worth of gratuitousness, or efficacious change, to the purely utilitarian purposes of a single, and self-serving, dimension of reality, namely (sinful) anthropolgical faith.[68]

Vis-à-vis the work of Faith, this means that sin makes it possible for human beings to parody the entropic function of Sin, to wear the efficacy of the Sin-Faith dialectic down, to impoverish it and inhibit its potential to create. Human sinfulness means that action can caricature the ecological density of freedom rather than welcome its tendency to produce gratuitous results.[69] By failing to incorporate the entropic aspects of Sin into creative syntheses of love, sinful human action can more or less successfully short-circuit or even cancel out the capacity for long-range efficacious results. By reducing the project-oriented character of action (concerned with the building of values) to purely object-oriented status (focused one-sidedly on ideological means), faiths and ideologies can influence reality in a negative way, human beings acting as if the universe were neither engaged itself nor engaging them and their freedom in anything like a project at all but were simply a sum of manipulable parts. Insofar as anthropological faith is capable of making the "parts" of reality into objects, it can provide what it believes to be sufficient justification for subjugating various elements of nature and second nature, or culture, to the purposive aims of a freedom made up—monstrously—of ideologies alone.[70] By giving over the ideological orientation of anthropological faith to purposive aims, action impoverishes freedom, distorting its essential structure.[71]

In short, sin is the expression of action's ingratitude to gratuitousness, a human "thumbing of the nose" at the ecological density of the Sin-Faith dialectic, with all the pain and yet efficacy the latter—when Sin is not exploited by sin—entails. In this sense, sin is a theological name for the willful (and infantile) refusal to cope with the logic and complexity of "efficacious inefficacy," to contend with the ecological density of Sin and Faith and their "circuit" of creative gratuitousness. It is a frantic search for the simple solution, a short-sighted clinging to ideological answers supposed to be highly effective and thought to be perfectly clear. It is the quest for some sort of magical antidote against the ethical ambiguities and objective requirements that make themselves felt in the course of every action. As such, sin entails a stupid belief—the result of an ecologically insensitive anthropological faith—that a mode of action as unrealistic as that of attempting efficacy through ideologies alone is not only definitively worthwhile but also ecologically possible.[72]

From Segundo's evolutionary perspective, sin thus involves a culpable lack of realism about both the teleology and ontology of action. It is a culpable abdication of the *charism* embodied in Faith's power to create a world that is good, a closing of the heart to the human vocation to self-transcending love. At the ontological level, where anthropological faith disregards the need to incorporate the entropic element of Sin into ideologies that would aim to be creatively efficacious, sin represents a glaring lack of realism about the structure of human action; and at the teleological level placed in a clarifying light by the gratuitous and yet "redundant" piece of Jesus-revealed "news" about grace, sin represents a lack of eschatological imagination, a failure to hope—and labor—for the definitive creation of the good. This suggests that, fundamentally, sin is a distortion of both the anthropological logic and ontological structure of action set forth in this and the previous chapters. It is a culpable by-passing of the circuit-like relations between Sin and Faith, a short-circuiting of the complex logic that for the sake of efficacious results must risk suffering the incorporation of Sin into the creative work of Faith.

As has already been seen, with respect to efficacious accomplishment of the aims of freedom, Sin plays a necessary and facilitative role. It is the evolutionary complement of Faith. When human social persons incorporate the logic of Sin into the projects of freedom in wise and flexible ways, they discover that action can and will be eschatologically efficacious, even if at the level of appearances it seems to have been merely provisional or even to have utterly failed. By contrast, when human beings do not incorporate the logic of Sin into their work, and when that failure is culpable, they turn Sin into sin. This forces ontological evil to serve the purposes of moral evil, with its anti-ecological, anti-eschatological and anti-evolutionary concomitants of enslavement, alienation and guilt.[73]

Unlike the ontological sense of the word, sin in the moral sense thus connotes the unwise, inflexible and destructive implemenation by freedom of its own eschatological logic. It is freedom's deliberate abdication of its own ontological structure, an over-simplification of the ecological density and anthropological causality inherent in the working of ideologies, faith's culpable failure to take up the vocation—intrinsically ethical—of eschatological responsibility for creation of a world that is good. In particular, sin entails a refusal by anthropological faith either to create and employ ideologies that are flexible and wise or, what is just as bad, a refusal to enter into the spirit, or constructively participate in the institutionalization, of ideologies of a more or less wise and flexible sort, ideologies that may already be in operation, however imperfectly, in the objective givenness of existing personal, societal, cultural and ecological structures. So far as Segundo is concerned, the evolutionary project can not go on and never has gone on as if a merely haphazard phenomenon. By its own logic, it demands that all contributing parts, including human freedom insofar as it is functioning as Faith, incorporate Sin into the circuit of gratuitousness, or grace, so as to labor to bring the creation of the world to term by means of an efficacy that is not only gratuitous but fully down-to-earth.

THE ROOTS AND *MODUS OPERANDI* OF SIN IN SEGUNDO'S THEOLOGY

As the preceding paragraphs suggest, what Segundo means by sin is significantly different from what traditional explanations of it convey. Ordinarily, Christian theologians have tended to define sin in terms of either pride or sensuality.[74] Typically, they speak of sin as egotism, self-will *par excellence,* human autonomy preferred to the will of God.[75] Of the two types of sin, pride is normally considered the more grave, for it is thought to represent the rebellious efforts of finite creatures to transgress the limits of finitude and set themselves up in place of God.[76] Carried to the extreme, this logic would almost make sin an offense against the canons of orthodox ontology. In practice, it tends to make sin an affront to the (alleged) "absoluteness" of God, i.e., an effort to displace the primacy of God's infinite being, uncreated and supreme, by setting up as a false absolute the finite being of creatures.[77]

Segundo rejects the devaluation of creatures—and reification of God—implicit in such a view.[78] From Segundo's perspective, sin flows less from rebellion against creaturely finitude than from the refusal—paradoxical and shocking to the ears of the righteous who possibly in fact are not—to accept justification unconditionally from God and be liberated by that acceptance to cooperate with God in the creative incorporation of Sin into the work of Faith for the construction of a world that is good. The root of sin is not pride but a timid fear of appropriating the creative power of freedom, a refusal to place the creative capacity of human Faiths and ideologies at the service of an eschatologically valid self-transcending love.[79] Such fear is utterly paradoxical insofar as it consists in a free decision to refrain from using freedom at all rather than risking the possibility of mis- or over-using it.[80] For Segundo, the fear of human autonomy is the product of a servile religious humility that is fundamentally self-deceptive: it makes human beings pretend that the *charism* of freedom is less than what God has revealed it to be—justification in Faith (liberation of freedom) for constructive participation in a love-building project with God. This pretense allows religious groups and individuals to allay their anxiety about justification with an alternative, and, in the short run at least, far more secure "vocation" of childish dependence on a law of "God," with its authoritarian (and magical) brand of purely sacred efficacy and its anti-secular program of religious self-justification through the piling up of "works."[81]

The self-deception caused by that false "vocation" then becomes a perfect excuse for what Segundo regards as the genus to which all species of sin belong: omission.[82] Omission is sin generically classified. It pertains to the countless ruses we human beings can and do invent for keeping away the costly task of investing the energies of anthropological faith in the creative realization of self-transcending love.[83] In this sense, sin points to constructive modes of action we could, and ought to, have created, ideologies of love in which we might, and should, have participated, but culpably did not. It represents a deliberate thwarting, or even witholding, of creative efficacy from the welfare of others.[84] Strictly speaking, in fact, sin is not really action at all but something more akin to "anti-action," a "poor excuse" for, or parody of, the real thing.

As "anti-action," however, omission is not the same as mere passivity. It is a more or less deliberate course of inefficacious action. Precisely as omission, it typically involves the "creation" of unjust social and ecological orders (or the perpetuation of their "run-away" effects, which is the same thing); it permits the formation and perpetuation of ideologies of domination and deprivation through anthropological faith's more or less consciously willed collaboration with and maintenance of sheer build-up (as opposed to constructive up-building through ideologies of self-transcending love). In this sense, sin represents the making of poor energy syntheses, badly integrated social and ecological circuits (structures which peripheralize and marginalize certain groups rather than integrating them in love); and ultimately, it is the tangible human aggravation of the cumulative weight of inertia through ideological reenforcement of mega-structures of destruction, suffering and death.[85] In this sense, omission can represent an active program of "anti-creation" as well as the simple failure to create.

For Segundo, the anti-creative effects of omission are most obvious in the countless ways that sin can, and often does, function in so-called "spiritual" realms like religion.[86] There, reliance on an extrinsic law is capable of providing sacred rationalizations for inadequate response, perhaps total blindness and deafness, to the ecological exigencies and this-worldly needs of neighbors.[87] In this way, sin serves to deprive both world and neighbor of good or goods so as to facilitate instead the pursuit of religious self-justification.[88] Fundamentally, this makes sin a matter of injustice, but with a reality denying twist. It is freedom's refusal to shoulder the task of creating with God a world in which Sin is a constructive constitutive part, a refusal to accept Sin as an ontological component of the circuit in which Faith must work for the creation of something good. In particular, sin is freedom's refusal to risk allowing itself to be conditioned by entropy, a refusal made for the sake of the immediate and anti-ecological security that results from treating world and neighbor in simplistic fashion as immediately manipulable objects.

For Segundo, this makes sin a matter of faith's timid, self-protective and ultimately anti-ecological preoccupation with religious purity, the self-righteous attempt to be "holier than God" by refusing to "contaminate" human projectivity—now deteriorating into mere purposiveness—with ideologies conditioned by the energies of Sin. In this sense, sin is a refusal to contribute to the building of love in a universe which, thanks to the ecological density of its evolutionary structure, is not only "a world of grace" but also, and scandalously, "a world of Sin."[89]

To imbalance the circuit between Sin and Faith is to a greater or lesser extent to distort the ecological density of reality. Rather than Sin's being built up into new realities by the synthesizing effects of Faith, sin tends to let Sin simply "build up" on its own. It keeps on piling up entropy until the latter displays itself, obscenely, in two principal ways: as ugliness and toxicity on the one hand and as violence and force on the other. The first consists in the mindless multiplication of sheer quantity, the accumulation of meaningless fragments of reality that appear in the lethal form of toxins and pollutants or are experienced oppressively as "overdose," "burn-out" and "junk." The second consists in the absence of vitality and freedom, the breaking down of communal relations that is experienced as mechanization, enslavement, ossification and death. In the end, both lead to the same result: the supreme anti-eschatological insult against the efficacy of Faith, namely a deliberately induced and widespread state of ecological *rigor mortis*. It is not the death of God that is the quintessential problem for theology today but the dealing out of death to God's most dearly valued project (and prophets), the killing of creatures' tentative efforts to create self-transcending love, the assassination of creative syntheses by which Faith is trying to contribute to the making of a world that is good:

> The central problem of our human condition today [is] the creation and maintenance of structures and power-centers that are bound to block all effective forms of loving our neighbors and our fellow human beings in either the public or the private sector.[90]

For Segundo, this means that sin is not arrogant pride but a double failure of freedom. First, it is a failure of anthropological faith, a failure to trust in human beings' having been justified by Faith, a lack of confidence in the fact that, even when we human social persons are still sinners—which in the present context must mean even though we are still capable of subverting the constructive potential of Sin, still capable of turning Sin sinward in the direction of destruction or havoc—God has declared us just.[91] Second, it is a failure to allow God's gratuitous justification to become the source of a creative liberty aimed not at justification of self but at the creation of Faith-filled ideologies that respond to the constitutively human and yet gratuitous *charism* of constructing a world that is good. In this sense, sin is not freedom exalting itself in pride but freedom abdicating its creative responsibility so as to cease being freedom at all. It is an abdication of the logic of Sin and Faith built into human action, a deliberate failure of freedom to welcome the liberation from anxiety that comes from God in Faith, a childish fear of learning to deal in a creative way with Sin, a timid "no thank you" by anthropological faith in face of the demanding task of trying to build with God in a medium of Sin ideologies that will last forever, ideologies creative of an ontological increase of goodness in the world.[92] As a double abdication, both of ontological realism about the entropic energies of Sin and eschatological responsibility about the creative work of Faith, sin is a refusal to expend the energies of faith for the sake of worthwhile projects, including that of God, in the world. It is an ungenerous no, aimed at short-term gain or fear of the loss of imagined profit, to the demands raised by Sin itself to spend the energies of anthropological faith on the search for love-building ideologies.

Ultimately, sin for Segundo turns out to be a willed distortion of the logic of action, a failure of freedom to accept the fact that the objective reality of the world, including its apparently definitive subjection to the reign of Sin, is a constitutive dimension of its own dialectical structure. It is a failure to integrate Faith and Sin into the creative *telos* of a loving project, a failure to invest the energies of anthropological faith in creative ideological responses in which are revealed the intrinsic worth of other beings, other centers of meaning and value, in the world:

> The sin with which the New Testament is familiar is not barefaced egotism. It is that brand of egotism which does indeed look for solutions but which is *unwilling to pay the price* for better solutions. The richer, less immediate synthesis is sacrificed in favor of more immediate, impoverished syntheses. *The intrinsic wickedness in this surrender to the easy way out lies in the fact that this approach ignores the differences of other beings: i.e., their character as centers. Facile syntheses—sin—reduce other beings to the common denominator of their short-term usefulness.*[93]

The source of wickedness in sin is thus the refusal of human beings to honor differences, the refusal to recognize and respect the worth of other beings and the value of their projects. It is the refusal to acknowledge those projects as worthy of both human love and the gratuitous love of God. Instead, sin turns other beings into sources of immediate gain and profit for purposive use alone, or worse, into sources of infantile security. It distorts the creative potential of human action in favor of the satisfaction of anxiety—i.e., the security that comes from this or that form of self-justification—at the expense of the worth of other beings as centers of meaning and value.

In this sense, sin ends up arrogating the value of others as if they were merely objects and their value a quantifiable sum. Is ends up being not only anti-eschatological but anti-ontological as well. Insofar as it identifies the value of others with the "raw" fact of their merely being, sin is the attempt to accumulate others' being so as to put it at the disposal of immediacy and purposiveness. It is the reduction of others to the generic level of impersonal being alone, followed by the utilitarian use of that being, now stripped of the value it would naturally come to aquire in a context of gratuitous love, as the bare stuff of commerce. In this sense, sin is the humanly caused depersonalization of the cosmos, the commercialization of intrinsically valuable created being for purposes of short-term profit or immediate apparent gain. It is an attempt, always fruitless in the end, to "cash in on" what God and creatures have already accomplished in the world without contributing anything constructive of one's own, without paying a fully human price.

THE KINDS OF SIN IN SEGUNDO'S THEOLOGY

Typically, Segundo believes, sin seems to take two forms. First of all, it can represent a free ceding of freedom to the easy way out, enslavement by the laws and mechanisms of objective reality made manifest in the entropic working of Sin. In this type of sin, the forces of degeneration brought to light by Sin are either deliberately pursued or else not actively or passively resisted; the dissipation of energies is not made into a source of energy aimed at greater and more creative syntheses but is pursued for its own sake, as if it were the point and goal of the entire project and as though the possibility of making creative syntheses did not exist, even inchoately.

The second form of sin is an overly anxious refusal to live gratuitously by Faith.[94] Refusing to pay the appropriate debt of gratitude to entropy in an incomplete and tragic universe, anthropological faith attempts to live instead by ideologies alone, by an unrealistic sort of magical efficacy that is anti-ecological and forced. Such efficacy is only apparent and dismally short-term. In fact, it is not efficacy at all but efficiency, i.e., the forcing of results by recourse to facile and simplistic means, the sacrifice of values to the short-term pay-off of an anti-evolutionary, "quick-fix" expedient, a cheap and immediate source of energy.[95]

Although the two types of sin may be distinguished, they are actually quite similar: each represents a deliberate deformation of the structure of human action. Each forms a parody of action, a setting out on the path of efficacy as if one or the other dimension of freedom simply did not exist. In the case of sin of the first type, action is reduced to the lowest common denominator of objective forces alone, to a facile slide along the one-way slope—to the extent that it is possible—of the law of least resistance. This is action negating the creative responsibility of freedom, a negation that resides in the failure of faith to create its own ideologies or participate in the creative ideologies of others—i.e., omission in the obvious sense. In the case of sin of the second type, action is reduced to ideologies alone; it becomes the search, to the extent that this is possible, for a pure and magical efficacy—e.g., Law—which would accomplish its aims anti-ecologically by the extrinsic energy of force. It is action negating its inherent dependence on the objective givenness of reality, faith abdicating its value-giving role to the utilitarian demands of ideologies (or an extrinsic norm or law), i.e., omission as a failure to live "an adventure in gratuitousness."[96] In both senses, sin is a refusal on the part of freedom to exercise itself as genuinely human

Faith. It is a refusal to "take a stand" one way or the other by choosing certain ideologies over others. It constitutes a culpable imbalance in the structure of action, what in the language of ecology Segundo calls inflexibility: a fundamental disproportion in the relations between faith and ideologies.

As the unjust deprivation of the freedom and being of others, sin thus constitutes a deprivation of others' intrinsic value and worth, and it does so in the context of their being participants in a community of distinct beings, each with different *charisms* on behalf of God's project. In other words, sin is injustice, an unwillingness to let the love-building projects and values of others participate in the gratuitous creativity of God, a refusal to be grateful to Spirit. And insofar as love is not a virtue among others but *the* evolutionary task, work of Faith *par excellence* and project aimed at creating a world still needing to be made good, injustice is synonymous with the omission of love. It is freedom's repudiation of its *charism*, the shirking of responsibility for creation of the world.

Segundo's Ecologically Conscious Theology and the Creation of a World that is Good

The theological relevance of Segundo's concept of Sin becomes most striking when its connection with the problems of society and culture comes into view. Already relying on evolutionary categories, and thus on an implicitly ecological starting-point in his study of Berdyaev in the early sixties, Segundo laid the ontological foundation for the eschatological value of freedom and established the main outlines of its dialectical relation with the laws and mechanisms of objective reality.

In the late sixties and early seventies, the social and political upheavals marking his own Latin American continent demanded that he turn more directly to the concrete situation of communities of Christians faced with the task of what *Gaudium et Spes* had called "finding more human solutions to the problems of the modern world" (*GS*, 11). In spite of the centrality of these social and political concerns in his work of this period, he continued to utilize evolutionary categories even while attempting to construct theological—and sociopolitically liberative—interpretations of church, grace, God, sacraments and sin.[97] These interpretations he elaborated in a thematic order noticeably different from the schemas of traditional theology. The innovative spirit of these works was a result of both their peculiarly Latin American context and their having been produced in the conversational (as distinct from academic) setting of adult lay discussion groups. At the same time, however, it is clear that the originality of these volumes derives as much from Segundo's use of evolutionary categories to interpret the doctrines of sin and grace[98] as from his concern with sociopolitical liberation.

The non-traditional schema of Segundo's *Theology for Artisans of a New Humanity* reflects his view that Faith can be liberated to seek "more human solutions" to the problems facing the world today only when its religious crystallization as a specifically Jesus-normed anthropological faith is freed from paralyzing fears and insecurities about the value of human freedom vis-à-vis the freedom of God. Segundo argues that, paradoxically, such fears often result from overly protective forms of ecclesial *praxis*.   People in Latin America were—and to some extent presumably still are—being prevented from searching in maturity and freedom for more human solutions to sociohistorical problems because their understanding of what makes for a specifically "Christian" religious faith was keeping them frightened and immature.

Large numbers of Catholics, for example, tended to be more anxious about their own salvation and the avoidance of Hell than about the quality of societal structures and the increasing amounts of suffering and repression on their own continent. People were often more concerned with obedience to the magisterium of the Roman church, from which were believed to descend a multitude of ecclesiastical, doctrinal and moral teachings allegedly sanctioned by the authority of "God," than with working together to eliminate down-to-earth injustices. This ecclesiastical dependency tended to prevent Latin American Christians from creating moral responses mature enough to contend with the increasing complexity of sociopolitical problems caused by the importation of consumerist life-styles and the peripheral position of Latin American nations vis-à-vis "developed" countries of the North. In short, Segundo perceived that a mass-oriented pastoral *praxis*--essentially reductionist with respect to the liberative message of the gospel—tended to keep the faithful in a position of subservience and support, witting or unwitting, vis-à-vis established sociopolitical and economic orders.[99]

Segundo was able fully to integrate the Latin American context of his theology into an evolutionary and explicitly ecological philosophical base, however, only with the publication of *Jesus of Nazareth Yesterday and Today* in the 1980's. In the volumes of that work, he shows how the political interpretation of Jesus' mission provided by the historical Jesus himself and recorded, along with specifically religious interpretations, in the gospels, can never be detached from a profoundly anthropological interpretation of the significance of Jesus such as that of Paul in Romans. He shows that in the context of the widespread oppression and suffering which characterize Latin America today, the bond uniting these different yet mutually illuminating interpretations of Jesus is nothing other than the need to admit (and humbly to welcome and allow to operate) the ecological density of human action.[100] In other words, theological talk about the value of action on behalf of God's kingdom will be meaningful and realistic vis-à-vis the kinds of suffering and oppression going on in Latin America today only in terms of categories sufficiently complex to ground disciples' action and hope for change in anything other than stoic passivity or utopian dreams. Chief among these would be ecological categories like humility, flexibility and wisdom—categories in keeping with the impassioned mode of action that in the first two chapters of these reflections has been called the costly, patient and laborious action of God's love.

In ways tempered by a wisdom learned from the laws of the universe itself, such categories lead to a more realistic understanding of what a gospel normed by Jesus' kingdom *praxis* means by loving action, particularly action on behalf of what Jesus called the at-handness of God's kingdom. Only categories such as these can serve to interpret the significance of human action in a constructive way in an evolving and problematic world. Action for change, in other words, must be tempered by an ecological realism that takes its major cues from the kinds of flexibility, open-endedness and wisdom which mark the evolutionary project. Such categories derive from the facts of experience about Sin. They are required by the ecological character of the structure of action, or the Faith-Sin dialectic, itself.[101]

As has been seen, so far as Segundo is concerned, the structure of that dialectic is identical with the working of grace, and it appears most clearly in Paul's existential description of the "divided human being" (Rom. 7: 14-25). Segundo's response to the anthropological schema of Paul, which forms a highly original exegesis of the first eight chapters of Romans, is to make the "divided human being" the basis for an evolutionary interpretation of the theology of grace and Sin. To do this, Segundo makes grace, *qua* Faith, an original, although gratuitous, dimension of God's eschatologically creative love. Because in an incomplete and tragic universe grace represents God's radical (and definitively powerful) impassioned love and God's gratuitous commitment to the creation with creatures of a world that is good, it liberates human action to participate efficaciously in God's eschatological project. As the gratuitous liberation of freedom, grace consists in God's original offer of friendship, the effect of which is to incorporate the work of Faith into the actual realization of what Jesus called the coming of God's kingdom.

Revelation of God's commitment to the values of that kingdom, embodied in Jesus' *praxis* unto death and ratified by God in Jesus' resurrection, constitutes a promise made to history and nature themselves: when all is said and done, the earth will not disintegrate. It will not disperse into a meaningless and undifferentiated smear of dust but will manifest what Paul calls "the glorious liberty of the children of God" (Rom. 8: 21). In other words, grace is aimed at glory, the definitive liberation of action and all of its constructive results. Grace transforms into eschatologically efficacious results what under the conditions of Sin (and sin) appears to be the congenital inefficacy of action. Such liberation takes place at the heart of action itself. It occurs not by a miraculous intervention from God but through the agency of a down-to-earth *praxis* of self-transcending love which shows itself to have been ecologically flexible and wise.

Thanks to the patient character of the love that is grace, human freedom turns out to be a constitutive dimension of the definitive creation of the world. The shape that creation will take appears to depend, at least on planet earth, on what we human social persons do and fail to do. Because that is so, the creation of the definitive reality depends in a radical way on what anthropological faith does with its experience of the mechanisms of Sin, and to the extent that it does, it can be said that the structure of God's gracious love is conditioned on earth by Sin. God depends on the results of Sinful Faith. God welcomes the agency of Sin-ful human action. God liberates faith for a God-like kind of self-transcending love, so as to make the exercise of freedom something that will be wise and efficacious in the face of Sin. In the love that is grace, Faith can become flexible enough to trust in ideologies that will work not to destroy the capacities of nature and culture but permit them to bring forth something new. In this way, Segundo believes, freedom learns however gradually both to experience and practice the definitive liberation of the Sin-ful cosmos loved gratuitously and irrevocably by God.

Segundo's notion that the experience of God's love gives action a consciousness of Sin and teaches it to be flexible and wise has two essential aspects. On the one hand, he believes that freedom learns in grace to become neither license nor force but humility. It learns to respect and love the objective givenness of its own make-up. Because the structure of freedom is *humus*, namely of the earth, earthly, action can learn not only to "fit" the requirements set by its own intrinsic logic but to rejoice in that logic and, through the Spirit-guided learning which defines the logic of Faith, to become utterly at home with God's radical way of loving the world and God's gratuitous yet appropriate commitment to its good.

On the other hand, Segundo believes, freedom can also learn to struggle against the path of least resistance which constantly remains a tempting escape mechanism for action.[102] Like a swimmer bouyed by water or a yogi at ease within the laws of gravity, Faith is enabled to learn a way of working in a medium of Sin. Through constant "practice," that is, by a *praxis* of self-transcending love, Faith more or less successfully gets the knack of trusting the Sin-dense structure of objective reality and allowing it to facilitate the aims of Faith without opting to short-circuit the natural operation of its laws. Such leading is the work of Spirit, who teaches that to give oneself uncritically over to those laws, to rush *tout court* into the pattern of the "rut" or, worse, to surrender to the "run-away" effects of natural processes or technological short-cuts, represents a hatred of one's own ontological structure, a rejection of nature's laws.[103] This means that freedom can learn to employ ecologically sound ideologies. When it does, in an utterly gratuitous and yet anthropologically coherent way action will turn out to have been eschatologically efficacious, even if according to appearances it seems to have miscarried or perhaps utterly to have failed.

THE ONTOLOGICAL VALUE OF SIN AND THE THEOLOGICAL SCANDAL OF GOD'S PATIENT LOVE

As a dimension constitutive of reality itself, Sin forms an essential element—what Segundo calls the quantitative and entropic one—of the ontological structure of the world. And since human freedom is a product of evolution and operates only in the context of an evolving world, Sin is a constitutive element of freedom, or action, as well. It is not the only essential element, since it has a powerful complement in the gratuitous yet no less constitutive element of Faith, but it is the more obvious and, judging from appearances, certainly the more widely operative of the two. Its effects in the human sphere are analogous to the effects of entropy in the sphere of physics: the universe and our action within it appear to the "naked" eye—what for Segundo is an eye uninformed by Faith—to be caught in a continual process of degeneration and breakdown, an irreversible dissipation of energy into constantly less usable, less effective states. Yet experience teaches that in spite of entropy, new syntheses of energy can be and continually are being made. In fact, when one looks at the universe more closely, one discovers that creative syntheses occur not in spite of entropy but precisely thanks to it. Entropy provides the seemingly endless reservoir of random events, disparate elements and just plain "time off" necessary for the creation of something new. In relation to Faith, therefore, Sin, like entropy, is actually constructive.[104] It is raw material for the creative construction of love. When human social persons put Faith into *praxis* in a wise and flexible way, i.e., when action incorporates the negative energies of Sin into the projects of freedom in a way that takes into account the debt that must be paid to entropy, Sin functions to facilitate the efficacy of ideologies.

By contrast, Segundo views sin as culpable human complicity—more or less deliberate—with the already-existing mechanisms of negativity in Sin. As moral evil or guilt, sin is a freely willed exploitation of the forces of breakdown and disintegration already taking place in the universe.[105] Thanks to the capacity of human freedom for guilt, the constructive potential of Sin can be turned against the projectivity of Faith. Sin can be diverted into sin; it can be made to serve the purposes of destruction. Yet even when freedom does this, Sin must still be understood as complementary to Faith, with which it can still contribute as a limiting, critical, even negative partner to provide the impetus to change. That is because as something out of joint with the Sin-Faith dialectic, sin can never be entirely successful at the attempt to co-opt the entropic energies of Sin. By permitting the anti-evolutionary impulse masked in sin to become openly visible to the eyes of anthropological Faith, freedom's dependence on Sin prevents sin from gaining total control over the objective givenness of reality. In the objective realm, in other words, Sin makes sin show up for what it is. Sin prohibits the more or less deliberate destructiveness represented by sin from being able to be definitively cloaked over or ignored. It makes the wickedness of sin stand out with glaring ugliness, the effect of which is to cause outrage, elicit protest, or at least create an ecological imbalance or unnatural void that whether one admits it or not shows up in one or another spot in the objective make-up of reality.

In this way, Sin serves as a self-corrective or regulatory device, a brake or alarm built into the structure of action. When things get so bad that people begin to think (even should they refuse to acknowledge it), "This has got to stop! Things—or I, or we—can go on like this no longer!" then that is Sin giving a warning to action that it is set on an anti-evolutionary course, a path moving toward destruction, a mode of action impoverishing reality, a constricting of Sin into sin. By the sheer weight of its appalling consequences, sin begins to signal anthropological faith in spite of itself that it is time to make a change of ideologies. Thanks to Sin, sinful human action has to come to terms with the limits set by its own objective reality and those of other beings, even if sin itself has no desire to come to a healthy stop. Vis-à-vis sin, Sin is the evolutionary "reality therapy" built into the structure of the universe.[106]

In a theologically scandalous way, Segundo thus poses the questions of evil and guilt in a fundamentally optimistic context.[107] Paradoxical as it may sound, he argues that Sin is an ontological guarantee built into the structure of the universe. Sin guarantees that in the creative projects of human action sin can never get the final word. Such a paradoxical view is possible because Segundo views the data of revelation about evil in evolutionary terms, in a context aimed at interpreting Sin in light of God's initial commitment to, and humans' subsequent responsibility for, the eschatological task *par excellence,* creation of a world that is good. Segundo believes that insofar as grace makes the two—God's initial-cum-eschatological commitment to the efficacy of that creation and human responsibility for its definitive realization—teleologically inseparable, it makes them inseparable at the everyday level of action. He thus sees Sin as a fundamental, constitutive vector of an unfinished universe that, in each generation, cries out to be completed and given lasting goodness. The latter can be accomplished not by the power of God alone but only by the power of God and human social persons working conjointly in a medium of Sin to create in Faith ideologies of self-transcending love.[108] For Segundo, Sin is the medium in which God and human social persons together create an enduring reality of love.[109]

What might seem scandalous to human beings, however, may not be so for God.[110] If the love of God can be characterized by the age-old theological notions of unbounded mercy and justice, then grace must signify God's love defined as mercy and justice; but if grace is precisely not the love of God alone, but the love of God conjoined in a project of definitive creation with the love of human social persons, then there are grounds in Segundo's understanding of Faith and Sin for saying that what the scriptures call the new creation will be the product not solely of the love of God in the form of eschatological mercy and justice, but of the love of God conjoined in grace with the love of human social persons in a humanly fashioned, secularly relevant "kingdom" of mercy and justice which is the "at-handness" of God's own love, incarnate.[111] Exactly such an understanding, translated into evolutionary terms by recourse to categories from ecological science, permits Segundo to say that what the scriptures call the new creation will be the gratuitous result of the human and divine loves working together in the realm of Sin to realize, in Faith, the justice and mercy which are the heart of God's values and the values of God's heart.[112]

In language borrowed from evolutionary science, Segundo demonstrates that the eschaton will be the outcome of human cooperation—action—in the task of incorporating the disparate energies of Sin into the synthetic energies of Faith. The reason for this is that the eschaton, as definitive realization of God's creative project, must result from a cooperative sharing of loves. It will turn out to have been the definitive mediation by earthly loves of God's initial and unfailing love for creatures, a work of justice and mercy in the realization of which creatures, and the world itself, gratuitously participate.[113] As was pointed out in chapter one, God's scandalous insistence that in a tragic and incomplete universe creatures actively participate in the creation of a world that is good makes God's action a passion and turns that passion into a theological embarrassment. The cause of the embarrassment is the patient character of God's love in face of the genuinely creative power of human action. This includes God's patient action, in the form of passion, in the face of negativity, for according to the single-hearted logic of God's impassioned love, God must be patient not only of the entropic working of Sin in Faith but of the creaturely suffering introduced into the creative project here and now by freedom's circuitous, time-consuming and possibly guilty way of participating in the creation of the new.

According to such an evolutionary interpretation of the doctrine of cooperative grace, the dilemma of guilt, or sin, remains as insoluble and scandalous as ever. Are theologians to understand that sin must serve the same purposes in the realization of grace as Sin, of which sin is a specific, characteristically human, case? If sin is fundamentally a special case of Sin, what can be said about the millions of deprived and oppressed in the history of the world, the countless victims of unrelieved wretchedness and humanly engineered injustice? How are their sufferings to be duly recognized, productively mourned, effectively protested against, somehow vindicated and redeemed? Does an evolutionary view leave room in the end for the outrage of the prophets, the grieving of the women, the cry of Jesus on the cross?

Yet Segundo is aware that the affront of human sinfulness is a far greater scandal for liberationists and activists today than the affront of objective evil, or Sin. While Sin can be understood in terms of God's patient love for suffering creatures in the face of entropy, time and chance—guiltless realities to which one does not appropriately respond with hatred but with which one finds it necessary simply to "put up"—sin raises the shocking question of God's willingness to forgive atrocities involving guilt. The trouble with forgiveness is that it threatens to swallow up God's justice with mercy. The theological affirmation of God's patient love—which logically must include a real and not merely notional affirmation of forgiveness—ends up creating a theological scandal. It seems to make God's impassioned love in face of the oppressive negativity of sin *too* positive. It portrays God as overly patient of human guilt and unduly slow to anger. Is God so blinded by passion as to risk *everything* in love, even the sovereign "birthright" of the divine wrath and the traditional prestige of the "divine reputation" as Judge?[114]

Looking at this dilemma from the perspective of the human *charism* to contribute ideologies of love to the realization of God's project, Segundo notes that the cause of the scandal is not that God "lets" Sin and sin "exist," but that each of them seems to be winning out over the values of what Jesus called God's kingdom, and apparently God does not mind. God's love is evidently so single-hearted, and what Jesus called God's kingdom is evidently so "at hand," as to be unable to be stopped even by the biggest evils imaginable. No evil can vitiate God's impassioned love, for its creative realization is the gratuitous outbreak in the here and now of an eschatological good that makes it worthwhile for God to put up with anything, even a negativity as enormous and expensive as the cumulative weight of human sin, for the sake of a single—and definitive—consummation.[115] Paradoxically, evil and sin thus delineate the ground of negativity in the face of which Segundo dares to affirm the theological priority of the positive: God's gratuitous love for creatures, invested in a shared, laborious and costly project with them in grace, will be efficacious unto good not only in the end but here and now on earth, even in the face of the obvious and seemingly permanent victories of Sin and sin in history and nature.[116]

Fundamentally, what Segundo seems to be saying with his theological analysis of the dialectic of Faith and Sin is that if we human social persons can not or do not contribute with God to the definitive shape of creation—if, in a universe of Sin, Faith lacks the power to create a world that is good—then life is not worth living. Freedom would have no meaning, and action—which for Segundo is synonymous with the creation of a world and the mediation of God's and our own love—is simply not worth the trouble.

NOTES

[1] The point at issue here is more germane to the logic connecting chapters one and two than might appear at first sight. I am suggesting that from the point of view of experience, action faces in two directions at once. On the one hand, it raises, and gives an affirmative answer to, the question of anthropological faith discussed in chapter one, *viz.*, is what we human social persons do and suffer ultimately worth the effort? On the other hand, at the level of ideologies it raises a more or less overwhelming doubt: in face of what we actually accomplish, it appears that the optimism of anthropological faith is unwarranted. The fact that the structure of action includes a disjointedness between faith and ideologies as well as an inseparability between them suggests that the logic of action manifests both positive and negative dimensions: looked at from the point of view of origins (Faith), action appears to be positive, but from the point of view of results (ideologies), it appears to be negative. In this chapter, I will attempt to show how Segundo understands Faith as that gratuitous way of contending with ontological and moral evil which permits disciples of Jesus to view the negative dimensions of action in a way that supports hope and not despair concerning the value of Faith's efforts to build ideologies of self-transcending love.

[2] Here, of course, one is talking about social sin, which, as has been suggested in the previous chapter, is also ecological. Not all sinful ideologies, however, start out intending to be unjust; many are designed to accomplish some more or less beneficial goal. One of the most distressing aspects of sin is precisely the concupiscent tendency of ideologies to fossilize or wander astray from their original goals, to end up betraying faith's aims or even accomplishing the opposite of what was originally intended. Segundo's understanding of concupiscence, borrowed from Rahner and augmented by the theological categories of Paul (*RC,* pp. 261-262), shows that this discrepancy applies as much to ideologies committed to evil (bad faith) as to those devoted to the perpetration of good (Faith): the forces of disintegration and breakdown keep *every* human ideology from being able to accomplish faith's aims in a completely efficacious way.

[3] That Segundo regards freedom as a value above every other is evident from the beginning of his career (*Berdiaeff,* pp. 95-128) but is given explicit expression

in *GHC*, pp. 44-45, p. 81 and p. 85. On the qualifications necessary with respect to Segundo's statements on this point, see chapter one, n. 99 above.

[4] Segundo sees as a fundamental hermeneutical requirement the need to make explicit one's operative theological *context.*   It forms a major element of the hermeneutical circle as described in *LT*, pp. 7-38 (see also *EAJN*, p. 110). In other words, it is necessary to "hear" revelation in categories that correspond to both the kingdom values of Jesus' gospel faith and the perceptions, problems and conflicts that make up human experience. This must be done not for the sake of theoretical understanding—impossible in the abstract—but for the sake of an understanding linked to practice, in other words, for the sake of action or *praxis* on behalf of the values of God's heart, in order to liberate freedom for the task of creating a world that is good.

[5] Like others who theologize from a liberationist perspective, Segundo believes that in order to be effective, the requirement to include the negative and conflictual dimensions of experience must be made as concrete as possible. In view of cries of solidarity and protest from persons and groups of good will everywhere, but especially in view of the cries of the suffering and oppressed themselves, it has to be demonstrated that the "news" of grace must come into contact with something already at work within the structure of its recipients which is capable of permitting them to receive it as news that is *good.* This means that the affirmations of Faith must be shown to meet the anthropological-epistemological demands for experiential verification, not in order to make Faith plausible or credible to a "modern mentality" (often equated with a mentality that is Western, North Atlantic and scientific) but to make it viable, practicable and productive in the lives of persons and groups who find themselves deprived of freedom in the concrete, linked in suffering and solidarity with those who are deprived, or both.

[6] These were presented in preliminary form in the first section of chapter one.

[7] This need was introduced as a formal requirement in *EG,* especially pp. 7-75, but has been present in Segundo's work from the beginning (see *Berdiaeff,* pp. 190-205).

[8] As discussion in this chapter will show, essential to understanding Segundo's evolutionary ontological categories is the distinction between Sin and sin. What he means by the Pauline notion *Sin* is different from but not irrelevant to what is meant by the more traditional notion of *sin* (or *sins).* The latter refers to the realm of moral evil, to wickedness or what is bad, to evil as it is more or less freely perpetrated by human beings and results for them in guilt. The former refers to what has traditionally been called objective or pre-moral evil, evil which does not involve subjective guilt, although, as will be seen, the fact that it is also structural and ontological makes it more complex than that. In order to distinguish the two senses in Segundo's work, I will designate the ontological term by the word *Sin* and the moral term by the word *sin.*

⁹ As will be seen, the significance of this difference is that, for Segundo, the logic of an evolutionary *telos* does not mean that negativity is gradually being superceded or overcome, but that it is continually impinging on freedom as a creative task; it is continually "crying out" to be incorporated into creative syntheses of self-transcending love. Such a logic is not chronological but ecological. It is not headed for a distant future but is concerned with the quality of the present.

¹⁰ *EAJN*, pp. 113-114. As was pointed out in chapter one, Segundo believes that if theologians have learned anything from evolutionary science, it is that an adequate understanding of the evolutionary project is inseparable from a humbling appreciation of its ecological complexity.

¹¹ As Segundo shows, newness is a key term in a Jesus-normed understanding of grace (*GHC*, pp. 117-122). He observes that both in the biblical tradition and outside of it, "newness expresses the complex experience of love. . . .[It] is the category which expresses the transcendence of love" (*ibid.*, p. 122). As such, it has to do with the phenomenon of transformation, which involves discontinuity or breakthrough but in a context of continuity (*ibid.*, p. 199). As will be seen in chapter four, newness is intrinsically eschatological. It pertains to *kainótes*, i.e., that which is new in quality as distinct from *néos*, new in time [Gerhard Kittel and Gerhard Friedrich, *Theological Dictionary of the New Testament*, abridged in one volume (Grand Rapids: Eerdmanns, 1985), p. 388].

¹² Although Segundo himself does not use this term, his appropriation of ecological categories permits my using it here as a means of access to his understanding of the ontological complexity of action. The term Segundo himself employs is *"el espesor de la realidad,"* [*HHJN* I, *Fe e ideología* (Madrid: Ediciones Cristiandad, 1982), p. 303]. Editing the divisions of Segundo's original text, John Drury renders this as "the dense complexity of historical reality" (*FI*, p. 248). I prefer the term *ecological density* because it stresses that, for Segundo, action has a constitutively ecological structure. In other words, the density of reality pertains not only to history but to nature or the cosmos as a whole.

¹³ As was pointed out in the introductory chapter, this concern is the starting point for all theologies of liberation, of which Segundo's is a particularly developed example.

¹⁴ On the heightened awareness of humanly caused evil in liberationist theologies, see Roger Haight, *An Alternative Vision*, (New York: Paulist Press, 1985), p. 68.

¹⁵ See, for example, Edward Schillebeeckx, *Christ* (New York: Crossroad, 1980), p. 725.

¹⁶ Of course few theologians would want to maintain that evil will be "overcome" at the existential level of history. What is being suggested is that evil demands a response from human social persons, and that response must take the form of some sort of this-worldly resistance. In short, it must take the form of ameliorative

action, what Segundo would call the attempt to deal creatively with the determinisms of evil and sin rather than simply letting them take over the capacity of human Faith, whatever its ideological expressions, to do something gratuitous and positive by way of response, to take one's stand or have one's say.

[17] For this reason, Segundo's account of the ontological complexity of action to be analyzed in this chapter forms the second half of the anthropological analysis begun in chapter one. There, the logic of faiths and ideologies was set forth with a view to grounding the charismatic quality of action that is graced. Here, the mapping of the logic of action must be done in terms of what forms the essential structure, with its ontological and moral complexity, of objective reality.

[18] The question remains, however, as to what (theologically) to do and say about the contrary experiences of (a) those who possibly are devoting their ideologies to the furthering of evil and (b) the "silent majority," those millions of the comfortable who feel no urgent need to act on behalf of change, and who, indeed, continue, however unreflectively, to act directly or indirectly on behalf of the *status quo,* precisely because they do not perceive as evil what the conscientized minority sees and possibly clearly knows is evil. The answer Segundo seems to provide is that no single person or group consistently fits into any single category in every sphere of life. All action is a mixture of love and egotism (*HCP,* pp. 130-131; *RC,* p. 261), and while people and groups might be contributing to evil at certain levels or in particular areas, possibly they are contributing to good in others. While this response does not solve the problem—in fact, in light of institutionalized injustices as massive, e.g., as patriarchy, apartheid, the Holocaust or the uneven distribution of wealth, it rightfully elicits protest—it provides a starting point for a solution by suggesting a way around the tendency of some liberationists and social and ecological activists to divide persons and groups simplistically into oppressed and oppressors.

[19] As will be seen in subsequent discussion, the point at issue in this challenge is not whether God has sovereign power; it is really whether human ameliorative action possesses power. Can human social persons, creatures though they be, realize lasting and worthwhile good? By initiating an impassioned project with creatures in grace, God is actually (and gratuitously) handing over to them an ontologically creative power. As was seen in chapter one, this means that the significance of grace is that God is "patient" before human action: God will not and can not accomplish in heaven what human action does not accomplish on earth. In the love that is grace, God freely and gratuitously—and some would no doubt say foolishly and scandalously— has placed God's eschatologically creative power (the definitive power over evil and sin) in creatures' hands.

[20] This question is different from that of traditional theodicy, *viz.,* given the existence of evil, how can there be God? At the practical level, the latter translates into: how is the coexistence of God and evil possible? The question about the efficacy of grace is being posed not in view of what is "possible" but in the (gratuitous) context

of the *actual givenness* of grace, taking as starting point the coagency of God's and humans' cooperative love, together with the questions love raises about the worthwhileness of suffering, the meaning of action in a universe that is fraught with evil, and the power of Faith to effect what is lasting and good. Traditional theodicies were ordinarily raised in the theoretical context of the abstract natures of God and evil as such. Creative power was ordinarily restricted to God alone, human "power" consisting in freedom's alleged capacity to "choose between good and evil" as between two opposed—and equal—objects.

21 Segundo regards teleology not as a progression or ascent toward eventual maturity (Platonic categories in the service of an Irenæan eschatology) but as a ceaseless circuit of gratuitous breakthroughs into the creation of something new (ecological categories in the service of a Pauline eschatology). According to Segundo, reality is structured for the continual and gratuitous achievement of efficacious results in the present rather than inexorably determined by either a pre-set mechanism (a deterministic view) or the jumbled working of chance [a scientific evolutionary view such as that espoused by Jacques Monod in *Chance and Necessity* (London: Fontana/Collins, 1974)]. For Segundo, evolutionary teleology maximizes human responsibility. It rules out the subordination of freedom to a "higher" and extrinsic principle of order or power, even if the latter be called "God". What Segundo's teleology does not rule out is that certain human beings, typified, e.g., by Quoheleth in *Ecclesiastes,* can contentedly live out anthropological faiths in which the presupposition of a coherence in life—an order in the universe—plays no part. There simply *are* people (whether theists or atheists) for whom life is not coherently meaningful, yet such people can still posit the value of acting responsibly in the face of evil. For an account of Quoheleth's view which also defends it, see Jerome Walsh, "Despair as a Theological Virtue in the Spirituality of *Ecclesiastes,*" *Biblical Theology Bulletin* 12 (1982), pp. 46-49.

22 Like the doctrines of creation and eschatology, from which it is inseparable, the doctrine of "original sin" can not adequately be accounted for by the lineal logic of chronological categories. As was observed in the introductory chapter, the logic of eschatology is concerned with the end not of time but of *evil;* it is a matter of deliverance from evil in fragmentary and incomplete ways in nature and history in light of a gratuitous yet able to be welcomed God-revealed promise that such earthly deliverances contribute to deliverance from evil in a definitive way in the end.

23 The essence of Niebuhrian pessimism is to doubt that human freedom has power unto good, to doubt that it can have definitive efficacy over the "principalities and powers" that rule the world, to think that only God can act eschatologically to create a reality that is good. Unlike Niebuhr, Segundo refuses to believe that creaturely freedom is powerless in the face of evil. On the contrary, he believes that although the efficacy of anthropological faith is conditioned by Sin and bounded by the apparent futility of disintegration, failure and death, freedom, *qua* Faith, is able

to make a difference that makes a difference in the face of Sin by creating efficacious and lasting results, qualitative ontological change. Freedom is not powerless but powerful; but unless persons and groups of good will learn how to release it, Faith will remain tied to a vicious cycle of inefficacy. The point of this chapter is to present Segundo's view of the release of freedom's power, *qua* gratuitous manifestation of Faith's creative efficacy in the face of Sin.

[24] This principle is first presented in *Berdiaeff*, pp. 99-100, but as discussion in the following sections will show, it forms the basis of Segundo's entire theology of Sin. It was the major point of *EG* and resurfaces in *JNYT* as key to the notion of Sin.

[25] In this sense, Segundo's theological appropriation of an evolutionary outlook is significantly different from that of Irenæus as presented in John Hick, *Evil and the God of Love* (New York: Harper and Row, 1966). Where maturity for Irenæus is achieved only in the end, in a time and place other than the present universe, maturity for Segundo happens repeatedly in the universe in each new generation, by means of action. The difference lies in their teleologies. Where Segundo stresses human responsibility in a conjointly shared divine-and-human *project,* Irenæus stresses human reliance on the plan of God in the face of a divinely led *process.* In Irenæus' view evil is overcome (in the passive voice and in a finally perfected world of the future) by God's eschatological recapitulation of the universe in Jesus, according to an over-arching and ultimately harmonious plan. The latter, as in the case of Augustine's æsthetic view of God's prevenient grace, is ultimately the accomplishment of God, who is actually the one who is at work in the exercise of human freedom. In Segundo's view, by contrast, God can not act to overcome evil either in the end or in the present unless human social persons act to do it and begin to do it now. The universe is not ruled by a harmonious and prevenient plan but is fraught with a conflict and strife that make it appear futile. God has no power on earth except in human action carried out in each new generation in gratuitous break-throughs of efficacious freedom. That "the glory of God is the human being fully alive" means not that God will make up for human immaturity and inadequacy by transforming an imperfect (human) being into a perfect (divinized human) being in the end, but that God passionately wants—and depends on for God's happiness and well-being as God—human maturity and adulthood right here in the imperfect world of now. For Segundo, to be "fully alive" is not to be finally perfect but rather to have been and to continue being ontologically creative in the midst of one's own and the world's imperfection. It is to exert creative power in the face of evil.

[26] The significance of Segundo's option for the priority of ontological over moral evil is thus that it highlights the importance of making a basic theological option: what does grace utimately *do* in and for creatures and, in particular, human beings? Does it primarily break the bonds of human guilt (Augustine, Luther, Niebuhr and the Protestant tradition); does it overcome the limits of human finitude (Thomas

Aquinas, Rahner and the Catholic tradition); or does it give action and the still struggling to be realized world in which action plays a part a brand new *raison d'être,* a sure and everlasting eschatological guarantee of definitive efficacy and validity? From Segundo's point of view, to limit grace to a breaking of moral bonds or an overcoming of finitude can be dangerously egocentric. It replaces the gratuitous and cosmocentric liberation of freedom with an unleashing of anthropocentric anxiety: it tends either to over-stress the enormity of sin and guilt or to hint that finitude is an overriding problem. For Segundo, what is important about grace is not that it gives human beings new *being* but that it calls them to participate in a new *project,* God's. And that presupposes the engagement of their fundamental human structure—a structure synonymous with action—in a brand new mission relation of kinship love with God. Along the way of introducing human beings to this mission relation, grace gratuitously replaces anxiety about justification (i.e., interest in one's own security) with a confidence in God's impassioned love and a willingness to accept the risk of creative freedom that participation in God's project implies. The effect of this change in emphasis is to give finite freedom, *qua* Faith, a genuinely efficacious *power,* the capacity to effect good in history and nature now. Such power must accompany every true freedom, since by definition responsibility presupposes power.

27 The logic of this demand has been explicitly grounded more by Edward Schillebeeckx than by theologians more generally considered liberationist in approach. See *Jesus: An Experiment in Christology* (New York: Seabury, 1979), pp. 621-622 and *Christ: The Experience of Jesus as Lord* (New York: Crossroad, 1980), pp. 653-666.

28 Of course, as the remainder of this chapter will make clear, evil is only one of two conditions for the ontological realization of good. The other is grace, represented in the human sphere by what Segundo, relying on the language of Paul, calls Faith.

29 *EG,* p. 129 (italics Segundo's); see also *ibid.,* pp. 126-127. Along the same lines, Segundo writes: "Sin is. . .*the base of our liberty,* which puts up resistance to that liberty" (*ibid.,* p. 84; italics mine).

30 Such a distinction is traditional in theology. What Segundo does is to translate it from immobilist (Platonic) categories into ecologically complex evolutionary ones, thus clarifying the nature of the continuity between the two, which is structural. The result is a redefinition of what traditional theology designates by the term *original sin.* What is "original" about "original sin" is not that it happened "in the beginning" or to an "original" set of human beings (a lineal-chronological view) but that, from the beginning, ontological evil, i.e., Sin, forms an essential and original element of the structure of a universe that is also and just as originally structured by God's gratuitous and creative initiative in grace (*EG,* pp. 51-103).

31 *HCP,* p. 147 (italics Segundo's).

32 On the anti-evolutionary character of sin, see *EG,* p. 127.

[33] Segundo discusses and twice quotes Teilhard's principle in *EAJN* , pp. 36 and 41. In the English version of *The Phenomenon of Man* (New York: Collins, 1959), p. 77, the text to which Segundo refers is translated as follows: "In the world, nothing could ever burst forth as final across the different thresholds successively traversed by evolution. . .which has not already existed in an obscure and primordial way."

[34] *EAJN*, p. 37 (italics Segundo's).

[35] *Ibid.* and p. 41.

[36] *EAJN*, p. 38. Again relying on Bateson's vocabulary, Segundo observes that in the evolutionary imagination, analogy and difference must always work together as equal partners in an incessant interaction between "loose and strict thinking" (*ibid.*).

[37] *EAJN*, p. 40 (italics Segundo's).

[38] *Ibid*, p. 39.

[39] *GHC*, p. 32.

[40] *EAJN*, p. 40 (italics Segundo's). For Segundo, who uses Bateson's categories to clarify E.F. Schumacher's notion that people need to start viewing the processes of nature as quasi-sacred (*FI*, pp. 257-270), this respect is akin to love, the most important anthropological corrective to the anthropocentric tendency to lose respect for natural processes and treat nature in purely utilitarian ways. Only love can prevent human beings from dividing reality into a dichotomy of persons and things, thereby legitimating the notion that "things" can be treated "non-personally" and can be placed at the service of human "persons" and their interests (*ibid.*). From Segundo's point of view, such love is self-transcending and can result only from a willingness to integrate the scientific and rational modes of knowledge with the sphere of meaning and values.

[41] The virtual identity between the approaches of contemporary evolutionary and ecological science makes it clear that to lack an ecological consciousness is to remain closed to one of the principal signs of the times (*EAJN*, pp. 12-15 and pp. 38-41). Just as it goes without saying that no responsible theology after Troeltsch can afford to be lacking in historical consciousness, so after the *conscientización* of evolutionary theory by ecological science neither can the option for the poor in a theology of liberation remain rationally coherent and morally responsible in the absence of a concomitant option for the deprived not only in the human species but in the whole community of living and non-living beings. A theology of liberation must therefore make an option not only for the poor and marginalized of the human community but also against the exploitation of other species and against destructive relations with the ecosystem. Theologians of liberation can not follow the exclusivist logic criticized in *EAJN*, p. 129, n. 65, where, alluding to a theatre piece based on Vercors' novel *Les animaux dénaturés*, Segundo points out the human tendency to sidestep with the familiar animal-human distinction the question whether animals

other than the human have rights: "We human beings have turned ourselves into a type of 'club,' fixed arbitrary standards for admission, and accorded rights only to those who qualify for membership. Other animals and things are used as mere instruments." By the same token, a theology of the affluent world that concerns itself with the problems of ecological crisis must make a political option for the human poor and marginalized, since, as Segundo warns (*EAJN*, p. 13 ff.), in the absence of theological sensitivity to the *social* ecology (*FI*, pp. 285-286), ecological concern in affluent countries can be used to mask economic forms of self-interest and divert attention from the needs of the deprived.

[42] *HCP*, pp. 114-115. As Segundo demonstrates, this dilemma is epitomized in the moving and anthropologically universal cry: "I do not do the good I want, but the evil I do not want is what I do" (Rom. 7: 19).

[43] The moral relevance of dividedness, which is also religious—what Segundo calls "the strange ethics of St. Paul"—will surface in the discussion of sin in section three.

[44] On the logic of circuits, which is fundamental to Segundo's understanding of ecological density, see *EAJN*, pp. 71-74; see also pp. 60-62.

[45] The instruments of Faith are what Segundo means by the terms *nature* and *second nature:* "Nature for us means all that which conditions liberty—on whatever level or plane of human existence it may be. And we know what 'conditions' means: *to make possible and to limit at the same time.* There is no liberty without these forces of primary nature (both those of my own being and those of my environment) and of our cultural 'second nature' (again both those of my own being and those of my environment); it is these forces that constitute its only instruments for carrying out its work. And there is no liberty that does not clash and compromise with them" (*GHC*, p. 32; italics mine).

[46] Insofar as that distance is visible both socially and individually, Sin in the human sphere is a socio-structural matter that can find an analogy—and accomplice—in the heart of each individual (*HCP*, p. 147). When it does, Sin can be turned into sin, i.e., moral evil or guilt, although it does not have to be. As was noted in the introductory section of this chapter, the dividedness at the heart of each individual and evident in every group and institution is not in and of itself a matter of moral evil or sin. It can become sin, however, when, incurring guilt, human freedom cedes itself to forces of alienation, breakdown and decay without attempting to incorporate them into more creative syntheses of love.

[47] As Segundo points out, however, paying one's debt to the entropic forces of Sin must be done with an ecological wisdom similar to that followed by Jesus in his own struggle (which ended up, as the resurrection shows, in his being definitively victorious over Sin's negativity). The "secret" of such wisdom is an "economy of energies" for the sake of self-transcending love, and Segundo states it with reference to the creative action of Jesus: "His freedom *never agrees, in bad faith, to be in*

complicity with an entropy greater than that required for the efficacy of his history project" (*EAJN,* p. 91; italics mine).

[48] It must not be inferred that what Segundo means by Sin is thus a light-hearted matter. On the contrary, it is utterly serious, since Sin represents the potential for considerable, although not total, destruction. Adverting to the "Shadaic" side of Sin is intended to point out only that Sin is something with which one inevitably must learn to live—and die.

[49] One thinks, for example, of the bold affirmation of life—against all odds—which is a saguaro cactus looming against the desert sky. Or one remembers the tears of joy experienced at the news of the "people's victory" in the Philippines in 1986.

[50] Of course, in the human sphere, where entropy is capable of being co-opted into the service of egotism or sin, what complicates this law is that the emergence of quality is not simply automatic. It is not guaranteed but depends on the exercise of freedom as self-transcending love.

[51] Segundo regards this hope as "'hope against all hope', wagering on a future that verifiable experience seems to belie" (*HCP,* p. 152). It is already present in human experience as "the assertion that *loving is worthwhile"* (*ibid.;* italics Segundo's), but it is reenforced by the "new way of seeing reality" provided by Faith. Insofar as such "seeing" refuses to accept the negative evidence of appearances as "all there is to see," it is a powerful no to the seeming futility of Sin. Segundo writes: "If Sin managed to alienate all human works, then nothing less than the entire universe would fail to achieve its intrinsic purpose. It would be a total failure in itself and for God, and all its mechanisms would have functioned in vain. Nothing would remain but the mute pangs of a birth that was stillborn. Death in its fullest sense would prevail. All the projects of life would sink into corruption and uselessness. Death would wipe out humanity and its works; and God, the Creator, would end up a failure" (*ibid.,* p. 153).

[52] *HCP,* p. 151.

[53] "Paul situates human existence on two planes: one visible and dominated by Sin, in which there is a greater distance between human intention and human accomplishment; the other invisible and lived by Faith, where the distance between intention and accomplishment is narrowed" (*HCP,* p. 159).

[54] Segundo writes: "Faith sees what we ourselves cannot see. . .[i.e., that] perhaps. . .in the life of every human being if we knew the whole picture, there *emerges* something that is profoundly human and personal, that marks a meaningful investment of giving oneself and one's life" (*ibid.*). As will be seen in chapter four, what "emerges" in the face of Sin is the new reality of the eschaton.

[55] On this subject, see, for example, "Concupiscence" in Rahner and Vorgrimler, *Concise Theological Dictionary* (London: Burns & Oates, 1983), pp. 86-87.

[56] It is interesting to observe that this interpretation is so widespread even in secular thought in the West as to permit "falling" to become a basic element of Heidegger's ontology.

57 Karl Rahner, "The Theological Conception of *Concupiscentia*," *Theological Investigations* I (Baltimore: Helicon, 1961), pp. 347-382, especially pp. 364-369.

58 In making this move, Segundo believes, Rahner releases concupiscence from the narrowness it had aquired in neoscholastic theology. But Segundo criticizes Rahner for failing to relate his existential categories to Paul's categories of Sin and Flesh in Romans (*EAJN*, p. 136, n. 161 and p. 133, n. 114; *RC*, pp. 259-261, especially p. 261, n. 4).

59 As has been indicated, this interpretation raises questions unable to be dealt with adequately here. The difficulty is that from Segundo's perspective, God does not seem to mind the enormity of evil which miscarried ideologies are capable of inflicting on victims. God continues to need and rely on ideologies, inefficacious though they be, and when the fire of God's judgment tests them in the eschaton, it will show them up for what they really are: works embodying mixed results and closer to either constructive love or egotistical destruction (*HCP*, pp. 130-131). The proportion of each ideology embodying egotism will be burned away, and the proportions embodying love will endure. The latter will be inserted into the definitive reality, where they will last with God forever. As was noted in chapter one, a crucial question in this context must be: can evil reach a critical mass heavy enough to prevent the breakthrough of love? Will the victims of torture find it helpful that the evil perpetrated by their torturers will be burned away into nothingness? Can evil assume an ontological gravity of its own?

60 *EAJN*, p. 84.

61 For Segundo, this "moment" has much in common with what the Johannine gospel calls the coming of Jesus' "hour." See ¿*Utopia?* Part II, pp. 47-62 and *GHC*, p. 81.

62 Timing is not to be confused with opportunism. On the contrary, it has more in common with sensitivity to the appropriate moment, the moment of *kairos* or grace. The full significance of the latter, which is eschatological, will surface in the discussion of love in chapter four.

63 For Segundo, love involves a complex correlation between efficacy and gratuitousness. It is epitomized in Jesus, whose love, understood in evolutionary terms, shows him "creating negentropy," taking "the initiative of *gratuitousness*" and integrating the marginalized (*EAJN*, pp. 62-64; italics Segundo's); in order to accomplish this, Segundo shows, Jesus had to integrate entropy—including what Paul calls "enslavement to corruption" and, ultimately, death—into the circuit of his love (*ibid.*, p. 87). (See also *ibid.*, p. 136, n. 163, on Jesus' also having to submit to the "social law" of loss of his autonomy and project.) In an earlier formulation of this same point, Segundo writes: "Jesus calls our attention to another kind of *efficaciousness* that is possible for love. It is a form of efficaciousness we tend to spurn in our normal

everyday lives: *the risky adventure of gratuitousness,* of grace-full living" (*EG,* p. 120; italics Segundo's).

[64] See chapter one. Such contact is not predictable. It can not be programmed in advance or placed under the control (or made the monopoly) of a particular church or ecclesial structure. Because grace is charismatic, God's Spirit blows where Spirit wills (Jn. 3:8). Creative efficacy erupts anywhere and everywhere there is found the tiniest movement of self-transcending love.

[65] *HCP,* p. 160.

[66] The laws of ecological logic are the laws of the circuit. They reveal that some forms of efficacy carry a very high price: death not merely figuratively speaking—e.g., sleep, "time off," randomization, disorder, breakdown, entropy—but death in fact, as was the case with the kingdom efficacy of Jesus (see n. 63 above); and this is true not only of the martyr-like efficacy of any human being cut down by a premature and violent death but ultimately of all persons who come to accept death as a condition for the arrival of new syntheses of life that are able to be realized only in the wake of their own decease and the death of their most valued projects (*EAJN,* pp. 70-74; see also pp. 87 and 113).

[67] Actually, as is evident when chapters one and two are taken as complementary parts of a single analysis, the advent of human freedom introduces a moral complexity into both Faith and Sin and not only into Sin. As fundamental dimensions of the structure of freedom in the human sphere, Sin and Faith are ontologically inseparable. It is thus inaccurate to abstract Faith from Sin as if Sin were ontologically inferior, an obstacle Faith must overcome or from which it must try to escape. On the contrary, Sin works by a logic which Faith must incorporate, for Sin is as essential to the efficacy of grace as Faith. Just as without chance, projectivity can not be efficacious, so without Sin Faith is unable to effect its work.

[68] In the context of Segundo's evolutionary categories, the adjective *sinful* does not carry the anthropologically derogatory connotations it often has in Protestant and Catholic versions of the Augustinian notion of sinful freedom, i.e., total depravity on the one hand or a freedom bent irreparably in on itself on the other. For Segundo, who moves away from neoplatonic categories of a philosophy of being to those of an ecologically conscientized philosophy of freedom, *sinful* refers not to a state of being (e.g., ontological worthlessness or moral alienation from God) but to a mode of action that does not contend creatively with Sin (i.e., the failure of anthropological faith to respond to the demands of entropy brought to light in the phenomenon of Sin, and therefore freedom's refusal to live and act gratuitously, to claim its creative power). Action is sinful when freedom refuses to be patient (i.e., loving in a self-transcending way) in the face of Sin, when anthropological faith abdicates its responsibility by taking the easy way out. Action is sinful when freedom fails to rise to the occasion of creating the new, surrendering instead to a run-away reaction that tries to "shift"

Sin into the ontologically inefficacious, never fully possible, "gear" of evolutionary reverse.

[69] In a paradoxical sense, *sinful* human action is an impotent caricature of the "real thing," which is *Sin-full* human Faith. From the point of view of eschatological validity, the former is inefficacious, while the latter is efficacious—i.e., capable of definitively creative power.

[70] An insight into this understanding of sin may be found in Gregory Bateson's description of the "Fall" as a human "head-trip" into purposiveness. See "Conscious Purpose versus Nature" in David Cooper, ed., *The Dialectics of Liberation* (Middlesex: Penguin, 1968), pp. 34-49.

[71] Segundo explains this distortion in terms of Bateson's categories of "digital" and "iconic" languages (*FI*, pp. 134-136 and pp. 155-159). Digital language is scientific and quantitative; it pertains to the realm of facts. Iconic language is symbolic or poetic. It strives to communicate a whole gestalt, and it relies on others' supplying what is "missing" or "left out"—what Bateson calls the principle of redundancy. Meaning is redundant because it overflows the boundaries of what is visible. Iconic language is thus the language of meaning and values while digital language is the scientific idiom of description, technology and fact. It is the language of ideologies alone, which in the absence of the iconic dimension tends to become monstrous, i.e., one-sided, or developed in only a single direction—efficacy—at the expense of meaning and values.

[72] The "rationale" behind the nuclear arms race furnishes a terrifying example of an unrealistic anthropological faith. It is an attempt to secure "peace," "life" and "freedom" (the "values" of "democracy") through war-inducing, death-dealing and biologically-cum-spiritually enslaving means, an ideology of destruction so widespread in its capacity for suffering and death as to be virtually irreversible.

[73] For Segundo's view of sin as anti-evolutionary, see *EG*, p. 27 and p. 127 and *EAJN*, p. 106. I add the words *anti-ecological* and *anti-eschatological* in order to bring out the cosmic and eschatological implications of sin and not only its anthropological relevance.

[74] See, for example, Reinhold Niebuhr, *The Nature and Destiny of Man*, Vol. I (New York: Charles Scribner's Sons, 1941), pp. 186-187.

[75] See Karl Rahner and Herbert Vorgrimler, *Concise Theological Dictionary*, second edition (London: Burns and Oates, 1983), p. 159.

[76] This is the view of sin put forth by Niebuhr in *Nature and Destiny of Man* I, pp. 178-240.

[77] Segundo believes this understanding stems from a collapsing of the realms of being and value into a single realm (*FI*, pp. 63-66). It seems to me that the crux of the problem shows up in a lingering theological confusion about what constitutes creatures' proper humility vis-à-vis the transcendence of God. It seems that humility should be based not primarily on an assessment of ontological difference (an abstract

"digital" approach) but on the "rightness" or truth of *praxis*—i.e., the validity or invalidity of creatures' justification. It is true that creatures are not God but finite. Yet the problem is not that finite beings should avoid trying to "be like" or "act like" the "infinite God;" on the contrary, "acting like God"—i.e., acting the way God acts— is precisely what, given the "news" of grace, we human creatures are *expected to do*, if we can judge by the self-transcending love which marked the kingdom *praxis* of Jesus. Rather, we must take care *which* " god" it is that we are trying to be like with our freedom, a task that can be carried out only by using Jesus' life-story and kingdom *praxis* as norm. (This is a major point of Segundo's critique of the "christological vacuum" in Ignatius' theology of God as Creator in *CIE*, pp. 41-50; it will also form a key element of the argument that unfolds in chapter three.) If "God" is a god of aseity, a self-sufficient "almighty" who is dominant over all, then with good reason we may suspect that we are imitating not God as Jesus revealed God but a false god fashioned in the image of human reason (see the following note). This suggests that the fundamental problem about sin is not pride but idolatry—a trait Segundo defines as human self-deception, motivated by injustice, about the values of God's heart. This is exactly what Segundo demonstrates in his exegesis of Romans 1-8 (see *HCP*, chapters one and two, especially pp. 18-19).

78 As Segundo points out (*OIG*, pp. 98-121 and pp. 139-142), reification is caused by attempting to "define" God rationalistically, according to the (anthropomorphic) requirements of reason (which can end up sacralizing injustice): "The fear of attributing 'too human' elements to God has unfortunately led theology. . .to 'purify' the notion of God by stripping all historical realism from it. Far from avoiding anthropomorphism, this procedure fell right into it. . .because this 'rational' version simply transposed to the divine realm the alienated relationships we have with persons through our use of impersonal, utilitarian categories for societal, political economic and juridical life" (*ibid.*, pp. 114-115). This is a type of "knowledge" which omits taking into account the data of revelation about God, specifically the data pertaining to God's actions and values in history. "Rational knowledge. . .consists in allowing reason, which can only distinguish natures, to present those natures to us as if they were the whole story" (*ibid.*, p. 113).

79 Such service, of course, must have a criterion; otherwise, it is capable of being twisted into all sorts of aberrant service—or worship of false gods—e.g., totalitarianism. Against the authoritarian rigidity of such service there can be little or no recourse. The need for a criterion is a central concern of this study, and forms the subject matter of chapter three.

80 Segundo explores the paralyzing logic of human immaturity operative in such fear in *GHC*, pp. 43-46. See also *OIG*, pp. 106-108.

81 *HCP*, pp. 64-66, p. 131 and p. 151. An instructive literary example of the social consequences of such religious twisting and legalistic self-justification may be found in Margaret Atwood's *The Handmaid's Tale* (New York: Fawcett, 1987).

82 *EG,* pp. 121-123; *HCP,* p. 177.

83 *HCP,* pp. 176-179.

84 In this sense, egotism is less a personal than a social reality: the ceding or abdication of freedom which constitutes a refusal to invest one's freedom for the sake of others, for the sake of building with them a world. Egotism is a refusal to shoulder the task of freedom—preeminently social—which pertains to human social persons by nature. It does not refer to satisfaction of one's own needs but to a refusal to satisfy the needs of others, particularly the deprived.

85 On the logic of this aggravation, which stems from the (self-righteous) sense of "purity from Sin" that people can develop when they say "No" in the abstract to dehumanizing powers and dissociate themselves from those powers from afar, Segundo observes: "While we [he and his study group engaged in reading Paul] could not find reasons to kill, we could find countless reasons for *letting people be killed,* ...and, worse still, for allowing thousands and millions to die even though no one had made a conscious decision to kill anyone" (*HCP,* p. 177; italics Segundo's). Nevertheless, as Segundo is aware, guilt "in the abstract" is equally inappropriate. His answer to this dilemma is to find ways of speaking and acting which are ecologically realistic, i.e., ideologies which attempt neither to locate efficacy in a single place (e.g., in an absolute norm like "non-violence") nor to find an efficacy that is believed to be qualitative and quantitative at once and thus capable of massive "overthrow" (e.g., the power of "the people" or "the poor" *alone*) (*ibid.,* pp. 179-182). Segundo believes that the latter effort raises false hopes which serve eventually to intensify people's desperation and despair, since in reality the poor are more powerless than powerful (*ibid.,* p. 179 and p. 224, nn. 254 and 257).

86 The domestication of God for oppressive or enslaving purposes—i.e., purposes that justify the failure to act creatively on behalf of the neighbor for the realization of liberation, justice and self-transcending love—is a particular temptation for religious persons and groups. According to Segundo, it is the sin against which Jesus rails in the synoptic gospels (*HJS,* p. 139), and it is the ideological mechanism of injustice which Paul sets out to unmask (*HCP,* pp. 38-41).

87 See *HCP,* p. 177, where Segundo notes that "the terrifying power of 'omission'" results "from immature subordination to secular or religious Law." The latter increases apathy and a false sense of powerlessness, promoting the (self-excusing, self-righteous) feeling that, once one has distanced oneself from the evils in question, "what else can be done?"

88 Segundo observes that "the only possible way to combat sins of omission is to leave the domain of Law, move out into the open, and face the whole panorama of human suffering" (*HCP,* p. 177).

89 The phrase "a world of grace" is the title of a book on Rahner's theology edited by Leo J. O'Donovan (New York: Crossroad, 1980). The phrase "a world of Sin" has a Pauline ring and is characteristic of Segundo's preferred way of thinking

about the ecological density of reality. The difference between the phrases and the emphases they represent suggests that insofar as Segundo takes the debilitating effects of Sin extremely seriously, he is more realistic, in a Niebuhrian sense, than Rahner, and yet, paradoxically, no less optimistic than Rahner (and perhaps more so) about the capacity of human freedom to love God. Where Rahner assumes that grace would have been a reality even were there to have been no sin, Segundo assumes that grace and Sin are structurally inseparable, and thus Sin and grace (rather than grace alone) must become theology's anthropological starting point. In other words, given Sin's undeniable perdurance and force, grace can be made theologically intelligible only in the face of a Sin which seemingly belies (but actually is incorporated into) the good news from God about the sure and everlasting efficacy of human realizations of self-transcending love.

[90] *HCP*, p. 175.

[91] Reinhold Niebuhr is quite right when he asserts that according to Christian revelation, what human beings are to be liberated from is not finitude but sin (*Nature and Destiny of Man* I, p. 178). But it would be important to ask whether he carries the implications of that insight through when he speaks about the origins of sin in anxiety. Like Niebuhr, Segundo begins his analysis of sin by rooting it in an anxiety that gets in the way of love (that Segundo relies on Niebuhr's understanding of anxiety is apparent in *HCP*, p. 209, n. 161). Yet, unlike Niebuhr, Segundo does not think the source of that anxiety lies in human beings' status as creatures caught between the infinite ambitions of freedom on the one hand and the finite limitations of nature on the other (for an example of Niebuhr's view on the latter, see *Nature and Destiny* I, p. 185). Anxiety for Segundo is not caused by finitude but is a servile fear about justification, a preoccupation with the status of human beings before God, or, in the case of those for whom concern about God is irrelevant, an anxious worrying about the demands of self-justification. For Segundo, sin is a question of the justification of anthropological faith. It is a problem of by what values human ideologies are to be justified and not a question about the limits of human finitude.

[92] It seems to me that Jesus' parable of the talents illustrates how, in a medium of Sin, human beings are liberated in Faith to create a world that is good. The point of the parable is that freedom is not to be buried or denied but invested in eschatologically constructive projects.

[93] *EG*, p. 127 (italics mine).

[94] According to Segundo, the efficacy of Jesus' love was realized not by adhering to an extrinsic norm (which is a reliance on ideologies alone) but by entering into "the risky adventure of gratuitousness" (*EG*, p. 120; see also p. 113 and pp. 120-121). See also n. 63 above.

[95] Segundo regards this type of sin as a ceding to the "mass" line of conduct of which every individual and group is capable. It is the tendency "toward simplification and immediacy" (*GHC*, p. 52), the surrendering of one's real efficacy

to the immediate and simplistic efficiency of cheap energy and the line of least resistance. Segundo writes: "Mass. . .is clearly not a specific social class but a line of conduct. Mass is defined here in terms of liberty, in terms of not thinking, in terms of allowing oneself to be led by others. Thus it is equivalent to inertia, passivity, nonliberty. And it should be noted that there is always a 'mass' element left in every [human being], however much [her or] his personality may be developed. There are zones and behavior patterns of nonliberty" (*ibid.,* p. 51).

96 *EG,* p. 121.

97 This was the five-volume series, *Theology for Artisans of a New Humanity.*

98 In *EG,* especially pp. 126-131, Segundo presents sin and grace as complementary vectors of the evolutionary project in such a way that they constitute original and integral dimensions of the structure of the universe. As has been seen in the preceding discussions, it is no exaggeration to say that from Segundo's point of view, Sin is the necessary presupposition of grace. It is the indispensible precondition of every manifestation of freedom and of love. This is the same original insight which underlies the development of the Sin-Faith dialectic in *JNYT.*

99 The same context marks Segundo's formulation of Latin American social and pastoral dilemmas during the mid-seventies. At that time he drew up a blueprint *(LT)* for the liberation of theology from the irrelevance it risked vis-à-vis the problems and conflicts of history by retreating from the complexity of sociopolitical affairs—an achievement which might just as accurately be called the liberation of the hermeneutical method from a fear of involvement in politics. For Segundo, the liberation of theology means freeing it to serve the needs of the oppressed. It means shifting the subject matter of theological discourse from concern for a purely religious or spiritual realm—the realm of "heaven" and "things that are above"—to the realm of earth and the ambiguities and conflicts of things that are "below." It means, in short, putting theology at the service of earth, which for Segundo means the service of human social persons and their historical, political, cultural concerns, and not reserving it exclusively for service to "God." This liberation can come about through two principal means: first, by adopting an openly partisan stance, what Puebla was eventually to name a "preferential option for the poor," as hermeneutical precondition for all theological interpretation about God and God's will, and second, by making the starting point for theology the actual problems raised by the "signs of the times," i.e., the concretely observable *realidad* of the sociohistorical context (see *LT,* chapter one).

100 See *FI,* Part III, Section B.

101 *HCP,* pp. 161-182. Insofar as the point of this chapter has not been to elaborate on the kinds of action Segundo advocates in various Latin American contexts, nor to prescribe the sorts of action a Segundo-like evolutionary perspective might suggest to persons and groups of good will in North America, I will not include either of these important topics here. I can only allude to my belief that it would be

a valuable project to elaborate a truly ecological, evolutionary ethics in the vein of Segundo's theology, a task which exceeds the scope of these reflections.

[102] As was seen in the earlier discussions, to learn to struggle does not imply that under the conditions of Sin (and sin) the struggle itself will ordinarily—or ever—be wholly successful.

[103] Taking the easy way out is bad not because it involves following "the laws of nature" but because it means trying to be "holier than God," refusing to work creatively and constructively with Sin. It is thus equivalent to refusing the Jesus-revealed kingdom mission of creativity and love to which God invites freedom and for the sake of which Faith puts its values to work. With regard to freedom, the laws of the Sin-ful medium of evolutionary reality are neither evil nor inferior but simply distinct, in the same way that in relation to one another two friends may be neither master and slave nor active and passive but simply completely distinguishable and utterly distinct at the same time that they cooperate in a loving communion.

[104] An obvious example of the constructive benefits of entropy may be found in the phenomenon of sleep. It provides the energies of living beings with the "time off" they need in order to function efficaciously during demanding periods of wakefulness. Sleep is effective, i.e., constructive, when it occurs in amounts and at times that are appropriate.

[105] The forces of entropy, or breakdown, of course, may be capitalized on at any level, from the sub-atomic through the biological, social and cultural spheres, to the cosmic, for every sphere of evolving reality participates in one way or another in all the other spheres.

[106] Like other therapies, the corrective aspect of Sin can be ignored. Segundo regards those who delude themselves into not "hearing" the alarm of Sin as being closed or hardened of heart. Their hearts are divided, and the division is cloaked over by self-deception (*HCP*, p. 22 and p. 190, n. 46). For Segundo, hardness of heart is the substance of bad faith.

[107] This remains true in spite of the fact that in his later works Segundo admits that his earlier Teilhardian optimism has been tempered (*EAJN*, p. 19 and pp. 22 ff.), presumably by an anthropological realism that reflects not only an interest in the pessimistic anthropology of Paul (*HCP*, p. 54 and pp. 113-114) and the ecological density of evolving reality (*EAJN*, pp. 29-41), but also a serious reading of Reinhold Niebuhr (reflected, for example, in *HCP*, p. 209, n. 161 and p. 214, n. 188). The principal reason for Segundo's optimism seems to be a love of and desire to celebrate the eschatologically creative power of human action, an exhuberance that seems to be in the spirit of Jesus' bold and high-spirited praise of genuine faith (e.g., Mt. 15: 28; Lk. 17: 6). Such theological *joi de vivre*, even if it should be shown to be wrong about particulars, seems fundamentally right. It recognizes the tragic side of creaturely existence but situates it in the context of an eschatological hope in the superabundant gratuitousness and utter positivity of love. When Jesus exclaims that

a human being with Faith can say to a mountain "Move," and it will move (Mk. 11: 23), he seems to be affirming the power Faith has to be ontologically creative in face of the seeming impotence and futility of action in a universe of evil. It is exactly on the issue of intramundane power, in fact, that Segundo disagrees with Neibuhr, observing that the latter's doctrinal position on *soli Deo gloria* causes him to imagine Jesus as rejecting all earthly power (*HJS*, p. 198, n. 17). For Segundo, Jesus' kingdom praxis *is* the eschatologically creative power of human Faith.

[108] What is scandalous about Segundo's view is that Sin, far from being necessarily negative, is actually neutral. As "raw material," it can go either way, depending on the quality of human action with respect to which it forms a necessary and beneficial part. When human beings permit Sin to enslave them, that enslavement shows up "symptomatically" in the anthropological fact of sins. Sin can facilitate sins, but it does not do so automatically or necessarily. Sin can also facilitate *love*, and, as will be seen in chapter four, Segundo views the latter as Sin's true and God-ratified function in the project that is grace.

[109] It is important to emphasize that it is Sin and not the world (and certainly not the beings who inhabit the world) which is to be the medium in which human freedom, in conjunction with the freedom of God, is to create. In other words, Segundo is not calling for the domination of some human beings over others or of human beings over other animals or "nature." He does not support interpretations of the scriptural notion of "stewardship" (Gen. 1-3) that in the name of freedom advocate human ownership of the earth or mastery over other species and resources. On the contrary, he calls for a historically sensitive heart, an ecologically conscientized wisdom, a responsive humility and responsible Faith in dealing with the apparent, but not definitive, contradiction Sin poses at the level of action.

[110] Indeed, one might ask what, if anything, scandalizes God. There seems to be only one answer: what the gospels call "the sin against the Holy Spirit" or "the unpardonable sin" (Mk. 3: 28-30). According to Segundo, the latter consists in the deliberate unwillingness—which is a lack of generosity, a failure in gratuitousness—to attribute to God every concrete instance of intramundane liberation, regardless of the "orthodoxy" or lack of it displayed by the apparent cause (*HJS*, p. 132). Such a line of thought suggests that, far from manifesting God as possessed of an (abstract) holiness and purity that are "offended" by Sin, Jesus manifests God as precisely the "impure One" who gratuitously enters Sin's domain, placing Sin in the service of an eschatologically creative project and incorporating it into an unprecedented act of definitive creation by coming to the defense of those whom Sin deprives of liberations (i.e., goods) that are rightly and properly theirs. This line of thinking sets the tone for a description of God as Neighbor of Neighbors in chapter four.

[111] An emphasis on justice represents a typically Protestant option concerning the significance of grace and an emphasis on mercy represents a typically Catholic one. It would be interesting to speculate (a) about the tendency of the first toward a

more prophetic spirituality and the tendency of the second toward a more "priestly," sacramental one, and about the political stance each would typically represent, of course without overlooking the need to temper such speculation with recognition of the critical elements in both traditions which nuance predominant views, and (b) about how Segundo's action-oriented perspective offers ecumenical advantages vis-à-vis development of a liberationist theology of grace and sin inclusive of both dimensions. The significance of this point will surface in chapter four.

[112] Without attempting to provide an answer, one might ask whether by stressing so heavily God's concern for justice, liberationist theologians give sufficient attention to God's love as mercy. By viewing grace as a mission-giving relation with God, Segundo seems to keep both justice and mercy in a healthy balance—which might just as well be thought of as an attempt to preserve a healthy balance between ethics and theology, or politics and mysticism.

[113] In the old Roman liturgy for Epiphany, there used to be a preface which stated that in Jesus, who is grace incarnate, God wills that what the preface called "redemption" be effected by humanity itself. Segundo seems to opt for such a view. In the spirit of Paul, he seems to suggest that such a "christological principle" can be expanded to cosmic dimensions to apply to the universe itself, which for Paul and Segundo is engaged in grace in a Spirit-led labor of bringing to term the eschatological project of creating a world that is good.

[114] According to the lyrical hymn to God's kenotic love in Philippians 2: 5-11, the answer seems to be yes, except that God is not "blinded" in the loving of creatures but rather is seeing with the only eyes capable of grasping what is worthwhile and real, namely the eyes of eschatological gratuitousness. In face of the gravity of evil, these eyes focus only on what is to be done and abstained from in self-transcending love in order to create the good. As will be pointed out in chapter four in the discussion of the ontological validity of love in the eschaton, this does not mean that God does not see evil, that God closes God's eyes to it or fails to recognize it for what it is, but rather that, seeing evil, contending with it and tasting its bitterness to the dregs, God acts in solidarity with suffering creatures, in eschatologically creative protest against the (dia-bolic) tendency evil has "to throw" the universe "apart." By countering the dia-bolic power of evil with the ontologically superior sym-bolic (i.e., creative) power of God's self-transcending love, God refuses to grant evil definitive ontological status in God's (and creatures') sight. In the face of this refusal, God gives suffering creatures new eyes (eyes of Faith) by which to discover that evil is not all there is to see. At the same time, such vision is an unleashing of freedom, the earthly manifestation of creatures' definitively creative power made real for them in grace, what Segundo means by the gratuitous anthropological dimension of Faith.

[115] To make such a scandalous—and dangerous sounding—affirmation is not the same as claiming that God thinks it is all right to *do* (or even "permit") evil for the sake of good. On the contrary, it is to claim that, judging from the data of

revelation, God thinks it is worthwhile to *contend* with evil, to struggle against its power insofar as it actually occurs or comes to pass. God neither wills evil nor welcomes the suffering it brings in its wake but rather suffers its occurrence in the same way that creatures must: because there is no other choice. There is no other way for God to preserve God's integrity, to assert God's "Godliness" or "holiness" *qua* God (which is different from God's "justifying 'Godself'" or saving an alleged "reputation"). There is no other way available to God than to suffer, like creatures and in solidarity with those who are deprived, the devastating effects of evil and sin. And this God does in the course of God's and creatures' conjoint commitment to create not a "better" or "perfect" world but a world capable in the end of being pronounced good. Yet, as chapter one pointed out, the suffering of evil by God and creatures is not the same as passivity. On the contrary, it is a creative passion and impassioned action that are efficacious and gratuitous; for in the face of evil, suffering is the willing investment of God's and creatures' creative energies (the power of grace and the power of Faith respectively) in the laborious, time-consuming and entropy-conditioned project of the construction of self-transcending love.

116 The priority of the positive is a fundamental datum of Jesus' revelation about God, and it is represented in scripture by God's own most characteristic *praxis* with regard to creatures. That *praxis,* made known by the unprecedented response of God's having raised Jesus from the dead and sealed by God's having given the Spirit as earthly "down-payment" on the eschatological efficacy of Faith, reveals God to be God preferentially not only of the marginalized and poor, but especially of those who are utterly marginalized and poorest of all, the dead. It is this scandalous love of God for the poorest of the poor, the forgotten and the dead, that is the most basic datum of what is revealed about the eschaton: God is precisely God who will not abandon the dead. God raised Jesus from the dead and raises and will continue to raise all the dead, and their just-as-forgotten, just-as-dead works of Spirit-guided Faith, to life. Love and not meaninglessness, love and not Sin, love and not failure, love and not death will have the final word about reality and its tragic streak of sorrow. Otherwise God is not Jesus' God and death must reign in the end. The resurrection of Jesus, which is the pledge of the resurrection of the whole creation, shows that on the last day, even in face of a failure as apparently definitive as death, love and not evil lasts. As chapter four will show, the gratuitously appropriate and creative power represented by the resurrection of both creatures and their projects is grounded in what Segundo calls the ontological priority of love over egotism (*RC,* p. 262, n. 8 and pp. 266-267). According to it, love alone is of lasting value in the eyes of God. Everything else—the enormous, cumulative weight of evil and sin bowing down the world and putting to death the projects of the just—will be burnt away at the day of judgment (*HCP,* pp. 203-204, n. 127). To the results of love and to them alone will God give life forever, even if they be seemingly obliterated by the negativity of injustice and buried deeper than the bodies of the forgotten dead.

III

BUILDING THE VALUES OF GOD'S HEART IN HISTORY AND NATURE: THE HERMENEUTICAL TASK OF ACTION AND THE REVEALED TRUTH CRITERION OF FAITH

Your will be done on earth as it is in heaven.

In a fundamental sense, the subject matter of this chapter is the nature and criterion of truth. The purpose of this part of the discussion is to show that truth is liberative, that theologically speaking there is only one criterion for truth, and that the criterion has to do with the liberation of the deprived. The thesis of the chapter, which is an attempt to combine these statements into a single hypothesis, is that liberation of the deprived is the only valid truth criterion of God's will. The intention is to arrive at a practical and realistic answer to questions posed by the previous two chapters.

By considering action as a hermeneutical phenomenon—seeing how freedom is intrinsically concerned with the realization of truth—and by maintaining with Segundo that the criterion for God's will is available only in Faith's down-to-earth capacity to read the signs of the times, I will attempt to show that action presents its own criterion for truth. Anywhere and everywhere there is liberation of the deprived—in other words, wherever and whenever anthropological faith responds to the signs of the times with a *praxis* suited to the needs of neighbors who are marginalized, forgotten or oppressed—freedom is liberated for the work of Faith and action is efficacious for the doing and making of truth. The question at issue will be how, from a theological point of view, such a radically secular standard—liberation—can be shown to be capable of discerning the sort of truth that is transcendent and that matches the will of God.

To ground the main hypothesis, I will attempt to link knowledge of God's will with participation in the values of God's heart, and I will do this by reflecting on Segundo's claim that the values of God's heart are revealed in a definitive way in the kingdom *praxis* of Jesus. Segundo regards Jesus' *praxis* as paradigmatic of God's love. Jesus' faith in what he called the kingdom of God grounds the values in which his message and action participate. Although historically conditioned and relative in content, his *praxes*--the ideologies that give expression to his faith—remain significant for disciples in every age.[1] In fact, Segundo says, Jesus' *praxes* demand to be interpreted anew in every situation, with a view to disciples' coming up with ideological responses congruent with the values of Jesus' kingdom faith. Like Jesus' *praxes*, these responses will be designed to realize God's will in works that effect an eschatological—and gratuitous—victory of Faith over the seeming futility of action in a world subjected to Sin and death.

    In the course of disciples' continuing efforts to make effective gospel interpretations of Jesus' *praxes*, Segundo argues, what is normative about Jesus— the God-revealing content of his kingdom faith—can be preserved from being relativized only by absolutizing what is relative about him, namely, his ideological *praxes*, giving them a normative value of their own. As in the case of Segundo's advocating an intramundane standard—liberation—by which to discern the will of God, the point at issue will be how such apparent contradiction—that what Jesus effected in the relative realm of ideologies has normative value for the action of disciples and definitive worth for the realization of God's project—can be shown theologically and anthropologically to hold.

    Against a backdrop of the significance of Jesus for people of good will today, the questions to be addressed in this chapter are therefore two. First, how can Segundo's paradoxical claim about the normative value of Jesus' kingdom *praxes* be shown to have adequate backing in the anthropological logic and ecological complexity of action as these were analyzed in the previous chapters? And second, what can such a claim actually mean theologically, especially from the point of view of the hermeneutical task disciples have of translating their Faith in Jesus' God-revealing *praxes* into ideological—and ethically decisive—*praxes* of their own? In particular, what significance do the ideologies of Jesus' kingdom faith have, historically conditioned and culturally limited as they were, for the quality and direction of disciples' liberation-*praxes* today—the Faith which gives them shape—vis-à-vis oppressive features like powerlessness, repression, failure, destruction, disintegration and death, features that in a particularly poignant way pose eschatological problems for human faith and give a social, political and ecological complexion to the face of Sin *qua* injustice and deprivation in our time?[2]

    In light of these questions, an additional aim of the chapter will be to speak about Jesus' kingdom *praxes* from a perspective of anthropological faith, i.e., immediate human interest, in Jesus in terms of the this-worldly significance of his ideologies for people of good will in the struggle to live a worthwhile life and do what is just and true rather than letting themselves be overcome by the sheer negativity and oppressive power of evil. The purpose of this approach is not to offer a christological reflection; rather, it is to highlight the significance of Jesus' message and action for an understanding of human action as a phenomenon that is constitutively hermeneutical, that ends up being lived and experienced under the ambiguous conditions of history and nature as a secular struggle for the realization of truth. The point, in other words, is to arrive at a practical criteriology for the knowing and doing of truth that can be of interest not only to those who want to be disciples of Jesus but to people for whom Jesus' *praxis* of liberation rings true whether or not they also happen to have a specifically religious faith in him.[3]

As will be seen in the concluding section of this chapter, an attempt to carry out the requirements of such a practical, liberationist task presupposes defining truth, including truth learned from revelation, in functional-hermeneutical terms. With Segundo I will assume that what is of interest about Jesus for many suffering and deprived people and those in solidarity with them today is precisely the this-worldly relevance of his kingdom *praxis* for the justification of eschatological hope, in other words, in the face of evil in *this* world, the bolstering of an already operative secular capacity to live each day "hoping against hope" in some sort of eventual liberation and to go on suffering, acting, working and dying for the sake of constructing good and not evil on earth.[4] In spite of the fact that this assumption (and its concomitant belief that eschatological hope is an intrinsic feature of the structure of human freedom[5]) is different from a christological attitude of (religious, disciple-like) anthropological faith—i.e., a faith that Jesus' person (inseparable from his *praxis*) provides a divinely sanctioned source from which to derive criteria for the knowing and doing of God's will—it can be shown to dovetail with it. And from a christological point of view, that seems to be its principal value.

The complementarity of these concerns shows up at the level of Segundo's christology—or rather, his refusal to engage in christology strictly speaking.[6] According to Segundo, the adequacy of any and every religious interpretation of Jesus' significance for people of good will today must rely, and even depend, on how convincing a picture of his social, political and ecological significance theologians and other disciples are able to draw in their preaching of the gospel. Unless present-day gospel interpretations of Jesus—the meaning of his action and the impact of his life—have a manifestly secular liberative significance, they are incapable from Segundo's point of view of conveying worthwhile religious meaning. Instead, they serve to add to the burden of idolatry that, in the name of "God," continues to weigh down the world with structures of injustice that are the watermarks of sin.

Because this insight seems to be one of Segundo's most decisive contributions to the task of making a truly Jesus-normed gospel interpretation of Jesus for people of good will today, I will draw on it to show why, from a theological standpoint, a knowing and doing of God's will according to the criterion provided by Jesus can be understood to have the same interests at heart—eschatological liberation from historical-ecological deprivation—as a knowing and doing of truth when it is sought after and practiced on behalf of liberation by victims of injustice and people of good will in solidarity with them anywhere in the world.

Of central interest in this chapter must therefore be a question to which Segundo has devoted a considerable portion of his writings: what are we theologians and other theists actually talking about when we use the word *God*? When it is not left a generic—and thus experientially empty, aloof and unimpassioned—term but is given concrete content with regard to specific instances of intramundane liberation effected in the lives of particular persons or groups and their histories, to which "god" does the word *God* refer? So far as Segundo is concerned, this question can be answered only when it is made synonymous with the central question of this chapter, namely, what did the kingdom *praxis* of the historical Jesus reveal about the values of God's heart?

In light of the centrality of faith and ideologies in Segundo's way of addressing exactly that question, I will begin explication of the central thesis of the chapter by reviewing from a hermeneutical perspective the logic proper to action itself. Taking action as a phenomenon capable of being observed from a strictly human point of view—i.e., apart from Jesus' revelation of God's love in grace—I will discuss why action inevitably poses for itself a hermeneutical problem: the appropriation of truth in ideologies. As a first step toward addressing the question, I will attempt to show that there is an anthropologically valid way of stating the thesis which is capable of being expressed in secular terms as follows: to seek truth is the hermeneutical task of action, and the liberation of the deprived is the only valid criterion for attainment of that truth.

What will be most striking about this step—and perhaps scandalous to some—is what it implies about the role of Jesus and his *praxes* vis-à-vis a theological concept of revelation. According to Segundo's schema, if Jesus' revelation of God is to retain its radical status as normative revelation, it must be relativized. In other words, it must be viewed not substantively but functionally. Jesus' uniqueness must be regarded not from a quantitative point of view, as if his life-story were a phenomenon occurring alongside and yet somehow above and beyond others, but from the point of view of quality. Jesus' *praxis* is a factor of key significance for disciples today because it makes a qualitative difference to the task of hermeneutical interpretation that action is engaged in from the start. Revelation qualifies the hermeneutical task with a datum about the eschatologically successful outcome of the project of love that is grace.[7] It is a difference that makes a difference to the appropriation of truth.

After discussing what these initial assertions can mean, I will move in the second and third sections to consideration of the hermeneutical task of action from the point of view of the human *charism* to build God's values on earth in the work of Faith. This part of the discussion will be carried out in two steps: first, a look at Segundo's twin theses that (a) the concept *God's will* is synonymous with the notion *the values of God's heart,* and (b) the criterion for discerning God's will must be derived from the kingdom *praxis* of Jesus; and second, a look at the nature and content of that criterion as it operates under the conditions of relativity and entropy in history and nature. Finally, in the last and most constructive section of the chapter, I will return to a discussion of the nature of truth, its actual substance and content, in light of that criterion.

For purposes of clarity, the content of the chapter may be divided into four sub-theses which here in the introductory section it is useful simply to list: (I) Human action poses a hermeneutical problem to itself, (II) the existence of which indicates that the nature of the human task—what in chapter one was defined as a *charism* to participate conjointly in love with God in the creation of a world that is good (and was in that way shown to be appropriate to the logic of action)—is intrinsically hermeneutical. (III) In the attempt to interpret the nature and meaning of the gratuitous project in which disciples and all human beings are invited to participate, namely building in Faith in a medium of Sin the values of God's heart (a vocation that disciples of Jesus know about because they act not only in grace, like everyone else, but also in the context of a sure and certain word from God given in revelation), disciples look not only to the message of revelation about what is God's will for human action "on earth as it is in heaven" but also, like everyone else, to the signs of the times, i.e., evidence available from the secular sciences and arts and in the depths of people's hearts when they are sensitive to the needs of the deprived. (IV) When disciples take into account these various pieces of data, they can learn, and come to know with a certainty that is reliable, that liberation of the deprived is the only valid truth criterion of God's will.

In outline form, these sub-theses define the logic of the chapter. They are intended to show that this part of the discussion is a matter of trying to turn the theoretical analyses of chapters one and two into concrete grounds for disciples' *praxis.* As a result, the sub-theses spell out the concern of these reflections with a fundamental question of ethics: given the nature of human action, i.e., its anthropological logic in light of grace (chapter one) and its ontological and moral complexity in light of Sin (chapter two), what are we human social persons to *do*? This question rules the logic of the chapter. Given the need to interpret the data of revelation by means of categories available from both the secular sciences and people's commonly shared experience of the anthropological logic of faiths and ideologies (assuming throughout the requirement of good will), it turns out that the theological question of a knowing and doing of God's will must be asked in practical, down-to-earth, hermeneutical terms as a secular question of ethics: in a universe subjected to apparent futility by Sin and death but called to participate in a gratuitous yet appropriate eschatological project initiated in love by God, what intramundane criterion can action come up with by which to test the quality of the contribution it must make to the creation of a world that is good?

The complexity of this question requires that before leaving this introductory section I include a word about the issues involved when one addresses the problem of an ethical criterion in a specifically theological context. At a minimum, it seems that such a criterion must enable theologians to do three things: (1) to determine with theologically reliable certainty what God's values are, (2) to determine with anthropologically reliable certainty what sort of action is appropriate to the realization of God's values and (3) to know theologically—and be able to ground anthropologically at the level of experience—that *that* sort of action is ethically appropriate and constitutes a distinctively human contribution to the realization of God's love, for the benefit of others, particularly the deprived, and not for self-serving, exclusively human purposes.

From the point of view of a theology that wants to norm itself by the life-story and *praxis* of Jesus, these requirements arise from three distinct yet closely related sources. The first is the ongoing relevance of Jesus' kingdom *praxis,* which, in light of the unprecedented experience of Jesus' resurrection, was initially and is still being experienced by disciples as revelatory in a definitive way of God's values. That experience is such that for those who have had it, it makes an ineradicable impact on their anthropological faiths and demands a fitting response at the level of ideologies. As will be seen in the next paragraph, revelation makes a qualitative difference to the *praxis* of disciples by turning their action into a *praxis* of truth that at the same time is also a witness—not only to values that are God's but also to God's revealed word that the eschatological outcome of God's project is going to be everlastingly successful.[8]

The second of these three demands presupposes an ethical requirement universally shared by human beings whoever they may be: to discern what are appropriate ways of acting. By reason of our acting at all, we human social persons decide, in and through our action and while it is still going on, how we *ought* to act. Because that is the case, the second demand flows from the constructive conversation, the mutually conditioning encounter or dialogue, conceivably the conflict and at times the bitter struggle, which can arise when the ideologies of disciples of Jesus (assuming their good will) concretely "mix" with the ideologies of other persons and groups of either good or bad will at the level of everyday *praxis.* This is the level at which the action of disciples can become *witness.* Like the kingdom *praxis* of Jesus, it can become capable of transmitting in a real—i.e., ideologically mediated yet definitively efficacious—way, the impassioned love of God. Such witness can be experienced by those living it as something negative (e.g., failure, passion, suffering, martyrdom) or positive (e.g., gratuitous instances of liberation from concrete deprivation). It can be the manifestation on earth of a freedom that is as gladsome as "the glorious freedom of the children of God." (For Jesus, such liberations and manifestations were cause for celebration and joy.[9])

The third demand—that of just treatment of others in history and nature, particularly the deprived, along with recognition of the intrinsic value of the interests and projects of others, including beings other than the human—flows fundamentally from human sensitivity to others. But it also derives from data of contemporary evolutionary science about the interconnectedness of living and non-living beings in a single ecological net, as well as from a basic theological datum of Jesus-normed faith concerning the impassioned love of God for every creature, but especially for the deprived.[10] When these factors are combined—in other words, when the impassioned love of God revealed in Jesus' *praxis* is joined to human sensitivity to others and to data available from ecological and evolutionary science—a new ecologically conscientized model of action is capable of arising, an ethics of appropriateness that can aim to be liberative for all creatures at the expense of none.[11]

The task of this third chapter may thus be summed up as four-fold: (1) to demonstrate that action establishes its own criterion of truth, (2) to explain from the point of view of a Jesus-normed revelation how compatibility between action's truth criterion on earth and the will of God in heaven may be derived and grounded, (3) to define what God's will is according to a Jesus-derived revelation and show how it operates in a liberative, eschatologically efficacious way under the conditions of Sin and sin in history and nature as self-transcending love and (4) to give an interpretation of how, as the embodiment in ideologies of exactly such love, liberation of the deprived relates hermeneutically to the universal anthropological task of realizing truth on earth. To fulfill this complex agenda, I am dividing the chapter into five parts comprising this introduction plus four additional sections dealing with the topics outlined above. The essential point occurs in the final section. There, I attempt to pull together the logic of the chapter as a whole, bringing the end of the argument back to the beginning by making a kind of hermeneutical circle in miniature: in and through the *praxis* of truth, those who want to be disciples of Jesus can come to know what God wills in order to do what God wills at the same time that they strive to do what God wills in order to know what God wills, and thanks to Jesus' kingdom *praxis*, disciples can do this in a way that gives a quite specific liberative content to the word (and the experience of) *God*.

Action Demands Its Own Criterion of Truth

Assuming the content of the two previous chapters, we arrive at this juncture suspecting that graced human action—i.e., Faith—presents a hermeneutical problem to itself, and we assume that the existence of that problem gives Faith an ethical-hermeneutical task: to interpret what to *do* (to learn how to act) and to *interpret* what to do (to keep on learning to learn how to act). All human beings share in this task. It reflects the existential complexity of human freedom, that restlessness of heart which gathers us human social persons together in a common pilgrimage after truth but points us via disparate anthropological faiths in various and sometimes mutually exclusive directions. Along the way, not only do we disagree, often violently, over which of these directions to take, but we also attempt to realize the values of conflicting—and sometimes identical—faiths through disparate ideologies. At times, indeed, often, these conflicting ideologies cause immense amounts of suffering to ourselves and other beings and lead to the destruction, or at least long- or short-term damaging, of the givenness of reality, blocking the creation of the new.

Regardless of the content of these ideologies, the fact that they exist, the fact that they can create or at least contribute to social and ecological evils on an increasingly damaging scale, aggravating suffering and injustice and adding to the build-up of more and more complicated varieties of sin—all of this serves to underline the fact that even when freedom is attempting to be constructive, its consequences in the sphere of objective reality are far from innocent. In spite of resistance from objective reality through the structural mechanism of Sin—a resistance that qualifies the spontaneous interests of freedom by preventing absolute realization of its original aims—ideologies represent more or less successful attempts to realize the values of this or that anthropological faith in optimally efficacious form. The fact that ideologies can have destructive consequences in the sphere of objective reality suggests that the faith which is their origin requires an objective criterion of truth.

As was seen in chapter one, central to faith is its social character. Its link with objective reality—the phenomenon of ideologies—means that faith is social, however, not only in origin but in structure and operation. Different faiths must attempt to deal with the conflicting truth claims of the ideologies they create by means of some sort of working together, some form of communal conversation and discernment, some type of consensus-building in order to determine which ideologies—and what sorts of anthropological faiths—are better than others for achieving not just any solutions to historical problems, not merely solutions that are more or less expedient, and beneficial to the interests of the few, but solutions of truth. The latter are solutions that "ring true" when they come up against the requirements, available at the level of consequences and results, of the objective givenness of reality. As will be seen, the phenomenon of "givenness" surfaces in the social sphere in the interests of others and the needs of the deprived.

Although Segundo does not spell it out, the link he makes between the social character of faith and the objective consequences of ideologies seems to derive from the nature of freedom as *praxis*. Precisely *qua praxis*, action is a mixture of thinking and doing that on the one hand embodies the values of a particular anthropological faith and on the other hand results in objectively perceivable consequences in the "outside world." This means that anthropological faith is the source or ground of *praxis* while ideologies—sets of lived and living *praxes* that necessarily include elements of both theory and practice—are *praxis'* objectively conditioned means.[12]

Praxis thus comprises not two elements (theory and practice) but three: faith (its guiding interest, epistemological premises or ontological grounds), theory (its scientific or rationally coherent self-justification), and practice (its perceptible encounter with—and effects upon—the objective givenness of reality). Considered in relation to objective results and consequences, the tension between source and means "polarizes" *praxis* with reference to truth, giving faith an intrinsically ethical charge. This results in anthropological faith's having to make practical, ethical choices—hermeneutical interpretations—about the truth of itself as faith, choices that tend from a social point of view to be either unifying or divisive insofar as their professed aims, embodied in ideologies, are susceptible of being tested in public against the givenness of objective results.

In order to interpret whether and to what extent any given ideologies are actually serving to realize truth in faith, freedom *qua praxis* tends to establish a criterion, and that criterion is bound up with—but not identical to—what Segundo calls the self-validating epistemological premises by which one punctuates the story of one's life or the history of one's social group and its faith-tradition. Such premises create a sensitivity to, but do not themselves constitute, a standard according to which human social persons judge the validity of their faiths. Vis-à-vis ideologies, the premises of anthropological faith provide a framework within which to interpret evidence available at the level of objective results and consequences in reality. Paradoxically enough, the interpretation is considered reliable—i.e., capable of mediating truth—precisely to the extent that it legitimates the values faith already has, values faith believes capable, given the premises out of which it is operating, of being counted on to "deliver" a long- or short-term result.[13] For example, if the absolute value of a government is national supremacy, of a sort that leads it to protect and enlarge a hegemony of power through ideologies like militarism and the accumulation of nuclear arms, and if these ideologies seem to that government to be capable of "delivering the goods," then even in the face of actual evidence to the contrary, that government will continue to "believe in" the *praxis* of arms escalation; it will "live by" and "trust in" ideologies of militarism and regard their seeming efficacy as (self-validating) "proof" that national supremacy as a value is "true."[14]

The self-validating character of anthropological faith and its link through ideologies to the interpretation of results thus supports the notion that action poses a hermeneutical problem to itself. Thanks to the three-fold structure of *praxis*, we human social persons and the traditions to which we belong experience knowledge as a *praxis* of faith-interpretation, a continual "reading" (and "writing") of the consequences of ideologies, a constitutively hermeneutical task. Since the consequences of faith show up in the objective realm at the level of ideologies, faith demands a criterion that is not extrinsic to the structure of action but intrinsic to its own internal logic. And since that logic includes not merely the intentionality of hermeneutical subjects but also the objective structures of already-given reality, its criterion can be arrived at only by a species of knowledge that includes the consequences of ideologies in objective reality as well as the original interests of faith. In this sense, the structure of *praxis* makes knowledge a hermeneutical task.

This suggests that in a way somewhat analogous to the working of the senses, *praxis* develops "eyes" and "ears" by which to "see" and "hear" the truth actually being accomplished by this or that particular faith and its attendant ideologies. From the point of view of the analysis made in the previous two chapters, the way these "eyes" and "ears" tend to operate is by "sensing": faith is continually engaged in a procedure of learning to learn to make "right" or fitting interpretations of the objective consequences of ideologies. In order to do so, it needs not only the values and interests underlying faith but also some form of theoretically coherent human science—what Segundo calls a "theoretical hermeneutical key" or "instrument of cognition" to complement the practical impulse inherent in ideologies—by which to assess what elements actually combine to make up any given situation. Faith needs such theory not only to be able to determine, through scientific analysis, what sorts of action will be realistic and constructive in any given situation, but also to become capable of learning to *guide* action.[15]   The scientific-analytical "theoretical key" and the practical-intuitive "appropriateness-sensing key" thus coincide with the values and interests of anthropological faith in the sphere of *praxis,* where they make a "hermeneutic circle" that has an impact on objective reality at the level of concrete results and consequences.[16]

As was pointed out in chapter two, Segundo shows that in an ecologically complex world subjected to the entropic logic of Sin and its perversion into sin, the capacity to assess the effects of ideologies can be learned only by experience. Such learning presupposes a good will that does not permit itself, through willing self-deception, to turn imperceptibly and gradually into an interest in self-justification, the vestige of an originally good anthropological faith gone bad.[17] Appropriately learned judgments of anthropological faith are interpretations mediated by critical sensitivity to the data of objective results. They are a matter of wisdom and flexibility about ideologies on the one hand and humility and self-criticism about faith on the other. Ultimately, they are a matter of sensitivity to truth.

At bottom, attainment of such learning is an experiential procedure, a gradual process of learning to learn to make sensitive judgments—in other words, appropriate hermeneutical interpretations—in light of the signs of the times. In this way faith learns to sound the depths of truth experimentally, so to speak. *Qua praxis* and in no other way, faith becomes capable of testing the direction in which ideological constructions, imperfect though they be, ought ultimately to tend. And, surprisingly or not, depending on one's perspective, it turns out that faith's organs of discernment are either dulled or sharpened by the cumulative effects, at the level of ideologies, of actual ongoing *praxes.*

Although Segundo does not speak in a fanciful way, from his point of view the ruling "mind" or interpretive principle which serves to guide faith along the way of its practical hermeneutical task is nothing other than the sensitive human heart. This is a heart that on the basis of the "signs of the times" considers the consequences of action vis-à-vis the objective givenness of reality insofar as the latter includes concretely observable evidence of the needs of the deprived.[18] The sensitive heart is a heart whose "eyes" and "ears" of anthropological faith are open, whose epistemological premises are attentive to objective facts, whose historical sensibilities are capable of picking up the signs of the times put forth in the sphere of objective reality by the early warning system—and ecologically conscientizing "reality therapy"—of Sin.[19] By bringing to light in the objective realm the devastating effects of injustice on victims, Sin shows up deprivation for what it really is: the injustice that is sin. Alerted to the concreteness of objective reality in this way, the sensitive heart "picks up" and discerns with clarity the actual substance of truth. The sensitive heart is thus the consciousness of anthropological faith which urges it to seek ideologies that respond to the signs of the times and the needs of the deprived.

The sensitive heart is not itself the criterion of truth but is the criterion's detector.[20] Because it is capable of correcting the interests of anthropological faith in light of the interests and needs of the deprived, it can realign faith's hierarchy of values by making it rely on data objectively available in the sphere of consequences and results. Although the sensitive heart cannot positively prove the reliability of the criterion it detects, it remains capable of testing it concretely by the fruits of action obviously at hand in the form of ideologies, evidence deriving from what is available to faith in the course of *praxis* itself. The cup of cold water given to the neighbor who is thirsty, the bodies of the Filipino people shielding, unarmed, the revolutionary soldiers from tanks, the refusal of the student to capitulate to competitive demands at the expense of intellectual honesty, the attempts of the struggling couple to model their everyday *praxes* about eating, love-making and owning goods on values responsive to the needs of others—these ideologies ring true to the sensitive heart because it is capable of interpreting their consequences according to a criterion—the needs of the deprived—that it knows and recognizes by the manifest objectivity of results.

Obviously, the sensitivity of the human heart can be dulled by *praxes* of deprivation and imbalance and misled by ideologies of self-deception for the sake of legitimating injustice as much as it can be sharpened by *praxes* of wisdom and flexibility. The heart can become hardened to the signs of the times and closed to the countless stimuli to truth[21] that impinge upon the eyes and ears of anthropological faith in the form of deprivations to be struggled against even if Sin and death cannot be definitively overcome. What, then, makes the sensitive heart capable of discerning truth? It can only be a willingness to take account of the needs of the deprived, the needs of the suffering neighbor.[22] And if someone should ask: Who is my neighbor? the human being of sensitive heart does not find it necessary to run off to this or that repository of Authoritative Teaching in order to consult something like a *"Theologische Wörterbuch* of Truth." Instead, she or he will be moved to point in the direction of those who, according to the results of our everyday methods of knowing and discerning, are obviously deprived.[23] These would include the marginated and dispossessed of whatever social and ecological grouping, human or not, living, inanimate or dead, all those living, once-living, potentially living and non-living beings who in the alleged name of "God" or any other oppressive power have had that which is rightfully theirs from the beginning taken away.[24]

The person or group of sensitive heart does not search for the splinter while overlooking the plank. To the deprived, the sensitive heart responds with a single-hearted simplicity: what has been taken away must be restored. Like the signs of Sin that impinge on Faith as a call for response and action, the deprivation of the neighbor appears to the sensitive heart as an obvious and unmistakeable criterion, a compelling cry of suffering and loss: it demands a compassion that is action and an action that is passion. As the core of *praxis,* Faith itself as a constitutive dimension of action tends of its own accord to discern a criterion for the knowing and doing of truth, and the name of that criterion is the deprivation being suffered by those most in need of a neighbor.[25] Ideologies or *praxes* of however unexpected—even scandalous—a source that serve by their fruits to liberate the deprived from actual evils and ills are capable of being recognized by the sensitive heart as meeting the criterion of truth.

In order to connect what is being said about the truth criterion of *praxis* in this section with what must be said in the next section about the criterion of God's will, it will be helpful ahead of time to consider the hermeneutical nature of faiths and ideologies in relation to a theological concept of revelation. As has been seen, all human beings share in the hermeneutical task of action, and all can know the criterion of truth.[26] Introducing a concept of revelation into the picture means that disciples of Jesus claim access to a reliability for the truth criterion as a criterion that derives not only from the logic of action but also and specifically from God. Introduction of such a claim shifts the discussion from an anthropological to a theological level.

From the point of view of a Faith that is derived from Jesus and normed by his kingdom *praxis,* the fact that action poses a hermeneutical problem to itself is pertinent to the concept of revelation insofar as the latter claims that action has a causal relation to realization of God's project. In other words, insofar as action is self-transcending love, it constitutes the efficacious eschatological mediation of God's love for creatures in grace.[27] As has been pointed out earlier, that datum of revelation makes it essential to consider in close connection with one another the criterion Faith arrives at in the course of fulfilling its hermeneutical task and what Segundo calls the "anthropological" or "historical" causality of action, its link with the eschatological realization of grace.[28]

As the first part of this discussion points out, it is precisely *qua* anthropological faith that Faith tends to establish a criterion for *praxis*. But since, according to revelation, Faith presupposes God's gratuitous invitation to embark on a relation of kinship and project-sharing with God (although it does not by any means presuppose belief in or even implicit or explicit knowledge of either of these), a Faith that is derived from and normed by Jesus' kingdom *praxis* faces the task of having to relate its anthropological truth criterion to the gratuitous context of what Jesus called God's kingdom. And that involves dealing with a word of revelation concerning what a truth criterion of liberative *praxis* might look like when viewed from the perspective of the heart of God. Making such a correlation—and arriving at the sort of reliability it provides—is not a cognitive problem. As was pointed out in the discussion above, the sort of knowledge that faith provides is not a rational certitude but a hermeneutically created sensitivity. It is a consciousness, the sort of knowledge that aptly may be described as the *praxis* of an art, an experiential-experimental type of knowledge that is proper to faith *qua* faith. Appropriation of God's revelation is not a cognitive but an *ethical* task: Faith has to work at the practical level to make fitting correlations between what God's revealed truth criterion is and what the hermeneutical bent of action seems oriented toward from the start, namely the settling on certain ideologies rather than others in the attempt to come up with liberative solutions to problems of secular existence and the needs of neighbors who are deprived.

Vis-à-vis knowledge of the will of God, the Faith of disciples of good will thus incorporates a revealed criterion on which it relies with moral (i.e., practical) and not cognitive certainty. The problem is, however, that while all human beings, whether their Faith is religious or not, have access to knowing and doing what the sensitive heart interprets ought to be done, no one has access to an experiential certainty about the inner mind and will of God unless God first make them known; and that situation creates, for certain theists at least, a temptation to look for some sort of extra-historical sign—what Segundo calls a sign from heaven or from "God."

Yet more than any other problem in theology, the demand for this sort of sign presents an insurmountable obstacle to those who—like Segundo and the anti-superstitious Jesus of the synoptic gospels—reject all claims to absolute certainty and cling to the criterion of integrity of heart and the intrinsic value of reading the signs of the times. For such world-oriented, neighbor-sensitive persons or groups, the idea of a sign from heaven—a purely transcendent criterion from "God"—is worse than a scandal; it is an alien demand, a historical impossibility, a theological contradiction. Unless one wishes to make a case for magic,[29] one must say that such a desire is—borrowing from the logic of Thomas Aquinas—utterly *inconveniens*. It simply does not work. It violates the integrity of the universe and distorts the logic of revelation. If one is a theist, therefore, one must ask with Segundo whether it is theologically *appropriate,* not to mention anthropologically possible, to look to God for a sign.

Segundo believes it is not, and I believe he has solid grounds for this theological restraint in the biblical virtue—and experiential realism—of humility.

Before exploring what Segundo has to say about this problem, however, it is necessary to discuss the meaning and use of the word *reliable* in the context of these reflections. First, it is not Segundo's word but mine. By introducing it into the discussion, I want to attend to not merely *what* Segundo says about the problem of deriving a criterion for God's will in history and nature but also *why* I think the derivation of such a criterion is fitting, or at least not alien to, the logic of action. As has been suggested above, the derivation of a truth criterion seems called for by reason of human beings' having to face the question "What must we—or I—do?" And the fundamental nature of this question shows up in every human action. In the very doing of one thing rather than another, we human social persons are already answering the question "What shall we do?" perhaps before we even ask it. And the fact that by our ideologies we are already giving an answer—good or bad as it may be—reveals the presence of a criterion for action that is at least implicitly operative in the logic of action itself. As was pointed out, it is operative precisely as a result of the ruling values of one's anthropological faith, and it becomes more or less efficacious in the form of the objective results or fruits of *praxis* in this or that particular ideology.

Second, the word *reliable* indicates that what revelation provides for human social persons and their action is not the criterion itself; on the contrary, that is supplied by each human being's anthropological faith when it is functioning in grace in its liberated form as Faith. Instead, revelation supplies only the testimony of a reliable *witness* that such a hermeneutically derived criterion matches God's will. The criterion for action is available to everyone in action that is graced; revelation furnishes a gratuitous—and secularly mediated—experiential confirmation that the criterion of liberation already guiding the sensitive *human* heart is compatible with values that are *God's*. Given the existence of anthropological faiths, we human social persons can say, "This or that criterion is or is not our or my truth criterion for action," and we can give our "reasons of the heart"—sensitive or not—for making such a statement. But then, if we are theists, we have to go on to ask: "Is this criterion of mine or ours compatible with God's?"[30]

The existence of these questions means that the problem of knowing the will of God does not lie in whether or not God's will can be known and done on earth. Theologians admit that it can be, and to a greater or lesser extent always is being, known and done anywhere and everywhere deprivations are being overcome and the needs of the deprived are at least tentatively being met. Rather, the problem lies in disciples' being able to know by reliable witness that the intramundane criterion of truth—liberation of the deprived—is also and specifically the will of God, and that problem is synonymous with the problem of revelation. As might be expected, this is a problem about which theologians, more than other people, tend to worry. Indeed, excessive worry about it can be for them an occupational hazard. Yet the fact remains that whether one worries about it or not, the gap between coming up with a hermeneutically valid criterion for action and linking it to trustworthy reliability about what are the values of God's heart can be closed theologically only by way of a viable concept of revelation. How this ought actually to be done, however, is a source of disagreement in present-day theological discussion and a matter of fundamental importance for the delineation of theological foundations for ethics.

Some would suggest that we human beings ought to derive criteria for action solely from God.[31] With Segundo, I think it is more realistic to admit that theists, like everyone else, must derive such criteria anthropologically, from the perspective of our various anthropological faiths and from the sensitive heart's spontaneous response to the needs of the deprived. Nevertheless we theists want to correlate what the sensitive heart comes up with on earth with what God has revealed in heaven. The central question thus centers on how to interpret, and thereby know and effect, God's values in an anthropologically coherent way, which is to say a way sufficiently grounded, from the point of view of ethics, in an experientially trustworthy criterion. And that brings the discussion directly back to the need for hermeneutics: to answer the question of what we must *do*, we human social persons have to *interpret* the objective requirements of the situation (the "signs of the times") and decide how appropriately to respond.

God's values, in other words, are to be sought not in heaven, from which a purely transcendent revelation will never come, but in realities that meet people's sensibilities on earth. The transcendent grounding for the criterion of truth is accessible only in the data of experience, which challenge human beings to respond to the deprived in ways appropriate to the alleviation of their deprivation. To test the reliability of whether *God* wills that this be so, such interpretation turns to the data of revelation about the values of God's heart, and these are provided in a striking and definitive way, although not exclusively, in the kingdom *praxis* of Jesus.

Segundo's logic thus leads to the conclusion that revelation supplies good news from God about the truth toward which the criterion of action already tends but for which it otherwise would lack a certain word from *God*. What Segundo's argument does not do is blot out the need to go through history and nature (to rely on the data of experience) to get it. In the *praxis* of Jesus, revelation supplies a reliable witness to the criterion of God's will, but it does not do away with the hermeneutical requirement of having to arrive at a knowledge of the criterion by means of the same down-to-earth interpretive procedure that all human beings use in daily experience.[32] By locating the source of revelation's reliability in the logic of action (i.e., in Faith and not only in God), Segundo keeps the truth criterion of anthropological faith, already valid and operative in liberative *praxis* on earth, in touch with the values of God's heart in heaven. By introducing God's revealed criterion into the logic of action as a gratuitous factor, something not required but able to be appropriated within the hermeneutic circle already at work in everyday *praxis,* Segundo makes sure in a realistic and not at all magical way that God's will can be made relevant to ethical reflection. Gratuitous but not extrinsic, revelation can participate in the task of guiding action according to values already valid for the release of suffering neighbors while neither invading the integrity of anthropological faith nor infringing upon the validity of its hermeneutical task.

The value of Segundo's approach thus lies in what it says about the anthropological "suitability" or fittingness of revelation.[33] It illumines how the Faith *charism* to realize God's values can be linked in a way that is gratuitous yet appropriate to the hermeneutical character of action. On the one hand, it shows that revelation is God's means of making sure that the values of God's heart will be operative on earth and will eventually be constitutive of eschatological reality, through however risky a route in the interim.[34] On the other hand, it shows that Faith's responsibility for the realization of God's project is confirmed in revelation precisely so that human freedom might participate in the shared realization of a lasting—and secularly liberative—friendship with God. What mediates the reality of this friendship is the realization of truth through a *praxis* of Faiths and ideologies that is liberative of the deprived; and what mediates the good news that such truth may also be named as coming in grace from the heart of God is nothing other than revelation.

Such a notion of revelation, centered on the eschatological success of grace as a project, shows that God achieves the end of grace—conjoint creation of a world that is good in a loving relationship of friendship and equality with creatures—by recognizing the ontologically constructive creative power of creatures' freedom, a freedom that surfaces in the hermeneutical *praxis* of neighborly love as the truth-making capacity of the sensitive heart. As has been seen, God does this by a bold and yet meek love that is patient of creatures' action.[35] In the course of revelation, God communicates this love gradually and gratuitously as a call to participate in a creative project that is operative from the beginning as something compatible with action's essential structure. As was pointed out in chapter one, eschatological creation of a world that is good is the objective of the impassioned love that is grace. In the context of that objective, God's invitation makes the fundamental human *charism*—Faith— a constitutively hermeneutical task. It is up to human social persons and their freedoms to interpret, and definitively to decide and accomplish, what the outcome of God's values ought (and in the end is going) to be at the level of ideologies.

What the eschaton is going to look like in the end, in "heaven," depends in causal fashion on what human social persons, through the hermeneutical *praxis* of Faith and ideologies, deem fitting and appropriate for the realization of truth on earth. And revelation confirms that such realization is synonymous with what God considers to be the knowing and doing of truth in heaven. Revelation insures the definitively liberative outcome of God's friendship with creatures in the creative project that is grace, but insofar as God's love is patient, God leaves it up to human freedom, the accomplishments of Faith and ideologies, to determine in detail what the dimensions and contours of the realization of the project will turn out to be in the end.[36]

Taken together, these points confirm Segundo's hypothesis that the nature of revelation is functional. They show that God's revelation is made in order to facilitate eschatological realization of God's creative project. Revelation furnishes a sure and gratuitous word from heaven about which values—but not which ideological expressions of them—God wants human social persons to mediate in the work of Faith on earth. For this reason, revelation for Segundo has a secular rather than a religious relevance.[37] In other words, Jesus' good news about God is communicated for earthly and not heavenly reasons, in order that vis-à-vis the sufferings of the deprived and the efforts of persons and groups of sensitive heart to solve the problems of the world, disciples might learn to convey a sure word from God that no love on earth is ever lost.[38] It is for the eschatological validation of self-transcending love, and not to give disciples privileged access to a sacred realm or quasi-magical religious efficacy otherwise out of reach of human capabilities, that God makes known the values of God's heart.

So far as Segundo is concerned—and I think he shows it to be both theologically and anthropologically sound—we human social persons do not need revelation to find an eschatological dimension in human freedom. That dimension is already present in freedom in the *praxis* of truth. It appears in Faith's tendency to learn a hermeneutical *praxis* of sensitivity of heart. Human beings need revelation in order to hear a word of good news from God that God cares "in heaven" about the same problems of suffering and evil, creativity and love, that people of sensitive heart care about on earth. They need it to know that God will give eschatologically enduring value to liberative *praxes* of self-transcending love, that in the eyes of God there is a "rightness," a trustworthiness or groundedness to action's own truth criterion according to which the sensitive heart can critique the interests of Faith and around which it can organize the content of ideologies and *praxes*. As the next section will attempt to show, in the working of revelation God provides a reliable witness—Jesus' kingdom faith and its *praxes*—by which, with trustworthy certainty, disciples can "hear" the good news that the values of the sensitive heart responding to the needs of the deprived are identical with values that are God's.

As will be pointed out in the final section of this chapter, Segundo's approach allows him to envision the relation between God's values and human action in anthropologically meaningful terms. It gives him grounds for saying that human freedom can know God's values only by acting to make them efficacious, which is to say that knowledge of God through revelation is actually dependent on the attempt to incarnate God's values by means of ideologies that effect liberation of the deprived, or the making of truth, in Faith. So essential is this to Segundo's perspective, that it explains why the risen Jesus of the gospel stories is able to be recognized and apprehended in faith only by those who hold dear the same values that Jesus did.[39] For Segundo, the problem of revelation can be adequately solved only at the level of *praxis*. It is optimally resolved by understanding revelation as a communion of values between the divine and human freedoms.

Concerning that last point, Segundo seems to be addressing revelation on a level at which cognition gives way to love and epistemology turns into anthropology. Insofar as knowledge of God becomes a matter of values and action, it is something in which creatures can participate. It refers to an interest that is meaningful and constructive on earth but which is also compatible with values held dear by God in heaven. The crucial reason for introducing the notion of heaven is that in theological discourse, heaven is not a spatial metaphor but a circumlocution for the transcendent power of love.[40] Revelation points out that whatever is done to neighbors on earth is being done to God in heaven (Mt. 25: 31-46); the transcendent referent of every action is nothing other than the value in God's eyes of the relative situation of the neighbor, wherein one continually approaches needs and requirements of crucial import to both the neighbor and God. This is the case not because God is somehow "present in" the neighbor in a quasi-substantive, mysterious way, but because over the course of repeated actions and manifest options in history, God has taken the suffering neighbor's part. God whose eschatological goal is to wipe away the tears from every eye has revealed Godself to be God who is on the side of the oppressed, God who is on the side of the deprived and needy, God who is on the side of the poor, God who is on the side of the neighbor whose capacity to participate in the eschatological project initiated by God in grace has been damaged or destroyed, the neighbor who has been stripped of goods such as freedom. dignity, hope, joy—goods that belonged to the neighbor properly from the beginning.

At this level, the realization of God's values can become an essential element of the hermeneutical structure of action, of which knowledge as a *praxis* of truth is part. In the anthropological context of action, truth ceases being a question of coordinating knowledge of two different levels of being—one eschatological, divine and of absolute value and the other historical, human and of relative value—and begins being a question of *praxis,* i.e., incarnating God's Jesus-revealed values in ideologies that are creative of something substantial and effective on earth— something ontologically real, altogether lasting and new vis-à-vis the needs of the deprived.

For Segundo, this means that the nature of revelation can be adequately described only when two apparent contradictions are affirmed: first, the absolute is accessible only in and through the relative, and second, the value of the relative is precisely that it *bears* the absolute, makes it flesh and empowers it to dwell in the *praxis* of creatures, to become incarnate in historically particular, ecologically discernible forms. Transcendence can be effective on earth only by allowing itself to be incorporated into the relative constructions of history and nature. "Where, then, is transcendence?" Segundo writes. "It passes through history, where the love of neighbor, made real, is *already* initiated transcendence."[41] Thus any criterion supplied by God in revelation cannot be purely transcendent. It must be hermeneutically perceivable, in other words, fully and thoroughly relative. Efficacy that is transcendent can occur in no other way than in relative efficacies belonging to ideologies on earth.

As was observed in section one, Segundo argues that in order to attain such efficacy it is necessary for disciples to discipline themselves—to be awake about the consequences of their *praxes* so as to be prepared to read the signs of the times in ways that can lead to the kinds of neighborly responses—ideologies of self-transcending love—appropriate to a Faith that, with or without the data of revelation, is creative of truth vis-à-vis both the needs of the deprived on earth and the values of God's heart in heaven.

Derivation of God's Revealed Truth Criterion from the Kingdom *Praxis* of Jesus

As has just been seen, from the point of view of a Jesus-normed theology, any criterion for knowing God's will must be shown to proceed in equally valid fashion from the logic of human action and the data of revelation. The rationale underlying these requirements was considered in the previous sections. Here it is necessary to look at the hermeneutical connection between revelation and action: the significance of Jesus' action for the action of disciples and, ultimately, for the action of others via the faiths and ideologies of disciples. This is a question of articulating the link between the realization of truth through hermeneutical *praxis* on the one hand, and confirmation of that truth in disciples' experience of God's having raised Jesus from the dead on the other.[42] For Segundo, the condition for disciples' actually making such a connection is the original historical content of Jesus' kingdom *praxis*, through which knowledge of God is available definitively but not exclusively. As definitive mediation of God's will in history, Jesus' *praxis* is normative of revelation but not the sole constituent of grace.

The theological reason for deriving the truth criterion of God's will specifically from Jesus' kingdom *praxis* centers on the inseparability of Jesus' *praxis* from the significance of the resurrection. In disciples' experience there is a link—grounded in the causality of Jesus' *praxis*—between what God has effected in Jesus' person by raising him from the dead, namely divine validation of his kingdom *praxes*, and definitive revelation of the values of God's heart. In other words, in light of God's having raised Jesus from the dead, Jesus' kingdom *praxes* were and still may be regarded as definitively reliable evidence concerning the values of God's heart.[43] This means that for Segundo, the historical particularity of Jesus' ideological

responses to problems of his time, his ways of making the values of his kingdom faith
operative and real—i.e., efficacious for liberation of "sinners" and the poor—these
historically relative *praxes* are capable of mediating in a definitive way the transcendent content of God's love for creatures in grace, the actual values of God's heart.

Yet a distinction must be made between the mediation of God's values that
took place during Jesus' life and ministry and the mediation of them that takes place
subsequently in history after Jesus' ascension and the sending of the Spirit. Although
both mediations are historical and both pertain to the realization of God's world-
creative project in grace, the first was a mediation of salvation-grace while the second
is a mediation of grace *qua* revelation. The mediation of salvation-grace was made
once for all, while the mediation of revelation—which takes place within the context
of grace—is ongoing and historically flexible. How do the two mediations differ?
The answer lies in the historical situation of disciples vis-à-vis the *praxis* of Jesus,
the location they have in history with respect to his life and work.

It makes a difference, in other words, whether one is looking at Jesus' *praxis*
from inside the immediate experience of his life and ministry (which includes the
violent death on the cross and his being raised from the dead) or from outside that
experience, from a perspective of historical distance punctuated by the additional data
of the ascension and sending of the Spirit. Living during the period of Jesus' life and
ministry, i.e., in the direct and immediate presence of Jesus' words and deeds,
"sinners" and the poor and people whom Jesus healed and set free—as well as those
who were disciples—were capable of experiencing in a direct and immediate way the
salvation-grace that Jesus proclaimed. They were able to experience the liberative
"at-handness" of God's kingdom that Jesus boldly called *salvation.*

Living in a period of history that post dates the ascension, however, disciples
become capable in Spirit of interpreting those salvation-mediating deeds and words
of Jesus that constitute his *praxis.* Such disciples live at a hermeneutical distance
between themselves and Jesus which, thanks to the work of Spirit who is to lead them
into truth, permits their being able to unlock the significance of Jesus' life and action
as a whole. Vis-à-vis the earthly task of building God's values, the distance between
disciples' own historical situation and that of Jesus creates the hermeneutical
conditions necessary to appreciate, and actively lay hold of, the revelatory function
of Jesus' *praxes,* their power to communicate a knowledge that at the same time ought
also to be a *praxis* of God's values in grace. A closer look at this important distinction
(which is not a separation) will help to clarify its significance for the rest of this
chapter.

As was seen in the introductory chapter, during his earthly ministry Jesus
mediated God's eschatologically effective salvation-grace to persons of his time to
whom his words and deeds brought gratuitous liberation from actual deprivations and
ills. After Jesus' resurrection and ascension, however, his disciples came to
understand those same *praxes* in a new and recapitulatory light as also capable of

mediating a definitively liberative revelation-content about the values of God's heart. In that light, which is the light of Spirit and of truth, they came to understand that if they want to know what *God* thinks salvation is about, they need to look at Jesus and his *praxis*. With respect to God's values, the *praxis* of Jesus constitutes a definitive revelation. It is the latter—Jesus' mediation of revelation—that this chapter is about, for the concept of revelation addresses the problem of how a historically relative kingdom *praxis* can be understood to have normative value for disciples' Faith and ideologies in every time and place.[44]

For Segundo, what is historically relative and particular about Jesus is significant not because it acts as a kind of "instrumental cause" of God's saving will in grace—a view traditionally put forth by neoscholastic theologies of a sacramental bent—but because it is capable of mediating revelation of God's values in a definitive and efficacious way.[45] An important difference between these views is that where traditional theologies stress the transcendent character of God's action by means of Jesus' work, leaving the contents of his kingdom *praxis* in a relative and secondary place, Segundo grants to those contents a normative, definitive status.

Segundo argues that the communication of God's will in grace is not an exclusively transcendent accomplishment, a work of God alone, effected through Jesus as by an obedient instrument; rather, the transcendent power of God's love depends for its efficacy on the original, historically relative and previously non-existent content provided by Jesus' humanly created kingdom *praxes*, ineffective as they might have appeared to Jesus and his peers from the point of view of his having ended up betrayed, condemned and abandoned before the judgment seat of Pilate (and, seemingly, also of God). For Segundo, in other words, there is a causal connection between Jesus' ideologies and the eschatological realization of God's love.[46]

Although Segundo does not spell out the christological implications of such a view, the notion of causality makes it possible to draw two important conclusions about the significance of Jesus' *praxis* and its relation to his having been raised from the dead. A first is that God's raising of Jesus from the dead was a gratuitous eschatological response to the ideologies that Jesus had created by his single-hearted Faith in God's kingdom. Although from the point of view of Jesus' premature and violent death, his *praxis* was apparently a failure—in other words, although what showed up on the cross was the victorious "hour" of Sin and the triumph of the forces of evil, from the point of view of the realization of God's project, Jesus' *praxis* turned out to be of incomparable worth and value. The resurrection of Jesus is God's testimony that Jesus succeeded in an original and creative way in doing God's will on earth as it is in heaven—i.e., making God's values operative in history and nature and permitting God's love to be made efficacious and real.

In other words, God's raising of Jesus from the dead was not an arbitrary act extrinsic to Jesus' life and work but a direct response to Jesus' action, a validation of the eschatologically creative efficacy of that action as a *praxis* of God's values on earth. In this sense, God's raising of Jesus was an announcement of good news in which God was moved to proclaim the truth of what Jesus' work had steadfastly accomplished. Yet if all of that is true, a second conclusion that may be drawn is that vis-à-vis successful eschatological realization of God's project, Jesus is neither principle of salvation nor conduit of grace (actually, these "roles" are more pertinent to the action of God's free and creative Spirit) but rather bearer of historical revelation, angel of God, prophet of the good news of God's liberative values, witness or *martyrion* to truth.[47]

In light of these conclusions, Segundo's approach has the paradoxical but theologically advantageous effect of distinguishing grace from revelation at the same time that it points out the link—Jesus kingdom *praxis*--that binds the two together. While, thanks to the hermeneutical character of action, every human being of good will lives existentially in the gratuitous context of grace and has access to the truth criterion of self-transcending love, not all human beings of good will can or do accept the *praxis* of Jesus as normative for their anthropological faiths; only those who are disciples of Jesus do, and these constitute only a small minority of the vast number of human and other beings living, dead and still to be born. The conclusion can only be that while grace is essential to the appropriation of salvation, revelation is not. And that is exactly what Segundo says.[48] More important, however, is what Segundo goes on to say after making this initial—and, for many theologians today, more or less commonplace—distinction. He claims that grace does not exist for the sake of revelation; revelation exists for the sake of the eschatological realization of grace.

Grace is at work in the world from the beginning, but the reason for its having been given is not so that sooner or later (all) human beings will come to accept God's revelation; in other words, vis-à-vis creatures, grace is not God's way of "exacting what is due." Rather, God gives revelation in the course of initiating a world-creative project in grace. God reveals God's values over the course of a long, shared history of working with creatures to create a world that is good, and God does this in order that the working of grace might achieve on earth the eschatological end within the context of which God has loved us from the start, namely the victory of Faith over the forces of evil and breakdown in a universe subjected to the seeming futility of Sin and death.[49] Even if a great many human beings—indeed, perhaps the greater majority of them—achieve this victory in utter absence of any reference to God, that is all right with God. God's will is not that God be recognized as God but that the suffering of the deprived be overcome. And this can be accomplished on earth only by the work of Faith, the courage to fashion constructive ideologies of self-transcending love, normed by the needs of the deprived. In a universe subjected to the apparent futility of Sin and susceptible to the injuriousness of dia-bolical (anti-ontological) sin, human beings can and do make themselves, like Jesus and God whom he revealed, neighbor to the deprived.

Yet the patient logic of God's love suggests that grace achieves this end not all at once but in a way appropriate to the gradually maturing character of the creatures (and their freedoms) to whom the invitation to participate in God's project has been offered. We human social persons cannot appropriate what Paul calls "the glorious freedom of the children of God" all at once; on the contrary, we must "take our time" and practice the hermeneutical art—painful, slow and arduous, but with its gratuitous moments of accomplishment—of learning by experience a *praxis* of the liberation of freedom in Faith.

In other words, the logic of Segundo's schema requires that revelation be given an educational function vis-à-vis the realization of God's project. In fact, Segundo argues, learning to learn what is true about God, namely, that God wills the liberation of the deprived from evil and that God equates the self-transcending love by which that liberation is achieved with the liberation of one's own freedom in Faith—this sums up revelation's entire point. Revelation is given in order to facilitate the earthly appropriation of something "heavenly" and transcendent, the doing of God's will in grace, and the latter consists in Faith's learning to create liberative ideologies on behalf of the deprived, which is a knowing and doing on earth of a truth that is willed in heaven.

Segundo proposes that such knowing and doing, which is actually a lived and living tendency inherent in Faith to arrive at the embodiment of truth in ideologies, can be achieved only through an appropriation of Jesus' *praxes* that is genuinely hermeneutical. The latter consists not merely in reflection on Jesus' *praxes* but in creative translation of their underlying values into entirely new ideologies, types of action constructive of the values of God and appropriate to the needs of the deprived. When Jesus' *praxes* are appropriated in this way, anthropological faith is capable of mediating a practical "fit" between the values of God and the truth criterion of human action. Such mediation is not only constructive of truth (which all Faith is from the beginning, with or without the revelation supplied by Jesus) but susceptible of being named by disciples, and being witnessed through ideologies, as a Faith that knows— and is a *praxis* of—the will of God.

What Segundo is saying is that theologically inconsistent—and socially divisive—ambiguities surrounding the meaning of the word *God* (and, ultimately, knowledge of God's true identity) can be removed only by filling in a generic concept like *God's will* with the clarifying contents of God's ways of acting in history and nature. And the latter are nowhere more clearly visible than in Jesus' action, those historically mediated concretions or "Jesus-specific" interpretations of the values of God's heart. For Segundo, the liberative efficacy of Jesus' kingdom faith is available only hermeneutically, through continual reinterpretation of the original "key" of his kingdom *praxis* according to requirements of ever-changing contexts created by the application of new interpretive keys sensitive to the needs of the deprived and proper to the signs of the times. There is no such thing as a "one-size-fits-all" hermeneutical key but only a constant need to shoulder the ever-changing requirements of an ongoing hermeneutical task.[50]

Segundo begins the task of interpreting Jesus' significance with an attempt to capture historical data about (the pre-paschal) Jesus available from the synoptic gospels. There, Segundo focuses on what was most unique about Jesus, namely his Faith, a phenomenon centered on the announcement of the coming of God's kingdom and key to everything that can be known with some degree of historical reliability about Jesus. From Segundo's point of view, the preferences of God (the values of God's heart) are accessible in Jesus' kingdom faith insofar as "the major theme of Jesus' message concerns the hermeneutical key to interpreting God. According to Jesus, that key entails attending to the human being and placing oneself in the service of humanity's full and complete humanization."[51] As was pointed out in chapter one, Segundo attempts to show that taking the "key" of Jesus seriously means admitting at the outset that the essential point about Jesus' kingdom faith is God's "bold preference for those who are suffering" and "God's joy. . .in rescuing sinners and the poor from the misfortune and marginalization in which they find themselves and in restoring their humanity to them."[52]

Segundo's reading of the synoptic data leads to the conclusion that Jesus' kingdom faith expressed itself in *praxes*—what Segundo calls ideologies—that were essentially conflictual.[53] These were motivated by Jesus' faith that what he called the kingdom of God was "at hand." In Jesus' politically volatile kingdom language, his provocative integration of the marginalized into the mainstream of social activity, his upsetting use of parables, his healing powers and miracles, his sermon on the mount or plain (the preaching of the "beatitudes"), his scandalous friendships, his table companionship with "sinners," his proclamation of the good news of God's kingdom free of prerequisites to the poor and granting of God's jubilee-favor to them *gratis*, his reputation as a glutton and a drunkard, his having been regarded by his family as out of his mind and by authorities and other groups as a political agitator or threat, his outrageous theological method concerning the priority of human needs over religious instruments like the sabbath and the law, his awareness of the increasing conflict surrounding his message and action, and his having been put to a violent death on religio-political charges—in all of these concrete data, Segundo argues, Jesus reveals the news of God whose kingdom is at hand, and reveals as well definitively significant content for a liberative rather than enslaving theological concept—and experience—of God.

What seems to Segundo to stand out most clearly about the conflict surrounding the announcement of the kingdom is Jesus' polemic against using God for religiously self-serving purposes. In the values-reversals set up by the beatitudes and parables, Segundo believes, Jesus reveals that "God is not just a compassionate God committed to those who suffer. . . .God is obliged to fight against the ideology that uses religious law as a tool of [human] oppression."[54] In other words, not only is God against suffering and deprivation because they are dehumanizing in themselves, but God is also against the ideological mechanisms of injustice that make—and keep—human beings subject to deprivation and oppression, particularly when some human beings wittingly or unwittingly subscribe to such mechanisms at the expense of others in the alleged name of religion or of "God."

Like Jesus' proclamation of a "year of favor from the Lord" (Lk. 4: 19), the beatitudes invert accepted religious and moral categories and sum up the scandalous datum that, according to Jesus, God offers the kingdom without moral, spiritual or religious prerequisites as good news to the poor—i.e., those who according to "dogmas" held by at least some of the religious establishment were considered irreligious rabble or "sinners."[55] Thus the beatitudes not only challenge accepted religious prejudices about what God really values; they also state that the kingdom of God is coming to invert actual situations of injustice: those who weep now will laugh; those who are hungry will have their fill. This is the greatest scandal of all, Segundo believes, for just as surely it means that, "those who have their fill now will end up hungry, because the advantage of the rich will end with the arrival of the kingdom."[56]

Ultimately, the impact of the beatitudes is that they create a profound *theological* scandal. Because they define what the nearness of the kingdom of God actually means, they bring to a head an underlying conflict about what God's closeness to the poor involves.[57] Segundo locates the cause of the scandal in the change of situation God wills by flagrantly giving the kingdom to people who are poor: the kingdom is coming because God cannot tolerate the inhuman situation of the poor. The cause of the scandal is not just that Jesus loves the poor—that could be dismissed as human idiosyncracy; rather, the scandal is caused by the fact that *God* hates the inhuman situation imposed on people who are poor. It is *God's* will that "poverty. . .cease to wreak destructive havoc on humanity":

> The poor possess the kingdom of God. . .not due to any merit of theirs, much less to any value that poverty might have. On the contrary, the kingdom is theirs because of the inhuman nature of their situation as poor people. *The kingdom is coming because God is "humane," because God cannot tolerate that situation and is coming to make sure that the divine will be done on earth.*[58]

Even more conflictual in Segundo's judgment are Jesus' parables. On the one hand they represent "a revelation and defense of the God who has chosen sinners and the poor as the preferred recipients of the kingdom," and as such, they are "specifically designed to combat the causes, real or alleged, conscious or unconscious, for rejecting the kingdom."[59] On the other hand, they represent "Jesus' attack on the ideological mechanism that turned. . .religion. . .into an instrument of oppression."[60]

For this reason, Segundo argues that the parables "were not meant to convince and convert the opponents of the kingdom. Their purpose was to point up *the wide chasm between two different, opposed value-worlds structured by equally opposed and irreconcilable premises* of both an ontological and epistemological nature."[61] The significance of the parables is that they "present a liberating conception of divine revelation (with its ontological and epistemological criteria) as opposed to a different conception of divine revelation that breeds and justifies oppression."[62]

What distinguishes Jesus' liberating conception of revelation from that to which the parables object? Segundo answers this question by concentrating on what he calls the "theological method" of Jesus.[63] This centers on how to derive the truth criterion for judging whether any given instance of liberation proceeds from God or has its source in evil. According to Segundo's reading of both the parables and Jesus' discussions with educated peers, use of criteria that are utterly down-to-earth—spontaneous response to the needs of the deprived and sensitive comprehension of the signs of the times—rather than reliance on historically extrinsic "signs from heaven" is what distinguishes the theological method of Jesus from that of religious experts and theologians of the established order.[64] Where the professionals who are Jesus' peers keep insisting on a need to begin theological interpretation with deductions and certitudes from above—signs from heaven—Jesus boldly declares that any and every earthly liberation, any and every release from deprivation, oppression or sin constitutes salvation from God in a strict and eschatological sense here and now. In the words of Segundo, Jesus "discounts totally any theological criterion applied to history which is not the direct and present evaluation of the event."[65]

In a particularly fruitful way, Segundo focuses on Jesus' scandalous practice of calling concrete liberations of the deprived "salvation" and identifying the results of those liberations with God's eschatological will, regardless of the historically visible, apparent source. Describing what he considers to be a major characteristic of Jesus' theology, Segundo argues that vis-à-vis concrete liberations such as healings and social transformations, Jesus' response to questioners shows that "*it does not matter at all who liberates [the human being] if [the human being] is really liberated.* . . . Directly or indirectly, in the liberation of [the human being] . . .God is always at work."[66] In fact, Segundo observes, so radically does Jesus invert established procedures for discerning the liberative action of God on earth that some would say that Jesus "absolutizes imprudently": he "calls the specific instances of liberation which he effects. . .the most absolute name in the theology of the time: salvation."[67]

Segundo takes Jesus' theological method as a model for any theology that hopes to be both liberating and liberative vis-à-vis the alleviation of deprivation and the solution of secular problems. Jesus' refusal to pull down pronouncements from heaven makes theology the second step of a risky interpretive procedure in which sensitivity of heart to the concrete needs of the deprived is first:

Jesus, unexpectedly, denies the possibility of starting from the theological level, from the level of certainties and of deductions from revelation. . . .Jesus points to a level where precisely a person has no other criteria than his or her own heart: *doing good or evil.* Theology only follows. The knowledge of God and of [God's] revelation is possible only *after,* not *before* this option.[68]

So central is this inversion of theological method to Jesus' revelation of God that in Segundo's eyes it becomes the criterion of "an obligatory hermeneutic circle" which requires that "before human beings resort to God to find a sure criterion of the divine presence in history . . .they should first develop their own sensitivity and judgment regarding the human being and its needs."[69] In fact, Segundo argues, so urgent is the demand of this practical hermeneutical requirement, that evasion of it constitutes the only unforgivable sin, "the sin of making God an accomplice in, and reason for, the oppression of the human being."[70]

About the nature of this sin, Segundo is very clear. It is a theological refusal to recognize the absolute in the relative, a failure to see God at work in the ideologies and causalities that liberate the deprived from actual evils and ills:

> The unpardonable sin is not to recognize as liberation what truly is liberation and to use theology in order to render the liberation of a [human being] something odious.   The sin against the Spirit is not to recognize with "theological" joy a concrete liberation happening before one's eyes.[71]

Segundo believes that this sin epitomizes opposition to the kingdom precisely because it consists in an" *inability to gauge correctly and fully between the absolute and the relative,* an ability which is the *proper mark of human existence.*"[72] In other words, the failure to recognize that the liberation of the deprived is a liberation willed by God is a failure to function in history and nature in a properly human way.

The overall impact of Jesus' message and action thus consists for Segundo in the conclusion that "whenever and wherever a human being is freed from some obstacle to the attainment of its full humanity, God comes out the winner."[73] And this is true however "socially unacceptable," according to established canons for interpreting God's will, the earthly agency seems to be through which such liberations come about—even if they seem to be coming from Satan.[74] In other words, the ability to recognize concrete instances of liberation—seeing the signs of the times that are in front of one's eyes rather than bypassing history and nature to search with what might be called "unearthly" eyes for infallible signs from heaven—must be the criterion for interpreting the will of God.   And this is the case no matter how scandalous, from a theological point of view, appears God's gracious will and no matter how inappropriate seems God's undue generosity in wanting to incorporate what Segundo calls "the dense fabric of historical causality" into the eschatological efficacy of grace.[75] According to the logic of that causality, human beings can know

God and do God's will "only when we sense profoundly what goes well or what goes badly in the life of men and women and *make of that our principal criterion.*"[76]

Segundo admits, of course, that the signs of the times are always limited and partial. No earthly liberation is going to be capable once and for all of effecting the kingdom of God on earth because intramundane causality is never absolute. In connection with the dangers this poses for theological interpretation of God's will, Segundo observes: "It will be remembered that, to the eschatological question of the disciples of the Baptist about 'he who is to come', Jesus replies with signs that are *historical, relative, extremely ambiguous, at a vast distance from the absolute and definitive.*"[77] Clearly there is great risk entailed when the sensitive heart must rely for its knowledge of the transcendent on the ambiguous—and fragmentary—signs of the times. Yet it is a risk that Jesus himself never failed to take, for he did not demand of those whose illnesses he cured that they ought never to get sick again; he never said to those whose sins he pronounced forgiven that, should they sin again, God's forgiveness would be revoked.

On the contrary, Jesus practiced a theological boldness in mediating salvation from God. Segundo believes that any effort to appropriate Jesus' values with equivalent confidence requires a similar reliance on the hermeneutical sensibility of the sensitive, open heart, even when it is a question—as it inevitably is—of having to make theological interpretations in the face of historical and ecological ambiguities that are all the more complex and dangerous because they are inherently political:

> Christian theology will have to be based much more on *a sensitive appre-*
> *ciation of what liberates [human beings] here and now.* This is opposed to
> the type of [theological] science which hopes to foresee and exclude *now* all
> the errors and dangers of the future by means of an adequate model, or which
> claims to criticize and relativize every historical step forward which cannot
> guarantee these safeguards.[78]

What Segundo is saying is that, in order to be efficacious at achieving any sort of liberation under the conditions of relativity and entropy in history and nature, Faith needs an ideology. It must make concrete political options. Not only is that the only way to make the liberative impact of its values felt, but it is also necessary if Faith is to come up with the kinds of scientific analysis and theoretical grounding needed to guide liberative *praxis* along the difficult—and ambiguous—path toward the hermeneutical realization of truth.[79] There is no such thing as a revelation from God purified of political implications.

Segundo's analysis of the synoptic evidence about Jesus' Faith thus concludes that the conflictual side-effects of Jesus' announcement of the nearness of God's kingdom resulted from scandalous theological interpretations—concrete *theological ideologies*—surrounding actual liberations of "sinners" and the poor.

These not only placed God on the side of the oppressed but shifted the locus of theological revelation in such a way that according to Jesus, access to the transcendent can be had only in the midst of the relative conditions of history and nature on earth. If those who were supposed to be regarded as "sinners" were being invited to sit down at table in the kingdom of God and those who were ordinarily considered "righteous" were being proclaimed sinners, it was because Jesus' *praxis* about how to recognize God's action and interpret God's will was charged with a passion that was human and historically conditioned. In other words, it was because Jesus' kingdom *praxis* had its roots in an impassioned faith-premise about God's own heart and values, and the impact of that passion (and of the experience which grounded it) was to invert established theological prejudices about relations between God and human beings, God and creatures, the absolute and the relative. Assessing the cumulative effect of Jesus' Faith—what Segundo calls "learning to learn" how to interpret the overall meaning and import of Jesus' ideologies—thus leads to the scandalous theological conclusion that not only the synoptic interpretations but Jesus' own choice of ideology, his use of the conflictual religious symbol *kingdom of God,* makes it necessary to interpret Jesus' life and mission primarily (although not exclusively) in what Segundo calls a "political key."[80]

So far as Segundo is concerned, the *praxes* of Jesus were conflictual because the three key terms of his message were intrinsically political: kingdom, poor, and good news.[81] As Segundo frequently repeats, to admit this is not to deny the obviously religious relevance of Jesus' message and action. Neither is it to insist that the political key is the only key by which to interpret the significance of Jesus' life.[82] Rather, it is to point out that, like all symbols used to express the content of religious faith, Jesus' choice of the notion *kingdom of God* carried consequences pertaining directly to people's ways of living together in this world. The kingdom of God preached by Jesus had a bearing on the interests and situations of people in his time and continues to have a bearing on what we recognize today as the sociopolitical structures and ecological relationships that form the basis of the present world-order.[83]

Segundo makes it clear that the political relevance of Jesus' preaching results from the fact that he did not simply announce the "at-handness" of the kingdom of God but actually began to set in motion an efficacious causality directed toward its realization:

> The preaching of Jesus is more than a mere *announcement*. . . .It also is the setting in motion of mechanisms that will be *constitutive* of the actual reign of God.[84]

That does not mean, however, that Jesus attempted to "force the issue" by provoking an apocalyptic showdown.[85] On the contrary, and unlike John the Baptist, Jesus intended that the news of the nearness of God's kingdom be greeted with feasting and joy.[86] Yet Jesus also taught that realization of the kingdom's values would be a hidden work, like the growth of a seed that goes into the ground and dies and only later, in an entirely different—in this case eschatological—season, springs up and bears much fruit:

> The kingdom of God is *already* present and at work *without drawing attention to itself.* The impossibility of seeing it now. . . is due to the *complex and in-depth* nature of the way it is operating.[87]

The coming of the kingdom -its intramundane logic and the hiddenness of its operation—thus depends for its efficacy not on the simplistic immediacy of an apocalypse but on what Segundo calls "the dense fabric of historical causality."[88] Realization of the kingdom's values must follow the long route of ecological density and patient action. These can arrive at eschatological completion only by way of achievements that, at the time they are taking place, remain largely unrecognizable, appear more or less ineffective, seem perhaps even utterly to have failed, and yet finally—and gratuitously—become recognizable, turning out in the end to have been achievements everlastingly efficacious and real.

What Segundo means by historical causality is that according to Jesus, human action has eschatologically creative power. Human beings are to have a hand—however large or small—in bringing the kingdom to definitive realization:

> There is a causal connection, however small and secondary, between the establishment of the kingdom and human activity directed toward it. . . .It is *from within* historical causality that human beings collaborate with the kingdom.[89]

The coming of the kingdom will not be a work of God alone, but the work of human beings and God together, the result of a "fundamental coherence of values" between them,[90] the product of a "conscious convergence between the efforts of human beings and the efforts of God" in such a way that problems like deprivation and injustice are shouldered and "all have their principal human needs solved."[91] As has been seen, so essential is the meeting of human needs to God's will about the coming of the kingdom that for Jesus, "perceived human needs. . .become the key to interpreting what revelation is trying to say."[92]

Segundo argues that concerning this crucial point, Jesus understood that the coming of the kingdom neither would nor could be received as good news by everybody. In announcing the nearness of the kingdom specifically to the poor, Segundo believes, "Jesus is doing *something more* than proclaiming a future event. He is *generating an historical conflict.*"[93] By setting in motion values constitutive of the kingdom, Jesus was not making the coming of the kingdom a *fait accompli,* but he was bringing out into the open an already-existing—and to that extent unavoidable—conflict.

Segundo argues that the announcement of the kingdom's nearness was good news for the poor because they were its gratuitous objects.[94] The kingdom was to be given to them without prerequisites not because they were worthy of it, not because they were good, not because God has a mysterious—and romantic—love of "poverty," but simply because they were poor. And the reason Jesus' *praxis* seems to supply for God's scandalous option is that the poor are victims of an injustice and deprivation that are all the more despicable to God to the extent that the sufferings thus caused can be shown to result from structural injustices and ideologies of oppression perpetrated in the alleged name of "God." Insofar as Jesus unmasks the phony values at work within already existing ideological mechanisms of injustice, his *praxis* makes clear a central tenet of his kingdom faith in God: "God's criterion and maximum value...is concern and compassion for the human being... particularly for those who are suffering."[95]

For those who upheld values like the ones Jesus critiqued, the nearness of the kingdom thus constituted not good news but bad: it precipitated a crisis of epistemological and ontological premises about how to interpret the salvation willed by God. The news of the kingdom's nearness to "sinners"—and its consequent farness from the self-proclaimed "righteous"—was either heard as a call to conversion and repentence, a call to radical realignment of the religious ideologies of anthropological faith with values of God revealed in Jesus' preaching and *praxis,* or else rejected as an insuperable scandal.[96] For those—disciples—who wanted to accept the invitation to participate in the kingdom project that Jesus himself had begun, the nearness of the kingdom became an urgent call to prophetic participation in bringing its values about. This meant shouldering the hazardous discipline of keeping awake, remaining alert to the kingdom's "secrets," working along with Jesus in the face of opposition to set in motion precisely the sort of gratuitous love and liberative *praxis* that would be capable of making the values of God as tangible a reality on earth as they are in heaven.[97]

Jesus' praxis thus had the disconcerting effect of making visible three distinct existential situations vis-à-vis the announcement of the kingdom at the time of Jesus' preaching—although, according to Segundo's logic, those same situations do not necessarily pertain to people in our own time and place. The three possibilities were: rejection of the good news as scandal, acceptance of it as a call to shoulder the yoke of discipleship, or, if one were a "sinner" (i.e., an outcast or one of the poor) joyful reception of the news of God's kingdom as an amazing favor, free of charge.[98]

Not surprisingly, the consequences of such a forthright political reading of Jesus' kingdom faith and *praxis* are especially important vis-à-vis the functional conception of revelation at issue in this chapter.[99] Segundo's reading of the significance of Jesus' life and *praxis* shows that what is historically particular about Jesus—

his ideologies—makes a hermeneutical demand on disciples, and this demand can be met not by disciples' attempting to copy Jesus' ideologies *per se* but by a creative effort to translate them into appropriate ideologies of their own:

> The means which Jesus used to reveal the Father to us in and through the concrete proximity of God's kingdom bear the stamp of history and its irreversibility. . . .In short, *they bear the stamp of any and every ideology.* . . .By the same token, to the extent that Jesus sinks his teeth into our history, in that way he acquires a past and a future. He is bound up with a tradition, and he obligates us to make *a creative effort* whenever we want to speak of him, or be faithful to him, in a new context.[100]

Yet because Segundo argues that "God can only be revealed in connection with values that are humanly meaningful,"[101] and because, as has been seen, Jesus steadfastly refused to give "signs from heaven" as extra-mundane credentials for his liberative *praxis*, it is clear that the "creative effort" involved in disciples' hermeneutical Faith-appropriation of Jesus' ideologies is conditioned by values already held dear by those to whom God's revelation is addressed:

> Heaven is mute for those who do not *already possess a criterion* for recognizing its voice in the human events that have an effect on human beings. The presence of heaven on earth—that is, something historical as a *revelation of God*—can be recognized only by those who already have a prejudice as to what constitutes the good of the human being.[102]

In light of such a statement, and in face of Segundo's theological exegesis of Jesus' God-revealing kingdom *praxis,* the question that must be asked is: how can such a scandalous state of affairs be the case? In order to arrive at an answer, it is necessary to take a closer look at the liberative content of the criterion of God's values, a task inseparable from the deeper question of the hermeneutical and educational function of revelation vis-à-vis eschatological realization of what Jesus called God's kingdom project in grace. This will be done in the next section.

The Educative Content of the Truth Criterion of God's Love

The preceding discussion was aimed at pointing out that according to Segundo's reading of the synoptic authors, the truth criterion of God's will is utterly secular: it consists in the release of the marginalized and unjustly treated from dehumanizing mechanisms and suffering. Jesus' message and action show that the values of God's heart center on the liberation of the deprived.

One might well ask what happens, however, when the political key of the synoptic gospels is joined to the anthropological key of Paul in Romans, in other words, when the hermeneutical interpretation of a disciple—in this case Paul as interpreted by Segundo—turns the liberative content of salvation-grace into an educative content of revelation. Segundo's answer is that an interpretation of God's values emerges which permits the particularity of Jesus' liberative *praxes*, his politically tinged ideologies about the values of God's heart, to take on a universal significance, to become anthropologically meaningful in every day and age, not only to people who want to be disciples but to people who are suffering and deprived as well as those who are or want to be in solidarity with them, with or without reference to God.

How does such a universalizing of the significance of Jesus' life and ideologies come about? According to Segundo, it results from a hermeneutical transposition of interpretive keys, a task Paul carried out with particular originality and creativity. Segundo shows that Paul begins by giving an anthropological name— Sin—to mechanisms and determinisms that in the sphere of human action can be turned into the enslavement and injustice that are sin. These Paul places in creative tension with Faith, the capacity of human freedom, gratuitously liberated in the Spirit, to contribute in the face of Sin and sin an earthly work of self-transcending love that will be meaningful and constructive to both the neighbor and God. Making this move permits Paul to translate Jesus' historically relative kingdom *praxes* into universally meaningful anthropological categories of liberation and enslavement, categories which embody the God-like values of Jesus' *praxis* of neighborly love *qua* gratuitous liberation of "sinners" and the poor from concretely observable ills. In other words, Paul sees Jesus' kingdom *praxis* not only as salvific for the people Jesus healed and cured, but as revelatory of a hope of salvation for struggling people today. Insofar as Paul translates the values of Jesus' kingdom Faith into existentially meaningful terms, he makes Jesus' work of salvation into a source of revelation about the values of God's heart, a piece of news from God capable of being welcomed as good not only by the poor who were contemporaries of Jesus but by people of good will and sensitive heart who are struggling against evil today.[103] Yet the criterion of God's will must still be recognized as liberation of the deprived, even though its theological locus in Romans 1-8 has shifted to the anthropological level of a Faith-appropriation of what Paul calls the "freedom of the children of God."

One might say, in other words, that the point Paul was able to grasp about the significance of Jesus, the creative transposition he was able to effect about the salvation Jesus handed to the deprived free of charge, is that Jesus' giving of the kingdom to "sinners" and the poor was not meant to sacralize either the kingdom or the poor, and it is certainly not meant to sacralize Jesus. It is not even meant to sacralize salvation. Rather, precisely because it is a historically particular revelation, it is meant to be interpreted. It must continue to be handed on anew in every time and place as a piece of good news from God.

This means that after the life of Jesus had been completed as a fact, i.e., after the resurrection made it possible to comprehend Jesus' life-story as a whole, Jesus' message and action are capable of taking on a universal meaning vis-à-vis the cosmic struggle between good and evil; for in the anthropological categories furnished by Paul in Romans, that struggle is one and the same with both the historically particular struggle of Jesus against the powers which held the freedom of "sinners" and the poor in check and the universal anthropological struggle in which Faith must put itself to work in a universe of Sin for the sake of intramundane realizations of self-transcending love and the creation of a world that is good.

What emerges as most important about Segundo's interest in the kind of creative interpretation of Jesus' significance being made by Paul in Romans is that it inevitably involves the more basic question of the values and interests of God: it raises the question, fundamental to revelation, of what God was "up to" when God validated Jesus' decision to name God's project a "kingdom" and give it "free" to the poor. According to Segundo's reading, what Paul claims God was "up to" is a revelation of gratuitous love that manifests the creative value of human freedom as self-transcending, neighbor-conscious love. In other words, according to Paul, Jesus' life story—what Paul now calls the paschal mystery—shows once and for all that it is God's will, made manifest in Jesus' life-story as a whole, that freedom be liberated to participate in the eschatological realization of what Jesus called the values of God's reign.

According to what Jesus' kingdom *praxis* revealed about the values of God's heart, it is essential to God's own Faith, to which Jesus' *praxis* bears definitive witness, that the ideological constructions of truth created by human freedom on earth be gratuitously productive and eschatologically worthwhile in heaven, both for neighbors and for God. The reason for this is that, insofar as freedom rings true to its own anthropological criterion, it is working *qua* Faith to make creative responses of sensitive heart to the needs of the deprived. In other words, the work of Faith is capable of realizing an everlastingly valid love on earth, even in face of the seeming futility of Sin, but only if it is a work that remains faithful to what Jesus revealed about God. Segundo thus demonstrates that God's own "Faith-stance," the values God holds dear and regards as truth in heaven, are humanly intelligible in a universe of Sin only vis-à-vis an already existing, intrinsically valid human Faith and its criterion of truth on earth.

As was seen in chapters one and two, however, Segundo does not consider the liberation of freedom in the abstract. He views it in terms of a freedom from and a freedom for, a liberation of anthropological faith from preoccupation with its own justification, for the sake of creating of a world that is good. And for all practical purposes, this two-fold liberation is synonymous with the theological concept *grace.*[104] As something profoundly linked to the definitive outcome and lasting value of history and nature, the liberation of freedom is therefore utterly concrete. It is the liberation of anthropological faith for the work of Faith, the release of faith for efficacious ideologies of self-transcending love, creative *praxes* of truth.

As freedom from, the liberation of freedom refers to the historical actuality, activated on earth in the "circuit" of grace, that Faith can be efficacious in the creative integration of Sin and sin, the apparent reign of entropy and break-down in the universe as we know it. As was seen in chapter two, from the point of view of experience, the universe appears to be running down (even though, at the same time, it gives evidence that "negentropic" breakthroughs are continuing gratuitously to be produced). When we human social persons consider the inefficacious effects of our action in the world, we recognize that it, too, is subject to the law of entropy, and we are tempted to think that that is all there is.

In retrospect, for example, what we have done often appears to have been ineffective and even counter-productive for the accomplishing of efficacious change. We are tempted to wonder what difference it could have made whether we did one thing or another. In fact, even when our actions are consciously aimed at the realization of truth in self-transcending love, we notice repeatedly that they seem to result merely in new patterns of breakdown and disintegration. A gift to one friend creates a raft of jealous responses from others. A speaking of truth about an agenda item at an important meeting creates a whole new series of subsequent lies in the drawing up of future agendas. A revolutionary rhetoric of freedom and national sovereignty born in one century generates the conditions for a rhetoric of repression and a denial of sovereign rights to neighboring nations in another.

From the point of view of the (Western, affluent, sociopolitically secure) individual, of course, the most entropic experience of all appears to be one's own impending death. It seems to represent the definitive victory of inefficacy over action since, in a culture that regards accomplishment as something pertaining to individual effort and merit, death rules out the possibility that any further action can be taken. From the point of view of one's own definitive absence from the spheres of causality and influence on earth, death represents the apparent—and possibly real—dissolution of everything we ever worked for and held dear. Yet as the wisdom of both non-Western religion and Western ecological science indicates, however much we modern peoples, especially in the power centers of the Western North, have learned to deny death and have tried to cloak over its presence so as to make it something almost invisible—and thus unthinkable as well—death is actually an intrinsic dimension of life. Tied inseparably together, death and life make up what might be considered *the* paradigmatic "circuit" of the ecological structure of the universe.[105] In the language of a Jesus-normed religious anthropological faith, in fact, the circuit formed by death and life has been "baptized" with a new theologically interpretive name: the paschal mystery.[106]

Pace existentialist thinkers who might be tempted with Heidegger to identify living to die or the act itself of dying (conceived of in the abstract) with definitive disposition or surrender of oneself in personal freedom, death is not *the* (on principle) oppressive power from which we human beings need to be liberated. It is not *the* theological scandal. On the contrary, that scandal consists in the oppresssive power of evil. It is evil and not death that raises the fundamental question of the Book of Job and causes the affront to Jesus' sensibilities in his ending up apparently abandoned on the cross: why all this innocent suffering? The theological scandal of enormous proportions is thus the affront to human sensibilities of what might be called inappropriate or "unnatural" death—death that results from injustice, e.g., the deaths of countless numbers of innocent victims whose dying could have been avoided were the situations surrounding it only different. Such deaths are the epitome of innocent suffering, for they are deprivations imposed on victims by ideologies not of truth but of falsehood, structures and means that violate the social and ecological equilibrium. Insofar as at the level of objective consequences in history and nature such deaths are not worth the price that has to be paid in individual negation and excessive suffering to "gain" them, they are abhorrent and inappropriate.

The laws of ecology do not require an economy that rules out suffering and death on principle. On the contrary, ecological equilibrium repeatedly shows itself to be a matter of creative incorporation of entropic elements like suffering, deprivation and death for the sake of greater syntheses of energy, or negentropic breakthroughs. Examples include the suffering involved in truly loving another person; the deprivation involved in respecting the lives and interests of other beings, in helping other persons when they are in need, or in focusing one's energies in a single direction to the exclusion of other projects for the sake of efficacious realization of a worthwhile long-range goal; or the death by old age which opens up new avenues for the work of freedom in individuals other than oneself in the future. [107] From the point of view of ecological science, in other words, death and decay are capable of being incorporated into a creative ontological dynamism, an ecological circuit that points in the direction of communal well-being, efficacious love and the successful transmission of life and values across the boundaries of time and space; and realization of those values can make the pain and suffering involved worthwhile. But the death involved in the heedless proliferation of unjust ideologies—ideologies of exploitation and expedience pursued for the sake of forcing unjust gains at the expense of the peripheralized, dispensed with and deprived—such suffering and death are far from worth the price. The injustice they create cries out for vindication and redress.

In a world subjected to the forces of Sin and death, the liberation of freedom can make sense—and, indeed, is justifiable as a theological idea—only if it is understood to consist in definitive liberation from the evil that is injustice—evil that, because it is not worth the price it costs in suffering and pain, is inappropriate not only from the point of view of the logic of ecological circuits but from the point of view of the logic of both the sensitive human heart and the impassioned heart of God. The preoccupation of this logic with the overcoming of evil and the alleviation of injustice turns Paul's anthropological question of the liberation of freedom into an eschatological problem.

Insofar as theologians not only can but must reflect on the experience of human freedom as something directed toward the realization of truth and love in a universe of Sin and death, Segundo believes they are capable of discovering in the spirit of Paul that in spite of the apparent victory of Sin and death on earth, freedom occasionally has what Segundo calls its "moments."[108] Every now and then we human social persons are capable of glimpsing even here on earth, under the ambiguous conditions of history and nature, more or less recognizable realizations of self-transcending love.[109] Although such moments are completely gratuitous, Faith can prepare for them, can practice in advance an attentive readiness that knows how to wait in hope for their arrival. Thanks to such readiness, for example, the women disciples who in fidelity and love attended to Jesus living, dying and finally dead and buried in the tomb, came to see that even a death as inappropriate and seemingly ineffective as that of Jesus was gratuitously efficacious: it made possible the realization of new, more complex forms of truth in history and nature, and, in light of the resurrection, actually shows up as having made an everlastingly valid contribution to the eschatological realization of God's project—its cornerstone, in fact. The "moments" of freedom people of good will experience here and now on earth thus indicate that the fruits of action, like the body itself, must be buried in the grave of apparent entropy so as to be able to produce efficacious results in the end.

In light of the preceding reflections, the second dimension of freedom, namely its being a freedom for, refers to the release of freedom for the constructive work of Faith, a *praxis* of truth by which human freedom participates even now under the ambiguous conditions of Sin and death in the eschatological realization of God's values. God wills the *praxis* of liberation in history and nature because that sort of *praxis* and it alone constitutes Faith's learning to construct ideologies of self-transcending love. In the *praxis* of liberation consists Faith's creative appropriation of God's will on earth as it is in heaven. Because ideologies of liberation result from human beings' acting on the basis of a sensitive heart, a heart tuned to the needs of the deprived and conscious of the ecological complexity of action in an evolving world, they are ideologies in Spirit and in truth. In this sense, they are also ideologies of love, works of a Faith that is fully human in content and utterly earthly in effects but at the same time capable of mediating in eschatologically valid terms the impassioned love of God.

Another way of saying the same thing is that according to Segundo, we human social persons have a responsibility for the success of the evolutionary project, which disciples of Jesus experience in light of revelation as one and the same responsibility for the eschatological success of God's project in grace. Revelation adds a gratuitous and clarifying witness to an already existing human responsibility, giving it its identifying name as a project, insofar as both its gratuitous source and criterion for success are revealed in Jesus' kingdom *praxis* as neighbor-liberative self-transcending love. Such ideologies have eschatologically efficacious value. So necessary are they to the definitive success of God's project that, in the words of Segundo, "Even celestial reality makes no sense unless human beings and their freedom can introduce into the definitive reality something of the love they carry as an aspiration in their inner humanity."[110]

If these observations are correct, then two theological requirements immediately come to the fore: the need for a liberative conception of morality based on what is appropriate, on what is fitting for efficacious mediation of God's neighborly love for creatures in grace; and a way of envisioning the relation between history and eschatology which takes account of the causal role of ideologies in the realization of eschatological results. Together these constitute the principal aspects of the liberation of freedom in grace, its earthly and heavenly aspects: the liberation of anthropological faith to function maturely as Faith, and the manifestation of the definitive value of the work of Faith that will be made by God in glory.[111]

Segundo's conception of a morality of appropriateness is grounded in the theological anthropology of Paul. It is based not on what is "permitted" by law but on what is appropriate to the fundamental human *charism*. It is based in the fact that, insofar as God has invited human beings to participate in a world-creative task and has liberated faith to work *qua* Faith at creative integration of the negative energies of Sin and sin into ideologies creative of truth, there is no "law" on earth except that of efficacious love:

> To love and to love efficaciously is the only law of the Christian—no longer the law that pins labels of "permitted" or "prohibited" on actions, independent from each person; but rather the law that points out to the liberty of human beings their unique and authentic path: always, in circumstances that are personal and unique, to create a love that is historical as well as irreplaceable and unique. . . .Christian morality is not a morality of licit and illicit but rather of *what is suitable or not for the construction of love,* for the efficacious gift of oneself.[112]

As was seen in chapter two, Segundo believes that a love that is efficacious is a love that knows how to strike an economical balance between the creative power of Faith and the entropic energies of Sin.[113] The complexity of efficacious love means that the "law" of efficacy demands a sure and reliable criterion, so as to enable the heart to be sensitive.[114] Such a criterion must enable Faith to recognize as valid only those ideologies which are genuinely efficacious insofar as they "ring true" to the needs of the deprived.[115] From this perspective, a morality of appropriateness is a morality of freedom both from and for: it is the liberation of freedom from the law, but it is a liberation for the creation of ideologies—i.e., ideologies of efficacious love. Like all achievements in a world subjected to the entropic energies of Sin, achievement of such creative freedom is, in the end, gratuitous. It is the product of a happy proportionality between the exercise of creativity or projectivity on the one hand and acceptance of the random contributions of objective reality on the other. The efficacy of self-transcending love results gratuitously from the generous wisdom and humble flexibility of the sensitive heart. It is the product of an artful *praxis* of neighbor-liberative love, the liberation of freedom in Spirit and in truth.

According to Segundo, such a morality has three main characteristics: it is creative, progressive and social.[116] It is creative because it has to know how to balance means with ends in such a way that the means do not simply escape from human beings, begin to take on a life of their own and end up blocking the possibility of realizing the very ends they were originally meant to achieve.[117] A morality of appropriateness is progressive because it takes seriously the fact that freedom neither can nor does become liberated all at once. Freedom takes time to mature and requires the long route of patient action, a learning to learn the *praxis* of self-transcending love by "suffering" ideologies the time and entropy they need to be conceived, gestated and born (i.e., allowing them to emerge). Freedom must have the opportunity to mature through various phases or stages of growth and must be given a certain amount of room in which to make mistakes.[118] In this way freedom is able to learn sensitivity to others rather than becoming preoccupied with interests centered on the self. Finally, a morality of appropriateness is social. It is focused on the interests of the neighbor and normed by the needs of the deprived in such a way that "concern must shift from wanting to know how we will be judged to finding out what we have done to help construct a world for [others]."[119]

Segundo believes that a morality of appropriateness has a critical sign-bearing function vis-à-vis the common human task of coming up with constructive solutions to problems of history, society and ecology.[120] It points to the kinds of projects in which we human social persons ought to be engaged and the sorts of ideologies by which we ought to be trying to put the values of our anthropological faiths into operation. These would be projects and ideologies designed to make the most efficacious contribution to the building of neighborly love in light of the kinds and amounts of energy available and the needs of the deprived.[121] In that way, ideologies are capable of being welcomed precisely from the point of view of the deprived themselves as ideologies that "ring true," i.e., are truly worth the effort.

According to Segundo, in other words, we people have to calculate the price of our projects. When the sensitive heart understands that it is the deprived and oppressed who normally end up having to do the paying, it knows that some projects are simply far too expensive. Efficacious love thus works on an economy: it tries to create an economical balance between the constructive intentions of Faith and the limitations imposed by the entropic determinisms of Sin. An example occurs in the conflict frequently experienced by proponents of radical structural change: should they opt for a rapid, and possibly violent, use of power in the short-run or for a program, likely to encounter countless set-backs, of long-range structural change from within? According to Segundo, sooner or later Faith must choose an option closer to one end of the spectrum or the other, since any attempt to effect change in the absense of an energy calculus "does not take into account the energy-limitations within which all human action, be it individual or collective, must operate."[122] The problem can be solved only when Faith attempts to take into account the price of efficacy over the long-term, weighing it against the needs of the deprived to determine whether, by the criterion they themselves constitute, the efficacy promised is really worth the price. Efficacious love must therefore learn to become flexible and wise from the point of view of both the laws of ecological equilibrium and the response of the sensitive heart to the needs of the deprived. It must embody a mode of acting that on the one hand is ecologically conscious and on the other is morally alert to the criterion held in common by both the sensitive human heart and the values of God's heart.

As the preceding reflections suggest, Segundo's conception of a morality of appropriateness ties the *raison d'être* of morality not to an extrinsic law but to the *charism* action receives in grace. This is a *charism* that can only be realized through loving participation with God in the creation of a world—not just any world whatsoever but a world that, in the end, can be found to be lasting and good. As has been seen, Segundo is able to arrive at such a morality by incorporating into the theologies of grace and Sin described in chapters one and two of these reflections the hermeneutical understanding of Faith described in this chapter—in other words, by characterizing action as a liberative *praxis* of truth. Key to Segundo's approach is the notion of the intramundane causality of action vis-à-vis eschatological realization of what Jesus called God's kingdom. The morality to which the latter gives rise is capable of maximizing human responsibility without sacrificing the transcendent reality of grace.[123]

If explicitation of a morality of appropriateness thus forms the first requirement for the making of a functional theology of revelation, the second, as was suggested in the preceding paragraphs, consists in finding a way of envisioning the relation between history and eschatology which can take account of the causal role of ideologies in the realization of eschatological results. A brief look at the causal connection between the creation of ideologies of self-transcending love and the eschatological realization of God's values will thus complete this description of the truth criterion of action and return the discussion to the underlying question of the functional character of revelation. Since the urgency of this question centers most obviously today on the necessity of linking Faith and politics, it will be helpful to consider it from that perspective.

Like many contemporary theologians, Segundo does not hesitate to recognize what he calls a "void" or "empty space" between Faith and political options, for as has been seen, Faith does not contain any blueprints for the solution of secular problems and revelation offers no ready-made answers to questions of liberative *praxis*.[124] Unlike some political and liberationist theologians, however, Segundo does not attempt to bridge this gap by positing the need for a rational intermediary, e.g., a utopian imagination.[125] Instead, he considers the gap itself—which is really an eschatological discrepancy, a matter of the inevitable (and ethical) distance between what is and what ought to be—from the point of view of the hermeneutical structure of *praxis*.

As has been seen, he regards that structure as a creative tension between meaning and efficacy which can be resolved only hermeneutically, i.e., by repeated attempts of human Faith to incarnate the values of Jesus' kingdom *praxis* in concrete ideologies. And this is true however provisional, relative and historically conditioned ideologies inevitably remain, even as a result of flaws as radical as inefficacy, failure and sin:

> Our theory...assumes that there is an empty space between the conception of God that we receive from our faith and the problems that come to us from an ever-changing history. So we must build a bridge between [them]. This bridge, this provisional system of means and ends is what we are calling ideology.[126]

Because Segundo does not hesitate to allow the transcendent character of Faith to enter directly into the provisional domain of relativity and Sin, it turns out that Faith gives eschatological direction, hence enduring value, to political options at the same time that it accepts from them the inescapable feature of being conditioned by history and nature.

The structure of faith and ideologies is thus as much a key to understanding the relation between history and eschatology as it is to understanding the nature of revelation.[127] Because revelation never comes to human beings in pure form, it is inseparably bound with attempts to incarnate its values in learned responses conditioned by circumstances and needs. Segundo believes that like the *praxis* of truth in which it participates, revelation comprises an educational process, led by God and guided by Spirit, to which persons and groups can whole-heartedly entrust themselves.[128] Through it, God teaches them how to recognize values that are God's.

Within this process, appropriation of God's values through ideologies is bound up with the relativity of historical circumstances and the entropic energies of Sin insofar as no single embodiment of Faith at any given time can pretend to the level of a definitive, "Sin-free" content presumed to be reliable for all time.[129] Where ideologies represent individual responses learned under particular conditions, Faith is "the total process to which [the human being] submits, a process of learning in and through ideologies how to create the ideologies needed to handle new and unforeseen situations in history."[130]

In this way, Segundo understands revelation as an educational process aimed at liberating human freedom by converting it into "freedom for history, which means freedom *for ideologies*."[131] Faith is a process of learning to learn the *praxis* of truth, and revelation is the means by which Spirit teaches Faith how to flesh out God's values in more or less efficacious systems of methods, means and *praxes* called ideologies and to do this in ways appropriate to the ever-changing signs of the times and sensitive to the needs of the deprived.

The logic of Segundo's approach thus implies that in the taking of political options, disciples must choose not between Faith and ideologies but among particular, existing ideologies. And they must do this in ways that reflect a commitment to values revealed quite specifically in the conflictual—yet no less revelatory—ideologies of Jesus. From the point of view of the values of God revealed in Jesus' kingdom *praxis*, Segundo argues that any political ideology which liberates deprived persons and groups from concrete oppressions, regardless of its form, source or expression, has eschatological value in the eyes of God, even in the face of Sin. Segundo maintains, of course, that distinctions and choices about ideologies must certainly be made, but they must be made using the down-to-earth criterion of what is concretely and politically liberative of the deprived rather than by recourse to an "eschatological proviso."[132]

Faith goes in search of ideologies, but it must use whatever ideologies are available in the situation the way it is. It can not afford to wait in a passive, politically uninvolved and, paradoxically, "im-patient" way for the advent of a "foolproof" ideology that will finally be perfect—and, from the point of view of doing the deprived any good, too late. Instead, it must suffer the risk of making political options here and now, imperfect though they be.

In the world-creative project initiated by God in grace, Faith thus needs ideologies, political and otherwise, in order to realize the values of what Jesus called God's kingdom. Without ideologies, the kingdom can not come and eschatology dwindles into an echo from a distant—and empty—future. As Faith without ideologies is dead Faith,[133] eschatology without ideologies is dead eschatology. By the same token, political ideologies without reference to the liberation of the deprived are meaningless. They are not creative of eschatological content but add up to what Ernst Bloch called mere chronological time, devoid of future. In the words of Segundo, "[The] very dynamism [of the transcendence of love] requires it to keep growing, transforming mere time into history."[134] In the learning process that is Faith, eschatology is to ideologies what meaning is to efficacy, intention is to realization, love is to the *praxis* of truth.

The Liberation of the Deprived and the Ontologically Creative
Character of Truth

Ruling the logic of this chapter has been a single theological presupposition. It may be stated in two parts. First, knowing and doing God's will is a matter of making truth. In other words, truth results from a union between knowing and doing linked to the values of God in *praxis*. This involves a practical view of the nature of truth: under the conditions of relativity and entropy in history and nature, truth is not something that already exists and simply has to be accomplished. Rather, it is something that must be made "by hand" according to the fresh requirements posed in each new generation. It is a result of action. Truth is the construction of Faith that cries out to be built, the substance of things hoped for.

Yet Segundo points out that the making of truth does not occur in the abstract. In fact, adequately to express the meaning of the phrase *making truth,* one must leave behind the abstract—and generic—sphere of infinitives and gerunds and move into the concrete, political and intrinsically conflictual arena opened up by the action (which includes the passion) of particular subjects and predicates, with all their historical and ecological conditionings and inequalities. The second aspect of the ruling presupposition is thus that truth is a matter of one's having to take real-life options: we human social persons give form and content to truth by fashioning action in one way rather than another, by choosing to live certain sorts of values and not others, by attempting to realize neighborly love in certain sorts of ideologies and *praxes* rather than others. Such options give ontological substance to truth. In fact, they are creative of a world, since they show that the making of truth is synonymous with the making of history and nature. Humanly constructed contributions to truth give history and nature a definitive meaning. They literally make truth "matter," and "matter" everlastingly, to the neighbor and to God.

When the parts of this presupposition are joined, they form a reliable presuppositional base for Segundo's main assertion: to do the will of God is to create truth. As has been seen, according to Segundo, to create truth is the hermeneutical task of human action, and the capacity to be able to correlate that task—essentially an ethical responsibility—with the theological or religious question of what it might mean in light of the data of revelation about a knowing and doing of God's will, requires disciples' learning to act with God in history and nature for the sake of mediating God's love and creating a world that is good. And this is accomplished through Faith's integration of the disintegrative forces of Sin and sin into Jesus-like ideologies of self-transcending love. In this concluding section, it is necessary to ask what such a making of truth might look like at the concrete level of everyday action. What can the phrase *to make truth* actually mean?

In order to answer this question, I would like to leave Segundo's thought-world for a moment in order to consider a story from the gospels that seems concerned with exactly this topic. As fruitful as any example that could be taken from contemporary life, it shows just how concrete and down-to-earth, how ordinary and familiar the making of truth actually is. The story in question is found in Mark 14: 3-9, the account of the unknown woman's anointing the head of Jesus with the expensive—and dangerous—fragrance of nard. As the story suggests, with this historically limited and yet meaning-giving action, the woman is creating truth. She is prophesying in Spirit and in truth about Jesus, bearing witness to a truth about who, by his message and action, he really is: he whom her action is recognizing and proclaiming is one who is about to be put to death but whose very life—its words and deeds and sufferings—continues to have a meaning and truth of its own, a truth Jesus has created by his own course of action: the truth of the kingdom of God.

Unlike Peter, the woman does not try to tempt Jesus away from the path on which he is set. She admits that his death is at hand, but in the very act of admitting it, she proclaims and prophesies in a public way that it will not be suffered in vain. In a way that perhaps Jesus himself, in the mounting fear of his violent destiny, was not capable of doing, she speaks a word of truth about the meaning of his death: in spite of every evidence to the contrary, she is saying, it is worth it. The kingdom of God for which Jesus is giving up his life is worth it.

According to the story as it is recorded in Mark, we find that the truth that the woman creates by her bold and unique action is a result of her faith in the kingdom project. It is the result of an option for Jesus and the values of his kingdom *praxis* that is specific and concrete. It is a product of her love, her sensitivity of heart, which makes an option for the most deprived, who in this instance is Jesus himself (by contrast with the poor who in this instance were being invoked only as a convenient pretense for Judas' objections). In fact, what Mark's version of the story brings out most clearly is the conflictual character of the woman's action: it elicits objections from some of the other disciples, for as the context of this action in the rest of the gospel makes clear, the disciples do not share her insight and seem to regard Jesus' death as unnecessary or at least not a serious possibility.

By contrast, the woman's action is recognized by Jesus as a testimony of true discipleship and a statement about the meaning and worthwhileness not only of his impending death but of his life and mission as well, for in effect they are inseparable. What she has done, Jesus exclaims, will be told in memory of her wherever the gospel is preached. Because she has done something that rings true to the values—and needs—of Jesus who is about to be put to death, she has created something new. As something never before accomplished and newly arriving on the scene, the truth created by the woman's action makes a substantial contribution to the meaning of Jesus' life and mission. It creates an emergence of meaning *for* Jesus that elicits a memorable response *from* him (and telling objections from his other followers). It concretizes a truth of definitive value not only within the universe of meaning that is the gospel faith but for Jesus himself, whose extreme—and very real—existential need it fulfills. The result is that Jesus, in turn, prophesies about the woman's action: by saying that what she has done will be told in memory of her wherever the gospel is preached, he is saying to her (and to those who have "ears to hear") that the value of the deed—its hermeneutical significance or truth—will last forever.

The manner in which such truth will last is crucial. Jesus' reaction suggests that the woman's action will not be remembered merely in the way that a past event is recalled or brought to mind. Rather, it will continue to live as an efficacious deed. It will go on bearing fruit, never ceasing to mediate meaning and power, not merely figuratively, "in the hearts and minds" of disciples, but in fact, in reality—i.e., in Spirit and in truth. Like all historical moments creative of truth, the woman's action is irrevocable. It will appear in the eschaton as a substantial contribution to what the scriptures call the new heaven and the new earth. In this sense, truth is not only something that must be created, fashioned or made on earth; it is not merely a fleeting work of human hands. It is an accomplishment that also cries out for eschatological verification, for testimony to its lasting genuineness. It must be tested against its own claim to be true. In other words, we human social persons must have grounds not merely for saying or intending to know and do truth; we must also be able to point to concretely observable results that show the knowing and doing of truth to be the case in a relatively efficacious way that can be perceived by others as making a difference to the outcome of their histories and their hopes.

The significance of efficacious results is that under the relative conditions of historical existence they permit ourselves and others actually to experience, in however incomplete and limited a way, a knowing and doing of truth that is God's will. Thanks to the woman's action, for example, Jesus was able to experience God's fidelity to the kingdom project, even in the face of negative evidence as enormous as his impending and seemingly ineffective death. The woman was doing something substantial and meaningful for Jesus: she was providing an opportunity—utterly gratuitous from Jesus' point of view—for him to experience a human Faith in God's fidelity and the worthwhileness of Jesus' own fidelity in keeping a steadfast faith in God. As unused as people may be to hearing this point, the woman's action effected a genuine liberation with respect to Jesus and his need; for wherever and whenever a human being or any being is liberated from concrete deprivations, evils and ills, there is caught a glimpse of God's eschatological salvation under the ambiguous conditions of Sin. There, as well, God's values are being realized, God's truth is being made, God's will is being done on earth as it is in heaven.

The story of the anointing is relevant because it shows that truth occurs not generically as "Truth" but rather here and there, in this or that particular action, wherever people respond in neighborly love to a suffering that is real, anywhere and everywhere the efforts of ordinary people "ring true" with respect to the needs of others, especially the wretched and deprived. As Segundo observes, disciples of Jesus, hoping against hope, "have to" wager that human freedom has the capacity to create truth in history and nature, because without it, their freedom (and all freedom) would be meaningless. It would be incapable of contributing anything of value to God's eschatological project, impotent to add a single jot or tittle to the creation of a world that is good.[135] Given the reality of that creative capacity, however, disciples believe that each human being can contribute something unique and lasting to the eschatological reality, no matter how large or small. For Segundo, in fact, someone's contribution may be as seemingly insignificant as a single smile, yet it will have lasting and definitive significance to the new heaven and new earth of the eschatological creation—and this remains true for Segundo even if the person *could* have contributed more and simply failed to do so.[136]

Given the examples of the anointing and the smile, it is possible to argue that truth is a matter of the realization on earth of self-transcending love, that human constructions of truth on earth are efficacious mediations of God's neighborly love. And that is what Segundo does. He argues that God's values are realized wherever and whenever the liberation of the deprived and the manifestation of freedom occur, wherever and whenever action is creative of self-transcending love. History is created and a world is made good wherever and whenever Faith makes a God-like initiative of self-transcending love in the face of Sin and death. As will be seen in chapter four, love that is built by the work of Faith has an ontological value of its own that God is able to illuminate by placing it in an appropriately eschatological setting.[137] There, its truth will be made fully manifest, revealing, in the moving words of Segundo, that "in the history we share with God, no love is lost."[138]

This translation-in-miniature of the gospel faith makes clear that revelation constitutes a piece of good news from God about the everlasting validity of self-transcending love. How that is the case with respect to the glorious destiny of action will be the subject matter of the final chapter. The significance of the good news as revelation, however, is relevant here, primarily because it pertains to Segundo's way of understanding the hermeneutical significance of Jesus' *praxis* for disciples' on-going efforts to create fitting expressions of truth.

In keeping with the logic of a functional conception of revelation, Segundo regards Jesus' life not as a repository of Truth or Revelation but as the gratuitous "setting" within which is definitively recapitulated the already effective hermeneutical orientation toward truth in the sensitive human heart.[139] Jesus' significance is that his life-story provides a context of "redundancy"—a superabundance of meaning—within which a truth criterion always more or less clearly known stands out with definitive clarity in relation to the values of God. Jesus' life-story shows that the values of human social persons of good will who work for the liberation of the deprived are also the values of God. In this way, Jesus' *praxis* "multiplies" or en-hances the already existing anthropological significance of the attempt to arrive at truth. It does this by communicating God's preferred hermeneutical method, God's favored model, for Faith's appropriation of truth. Although this communication is redundant to the logic of action, it is nevertheless able to be welcomed by it in grace, for it gratuitously reaffirms (as opposed to showing for the first time, indicating a necessity or proving) that the two—truth on earth and truth in heaven—are actually one and the same.[140]

What becomes clear in the light of Jesus' life-story is thus not "The Truth," nor even "The Meaning of Life" or of "God"—these can never be fully grasped during the course of a lifetime or under the conditions of Sin and relativity on earth—but rather a *way* that must be followed, a course that must be run, a *Tao* or *Zen* of gratuitous living, an art of liberative *praxis* according to which one's heart can learn to pick up, and resonate with, the values of God's heart. And the name of this way is not "Jesus" but Faith, concerning the truth criterion of which Jesus provides not a necessary means but rather an utterly gratuitous testimony, a God-revealing witness of liberative *praxis* and self-transcending, neighbor-making love.

This approach sees Jesus not as *"the* answer" (to a question human existence poses) nor as *"the* savior" (of a multitude of sinners who otherwise would be lost), nor as *the* most intense historical expression of God's truth (among a host of other less explicit expressions of truth—a quantitative, substantive view). Instead, it sees Jesus as God's highly favored witness, God's "eschatological prophet" or truth *martyrion* anointed by God; for thanks to the resurrection, it is plain that on the kingdom faith of this particular witness God's favor rests in a new and definitive way. This means that the revelation of God (and truth) that Jesus brings is not "other-worldly." It is not extrinsic to history and nature, providing "divine"—and alien—content for a truth criterion of action or laying bare the inmost secrets of the interior life of God. On the one hand, a hermeneutical notion of revelation rules out the methodological unchastity of seeking privileged access to knowledge of God, and on the other hand, the criterion for truth (and thus the values of God's heart) is already available to anyone and everyone of good will in and through the hermeneutical dimension intrinsic to the working of Faith. Rather, what God's validation of Jesus and his kingdom *praxis* supplies is a reliable, revealed, passionately redundant gratuitous testimony that such a secularly derived truth criterion—a criterion like Jesus'—is also and surely God's. God's raising of Jesus from the dead bears witness to a gratuitous yet appropriate congruence between liberation of the deprived as humanly constructed truth criterion of self-transcending love and liberation of the deprived as revealed truth criterion of the values of God's heart.

Like Jesus' entire life, which ended in a martyr's death yet was gratuitously redeemed by the unprecedented act of God's raising Jesus from the dead, Jesus' kingdom *praxis* constitutes a trustworthy and reliable witness. In light of its validation by God, it shows that what the hermeneutical bent of action is already capable of judging to be the truth criterion of neighborly love on earth—namely, liberation of the deprived—is identical with what God calls the truth of love in heaven.

Truth thus occurs in and as action and can be appropriated in no other way. If truth is what makes us free, it can do so only as a *praxis* of liberation that is constructive of self-transcending love. As a *praxis* of the values of God's heart that lives the anthropological *charism* of self-transcending love as a hermeneutical liberative task, action is the place where religion and ethics become one. Phrased in the secular language of ethics, this means that the task of human action is the making of truth through self-transcending love. Phrased in theological terms, it means that the mediation of God's love for suffering creatures takes place in love-building action and is experienced as a demand for the liberation of the deprived. Phrased in a language of the gospel, it means that the task of a Jesus-normed Faith is discipleship— what Jesus called praying (and working) for the coming of God's kingdom, i.e., laboring that the world be filled with grace and truth on earth as it is in heaven, and participating creatively in the neighbor-liberating project of making that love a reality.

To translate these observations into practical terms, one must finally say that, for those diciples of Jesus who act in good faith, love is a matter of appropriate action or discipleship, with Jesus' kingdom faith and ideologies serving as revealed truth criterion. Obviously, this is to state the thesis in a religious language peculiar to a specifically Jesus-normed anthropological faith. Phrasing the question this way translates into a particular theological language about the discerning of God's will a more or less universally intelligible anthropological language about the task of arriving at a valid truth criterion for action. In effect, the theological problem is a matter not simply of how correctly to discern the will of God but more fundamentally of how to know and do the will of "the right 'God,'" i.e., how to discern the will of God from the perspective of an anthropological faith that is not false or misleading in its perception of God's values but rather reliable and true.[141] For disciples, in other words, it is a question of discerning the will not of "God" in the abstract but of God whom Jesus called *Abba*.

From a Christian point of view, such a Jesus-specific mode of discerning God's will involves an undivided interest in and single-hearted following of Jesus' way, a commitment to Jesus and the values of his life-story that seeks to express itself in concrete *praxes* of truth modeled on his God-revealing kingdom faith and its corresponding ideologies. In short, a faith that is discipleship entails a theology that is hermeneutics; it has no choice but to function as a *praxis* of God's values. At bottom, this is what is most accurately denoted in theological circles by the category *spirituality*.

Segundo believes that as practical expressions of a faith that is a spirituality of discipleship and a theology that is hermeneutics, the ideologies of disciples must strive to attain a Spirit-taught equilibrium—what in gospel-language Paul calls the liberation of freedom in Faith—between knowing the will of God whom Jesus called *Abba* in order to do it and doing the will of God whom Jesus called *Abba* in order to know it. Such striving is a theological education in ethics. In other words, given the *charism* of grace—the vocation disciples have to build God's values and thereby assist in the common secular project of creating a world that is good—the spirituality that puts that *charism* into *praxis* is a learning what to do. It is a discipleship. From the point of view of the hermeneutical subject—the person or persons living a Faith of discipleship—this means that truth is a matter of giving oneself over completely and devoting one's energies wholly in service of values embodied in one particular project above every other, in this case the project not of any god at all but of *Jesus'* God, God revealed by Spirit in Faith and made accessible through the *Abba*-faith and kingdom *praxis* of Jesus, i.e., God who wills the liberation of "sinners" and the poor.[142]

Disciples' preoccupation with knowing the will not of "God" in the abstract but God whom Jesus called *Abba* makes truth a matter of freedom's being liberated for Spirit-like action in grace, namely for what Paul calls the work of Faith. Because it involves participation in a project appropriate to the tragic character of the universe—creation of a world that is good—and because it involves knowing and doing the will not of "God" in the abstract but of God revealed in Jesus' kingdom *praxis*, it rejoices, like Jesus, in the liberation of the deprived. In short, truth in this perspective becomes a practical hermeneutical task, a matter of Faith's constructing ideologies of spirituality or discipleship, a question of disciples' learning in Faith how to translate the historical particularity of Jesus' kingdom *praxes* into liberative ideological responses of their own. By means of such ideologies, Faith will attempt to find liberative solutions to debilitating problems of the deprived and will invest its energies in a *praxis* adequate to meeting still-outstanding cultural-ecological needs in a world subjected to apparent futility by Sin, sin and death.

Yet as has been suggested earlier, the capacity to make such ideological translations actually liberative of the deprived—not to mention anthropologically meaningful and ecologically wise—depends in a radical way on how one conceives of "God" for the realization of whose values one sets one's Faith to work. Which "God," or perhaps what sort of god, was Jesus' *praxis* actually revealing? So many different and even contradictory contents are contained in the same word *God* that one might well ask of someone who uses phrases like "the kingdom of God" or "a knowing and doing of God's will"—god who? whose god? god according to which interests and criteria?[143] In the context of a liberationist hermeneutic, in fact, the asking of such conflictual questions is not a methodological option but an essential starting-point.[144] As has been seen, it is called for by the way the kingdom *praxis* of Jesus actually strikes victims of injustice (and those in solidarity with them and sensitive to their cries) when such persons and groups listen to accounts of Jesus' words and deeds in the gospels. Yet it is also required by the hermeneutical nature of biblical interpretation as a whole, which for Segundo involves approaching the Bible as a collection of extremely varied (and sometimes mutually contradictory) ideological expressions of a constant, coherent and underlying anthropological faith in God that at the same time is specifically religious.

Segundo argues that biblical interpretation is a process of learning to learn.[145] It is an endless educational circuit. By approaching the biblical contents in light of questions of the time and by repeatedly comparing and contrasting one's own interpretations with interpretations recorded and deposited over the course of thousands of years of biblical faith, disciples follow an endless circuit of learning to learn what is God's will, and they continually arrive at new interpretations of who God is and what God's values are. These interpretations are helpful not because they are always new but because, insofar as they are genuinely hermeneutical, they allow God to communicate God's values efficaciously on earth under the changing conditions of each new era. They insure that God's values will be fruitfully received by disciples in every time and place, so as to become operative in their anthropological faiths as a liberation of freedom for truth-making, love-constructive *praxis*. They make it possible, in other words, for truth to become a reality on earth as it is in heaven.

In the case of the gospels, for example, a hermeneutical appropriation of biblical revelation makes it possible for Jesus' disciples to embark in Faith on a Jesus-like *praxis* of God-like self-transcending love. In that way the ideologies of disciples—the ways they go about concretely living out the values of the gospel faith—become capable of mediating God's values in spiritualities relevant to problems of the time and pertinent to issues close at hand. Precisely as a faith that is acting as Faith, freedom learns to incarnate a living Faith in God by appropriating God's values in forms more or less efficacious with respect to the liberation of the deprived and the negativity and apparent futility of Sin, but in ways entirely new and suited to the ever-changing situations of disciples' preunderstandings and the signs of the times.

The hermeneutical process of learning to learn can not be without a criterion, however, and that is the key that unlocks the ethical relevance of this chapter. Because Segundo regards the Bible as a complex evolutionary phenomenon—he believes it covers four major developmental stages of recurring revelations of God[146]—and because he regards the kingdom *praxis* of Jesus as a new and original stage vis-à-vis other (no less valid) revelations of the values of God's heart, he regards the content of Jesus' faith as definitive. When it is a question of discerning the values of "the right 'God,'" in other words, one must consult the kingdom *praxis* of Jesus, limited and historically relative though it remain;[147] for in that set of culturally conditioned ideological responses unique and original—one might say idiomatic—to Jesus' faith experience of God, there are revealed values of God's heart to which God testified in an unprecedented, impassioned and redundant way by raising Jesus and his seemingly defeated kingdom *praxis* from the dead.

To determine exactly what such wholehearted following of Jesus might mean, it is helpful to recall Jesus' response to the disciples when they asked him to teach them to pray. He instructed them to voice a cry for the coming of the kingdom.[148] According to Segundo's reading of Jesus' *praxis*, the way to pray for the coming of God's kingdom is not to hope for a future that does not yet exist and that God will someday effect, but rather to will what God wills, to want what God wants, to work now and today on earth for realization of the same values that God works for and holds dear in heaven. To pray in Faith for the coming of God's kingdom is a learning to practice here and now the values of God's eschatological promise. It is a learning to make real and operative on earth, in action carried out for the sake of realization of God's project, a hope that guarantees the gratuitous actuality of achieving efficacious results on behalf of the success of God's project in the eschaton.

As a result, to pray in Faith for the coming of God's kingdom is to express and deepen both faith and hope: it is to state out loud and "right up front" that in spite of the obvious, and, at times, seemingly or actually debilitating limits imposed by Sin and sin, one is placing one's anthropological faith in the efficacy of self-transcending love and one's eschatological hope in the efficacy of Faith. Such prayer, Segundo observes, is not equivalent to asking God for miracles. Rather, it is "voicing the limit confronted by our love, and the victory of our hope over that limit."[149] Such prayer shows that at the level of graced human action, which gives concrete expression to that hope in a liberative and truth-creative *praxis* of self-transcending love, Faith and hope turn out to be mutually informative if not synonymous. The merging of anthropological faith and eschatological hope in the single medium of action that is graced (i.e., Faith) opens up an earthly avenue to heaven. It constructs on earth a humanly fashioned means—love—by which eschatological realizations of the gratuitous project initiated by God might take root within the relative realm of earthly action, there to give human ideologies definitive value as true and lasting mediations of God's love for suffering creatures in grace.

The relationship between action that rings true and the destiny of the evolving cosmos leads directly into chapter four. There, I will discuss how ideologies that "ring true" to the needs of the deprived—historically limited yet eschatologically valid contributions to the creation of a world that is good—constitute what theologians from the time of the prophet Isaiah, through the time of the evangelist John and up to our own time have been describing as God's proper and transcendent glory.

NOTES

[1] For purposes of clarity, I define a disciple of Jesus as a human being of good will—irrespective of religious affiliation or lack of it—who *consciously* makes Jesus' kingdom *praxis* the norm of action. This rules out anything like "anonymous Christianity" or "anonymous" discipleship and excludes persons and groups who may call themselves "Christian" but do not hold the values Jesus did. The vast number of persons who have done or are trying to realize truth without reference to God or who have done or are trying to do God's will without reference to Jesus are acting in a grace that is not and does not need to be mediated through Jesus.

[2] An articulate and prophetic-critical expression of how evil and sin pose eschatological problems occurs in Timothy Findley's novel *Not Wanted on the Voyage* (New York: Delacorte, 1985), a contemporary retelling of the story of the Flood. Findley's description of a world destroyed is sensitive and touching and thus raises all the more poignantly the question of the meaninglessness of suffering and evil, particularly as humanly caused. On the lips of the rebellious angel Lucy, Findley places the pessimistic question: "What for—the human race?" and through Mrs. Noyes (Noah's spirited wife) he declares that to create the world anew, to begin again, is not worth the pain and suffering that would be caused by the resumption of the old ways of evil, in this book epitomized by the tyrannical and destructive Noah and his depressing minion "Yaweh." The story ends with Mrs. Noyes surveying the aftermath of the Flood from the deck of the ark, praying not to the absent "God," who has become irrelevant, but to the empty sky; and she is praying not that the waters recede but for rain.

[3] This matches Segundo's purpose as expressed in *HJS*. Of course, like Segundo, I have a religious faith in Jesus, but to present such faith in doctrinal terms is not the point of this study, just as it is not the point of Segundo's theology of Jesus, which Segundo wryly terms an "antichristology" (see n. 6 below). Even less is it the point to show that Jesus himself, in his person, must be accepted—whether explicitly or "anonymously"—by all human beings as constitutive of salvation. With Segundo, I regard the point of human existence to be not acceptance or confession of Jesus as LORD, but rather *praxis* of neighborly love in spirit and truth, which in a Jesus-normed

religious language is equivalent to a knowing and doing of God's will on earth as it is in heaven. Like Segundo, I do not believe that a Jesus-normed religious faith should regard Jesus as savior in a simplistic sense, as if salvation consisted in acceptance of his person and as if his person were a sort of fetish of God. Rather, Jesus' life-story supplies the gratuitous interpretive "setting," the unsought for yet able to be welcomed news from God that action's own secularly derived truth criterion of the liberation of the deprived constitutes the criterion of salvation in the eyes of God. Jesus' life-story shows that according to God, salvation is already being effected in any and every action that embodies self-transcending love, and in a universe subjected to apparent futility by Sin, such news is capable of being received as good. "Antichristology" thus focuses not on Jesus' mode of being related to God but on Jesus' significance to whichever persons or groups of good will for whom the story of his life happens to become of interest. It puts what is first of all an anthropological and secular question to Jesus, which in the words of Segundo is: "Why are you talking to *me*?" (*HJS*, pp. 17-18).

[4] See *HCP*, p. 152. As has been noted repeatedly throughout these reflections, it can be reasonably argued that in the thinking of Jesus' time, eschatology had to do more with a hope in the overcoming of evil than with the expectation of a life after death. It was a social rather than individual hope and was markedly this-worldly in focus. It concerned what today might be called the utopian impulse built into the structure of freedom (Ernst Bloch), a human refusal to grant to evil the final and definitive word. This is the view of eschatology operative in this study, and as this chapter is intended to demonstrate, it is also Segundo's view.

[5] This dimension of the question will appear in chapter four.

[6] Strictly speaking, Segundo neither has nor does a christology, even in his making of an evolutionary interpretation of Jesus' significance in *EAJN*. Rather, as was pointed out in n. 3 above, he does what he calls "antichristology," the effort to interpret Jesus' significance in anthropologically meaningful categories from the context of today, for the sake of contributing to the common human search to find solutions that are just and wise in the face of secular problems (*HJS*, pp. 13-21).

[7] *HJS*, pp. 172-177; *HCP*, pp. 152-153.

[8] In other words, revelation affects disciples' *praxis* by letting them know what kind of *praxis* is in line with the values of God's heart. Revelation gives them the gratuitous and "redundant" news that the struggle to realize such values is guaranteed in advance to be worth it, and worth it forever, in the eyes not only of the world but of God. For evidence that Segundo believes the resurrection furnishes exactly this kind of clarification, see *HJS*, pp. 172-177.

[9] *HJS*, pp. 147-148 and p. 215, n. 17.

[10] Although the *praxis* of Jesus did not address ecological relationships directly, it did convey the reality of the impassioned love of God, and thus it can be demonstrated theologically that the validity of the third demand has solid grounds in

revelation. As Segundo demonstrates, it is not necessary to look in Jesus for a source or norm for every action (*HCP*, p. 163; see also *LT*, pp.110-120). For Segundo, "there is no Jesus-Jesus" (*HJS*, p. 19)—disciples can not hope to grasp any "real," historically pure and uninterpreted Jesus; there are available only interpretations of Jesus made throughout history. When these various and at times contradictory interpretations are contrasted and compared, they provide what Segundo calls a "hermeneutical distance" between them and Jesus which permits disciples' being able to ask and answer questions of their own that were never posed to Jesus or his interpreters in the gospels (*ibid.*, pp. 13-21). Segundo follows exactly this procedure in the course of creating his evolutionary-ecological interpretation of Jesus' significance in *EAJN*.

[11] The morality of appropriateness that such an ethics would call for will be discussed in more detail in section three below.

[12] Such an understanding is different from a dialectical notion of *praxis* as theory and practice without reference to the role of values and interests in faith. Where reference to values makes *praxis* an anthropological matter and gives it ecological relevance by focusing on action's effects in the sphere of objective reality, a simple dialectic risks remaining at an epistemological level primarily concerned with the effects of practice on the acting subject. Its conception of "the theory-practice relation" tends to be abstract and dichotomous, e.g., when it comes to the question of deciding on the locus of action's truth criterion, priority sooner or later has to be given to either practice as orthopraxy or theory as orthodoxy. By contrast, *praxis* understood as a politically charged tension between values and efficacy creates a hermeneutical "circuit" between both theory and practice (ideologies) on the one hand and their underlying premises or grounds (faith) on the other. Its logic includes the objective structure of reality.

[13] *FI*, pp. 91-95 and p. 266 and ff.

[14] Such examples need not be political in the usual sense, however. The same dynamic holds in the case of individuals and groups. For example, if the absolute value of someone's life is the accumulation of power through money, and money seems to that person to be able to "deliver the goods," then in spite of evidence to the contrary, that person will continue to "live for" money and value its efficacy as "true."

[15] This is the point of Segundo's discussion in chapter four of *Masas y minorias* (especially pp. 107-109), of what can be meant by a "specifically Christian commitment" (Assmann) to the struggle for liberation. In an important article entitled "Fe y ideologia," *Perspectivas in diálogo*, (November, 1974), p. 233, Segundo illustrates that any given anthropological faith is nothing without an ideology. Using Christian faith as an example, he writes: "Christianity is nothing without an ideology, it demands an ideology. In order to realize Christian values efficaciously, one will search for an ideology: Marxism, for example, although this is not necessary if another ideology exists which gives me a more exact system of means and ends.

. . .I am not wedded to any ideology, but I do seek one which is more coherent, more scientific, and more efficacious, while I remain faithful to the meaning that I accept in faith" [translated by Alfred Hennelley in *Theologies in Conflict* (Maryknoll, N.Y.: Orbis, 1979), p. 172, n. 17].

16 Throughout his writings Segundo insists on the need to combine three factors in a hermeneutic circle in order to guide *praxis* along the way of its hermeneutical task: (1) the values of a particular anthropological faith; (2) data provided by a particular historical ideology and the scientific-analytical tools it provides; and (3) sensitivity of heart expressed in commitment to the oppressed.   The clearest expression of this circle occurs in *Masas y minorías*, pp. 91-110. Segundo regards this combination as indispensible to the task of attaining an adequate hermeneutical preunderstanding vis-à-vis a *praxis* that hopes to be efficacious on behalf of ameliorative structural change. On the complex nature of *praxis*, see also *HCP*, pp. 172-173.

17 For Segundo, bad faith is "consciously responsible in origin but unconscious in its further developments" (*HJS*, p. 99).

18 Segundo defines the sensitive heart as possessed of a historical sensibility, a capacity to judge events on their own (intramundane) terms from the point of view of whether thay are of liberative value to those who are suffering deprivation, oppression or need ("Theological Crux," pp. 119-120). Elsewhere, he writes: "From where does a human being. . .derive his or her value-criteria? [They] arise from a sense of responsibility *in the face of the visible needs of one's fellow human beings*" (*FI*, p. 43; italics mine).

19 Discussion of Sin as a built-in regulator of the projectivity of freedom occurs in chapter two.

20 The criterion consists in the deprived themselves, in the actual faces, minds and bodies of the marginalized and poor, the outcast and oppressed. It is visible in the misery of the weak and little ones of the earth who are rendered dispensible by ideologies that serve the high and mighty.

21 *HCP*, p. 22.

22 See *Masas y Minorías*, pp. 92-93.

23 Discussing the parable of the "good Samaritan," Segundo observes that the person of sensitive heart does not ask "Who is my neighbor?" but, instead, attempts to *become* neighbor, i.e., make herself or himself neighbor, to whomever is in need: "Neighborliness *is fashioned* precisely through human love. A heart sensitive to others, a loving heart, finds *neighbors* wherever it gets a chance to approach a needy person with love" (*HJS*, p. 130; italics Segundo's).

24 Although like many contemporary theologians Segundo continues to limit terms like needy, deprived and oppressed to suffering *human* beings, I believe it is necessary to expand the concept of neighborliness to include making oneself neighbor to all beings who suffer deprivation.

[25] That Faith tends of itself toward sensibility to neighbors' needs is supported by Segundo's view that Faith and its impulses are always good. As the inner core of freedom, Faith is rooted in Spirit-initiated impulses, i.e., the impassioned love of God who knocks in grace at the door of anthropological faith. Where faith can and does go wrong is where it finds itself attempting to legitimate injustice vis-à-vis the neighbor. Caught in this dynamic, faith abdicates its freedom: it deceives itself by creating idols, "false gods" not congruent with Spirit—whom it employs in the creation and perpetuation of ideologies that allow and encourage injustice (HCP, pp. 18-21 and p. 38). For Segundo, this act of self-deception defines the basic dynamic of sin, which takes unfair advantage of Sin by riding the crest of the entropic mechanisms of objective reality on waves of egotistical self-interest, allowing anthropological faith (which is now no longer the "good will" of Faith but rather a self-deceived "bad faith") to be carried adrift of the needs of the deprived.

[26] According to Segundo, all who love already act in Faith; therefore, those who love already know—or in the logic of faiths and ideologies at least have access to knowing—the criterion for action. Anthropological faith is liberated (and made manifest as Faith in the eyes of God) wherever and whenever self-transcending love is done. In other words, self-transcending love is the sure and unmistakeable sign that any given anthropological faith is, from the point of view of God's values, already functioning as Faith, insofar as it is functioning according to the liberative criterion that is God's. It is neither necessary nor desirable that Faith of this sort become either implicitly or explicitly conscious that it is Faith; it need only be interested in determining whether or not it is *love* (and the criterion for doing so is available in the logic of action).

[27] As the previous note indicated, of course not all Faith is "Christian." In fact, much of it is not even specifically "religious." Yet from the point of view of Segundo's understanding of a Jesus-normed revelation, all Faith, religious or not, is anthropological faith that is gratuitously ruled by sensitivity of heart, that recognizes the needs of the deprived and tries to respond in self-transcending love.

[28] HCP, p. 94 and HJS, pp. 158-160.

[29] Segundo defines magic as "the absence of historical realism. It is invoking a-historical powers to solve the problems of history. So magic is any and every procedure which rejects the criteria of historical causality because it sees them as merely human and sees God as someone who operates through other mechanisms that are known only to the initiate" (ST, p. 63).

[30] The real force behind this question is actually something of the reverse of the way it is stated here. For human beings who believe in God, it is important to be concerned with God's values, not so as to codify them into a law to be obeyed but because believers *qua* believers are interested in receiving a word from God—a piece of news which is entirely gratuitous—that would reveal whether God cares about the same problems we do: evil, suffering, injustice, oppression, the needs of the deprived.

"Hearing" a word from "heaven" that, indeed, God does, makes the news from God good.

[31] One could ask, for example, whether this is not the ultimate effect of the *sola Dei gloria* underlying the theocentrism of James Gustafson, *Ethics from a Theocentric Perspective* (Chicago: University of Chicago Press, 1981)

[32] Speaking about Mt. 25: 31-46, in which God's revealed criterion is explicitly stated, Segundo notes: "Contrary to all the previsions of those who possessed divine revelation, God's judgment is based not on the law promulgated, studied, and elaborated over centuries, but on the help offered 'the least.' But this does not and cannot signify the abolition of the law and the prophets, that is, divine revelation (see Matt. 5:17). Perceived. . .needs thus become the key to interpreting what revelation is trying to say to human beings" (*HJS*, p. 129). Elsewhere, he writes: "God's revelation. . .is a factor added to the analysis of history by itself" (*ST*, p. 133).

[33] To say that revelation is anthropologically fitting is different from asserting an epistemological *necessity* concerning it. The latter seems to be a trap, or at least a temptation, for apologetical or fundamental theologies that try to "prove," or give indisputable evidence of, the existence of transcendent realities. That this is an error is a major point of Blondel's *Letter on Apologetics* in *The Letter on Apologetics and History and Dogma* (London: Harvill Press, 1964).

[34] What makes the interim risky is that God hands over to creatures the project of creating a world that is good, and God does this in an anthropologically liberative way as a loving trust. This is not the same as thinking that God hands over the world itself to human beings, which God precisely does not. God hands over the hermeneutical task, but not any of God's creatures, not even the smallest filament of hair. Why make such a distinction? Because stewardship is not the same as ownership. In initiating a project, God wills in love to put the success of God's most cherished values freely at the mercy of creatures. Yet God does not simply abandon the creation of the world to them. By inserting revelation into the project that already exists in grace, God insures that no matter how far astray anthropological faiths may go—no matter how hardened human hearts might become to the needs of the deprived—there forever remains a heart-felt word and promise that cannot be revoked, that can not be obliterated by the sheer bulk of Sin, sin and death: in the end evil will not prevail, no matter how high it has accumulated and how deeply it has scarred the earth. Like Jesus, victims of injustice will be vindicated by a fitting yet no less generous and gratuitous eschatological response of heart-felt love from the Neighbor of Neighbors who is God.

[35] As was pointed out in chapter one, in making this move Segundo seems to be in sympathy with the intriguing assertion of Blondel that God is "patient" before human action: in a universe subjected to apparent futility by Sin, God depends on the efficacious results of action for the realization of God's love, for the eschatological success of God's project.

[36] What God's "patience" entails for the eschaton, vis-à-vis both creation of a world that is good and manifestation of the glory of God, will be considered in chapter four.

[37] For Segundo, the religious relevance of revelation *is* its relevance to the solution of secular problems. What is perhaps Segundo's most explicit statement of this occurs in *ST*, pp. 133-134.

[38] Consistently throughout his writings, Segundo regards this message as the "bottom line" of revelation's content. See, for example, the transcript of Segundo's methodological observations in "A Conversation with Juan Luis Segundo, S.J." in Teofilo Cabestrero, ed., *Faith: Conversations with Contemporary Theologians* (Maryknoll, N.Y.: Orbis, 1980), p. 175. See also *HMPA*, p. 115 and *OIG*, p. 46; *ST*, p. 83.

[39] *HJS*, p. 171.

[40] Segundo writes: "A mature notion of *heaven and eternal life* does not consist of a reward to replace what we have done or suffered. Rather, it *situates on the plane of the absolute all that we have done freely out of love*" (*GHC*, p. 163; second italics mine).

[41] *TC*, p. 72 (italics Segundo's).

[42] In a contemporary theology that takes cognizance of the working vocabulary of Karl Rahner, this connection is sometimes viewed as the link between general and special revelation. It can also be subsumed under a christological rubric (the link between grace and the person and work of Jesus). By phrasing the issues in the way that I do here, I believe it is possible to show how Segundo's formulation takes the question in a liberative and pragmatically fruitful different direction. It liberates theology from the unbearable burden of trying to establish the uniqueness of Jesus' revelation of God solely on quantitative grounds. Where the latter are represented by arguments such as "all human beings have access to truth in partial ways but Jesus offers the whole and perfect truth," Segundo's approach suggests that, thanks to grace, everyone of good will already has access to the whole truth in and through the hermeneutical character of action. What Jesus adds is not "more"—or "better"— truth but a reliable witness to the "match" or "fit" that revelation validates between the truth criterion graced action comes up with on earth and the values of God's heart which are simultaneously in heaven and on earth insofar as they have been revealed in the kingdom *praxis* of Jesus.

[43] As the following paragraphs will show, this does not imply that Jesus' significance derives solely from the resurrection. The resurrection was not originally— and may not be today—regarded as something meaningful and effective in and of itself, a miraculous sign from heaven, a "proof" or cause for faith (*HJS*, p. 176-177 and p. 219, nn. 12 and 13). On the contrary, faith in Jesus and a grasp of his significance can be rooted only in an experience of Jesus' life as a whole, a life defined primarily by his mission, *praxis* and death as well as by the resurrection which makes

sense only when it is seen as intrinsically connected to them. The resurrection means nothing apart from the original historical content of Jesus' life as a whole, the most constructive and original contribution to which was his God-revealing kingdom *praxis*.

[44] Segundo's understanding of revelation implies that human beings who pre-dated Jesus, as well as those who came after him in time but were or are not his disciples, certainly may be living and acting in grace and certainly have access to revelation. In other words, Jesus is relevant to human beings from the point of view not of salvation but of Faith. This is the meaning of Segundo's axiom that "love is Faith that is beginning" (*CCC*, pp. 55-57; *TC*, pp. 75-77). According to Segundo, Faith has two historical forms: *grace* (which is evident in love that is Faith beginning) and *grace plus revelation* (which is evident in love that is Faith made capable by revelation of thinking of itself as Faith and knowing itself to be Faith in Jesus' God). The second is neither better nor more "developed" than the first; nor is the second an explicitation of the first. The two are simply distinct—and, for Segundo, dialogically related. Because the point of human existence is not to move from the first kind of Faith to the second but rather to engage in a running dialogue between the two for the sake of coming up with constructive solutions to problems of injustice and evil in the world, the two are not in competition but in conversation.

[45] It seems that where the neoscholastic approach was intent on "getting souls to God," Segundo's approach is intent on "getting God to the world," or, better, getting God and the world together without blurring the distinction which must obtain between them. Early in the 'fifties, Rahner wrote an important essay on nature and grace in which I believe he was attempting to address exactly this question. By attributing what he calls a "quasi-formal causality" to God's initiative in grace, he ends up (without coming right out and saying so) granting to the historical relativity and particularity of human existence (what for him in this context is "nature") precisely the sort of intramundane efficacy or causality—a "quasi-material" causality, so to speak—for which I believe Segundo is arguing in his liberationist theology of cooperative grace. In the case of Segundo, however, the qualification *quasi* is boldly removed. In Segundo's schema, grace is the making of a new creation through the inclusion of intramundane causality and thus reflects the patient "style" of God's love. The practical aspects of Segundo's conception of intramundane causality are presented in "Intellect y salvación" (p. 77 and pp. 87-93), where Segundo points out that the essence of salvation is intramundane accomplishment.

[46] *HJS*, p. 158.

[47] It would be exciting, but beyond the scope of these reflections. to explore the significance of these conclusions further. They point toward a christology that sees Jesus as God's living witness, made credible by solidarity with the suffering and deprived, that what we human social persons do and suffer really matters, both to the deprived on earth and to God in heaven. Thus, from the point of view of ethics, Jesus'

significance would be that those who want to be disciples must get involved in appropriate projects—projects aimed at truth, i.e., the overcoming of evil and the creative incorporation of the energies of Sin into works of Faith, projects normed and critiqued by the liberation of the deprived and summed up in the values revealed in Jesus' kingdom *praxis*. Out of this could grow a Spirit-christology of practical, ethical relevance to people of good will in the struggle to respond with self-transcending love to suffering and deprivation in this world. (On this topic, see also chapter one, n. 122).

48 See *CCC*, p. 11.

49 See "Intellecto y salvación," p. 79.

50 See *HJS*, pp. 88-89 and 178-188. Segundo points out that, like every human being, Jesus had to choose a preferred symbol for unlocking his understanding of the world-situation of the time. He chose the key represented by the (already existing Jewish) notion of the kingdom of God. Two thousand years later, the most studied observation disciples can make about this choice is that it was a profoundly political religious symbol. Its political character was necessitated not by any arbitrary preference for politics on Jesus' part but by the circumstances of his time. The latter make up part of the historical conditioning that helps to determine the contours of Jesus' life. For that reason they may not be overlooked. If today disciples (rightly) continue to make a religious judgment about the significance of Jesus' choice—a judgment that can have been made with certainty only *after* the events of the resurrection, ascension and manifestation of the Spirit—that does not excuse them (just as it did not excuse the gospel-writers) from adverting to the historical reasons (as distinct from theological ones) for Jesus' violent death. These reasons were *political*. The data indicate that Jesus was put to death as the result of a conflict of which he was the center. Paul's interpretation constitutes one of the earliest christological interpretations of the original data. Thus while christological interpretive keys will shift with the passing of each generation, Jesus' preferred key—the politically charged one of the coming of the kingdom of God—remains, to the best historical-critical knowledge to date, part of the data of Jesus' history.

51 *HJS*, p. 128. It is significant that Segundo immediately goes on to say that "from that standpoint, the fundamental conversion of those to whom the word of God has been revealed involves shifting from the notion of privilege to the notion of responsibility, ceasing to regard oneself as an end and considering oneself as a means. One is working with a mistaken hermeneutic key if one considers God's revelation as an acquisition. That key unwittingly causes 'hardening of the heart.' The other person—and inevitably the poor person in the end—comes to take a secondary place vis-à-vis the divine treasure one thinks one possesses."

52 *HJS*, p. 124.

53 For Segundo, as for other liberationist theologians (and, indeed, for communities of disciples as a whole since the advent of the option for the poor in

ecclesial teaching), the basic requirement for a hermeneutical preunderstanding appropriate to the interpretive task of theology is an option for the poor: "Only being in tune with the poor and their interests will open one's heart to the correct interpretation of God, of the law and the prophets, and ultimately of Jesus himself" (*HJS*, p. 131). Such preunderstanding is partisan (*LT*, p. 13 and pp. 33-34) and conflictual insofar as it admits that "the stance of Jesus vis-à-vis the conflict of opposed interests in the society of his time is not that of a man who places himself *above* them or *transcends* them. Far from it! The (eschatological) reconciliation sought by his message will entail the unmasking and accentuation of that conflict and its hidden mechanisms, *in order to turn its victims into conscious, active subjects in the struggle*" (*HJS*, pp. 132-133; italics mine). In n. 18, attached to this statement, Segundo specifically refers readers back to his work *The Liberation of Theology*, presumably because he regards the hermeneutical circle outlined there as an attempt to create a theological preunderstanding capable of leading to conscientized participation by the oppressed themselves and all in solidarity with them in the struggle to come up with liberative solutions to the world's problems.

[54] *HJS*, p. 118.

[55] *Ibid.*, pp. 107-109 and pp. 115-117.

[56] *Ibid.*, p. 114. Just how scandalous (at least the Lucan version of) Jesus' beatitudes can be was brought home to me on Christmas Day, 1987, during a WQED Pittsburgh radio broadcast during which the canticle of Mary (the "Magnificat") was recited as part of a holiday performance by the Robert Shaw Chorale—and the verse stating that "the rich will be sent away empty" was expunged from the text!

[57] Segundo does not attempt to tone down the conflictivity of the beatitudes but on the contrary brings it more fully to readers' attention. He states: "The theological scandal of the Beatitudes lies in the fact that there is a period after 'the poor.' In their clearest and most ancient sense, they tell us that there is an intrinsic and positive relationship between the kingdom and the *situation* of *every* poor person, between the happiness brought by the kingdom and being poor *(period!)*. Any and all added comment is speculation; it does not come from Jesus" (*HJS*, pp. 108-109; italics Segundo's).

[58] *HJS*, p. 107; (italics mine).

[59] *Ibid.*, p. 120.

[60] *Ibid.*, p. 146.

[61] *Ibid.*, p. 138 (italics mine).

[62] *Ibid.*, p. 137. Although Segundo is not always so careful in his choice of words as he is here, it is important to notice that it is not theologically helpful to regard "opponents of the kingdom" as this or that particular group. It is more accurate to view opposition to the kingdom in terms of already-existing religio-political structures and mechanisms of injustice, for it is those mechanisms—and the life of their own that they can take on, especially in the absence of prophetic critique—and not

necessarily individual people or groups whose values are irreconcilable with the values of God. What is really at issue in Segundo's reading of Jesus' polemic is thus *two different and opposing theological methodologies* and not two different religious groups. Segundo brings out this point in an ecclesial application of Jesus' theological method to modern-day problems of evangelization in "On a Missionary Awareness of One's Own Culture," *Jesuit Missions Newsletter* 1 (1974), pp. 1-6. That Segundo's emphasis on the polemical nature of Jesus' parables and preaching is not *intended* to contribute to an anti-Jewish mentality is evident in his pointed observations that Jesus' critique is directed against religio-political mechanisms of injustice in ecclesial communities of disciples today just as intensely as it was directed against mechanisms of injustice in his own time (see, for example, *HJS*, p. 126 and "Missionary Awareness," p. 6). In other words, for Segundo, the point of Jesus' criticism is to unmask ideological mechanisms of injustice that legitimate enslaving interpretations of revelation, not to condemn this or that group of religious believers.

63 Segundo discusses Jesus' theological method in virtually every one of his writings since the early seventies. Most notably, see "Capitalism—Socialism: Theological Crux," pp. 119-121; "On a Missionary Awareness of One's Own Culture," *Jesuit Missions Newsletter,* pp. 4-6; *OIG*, pp. 150-154 and p. 172; *LT*, pp. 77-82; *FI*, pp. 48-49; and *HJS*, pp. 131-133.

64 In keeping with the observations made in n. 62, it must be mentioned that much discussion surrounds the question of exactly who were the professional peers against whom Jesus polemicized. Segundo identifies them as Pharisees (*HJS*, pp. 99-101) and gives them a historically unjustifiable negative rating. Among Jewish scholars, Geza Vermes [*Jesus the Jew* (London: SCM, 1973/1983)] identifies them as Shamaites, and Harvey Falk, who regards Jesus as a Pharisee among Pharisees, identifies them as Sadducees [*Jesus the Pharisee* (New York: Paulist Press, 1985)]. Among Catholic scholars, neither Pawlikowski nor Swidler makes any statement defining who the opponents likely were but rather each argues who they were not: e.g., Swidler maintains that they were not the Pharisees "as a whole" [for the views of both of these writers, see Leonard Swidler, "The Pharisees in Recent Catholic Writing," *Horizons* 10 (Fall, 1983), pp. 267-287]. While a clearer knowledge of the identity of Jesus' adversaries would be helpful from a historical point of view, and while research on the Jewishness of Jesus would certainly go a long way toward overcoming Christian anti-Jewish stereotypes, refutation of Segundo's historical perceptions does not alter the validity of his theological observations, since, whoever Jesus' actual opponents might have been, their significance is not that they represent a religious group but that they specify *to what sort of theological method* Jesus' kingdom faith and its attendant *praxis* is opposed.

65 "Theological Crux," p. 119.

66 "Missionary Awareness," p. 5 (inclusive language substituted; italics Segundo's). Segundo paraphrases the same observations in *LT*, p. 79.

67 "Theological Crux," p. 120.

68 "Missionary Awareness," p. 5 (inclusive language for God substituted; italics Segundo's). See also *LT*, p. 79.

69 *HJS*, p. 132.

70 *Ibid.* See also *OIG*, p. 45 and *FI*, p. 48.

71 "Theological Crux," p. 120 (inclusive language substituted).

72 *HJS*, p. 157 (italics mine).

73 *HJS*, p. 132.

74 See "Theological Crux," p. 119.

75 *HJS*, p. 160.

76 "Missionary Awareness," p. 6 (italics mine).

77 "Theological Crux," p. 119 (italics mine).

78 *Ibid.*, p. 122 (italics mine; inclusive language substituted).

79 Segundo analyzes this problem in detail in *Masas y minorías*, especially pp. 91-110. On this point elsewhere, he registers a complaint against Christian theologians and ecclesiastical spokespersons who would want to prohibit the taking of concrete political options such as a move toward socialism out of a fear that it cannot guarantee perfect justice in advance: "When the political theologian of Europe requires Latin Americans to put forward a project for a socialist society which will *guarantee in advance* that the evident defects of known socialist systems will be avoided, why do we not demand of Christ also that before telling a sick man who has been cured 'your faith has saved you', he should give a guarantee that the cure will not be followed by even graver illnesses?" ("Theological Crux," pp. 120-121; italics mine).

80 On the nature of this key, Segundo writes: "From start to finish, from his adversaries to Jesus himself, everyone and everything make clear that the revelation of God in Jesus was *intrinsically political, without ceasing thereby to be religious:* that is, to appeal to a faith that is truly such. God cannot communicate with humanity except by taking up, in the limited way that is part and parcel of everything in history, the language of human meaningfulness and values of one or another of the planes of existence. The political plane is no more unworthy than any other plane of serving as the vehicle of God's revelation. It does not compromise or obscure the religious content God wishes to interject into it any more than any other plane does" (*HJS*, p. 102; italics mine).

81 *HJS*, p. 87.

82 Segundo clearly states: "The fact is that no single key, rooted in one area of a human life, can account for all a person's ideas and actions—particularly when that life is rich and deep.... Here I have been using a political key to explain the prepaschal Jesus. But I am not thereby suggesting that the religious should be relegated to a secondary plane. . . .Still less am I suggesting that *everything* about Jesus can be explained by the political key. All I am saying is that the political key is the best code for deciphering his destiny and teaching *as a whole*" (HJS, p. 160; latter italics mine).

And in *ibid.*, n. 2, p. 219, Segundo reiterates even more strongly: "I am not suggesting that any one key can explain the whole life of a human person. In the case of Jesus, for example, we have religious and moral teachings that cannot be explained solely in a political key; such an explanation would be sheer reductionism."

83 Segundo remarks, "Even in choosing the term [kingdom of God], Jesus could not have been unaware of the *political* content it *already* had in the minds of the people" (*HJS*, p. 88; italics Segundo's).

84 *HJS*, p. 158 (italics Segundo's). See also pp. 159-160 and pp. 148-149.

85 Segundo opts for an exegetical position that regards Jesus' own understanding of the nearness of the kingdom in non-apocalyptic terms (*HJS*, pp. 152-155). Whether such a position is exegetically justifiable remains open to debate. Whatever Jesus' own thoughts on the matter might have been, however, they do not invalidate Segundo's theological interpretation [on this point see Roger Haight, "A Political Interpretation of Jesus," *Cross Currents* 36 (Spring, 1986), p. 89]. Theologically, Segundo is on solid ground when he argues that Jesus did not regard the kingdom of God as something that must—or will—be realized definitively on earth.

86 *HJS*, pp. 146-147.

87 *Ibid.*, p. 160 (italics Segundo's).

88 *Ibid.*, pp. 159-160.

89 *HJS*, pp. 158-159 (italics Segundo's). As will be seen in the final chapter, Segundo believes that the relation between heaven and earth, eschatology and history, is not temporal but causal. The link that binds the two together is action that is creative of truth, a *praxis* of self-transcending love. Realization of what Jesus called the kingdom of God will thus be made fully manifest only eschatologically, but not without substantial and necessary causal contributions from human action on earth.

90 *HJS*, p. 144.

91 *Ibid.*, p. 159.

92 *Ibid.*, p. 129.

93 *Ibid.*, p. 148 (italics Segundo's).

94 That the poor are first of all the objects of the kingdom does not negate for Segundo the important fact that they are also called to be subjects of the liberation it entails (*RC*, p. 125).

95 *HJS*, p. 128.

96 *Ibid.*, p. 119.

97 *HJS*, p. 139 and pp. 158-159. As was pointed out earlier, however, it must not be inferred from Segundo's reading of the synoptic data that Jesus' enlisting of disciples meant the kingdom of God was to be realized definitively on earth. The causality of human action refers not to when the kingdom is going to "come" but to how. And that "how" is a matter of cooperation between God and human beings at the level of the work of human Faith vis-à-vis the forces of Sin and death. According

to Segundo, disciples are those who not only work along with Jesus at a task as hazardous as his own (*HJS*, p. 139) but also claim—thanks to God's having raised Jesus from the dead—to know for sure, in advance of the end, the successful eschatological outcome of God's world-creative project (*HJS*, pp. 175-176).

[98] See *HJS*, chapters VII, VIII and IX, especially pp. 90 and 119.

[99] So far as Segundo is concerned, God's revelation can be expressed only in connection with human values, and although the political plane is no less—and no more—suited than any other for accomplishing this goal, it remains relevant to Jesus' kingdom faith for an important reason: the political sphere is the sphere in which love is able to be made efficacious at a universal level, and if Jesus' message was about any value of God's heart, it was certainly about the value of love (*HJS*, p. 83). Segundo surmises that from the perspective of Jesus' religious aims, he realized that only an intrinsically political religious symbol could be capable of conveying God's value of universal love, for only it is capable of challenging people to conversion to a worthwhile project, to participation in a mission or a task, namely a self-transcending love of neighbor that, like God's own, is agapic and universal—i.e., creative of justice. Paradoxically, what this move of Segundo's does is to free the transcendent value or religious significance of Jesus' message—i.e., preserve its normative significance for the ongoing hermeneutical task of interpreting God's will on earth —precisely by recognizing and pointing out its historical relativity and limitedness as something intrinsically political (*HJS*, pp. 109). The fact that we today can admit that Jesus used a political key in which to express his religious message means that we are free to transpose that key into relevant keys of our own—e.g., feminist keys, ecological keys, evolutionary keys, liberationist keys—so long as in doing so we remain faithful not to Jesus' particular ideologies but to the values of God's heart that undergird them.

[100] *HJS*, p. 165 (italics mine).

[101] *Ibid.*, p. 85.

[102] *Ibid.*, p. 132 (italics mine).

[103] Segundo warns, however, that this does not mean that Paul may simply be regarded as the only or best interpretive key for disciples today, or that modern disiples, having Paul, may ignore the categories and critical-analytical intellectual framework contributed by the social sciences, e.g., the work of Marx, Freud and others (*HCP*, pp. 166-167).

[104] This was the point of chapter one.

[105] It is interesting to speculate on the gospel stories recounting Jesus' actions of restoring people to life. There is nothing in the data to indicate that Jesus, as a first-century Jew with biblical roots in the Torah, prophets and writings, would have abhorred death on principle, as a simple "fact of life." Rather, the gospels suggest that there always seemed to be some other reason involved in his restoring the dead to life: e.g., the widow could not survive socio-economically without her son, the raising of

Lazarus had a theological sign-value. This does not mean, however, that Jesus viewed his own or others' deaths lightly, or that death is not a negative reality and a cause of suffering in the extreme (see following note).

[106] To speak of death in the "wisdom tradition-like" context of an ecological circuit and the religious context of the paschal mystery does not have to be equivalent to erasing the blatant negativity of death, whether one's own or that of others. Although Jesus raised Lazarus from the tomb and that action was interpreted theologically as a sign, Jesus nevertheless wept. To speak of death in the context of the paschal mystery is not to "spiritualize" death or gloss over its negativity but rather to raise the deeper question of the theological need to distinguish among varying kinds and causes of death: kinds that are unjust and causes that are obscenely inappropriate. In other words, it is to attend to the theological connection between certain types of deaths and the doing and suffering of *evil*. There is a qualitative difference, for example, between the death of a human being by murder and the death of a human being from old age, even though both types of death are negative.

[107] Segundo observes that the ecological logic of (ontologically creative evolutionary) circuits obliges us to remember that "death has its 'moment' in the circuit" (*EAJN*, p. 78). For example, he muses, if Einstein had lived forever, the discovery of relativity would have been unable to be so efficacious as it has become by its having been placed randomly at the disposal of others who came after him: "Einstein and his discovery have to be 'randomized', turned once more into an object of chance in order to be effectively continued" (*ibid.*, pp. 73-74).

[108] *GHC*, pp. 158-161.

[109] Segundo observes: "Every now and then, imperceptibly, the distance between intention and performance in a project of love will almost disappear. It is not a matter of minute 'verifications' but rather glimpses of a reality that will be made manifest only later in another dimension: the transcendent dimension" (*HCP*, pp. 131-132).

[110] *EAJN*, p. 105.

[111] As will be seen, the eschatological ramifications of these same aspects will furnish the proper subject matter of chapter four.

[112] This quotation from Segundo's essay "Intellecto y salvación" appears in English translation in Alfred Hennelley, *Theologies in Conflict* (Maryknoll, N.Y.: Orbis, 1979), p. 94 (italics mine). For Segundo's later discussion of a morality suitable for the construction of love see *EG*, pp. 118-121 and *HJS*, pp. 81-85.

[113] See especially notes 64 and 67 in chapter two.

[114] *ST*, p. 58.

[115] Segundo writes: "Our love-based attitudes must flow from the concrete needs of those around us. Thus the liberty of the Christian, as a creative force, is in the service of the needs of those who are nearby, i.e., *our neighbors*" (*CCC*, p. 111; italics Segundo's).

116 See *CCC,* pp. 104-112.

117 Segundo does not scruple to state that the end justifies the means, but he is extremely careful to qualify that statement by pointing out that the end must be judged by the criterion not of efficiency (expediency; short-term profit for the few) but of the needs of the deprived (gratuitousness; Jesus-like neighborly love). On this topic, see *LT,* pp. 170-175 and *FI,* p. 258 and ff. Segundo is therefore not utilitarian in the sense of "use whatever works." On the contrary, as his extensive criticisms of a one-sided emphasis on rationality and scienctific know-how point out, he is opposed to over-purposiveness, i.e., the overdose of efficacy, or ideologies, at the expense of values, or faith (for a statement of purpose about this, see *FI,* p. 264). Instead, he advocates an ecological wisdom and flexibility that take into account "the dense complexity of reality" (*FI,* p. 261) the need to balance means against the price that must be paid to make them efficacious (this is the point of *FI,* Part Three, sections B and C, chapters ten through thirteen). For Segundo, the cost of true efficacy—as opposed to expediency or efficiency, which are cheap and profitable for victors but exhorbitantly expensive and even death-dealing for victims—can and must be calculated only by judging it against the criterion of the sensitive heart, which is constituted by the needs of the deprived, in other words, against values which are non-purposive, not purely rational-technical but rather akin to gratuitous love. Speaking of efficacy's inevitably being conditioned by the objective givenness of reality, Segundo remarks at the outset of *FI,* "All the great problems of our civilization can be summed up as one problem: i.e., What is the best and most economical way [in the ecological sense] to combine the *meaning* of human existence with the *know-how* to manipulate reality?" (p. 26; italics mine). At the end of that lengthy study, he reiterates this question in terms of the need to make a "necessary shift in emphasis today from the realm of means to the realm of ends, from the pole I have called 'ideology' to the pole I have called 'faith,'" a shift he describes in terms of "an increasingly greater role for a type of knowledge concerned with the realm of life's meaning and meaningfulness," i.e., a knowledge deriving from the "explicitly anthropological factor" of "the inner disposition of the human being. . . [specifically,] human perception and valuation of means and ends" (*FI,* p. 263). For Segundo, this problem can be solved only by gratuitousness, what in secular language Gregory Bateson calls "grace" and Segundo calls "flexibility" (*ibid.,* pp. 309-310), i.e., anthropological faith's consciousness of the fragile nature of the "social ecology," the awareness that it can be destroyed insofar as purposiveness or a one-sided emphasis on means can produce "unexpected chain reactions far beyond the concrete, simple intentions of the people employing them" (*ibid.,* pp. 285-286).

118 Segundo observes that the attempt to impose truth on freedom prematurely, or at an inappropriate time, even if it be truth pertaining to the moral sphere, does more harm than good. There is an appropriate moment in which truth can be integrated into the educative circuit, and, according to that moment, even an error (and its future

correction) could be better than a truth introduced at the wrong time (*RC,* pp. 214-215, n. 19). In making this point, Segundo refers to a well-known (but in ecclesial circles often neglected) argument of Cardinal Lercaro in favor of the tolerance for error for the sake of a higher good, even when such error could have been prevented (see *ibid.,* p. 237, n. 15).

119 *CCC,* p. 110 (inclusive language substituted).

120 *Ibid.,* pp. 111-112.

121 "Faith," Segundo writes, "liberates us *from* the temptation to seek security in the law and *for* the work of achieving the most perfect possible love with the instruments provided by our own age and circumstances" (*HJS,* p. 83; italics Segundo's).

122 *HJS,* p. 181.

123 Segundo believes that a significant religious contribution of a morality of appropriateness is its potential to offer an ecumenical corrective to the problems surrounding the relation between grace and human freedom inherited from reformation and post-reformation approaches. Both what he calls Lutheran "passivity" with its deprecation of freedom by reliance on a doctrine of *sola gratia* and Catholic "legalism" with its deprecation of freedom by reliance on the authority of law can be overcome by rehabilitation of a doctrine of cooperative grace, the recognition that human freedom contributes in a causal way to eschatological realization of what Jesus called God's kingdom (*LT,* pp. 150-151).

124 *LT,* p. 144.

125 The mediatory function of the utopian imagination plays a central role in the theologies of Gustavo Gutiérrez, *The Theology of Liberation* (Maryknoll, N.Y.: Orbis, 1973), pp. 232-239 and Gregory Baum, *Religion and Alienation* (New York: Paulist, 1975), pp. 283-292.

126 *LT,* p. 116.

127 This point will return with added significance in the discussion in chapter four.

128 *LT,* pp. 178-179.

129 *Ibid.,* pp. 116-120.

130 *Ibid.,* p. 120 (inclusive language substituted); see also p. 181.

131 *Ibid.,* p. 110 (italics Segundo's).

132 The latter is Metz's term and is criticized by Segundo for what he believes is its tendency to devalue the taking of actual political options by relativizing all options equally. See *LT,* pp. 144-145; see also *RC,* p. 23, n. 9.

133 *LT,* p. 121. See also *FI,* p. 126. Actually, "dead Faith" is a contradiction in terms.

134 *GHC,* p. 122.

135 *HCP,* pp. 152-153.

136 *Infierno,* p. 55.

137 On Segundo's understanding of Jesus' resurrection as a clarifying, value-manifesting "setting," like the setting of a jewel, see *HCP*, p. 143 and p. 216, nn. 212 and 213.

138 *OIG*, p. 46. As will be seen in the final chapter, from Segundo's point of view the everlasting validity of love *is* the good news. In the face of apparent futility, the projects of love that anyone has built in Faith will come back to life and live with God forever.

139 *HJS*, pp. 176-177. In these pages, Segundo writes, "Once their [i.e., disciples'] experience of the risen Jesus took place and opened up a meaning to them, *they discovered that this meaning was already present and expected in what they knew before*" (italics mine).

140 See previous note. That Segundo regards the resurrection as a redundant communication from God means that the message about what God's values are and how God goes about loving was already clear even without it. In light of it, however, the clarity it brings to the message is like the insight that arises from the words "I love you" when the love has already been experienced by both the one loving and the one being loved. Redundancy is gratuitous and iconic. Like the insight that arises from a poem, it surprises us with truths we've always known (Robert Frost). This is the meaning of Segundo's discussion of resurrection *qua* manifestation and recapitulation; it is "an opening up to the true vision, an *epistemological conversion. . .*a new way of punctuating the flow of events" in which there will finally be revealed "a correct and manifest estimation of 'the quality and value of each person's work' (1 Cor. 3:13)" (*EAJN*, p. 105; italics Segundo's).

141 The latter makes apparent that the hermeneutical task is highly complex, that, perhaps, it is a matter of disciples' being "wise as serpents and innocent as doves" (Mt. 10:16). It not only requires that interpreting subjects make clear exactly who they, the subjects of the discernment, are and in what their preunderstandings consist—a requirement defended, for example, by Gadamer in *Truth and Method* and carried out according to the requirements of an existential preunderstanding by, for example, Bultmann—but it also requires that interpreting subjects clarify with a reliable degree of objective certainty exactly what sort of "God" is being discerned and in what God's "preunderstandings," or values, consist. Approaching the hermeneutical process this way, which is Segundo's way, demands an objective criterion about God, i.e., data of revelation. Otherwise it risks falling into a cultural reductionism that limits interpretations of God, for better or worse, to being merely human interpretations, i.e., projections or speculations.

142 It seems that what is of importance about the fact that Jesus called God *Abba* is not that Jesus *called* God *Abba*—in other words, that after Jesus' arrival on the scene God is somehow to be known by disciples as *"Abba"* (and is therefore limited to being described in terms of allegedly father-like traits; as feminist theologians have shown, this is far from being a helpful approach for all human beings, and in

popularized form it can become sentimental and silly). Rather, what is important about Jesus' calling God *Abba* is that *Jesus*—with the particular values his kingdom faith and its *praxis* displayed—called God *Abba*. In other words, what is important about Jesus' relation to God is that God as Jesus revealed God is shown to be concretely committed to certain values and not others. Specifically, God whom Jesus called *Abba* takes the side of the deprived and dispossessed, wills the return of that which ought rightly to have been theirs from the beginning, rejoices in the restoration of unjustly deprived goods, and by raising Jesus from the dead validates the truth that, indeed, the actual instances of liberation which Jesus termed *salvation* on earth also constitute salvation from God's point of view in heaven.

[143] Two particularly chilling literary examples of what the word *God* can mean in the context of a North Atlantic culture of the West—and of the debilitating, death-dealing connotations the word can carry at the sociopolitical and ecological levels in the absence of a prophetic critique—occur in Sartre's *The Flies* and Findley's already mentioned *Not Wanted on the Voyage*. In Sartre's play, "God" is portrayed as almighty upholder of a pre-established order and destroyer of human freedom, and in Findley's novel, "God" is portrayed as impotent destroyer of the world itself, feeble and more or less irrelevant accomplice of a genuinely destructive Noah in the decision to drown all the beauty, wonder, flexibility and communality of life on earth and wipe out the possibility of gratuitous relations. In both examples, tyranny and cruelty are traits central to the meaning of "God," even though in the second example, it is Noah and not actually "God" who is tyrannical and cruel and "God" becomes irrelevant.

[144] *HJS*, pp. 11-12.

[145] *LT*, pp. 97-124 and pp. 179-181; *RC*, 161-197, especially pp. 170 ff.

[146] *RC*, pp. 170-195. See also *Etapas*, p. 11 to the end. There, Segundo distinguishes the four stages as follows: the sacral stage (emphasis on God's mysteriousness); the covenant stage (emphasis on God's moral providence); the justice stage (emphasis on God as creator); and the Wisdom stage (emphasis on God's interest in human justice-doing and in the significance of freedom for attaining human destiny). Although much in the Wisdom stage (which Segundo sees as underlying the religious outlook of the Pharisees) is similar to what is presented in the gospel revelation of God, the novelty of Jesus' revelation of the values of God's heart goes beyond it—principally, Segundo believes, because of the gospel notion that freedom is not a test but a creative sharing in love with God. For a brief summary of these points in English, see Alfred Hennelley, *Theologies in Conflict* (Maryknoll, N.Y.: Orbis, 1979), pp. 53-59.

[147] Yet, as this chapter has attempted to show, Segundo does not argue that God's values are revealed solely or exclusively through Jesus' *praxis*. He does not advocate a view of revelation that requires a "christology from above." On the contrary, he urges theologians to incorporate into their theological preunderstanding humanly created categories deriving from values underlying religion, art, philosophy

and science. These arise out of the context peculiar to each historical time and, if compatible with the values of Jesus' kingdom faith, can serve as correctives—in our day, for example, as ecologically conscious ones—to one-sided hermeneutical preunderstandings that tend to limit God's relations with creatures to a too-subjective, overly anthropocentric, purely redemptive significance. More inclusive sorts of categories, particularly those that today lead to an ecologically conscientized human wisdom and a sensitivity to the deprivations, needs and interests of other beings, serve to remind disciples that grace is not merely redemptive but creative. In no way ought such a gratuitously generous and all-embracing project of agapic love be limited— arrogantly—to God's having to "repair" what "went wrong" with human beings and their relations with God and others due to the reality of sin. In other words, ecologically sensitive, politically liberative categories, even though humanly devised, can help disciples to remember that God's project is concerned with the "big picture": it is centered on the priority of the positive, the creative incorporation of Sin into Faith, and is not preoccupied with the negative dimension of the forgiveness of (human) sins.

148 Prayer for the coming of God's kingdom is relevant to the question of the nature of truth because from the point of view of what is demanded by discipleship, the way one thinks about the coming of God's kingdom is paradigmatic of the way one conceives of the gratuitous love that is grace. The way one prays for the coming of the kingdom is an indicator of the way one conceives of the eschatological realization of God's will, and thus of the efficacy of grace, on earth.

149 OIG, p. 46.

IV

THE GLORIOUS DESTINY OF HUMAN ACTION AND THE ABSOLUTE VALUE OF ITS EFFICACIOUS PROJECTS: SELF-TRANSCENDING LOVE AS EMBODIMENT OF THE NEW HEAVEN AND NEW EARTH

...Who are in heaven, hallowed be your name.

When disciples of Jesus precede their prayer for the coming of God's kingdom with appropriately chosen meek and yet bold words of loving address to God followed by the proclamation "Hallowed be your name," they are acknowledging the transcendence of God.[1] They are recognizing God's "Godliness" and juxtaposing affirmation of it with the proclamation of God's impassioned love, acknowledging that God is God and that there is no other, that they themselves are not gods, and yet proclaiming that God in the coming of whose kingdom they want to participate is manifestly gracious, utterly committed to the creation of good and not evil in the universe, intimately involved with creatures who can love God not by necessity but in response to a gratuitous initiative of love. In short, with this Jesus-normed style of direct address, disciples are acknowledging the unique and irreplaceable identity of God, God's sheer gratuitousness with respect to creatures.

As was seen in chapter one, the task of reconciling acknowledgment of God's transcendence in heaven with recognition of God's gratuitous involvement in a logic of action that proclaims its own validity on earth is a theological problem of the conjunction of the divine and human freedoms in grace. The crux of the problem is that each of the freedoms must be permitted to remain autonomous while working together at a common task of meaning and value to both. At the same time, the possibility and actuality must be acknowledged that human freedom can have a project in its own right with a secular validity that neither implicitly nor explicitly requires religious participation in a project of God.[2] Chapter one was an attempt to demonstrate that the theological solution to the problem of establishing such flexible continuity is the logic of action in grace. It is capable of solving at the level of theory what is already in process of being worked out with greater or lesser clarity at the level of everyday practice.

In this chapter, I am concerned with the eschatological consequences of making such a link. This focuses attention on the question of a continuity of destinies between God and the world.[3] If such continuity is to remain in touch with the revelation of the values of God's heart communicated in Jesus' kingdom *praxis*, it must be shown to pertain to the unbreakeable connection between grace and glory, i.e., the connection between God's initiation on earth of a salvific project that is liberative of the deprived and God's manifestation in heaven of a definitive creation that is found to be lasting and good. In other words, the positing of continuity between God and the world must point to the eschatological character of what Jesus called the kingdom of God. It must bring to light the point of intersection between creatures' participation in God's project on earth and their enjoyment of its eschatological realization with God in heaven.[4]

Ultimately, the affirmation that grace is headed for glory has to do with giving a theologically intelligible meaning to the datum of revelation that God's love for creatures is real. It has to do with attributing to the love that is grace a sure eschatological efficacy, a definitive power over evil, suffering and death. The concern of this chapter is thus the question that has motivated these reflections from the beginning and now appears in these final pages with reference to eschatological hope: in a universe in which action is subjected to apparent futility by the cumulative weight of its own inefficacious results, what does it mean that creatures are loved passionately and unfailingly by *God?*

The task of these final pages is to make a theologically coherent response to that question. It is to try to put into words the news about God's love that Jesus brings from God, a news that is capable of coming to persons and groups of sensitive heart as news that is good only insofar as it is capable of grounding a seemingly incredible hope: the drowning of ameliorative action in what, under the conditions of Sin, looks and feels like definitive defeat is actually, at the level of God's eschatological project at work in the universe in Faith, the definitive manifestation of the efficacy and worthwhileness of exactly such action in heaven. As discussion in the following pages is intended to show, the theological name for such efficacy is self-transcending love, and the manifestation of its worthwhileness in the definitive reality of the eschaton is constitutive of God's everlasting glory.

As has been mentioned in the earlier chapters, but in this final stretch of the discussion must be recapitulated in a clarifying way, the theological category signifying Faith's resilient capacity to stick with the struggle in the face of Sin and participate in the building of love on earth is eschatological hope. As the earlier chapters have shown, the theological referent of eschatology is neither the end of the world nor the end of history but the end of evil, the end of the reign of Sin. As a theological category, eschatology pertains to the definitive overcoming of evil, suffering and death. It points toward the bringing to term of the costly labor of creation, the jubilant celebration of the long-awaited arrival of a world that is finally good. In this sense, it represents definitive completion of the project that is grace, full realization of God's and creatures' conjoint investment in a world that is built out of love. In talking about the definitive realization of that project, I want to show why a meek and yet bold earthly hope in the everlasting worthwhileness of self-transcending love can be as sure and steadfast in the face of Sin as God's eschatological promise in heaven.

In the following sections, I will look at the eschatological significance of such hope and promise from the point of view of the present-day disciple of Jesus who tries to respond to two urgencies at once: the need to make a theological justification of eschatological hope that is actually a *praxis* of discipleship of Jesus, whose revelation of God it accepts as normative, and the need to find a way of talking about Jesus' revelation of the promise of God that can emphasize its secular significance, its relevance to the longings, sufferings, projects and hopes of the sensitive human heart. The urgency of these tasks stems from the ever-present need for disciples to engage in a *praxis* of Faith that is appropriate to the needs of the deprived and attentive to the signs of the times.

In approaching the question this way, I am making the assumption that, given Jesus' revelation of God's passion for and jubilation at the liberation of the deprived, the point of eschatology, and thus of Jesus' revelation of God's promise, is to say something meaningful about the value of history and nature. I am assuming that to say eschatology is to speak about the worthwhileness of self-transcending love and the creation of a world that is good from a perspective that can make sense to both a secular anthropological faith in the value of ameliorative action on earth and a religious, specifically Jesus-derived anthropological faith in the value of such action in heaven. A preliminary consideration of this double referent in the conception of eschatology will help to clarify the importance of beginning with this assumption and will set the stage for the theological affirmation of the definitive worthwhileness of love that rules the logic of this chapter.

The Relevance of Eschatology to Heaven and Earth

At the secular level, to raise the question of eschatology is to ask about the meaningfulness of hope. It is to raise in anthropological categories the theological question at the heart of this chapter: in what does hope actually consist? When all is said and done, one must admit that the answer to this question is a matter of people's going on living—and dying—night and day, a matter of their continuing to act and suffer in the face of incredible odds, in a way that, even in the face of evils as overwhelming as injustice, suffering and death, never definitively ceases positing the worthwhileness of self-transcending love.[5] To ask about the meaningfulness of human hope is thus to consider how love can continue to be made intelligible under the conditions of frustration, failure, suffering and injustice that mark experience on earth. Given the apparent futility of action in a universe subjected to Sin—the blatant determinisms of the laws of randomness and breakdown that often mean suffering and death rather than happiness and success—and given the seeming obliviousness of the mechanisms of nature and culture to the sensibilities and impulses of the sensitive heart, why is it worthwhile for persons and groups of good will to continue acting toward the making of neighborly ideologies, to keep on working toward the making of a heaven on earth, to go on hoping against hope for a time when the evils of suffering, failure, injustice and death will no longer prevail?

The persistence of more or less meaningful, not always explicit, responses to these questions—evidence that, irrespective of people's affiliation or lack of affiliation with religion, love continues to be practiced on earth among persons and groups of sensitive heart in spite of the fact that injustice and evil have not been definitively wiped out but actually seem to be accumulating at a greater and more oppressive rate—all of this means that the yes of anthropological Faith to the question whether it will turn out in the end to have been worthwhile to hope in love's definitive value *now* is a matter of human beings' continuing to posit meaning and value in history and nature themselves, in a way intrinsic to action's structure and its laws. In this sense, the phenomenon of hope seems to display an inherently eschatological "valence." It seems to pertain to a resilience built into the structure of the universe from the start, an irrepressible logic of positivity which appears in the sphere of anthropological Faith as a utopian tendency to construct ideologies of efficacious change aimed at the overcoming of evil on earth. [6]

SECULAR UTOPIAN STRIVING AND RELIGIOUS ESCHATOLOGICAL HOPE

It is important to note that the word *utopian* is not necessarily a synonym for a lack of Niebuhrian realism.[7] As a secular category relevant to the making of eschatology, utopia does not have to pertain to either a utilitarian striving for a perfect society of the future or a nostalgic attempt to return to a golden age of the past. On the contrary, it can serve as an intrinsically *ethical* category, inseparable from the secular struggle to build a heaven on earth.[8] It refers to the repulsion of the sensitive heart by evil in the present, the repugnance at suffering and futility which elicits a moral striving to alleviate injustice now. Utopian hope thus has a sense of moral urgency attached to it. It pertains to the spontaneous response of the sensitive heart to the wretchedness of the deprived, the persistent struggle against all odds to work for a more just world.[9]

Understanding utopian hope as the ethical impetus of the sensitive heart, the motivational "engine" of anthropological faith, suggests that the concept *utopia* in the realistic sense has a genuine "affinity" for eschatology.[10] In spite of the tendency of some theological traditions to make pessimistic assertions to the contrary,[11] the phenomenon of utopian striving can give rise to the optimistic hypothesis that eschatology is a category pertaining to the value of ameliorative action on *earth*. Yet once that hypothesis is accepted, it leads to the making of another. As the religious expression of a sense of urgency about the making of a world that is good—a sense that *qua* ethical and anthropological is meaningful at the level of secular and not only religious experience—eschatological hope has the capacity to illumine the utopian logic at the heart of the commitment to liberation, to confirm it *qua* hope and offer it good news from Jesus about the gratuitous surety it can find in the eschatological promise of God. A brief look at the utopian character of the commitment to the deprived will show the feasibility of making these hypotheses.

As was seen in chapter three, the commitment to liberation that characterizes the Faith of the sensitive heart is measurable in an objectively reliable way by the intramundane truth criterion of the needs of the deprived.[12] The truth of this commitment shows up in action as neighborly love, a solidarity with the deprived and sensitivity to their cries that, like the response of the Samaritan to the man beaten by robbers, is heart-felt and gratuitous, self-transcending and costly and thus taxing on one's energies, one's loved ones and oneself. The ideological concretions of such love are impassioned and prophetic. They are creative of truth like the bold (and yet meek) action of the woman who, in the face of Jesus' apparently futile approaching death, anointed his head with an oil of gladness that, in spite of appearances to the contrary, proclaimed in both her eyes and God's a stubborn affirmation of the worthwhileness of Jesus' kingdom message and the validity of his life.

Taking shape in exactly such circumstances, the neighborly commitment to the liberation of the deprived is profoundly hope-filled and utopian: it tries to put into existence "somewhere" in reality what had hitherto existed "nowhere"—an incarnation of truth. By directing Faith earthward, the commitment to the deprived plants the seed of truth firmly in the soil of reality. There it can grow into ideologies of self-transcending love, the results of which, even if they die, will have succeeded in however small a way in opening reality "heavenward" to the gratuitous realization of results. Although the flowering of love is always in the minority in face of the massive determinisms which threaten to carry away the initiatives of Faith in the wake of Sin or lose them under the momentum of a law of diminishing returns, love embodies the logic of gratuitousness at the heart of evolutionary reality. It opens the "muddle" of entropic energies to the surprising yet appropriate experience of the emergence of something new. By completing the circuit in which Faith "senses" the moment of ontological breakthrough and "comes out to welcome" the gratuitous arrival of truth, love allows something new to find a place in the universe. It prepares the ground for a hearty "amen" to the gratuitous emergence of new reality, asserting the accomplishment of an ontological gain in the face of Sin's apparently definitive negations. In this sense, love enables Faith to be ontologically powerful and creative. It allows it to work in an eschatologically efficacious way in the face of Sin by contributing substantial content to the creation of a world that will not degenerate into the futility of death but will spring back to life, capable of being pronounced definitively worthwhile and good.

By comparison with the high visibility of entropy in the universe, the negentropic energy of love seems hard to come by. In reality, however, its realization is neither scarce nor rare but rather not yet fully visible. Both the actual occurrences of love and the durability they have in the eyes of God are more or less obscured on earth by the quantitative energies and sheer ubiquity of Sin. The value of love will appear in its entirety only against the definitive background of the eschaton, where like a jewel placed in an appropriate setting, love will finally be made manifest in all its beauty; and its value, which is absolute, will shine like the morning star.

As a category of gratuitous breakthrough relevant to the realization of ontological results that are going to last with God forever, eschatology has a three-fold connection with the logic of utopian striving. It has a cosmic connection insofar as it pertains to the work of conjointly creating a world; an ethical connection insofar as it pertains to the creation of a world that is good; and a temporal connection insofar as it pertains to the willingness to suffer and celebrate now the emergence of a new reality that will be capable of being pronounced definitively good only in the end. This means that the eschaton is best linked to the project that is grace neither lineally nor chronologically but by the logic of utopian hope. This is the logic of action's constructive project-mindedness which is analogous to the logic of grace and thus compatible with God's eschatological promise. It shows that human utopian hope and God's eschatological promise have exactly the same interests at heart: creation of a world that is good. It allows one to see that although the emergence of the eschaton is gratuitous, it is not extrinsic to action but intrinsically related to its logic. Finally, it shows how the eschaton can be said to pertain to Faith's utopian orientation toward the objective realization of results, for it focuses on the creative impulse of the sensitive heart to invest the energies of Faith in ideologies aimed at building a reality that does not as yet exist.

Insofar as the logic of eschatology is spontaneously congruent with the logic of utopian striving, it tends to move action away from interest in the world as it is toward interest in the world as it ought to be. Yet insofar as it is normed by the liberation of the deprived, it is the anthropological version of the patient and impassioned love of God, the counterpart on earth of the definitively creative power of God over evil, injustice and death. Eschatological hope thus embodies the deepest and most proper meaning of human freedom, i.e., the inner logic of its *charism*, which, in the words of Segundo, is "a creative impulse, like [God's] own, one that was destined to create love."[13] If, in the glorious setting of the eschaton—the ontologically good and enduring world which freedom will have created with God by the work of human Faith—the actual results of eschatological hope (what Paul calls "the substance of things hoped for") will show up at last as glorious manifestations of the ontological value of love, the reason can be found in the eschatological logic which inheres in action from the start:

> Eschatology. . .has to do with actions in history that are building something lasting and definitive even though they may seem to be going astray and heading for corruption and death. The definitive reality will not come about without the creative freedom of God's children; but only at the end will we see its *manifestation,* its full positive visibility or *glory.*[14]

Paying theological attention to a Jesus-derived eschatological hope thus involves paying anthropological attention to the secular phenomenon of utopian striving. It involves wanting to speak about the definitive worthwhileness of self-transcending love in a way that can make sense to victims of deprivation and injustice as well as neighbors of good will concerned about releasing them, whether such persons and groups have a religious eschatological hope in God (and Jesus) or not.[15] In other words, speaking theologically about the worthwhileness of love involves wanting to give eschatology a practical, which is to say ethically significant, foothold in *this* world, wanting to place ameliorative action and utopian striving in a context of theological realism which is intelligible from a secular point of view.[16] This desire is based on the premise that eschatology is an anthropological concern, a matter pertaining to the hopes and sufferings of the deprived and persons and groups of good will in solidarity with them—in other words, the making of a good world on earth. It is not a matter of a separate world pertaining to God in heaven.

Yet the pertinence of eschatology to the this-worldly phenomenon of utopian hope does not simply make it irrelevant to theological interest in heaven. It is precisely the experience of historical provisionality—the coming up of utopian striving against the limits of incompleteness, inefficacy and failure—to which revelation from God speaks a word of promise about definitive liberation. Revelation validates utopian hope on earth with news of the everlasting value of secular liberative striving, not merely its accomplishments but also, and especially, its failures. It is precisely the eschatological value of failure to which the datum of Jesus' resurrection testifies, and that datum comes specifically from heaven.

THE SECULAR RELEVANCE OF ESCHATOLOGY AND THE NATURE OF THEOLOGICAL DISCOURSE

The result of this double referent in the conception of eschatology is that if anyone wants to talk about eschatological hope in the context of making a theology, she or he must be alert to issues involved in trying to take account of data from both heaven and earth. This is a complex task requiring initial clarification about to whom theological discourse is addressed and how it should be carried out. Insofar as it is theological, such discourse is primarily, but not exclusively, addressed to persons and groups for whom revelation from heaven—"news" pertaining to an eschatological promise coming to earth from God—is a relevant datum. Insofar as it is discourse, however, it must be intelligible to others. It must be capable of coming across to persons and groups of sensitive heart in general, not merely as a rationally coherent justification for the sort of eschatological hope that is in persons and groups who want to be disciples of Jesus but as a piece of good news having direct bearing on the concerns of any and every sensitive heart, wherever is met a liberationist striving, a creaturely suffering, a utopian hope for the overcoming of injustice, deprivation and death.

In other words, theological discourse about eschatology ought to be aimed at funding disciples' *praxis* of liberation of the deprived, the *praxis* of truth outlined as the hermeneutical task of action in chapter three. It ought to lead to ways of talking about God's promise of definitive salvation that can be "related, in each problem, to every vicissitude of history."[17] In that way, disciples will be made capable of contributing side by side with other persons and groups of sensitive heart to an intramundane project in which revelation from God can be put in touch with down-to-earth secular problems. Then, in the face of obstacles as formidable as action's apparently congenital inefficacy in a universe of Sin, the Faith of disciples can participate with the Faiths of other persons and groups of sensitive heart for the sake of making appropriate responses to both the needs of the deprived and the signs of the times.

In order to incorporate the concerns of both heaven and earth in such a secularly relevant way, it is necessary to consider eschatological hope in light of the many persons and groups of sensitive heart who are neither theists nor disciples of Jesus and whose anthropological faith provides a utopian hope in the worthwhileness of ameliorative action which is identical to the hope of disciples that is grounded in the resurrection of Jesus and set forth in this study as a promise validated by God.[18] Yet this must be done not in order to supply for those persons a convincing story about the link between God's eschatological promise in heaven and human utopian striving on earth—for persons and groups who are not theists, the question of such a link is irrelevant—but because acceptance of heaven as a datum of anthropological faith poses a theological problem for the *praxis* of *theists*, in particular, theists who want to be disciples of *Jesus*.[19]

In other words, the purpose of theological discourse about eschatology is to enhance the effectiveness of Jesus' revelation of God's promise by means of disciples' *praxis* of eschatological hope on earth, to enable them to "place revelation at the service of human [i.e., secular] problems and their solution, and so come to hold revelation always anew, guided by the Spirit."[20] Theology is not a contest of religious doctrines but critical reflection on, and practical response to, secular problems in light of data of revelation. Making the whole of theology into something like apologetics or fundamental theology, which, from Segundo's point of view, is and ought to be "in the process of disappearing" tends to remove eschatology from the arena of public relevance.[21] It keeps the language of eschatological hope inside the boundaries of the Christian religions, preventing data from heaven from making mutually productive contact with the liberationist *praxis* of sensitive hearts elsewhere. By contrast, permitting theology to translate data from heaven concretely and directly into the language and experience, sufferings and hopes that are part of disciples' and others' secular *praxis* opens up a route along which disciples of Jesus can walk as companions, in continuing conversation with persons and groups of sensitive heart of other anthropological faiths, for the sake of constructing ideologies appropriate to solving the problems of the times and meeting the needs of the deprived. Such *praxis* serves to solidify the values of persons and groups of good will—the faiths behind their ideologies—into a shared hope that does not need to rely for the commonality of its vision and *praxis* on a prior act of adherence to (or severence from) this or that "religious" or "secular" ideology.

Doing theology in the latter mode presupposes that a basic requirement for talking about the relevance of heaven to earth is a capacity to critique eschatological statements with objective evidence from the signs of the times, to test disciples' *praxis* of hope against its consequences for suffering neighbors and the solution of problems in history and nature. No less importantly, however, such theology must be capable of justifying and bolstering the eschatological hope of disciples themselves, particularly in face of Faith's constant temptations to discouragement over the seeming inefficacy of neighborly ideologies and the apparent futility of self-transcending love under the conditions of Sin and sin.[22] On the one hand, such an approach assumes that the theological significance of eschatology is something disciples work to realize on earth, a lived and living *praxis* relevant not to heaven alone, especially not a purely transcendent realm above and beyond history or accessible only in the interior or "spiritual" reaches of the heart, but to the countless vicissitudes of life which, at the this-worldly level of action, constitute decisive points of intersection between heaven and earth, the absolute and the relative, precisely here in history.[23] On the other hand, it assumes that disciples' interest in liberation includes interest in a confirmation of utopian hope that is redundant to its already existing secular logic yet highly appropriate to it. Such confirmation is theological and religious in nature. It consists in an able-to-be-welcomed ratification of—a revealed contribution to—utopian striving that, in the end, can be made and manifested as such only by the gratuitous initiative of God.[24]

The theological name for God's redundant, which is to say gratuitous yet appropriate, contribution to utopian striving is salvation. It is the unfailing fulfillment of God's initial pledge that the utopian passion for secular liberation, even when it has seemingly failed to achieve efficacious results, will be manifest in the end as having been efficacious and worthwhile in an eschatological sense, i.e., capable of having definitive value for the overcoming of evil, suffering and death. The ontological durability of secular liberations will be made fully visible only "after the fact," so to speak.

Placed in the "heavenly" setting of the eschaton, the reality love already possessed on earth in spite of its always having been more or less obscured there by the entropic trappings and time-consuming circuitousness of Sin and sin will at last be fully manifest. It will be made visible in all its aspects as an ontologically real accomplishment, a labor of Faith effected for the sake of making oneself neighbor to the deprived, a work "of the earth, earthly" that, in the eschatological perspective of the end, is nevertheless capable of being also ratified as a definitive work of the love of God in heaven. As such, self-transcending love is a work of Faith that in the eschatological concretion of the new heaven and new earth is being salvaged, cherished and made manifest in glory by the Neighbor of Neighbors who is God. In the end, such love will be shown to have been the effecting on earth of a reality that is eschatologically valid and lasts with God forever, a work that is ontologically new.

ESCHATOLOGY, LIBERATION AND SALVATION

The pertinence of eschatology to both heaven and earth is thus key in theology to a complete rather than partial understanding of salvation. It shows that salvation must consist in two aspects at once: the turning of anthropological faith earthward toward a project of secular liberation of the deprived, and the directing of ideologies heavenward toward definitive realization of the promised creation of "a new heaven and a new earth"—a world that is lasting and good. And this will be accomplished by the intramundane causality of more or less efficacious, seemingly provisional ideologies that are nevertheless capable of being made manifest in heaven for what all along, in a not yet fully visible way, they already were on earth, namely definitively valid works of self-transcending love.

As was seen in chapter one, the turning of faith earthward takes place in the working of grace in Faith. It reconfigures the epistemological premises of anthropological faith by locating the latter in a gratuitous new context, a relationship of kinship with God (what Segundo calls "adoption as adult children of God") and community with creatures (what Segundo calls variously a "synthesis of centers" or "brotherhood and sisterhood with Christ").[25] Together, these new and gratuitous relations liberate anthropological faith from the debilitating effects of insecurity, alienation and fear. Freed from enslaving preoccupation with the justification of its own inadequacy before God and others, anthropological faith is liberated for participation in the second aspect of salvation, the turning of ideologies heavenward, toward realization of God's eschatological project and promise: creation of a world that is good.

Specifically at issue in this schema is the connection between the traditional theological notion of salvation and what liberationist theologians ordinarily call liberation.[26] By the former is traditionally meant "salvation with a capital 'S,'" the *definitive* liberation from evil, sin, suffering and death, the eschatological completion and gratuitous fulfillment variously describable in religious terms as the coming of the kingdom of God, the resurrection of the body or the creation of a "new heaven and new earth."[27] Although the contents of these symbols vary to some extent, salvation is understood in all of them as the efficacy of God's promise, the definitive eschatological victory of God's of love over injustice, suffering and death, the evils and ills resulting from the entropic energies of Sin. Such victory is understood as coming from heaven in grace, becoming operative on earth through human action in Faith, communicating its hope-building, love-making power in history and nature through revelation, validating its truth and reliability in Jesus' life-story by God's unprecedented action of raising Jesus from the dead, and destining the earthly realization of human love for everlasting fulfillment in glory. According to Segundo, eschatological salvation in this definitive sense includes the saving or "salvaging" not only of persons but of their projects, what Paul calls the whole "tent" of the body with all its loves, values, interests and concerns, together with everything of meaning and value that human beings have made and suffered in their lives, i.e., have allowed gratuitously to emerge.[28] In this sense, salvation can be understood to include the eschatological culmination of the whole of objective reality, the resurrection of the entire cosmos and the immense riches of the givenness of nature and culture thanks to the sheer abundance of which the projects of human Faiths have been gratuitously facilitated and made efficacious.[29]

By *liberation,* on the other hand, is meant the historically and ecologically provisional, fragmentary and incomplete instances of gratuitous accomplishment, the random manifestations of creative freedom that characterize life in a universe not only subjected to apparent futility by determinisms of Sin but capable of negentropic breakthroughs. In Segundo's evolutionary language these may be described as ethical appropriations of gratuitous love made real on earth in the complex structure of the Sin-Faith dialectic or the ecological density of human action, where often they exist in the apparently unrealized state of a suffering utopian hope, the brokenness of human failure. They are the everyday output of anthropological faith at work in ideologies, the ambiguous and provisional results of neighborly responsibility— actual experiences of and concrete efforts at the realization of self-transcending love—by which people of good will learn to embody utopian hope in ameliorative action on earth.

For Segundo, relying on the complicated anthropology of Paul, such fragmentary liberations are a result of the gratuitous lessening of the distance between the origins of action and its objective results, i.e., the gap between Faith and Sin.[30] As was stressed in chapter two, the experience of this distance means that, ordinarily, under the conditions of apparent futility resulting from the givenness of Sin, the results of human projects are not recognizable as faith's own. The intentions of the inner "I," even when they proceed from fidelity to the truth criterion of love and are the expression of a hope in its value, do not carry through. They are inefficacious and can contribute to the perpetuation or increase of the forces of breakdown in the universe. Under the tragic and incomplete conditions of action in a universe of Sin, this distance is a result of what Paul calls the subjection of Faith to the "law of the members" (i.e., ideologies *qua* Faith's indispensible but never entirely efficacious instruments for the effecting of historical-ecological change). The law of the members is thus synonymous with what Paul calls the law of Sinful Flesh and Segundo calls the law of concupiscence.[31] While the inner "I" of Faith is serving (or at least is intent on serving) what Paul calls the law of the Spirit, the "members" or instruments of Flesh which Faith must use in the attempt to be efficacious in ideologies are caught up in the service of Sin.[32]

The concupiscent effects of action's service to Sin come close to making the utopian hope for this-worldly liberation appear unrealistic. They tempt the deprived and persons and groups of good will in solidarity with them to think that any affirmation of hope, whether anthropological or religious, is more or less equivalent to an idle dream:

> Analyzing history, we see that progress turns on humanity and goes against it. Even the most humanitarian and promising revolutions go astray. Social consensus, the pledge and jewelpiece of any democracy, has buried within it a crushing mass force. The ideologies of liberty, [sisterhood/]brotherhood, and love become sclerotic and bureaucratic. The martyrs are lost in the mists of incomprehension and forgetfulness. The sacrifices, in the long run, are made in vain.[33]

Complicating the situation even more is the experience of sin: action is not automatically set on a course of liberation of the deprived. Seemingly, human freedom can be "anti-creative" more easily than it can be creative. Getting efficacious results out of action is a complex matter taking a life-time of learning and experience. More than anything, it is a matter of taking the risk of gratuitous, self-transcending love.[34]

In the context of gratuitousness and love, freedom is a discipline requiring a tolerance for error and a susceptibility to suffering that involve a fundamental willingness to "begin all over again."[35] In the space opened up by that discipline, Faith must allow itself flexibility—room enough, but not too much—to learn from bungling mistakes. It must challenge itself to construct new syntheses of love out of the increasing entropy and breakdown sin inevitably creates.[36]

Hope in the value of self-transcending love does not pertain solely to the experience of negativity, however. Occasionally, even while Faith is still subject to the entropic law of Sinful Flesh, persons and groups of good will experience glimmerings of the way their projects appear from the negentropic perspective of Spirit. They experience a taste (which theologically speaking is a foretaste of Spirit's boundless positivity, an earthly "downpayment" on the heavenly reality) of having accomplished results that are gratuitously recognizable as Faith's own, results that are truly the work of the inner "I" of Faith even though the ideologies enfleshing it are not completely efficacious. In the language of some of the early Jesus-derived communities, such moments are gratuitous experiences of what the scriptures call *kairos*--Spirit-filled moments of grace *qua* salvation. For Segundo, they are instances of the gratuitous realization of what Paul refers to as the "fullness of time" and John calls Jesus' "hour,"[37] what today the language of evolutionary science would call the efficacious flexibility of an ecological circuit, the reaching of a creative equilibrium between the quantitative and qualitative dimensions of reality,[38] and what in the categories of communication theory Gregory Bateson calls the attaining of "right" or appropriate proportions between the digital and iconic dimensions of creative action.[39] In such moments of gratuitous breakthrough, there "dawns on" Faith a truth about eschatological reality that is appropriate to experience yet still somewhat surprising: earth is sometimes very much like heaven.

For Segundo, there is no need for eschatological hope to flutter about in the heavens. Hope can be firmly rooted right in front of our eyes on earth.[40] In the self-transcendent loving of the neighbor, it can occur to Faith that it is already engaged in the task of constructing a heaven on earth. In those moments of gratuitous breakthrough where the distance between Faith and Sin is lessened or becomes almost imperceptible—moments of liberation or perhaps of mystical intensity in which the power of heaven is made tangible on earth through a kind of "crossing of a threshold" into a new apprehension of the meaningfulness of reality, a shift of gestalt or grasp of truth which is new to Flesh yet not discontinuous with its previous experience but related to it as clarifying culmination—in those moments, there is manifest the promise of, and Spirit's "down-payment" on, a new reality. In the apprehension of that promise—which at the same time is an experience of the reality and value of the present—there is confirmed that what Faith has carried out within the earthly boundaries of utopian hope, what it has done or not done through the expending of costly energies in the *praxis* of neighborly love, in short, what freedom has achieved through the fragile work of a seemingly impotent but actually powerful Faith: these are caught sight of in such moments as indestructible accomplishments forever and irrevocably valid. Such experiences open the eyes of Faith for even the briefest of seconds to a vision of the new and definitive reality in heaven that is being created by self-transcending love.[41] That vision confirms the inkling of utopian hope, an eschatological suspicion it has already had but of itself is unable to confirm, that whatever is done on earth with even the smallest dose of love is everlasting; it is worth it, and worth it forever.[42]

Insofar as such moments are utterly gratuitous, the breakthrough of new reality is the result of an efficacy that in the iconic language of religious experience is said to be "coming down from heaven," while according to the digital language of empirical experience it is said to be proceeding laboriously from earth.[43] The logic of moments of gratuitous breakthrough is thus similar in operation to the logic of evolutionary reality: it is entropic and negentropic at once. As Segundo points out with increasing clarity in his later works, entropy and negentropy are not opposed to one another in Manichæan fashion.[44] They are not to be conceived of as synonyms for evil and good, Sin and grace, negativity and positivity, powerlessness and power, inefficacy and freedom, egotism and love. On the contrary, they are the two essential and complementary vectors of efficacious change at the heart of reality; they define the structure of the universe.[45] Each is entirely necessary to the creation of new reality; one can not operate in the absence of the other.

In this sense, entropy and negentropy are equally constructive of new reality. They are equally contributive to love. From the point of view of the gratuitous realization of efficacious change, each of them has its moment, each its distinctive contribution to make, and Faith has to learn by experience and in conformity with the truth criterion of self-transcending love how to incorporate entropic energies into the circuit of flexibility and wisdom by which it can "rise to the occasion" of welcoming negentropic breakthroughs and celebrating their arrival with joy. As Segundo puts it, relations between entropy and negentropy, which in the anthropological categories of Paul translate roughly into Sin and Faith, are a matter of *"a difficult dialectic,"* [46] a case of the simultaneous working of "a victory and a defeat, but on different levels."[47] According to the circuit-like logic of such a dialectic, action can be conceived of as engaged in the service of Sin and Faith at once. It can be understood to be operating on two different logical levels, the visible and the invisible, i.e., Flesh and Spirit respectively, and to be doing so in a way that is capable of producing efficacious results at the level of Spirit or Faith, while producing apparently inefficacious results and perhaps even seemingly utter failure at the level of Flesh or Sin.[48]

Like the resurrection of Jesus from an apparently useless death, the economy of Sin and Faith is thus the result of "a *gratuitous* and risky venture on the incalculable."[49] It is charismatic. It shows that the power of God's Spirit does erupt on earth. It reveals that, occasionally, the fruits of Spirit actually do break forth, like the evanescent expression of serenity which passes for only the briefest of seconds, but nevertheless really passes, across the otherwise pained and contorted features of a terminally ill person who lies struggling against death. Every so often a dictator falls or people turn out by the thousands to demonstrate against the destructive multiplication of worn-out ideologies of death. Every so often—perhaps only rarely, perhaps once in a single life—the beautiful and death-defeating efficacy of love breaks over the features of the weary world like the resurrection of Jesus breaking over the face of Mary Magdalen in the early Easter morning.

If that is true, then it is true that in the beginning was the eschaton. What the eschaton involves is the creation of something new. Yet the newly created reality is neither discontinuous with the "old" nor different in a radical way from what preceded it but rather its creative "recapitulation," its radical culmination.[50] The logic of newness is marked not by discontinuity but by a superabundance of meaningfulness, a liberative "redundancy" which is the gratuitous result of a creative tension between continuity and discontinuity.[51] In the words of Segundo, the gratuitous breakthrough of the eschatological reality represents "the immense power of what we today would call 'negentropy' to place all the energy of the cosmos in the service of meaning."[52] This power, which is the power to create heaven on earth, is utterly continuous with the power of the earth itself. It brings to completion and recapitulation the intramundane struggle for the realization of self-transcending love, making manifest the earth's definitive significance as the newly created home of both human beings and God:

> The "new earth" is the "new heaven" of God (Rev. 21:1). In other words, God locates [God's] new and definitive dwelling there where the values of the human being, now liberated, flourish in full bloom. Thus the meaning of history in which humanity takes part and struggles, is not going to be replaced by something else; it is going to be absolutized in the new, definitive creation. God is not presented as spectator to the human struggle for meaning. Instead, God is identified with its culmination.[53]

Viewed in the light of such an eschatology, creation is not initiated for the sake of grace but grace for the sake of creation. Because grace is a matter of the definitively efficacious power of self-transcending love, it pertains not to the fulfillment of a distant past but to the creation in the present of a good and worthwhile future. It must be interpreted not by the Book of Genesis but by the gospel of God's having raised up Jesus and his apparently defeated kingdom project to new life. Creation is a question not of origins but of destiny. It is a matter of conjoint loves. Thanks to the impassioned love that is grace, the destiny of heaven is something God has tied irrevocably to the destiny of earth. God's creative project of love is ongoing and cooperative. It will be completed only by the freely validated contributions of self-transcending love. These will become everlasting incarnations—simultaneously achieved and gratuitous—of a new heaven and new earth which God will insert into the definitive reality on the day of the eschaton. There God will make their newness visible as the definitive contours of a world of bliss and freedom in which the lion lies down with the lamb, the fig tree blossoms and is never barren, the deprived have the good news freely handed to them that they are definitively and abundantly blessed.

As the previous section suggests, the question of making a theological link between a liberation that is provisional and a salvation that is definitive is a question of combining the religious meaning of God's eschatological promise with the secular import of utopian hope. The theological response to such a question must be to explore the religious meaning of salvation, the definitive liberation that is mediated by a religious anthropological faith in Jesus' revelation of the values of God's heart and grounded in a religious eschatological hope in the making of a new creation that is said to be "coming down out of heaven from God."

The effort to understand what such a salvation means must include all three dimensions of eschatological hope mentioned in the previous section: what Jesus called the at-handness of the kingdom of God, what Paul calls the resurrection of the body and what the book of Revelation calls the making of a new heaven and a new earth. Stangely enough, the three are seldom brought together into a single eschatology.[54] How then ought they to be combined? Jesus' revelation of what he called the kingdom of God, the traditional credal doctrine of the resurrection of the body, the scriptural notion of the new creation promised by God—if these are to remain inseparable elements of a single eschatology that derives from the life-story of Jesus and is relevant to the contemporary anthropological consciousness of utopian hope, it will have to be demonstrated that the continuity of destinies effected between God and creatures in grace is inclusive of every dimension of self-transcending love on earth: the social as well as the individual, the political as well as the religious, the ecological—what might be called cosmic—as well as the historical. Exactly how these varied symbols of one and the same eschatological hope actually function to incorporate the totality of those dimensions will be treated in a later section. Here it is necessary to recall the interrelatedness of the eschatological symbols themselves, in order to point out their value in trying to make a theological interpretation of definitive salvation that illumines the value and destiny not only of history but of nature or the cosmos as a whole.

Insofar as the logic of the preceding chapters has been an ascending one, it has prepared the ground for making exactly such an interpretation. But insofar as the nature of such an interpretation is religious and theological, it requires that the direction taken in the first three chapters must now be reversed. Where the earlier chapters were concerned with saying a theologically intelligible *human* word about what makes the good news *good*, i.e., what makes Jesus' revelation of the values of God's heart appropriate to the concerns of sensitive hearts on earth and capable of being welcomed there as compatible with the logic of action in the secular realm, this final chapter is concerned with conveying an anthropologically intelligible word from *God,* a word of gratuitous revelation about what makes the good news *news.* Together, the goodness and newness of God's revelation form a single Jesus-derived gospel. They constitute two sides of a single theological datum about the meaning of God's eschatological promise, a datum that in categories appropriate to the secular experience of utopian striving must attempt to embody the religious content of a salvation that is not only liberative on earth but creative of a world that is good and inhabitable, that is "coming down out of heaven from God."

The questions ruling the logic of the following sections must therefore center on the sheer gratuitousness of the eschatological content that breaks into the world from God, a news from heaven that can be recognized on earth only by the truth criterion of neighborly commitment to the liberation of the deprived and yet can not simply be reduced to concrete instances of secular liberation in nature and history. If the story of God's project were to end with the accomplishment of historical and ecological instances of liberation through neighborly love on earth, if it were to conclude with an interest in the relatively efficacious ideologies of the Faith of sensitive hearts, then there would actually be no point in disciples' being interested in getting any news from heaven. Concrete instances of secular liberation would serve not merely as the only reliable truth criterion of a salvation promised by God but would focus eschatology exclusively on earth. Fragmentary experiences of liberation and the manifestation of freedom on earth would become sufficient to exhaust the religious content of salvation, and heaven would be made permanently irrelevant.

Such an approach would obviously present serious theological problems. A first is that salvation would become a purely immanent affair, a utilitarian matter of intramundane achievement. Emphasis would fall on the need for efficacious results in such a way that, were evidence for success visibly lacking, the efforts themselves would be dismissed as having little or no salvific value to anyone, including God. Salvation would be considered real and effective only insofar as it could be seen to be already realized or actually "working" on earth. Carried to conclusions, the logic of salvation according to such a view would consist in pursuit of an efficacy that would be "utopian" in the worst sense: namely, representative of an unrealistic search for immediate solutions in the direction of "whatever works" or "whatever it takes" to liberate or be liberated here and now, regardless of the cost. Segundo rejects such views as anti-evolutionary.[55] They neglect to take into account the dimensions of meaning and value and focus instead on the dimension of efficacy. And they do this at the expense of evolutionary factors like flexibility, wisdom and a tolerance for error which, from his point of view, are integral to the discipline of learning what it means to be possessed of a freedom that is socially, politically and ecologically contextualized and thus essentially limited by the givenness of reality.[56]

As was seen in chapters one and two, a limited freedom is a disciplined freedom, a freedom made humble by self-transcendent contact with reality.[57] It is a freedom that is trying to learn respect for the ecological density of efficacious love, that is trying to incorporate into its essential structure a love-like gratitude to the determinisms of Sin and the mechanisms of nature and second nature on which Faith depends for the achievement of efficacious results. Refraining from the temptation to immediacy and facility, a humble freedom refuses to short-circuit the creative energies of natural processes by either an overload of purposiveness or a timid failure of creative imagination. It is committed to learning a *praxis* of truth that is ultimately the impassioned action of suffering, a patient love which does not force the creation of the new but allows it gratuitously to emerge. Such freedom is a discipleship of self-transcending love.

A second danger is that the commitment to secular liberation would be thought to constitute, or, rather, would simply be made equivalent to, religious faith in God, and everyone on earth, possibly against their wills and in likely violation of their consciences, would end up being categorized as an 'anonymous theist.' God's universal salvific will would be made the theological means to a no doubt well-intentioned but certainly distorted end: the blurring of ethics and religion. Such blurring would make the striving for liberation of the deprived "anonymously synonymous" with religious appropriation of the datum of revelation about eschatological salvation. What is worse, it could serve to make theology an elitist ideology, the prerogative of religious groups who in the name of "God" could employ theological categories as ideological tools to point out the "anthropological flaws" in others: if not to indicate the so-called "sinfulness" of secular reality (by drawing false dichotomies between 'sacred' and 'profane,' 'secular' and 'religious') then to suggest the existence of an alleged "incompleteness" in the experience of professedly a-religious human beings and groups.

But that oppressive scenario does not have to occur, and it can be prevented by maintaining an appropriate theological distance between religion and ethics. The problem of a loss of equilibrium between the two is most pertinent, and therefore optimally solvable, at the level of eschatology. While concretely experienced instances of secular liberation are sufficient on earth to constitute love—and therefore sufficient to realize for earthly reasons in Faith the same values God wills for heavenly reasons in grace—such instances are not simply coextensive with a religious anthropological faith in Jesus' revelation of God. The religious difference made by an anthropological faith in God whom Jesus revealed is a matter of human beings' being able to pray the way Jesus taught, a matter of their being able to address God with the kind of "Hallowed be your name" which stands at the head of this chapter.[58]

A Jesus-centered religious anthropological faith pertains to a free appropriation of the gratuitousness of God's love for "sinners" and the poor, a Jesus-like preoccupation with God's single-hearted passion to work with suffering creatures at the project of liberation of the deprived and to make in the face of Sin and death a world that is inhabitable and good. Ultimately, a religious response of anthropological faith to the initiative of God's love is *voluntary*. It involves conscious and not 'unconscious' participation in what, for disciples, is God's gratuitously revealed yet strangely familiar and appropriately earthly work: the costly construction, conjointly with creatures, of a new heaven and new earth through the labor of self-transcending love.

For Segundo, it is particularly significant that Jesus taught the disciples only a single prayer, the "Our Father". The significance does not lie in the fact that the formula is unique, the only words by which disciples ought to address God. Rather, the significance is that the prayer of Jesus contains and defines the orientation of prayer as such, which is to put disciples directly in touch with the values of God embodied in what Jesus called the coming of God's kingdom. In the prayer that Jesus taught us, disciples find themselves before the project dearest to God's heart, a project which is also their own. From the human situation of relative impotence, disciples place themselves at the service of God's project, asking that the power of God be effective on earth to realize the values of the kingdom project by incorporating disciples in its work.[59]

The questions ruling the rest of the discussion may therefore be summed up as expressing a theological interest in hearing a word of news from God about the definitive worthwhileness of what Jesus called the kingdom project. If this project is also an unfailing promise of definitive salvation, a present downpayment on the future manifestation of the everlasting value of self-transcending love, what new content is going to "come down to earth" from heaven? Of what is God's eschatological validation of neighborly love going to consist? On the other hand, what difference can, do and ultimately will, the earthly realization of neighborly love actually make to God? If God's will is that God's love for suffering creatures be realized on earth as it is in heaven, does it not follow that what happens to and among creatures affects the happiness and heart of God?[60] What, in other words, is the definitive significance of God's having initiated and revealed the project that is grace, from the point of view not just of creatures but of God?

In spite of the pertinence of these questions to a theological interest in heaven, a reading of the remainder of these reflections will show that, in the end, the purpose of asking about the "heavenly" dimension of eschatological hope remains tied to a stubborn theological interest in its earthly significance. Such a stress seems justified in light of the ease with which present-day emphases on religious anthropological faith can risk obscuring the earthly relevance of eschatology with purely religious, essentially other-worldly interpretations of salvation.[61] Indeed, the news of God's promise of creation of a *world,* the revelation from God about the building of a new heaven and a new *earth,* the promise of a new creation in which every tear will be wiped away and deprivation and death will be no more—in short, the ethical dimension of God's promise of salvation in a universe subjected to Sin—all of this is in danger of being overlooked or forgotten in favor of a purely religious understanding of eschatological salvation that is said to pertain strictly to God in heaven.

The remainder of the discussion will be tied to the earthly relevance of a Jesus-normed eschatology in two ways. On the one hand, I will attempt to pull together and recapitulate what the argument up to this point has been intent on establishing, namely that in the logic of action there can be found a sort of anthropological fittingness, a kind of "eschatological readiness" on the basis of which the destiny of creatures may be linked to that of God (a readiness, however, does not of necessity have to be "met"). Yet I want to add to that affirmation the eschatologically relevant datum of gospel revelation that the structure of that continuity—the actual content serving to connect the earthly power of ameliorative action with the heavenly power of the impassioned action of God—is the capacity of anthropological Faith to build ideologies of self-transcending love. I want to show that love inheres in action by a logic that is eschatological, and I want to speak a theological word about that logic from the perspective of revelation; for revelation claims that, when viewed from the vantage point of God's own initiative of love in grace, action that is normed by the liberation of the deprived is capable of bearing fruits on earth that will show up in heaven as constitutive elements of, and everlastingly valid contributions to, God's proper and transcendent glory.

On the other hand, I wish to elaborate more fully on the this-worldly significance, the historical and ecological relevance, of an eschatological hope in the worthwhileness of love in light of the problems of our time. This aspect of the task seems especially crucial given the desire to remain faithful to a *praxis* of Faith that is a discipleship of Jesus in Spirit and in truth. Insofar as the latter would attempt to be a theological reflection on the project and promise of God that functions as rationally coherent ground for hope and ethically justifiable impetus for action, it must be conducted in a secular context of the most pressing problems of the times. The point is that in our time it seems inappropriate even to attempt an account of the theological continuity between God's project in heaven and utopian striving on earth in absence of eschatology's double referent to both the values of God made known in revelation and the troubled questions of the sensitive heart, religious or not, about the increasingly violent and long-term effects of injustice in this world, the burden of unrelieved debilitation and deprivation for increasingly vast numbers of suffering creatures on earth.

As the preceding discussion has indicated, theological concern over love's failure to eliminate this burden creates a need for a hope-confirming account of the eschatological significance of action in history and nature, a need made all the more urgent insofar as theology has recently gained a new hermeneutical consciousness. Theologians are becoming increasingly aware that God's salvation has been revealed in Jesus' kingdom *praxis* as a *praxis* of liberation ruled by the values of God's heart. Chief among the latter is the release of suffering neighbors from injustice and deprivation, a liberation that must be made a preoccupation of the heart on earth just as it is willed by God in heaven. Just as liberation of the deprived is the only truth criterion of love on earth by which to determine the will of God, so is the preoccupation of the sensitive heart with the liberation of the deprived the only valid criterion in heaven by which God can recognize, and eschatologically validate, the substance of neighborly love. Love is recognizable on earth as it is in heaven not by its efficacious results but by the sensitivity of neighbors' hearts and actions to the needs of the deprived.[62]

For Segundo, this means that the efficacy of action has to do not with whether Faith actually "works," not with whether it is "successful," but with the *quality* of its work, with whether action rings true to the truth criterion of self-transcending love. The significance of this criterion is that it permits what is a work of human Faith on earth to effect in the sphere of eschatological reality a work that is the love of God in heaven:

> In deciding what is 'suitable' [to the liberative work of Faith], human beings must consider what 'builds up' their brothers and sisters (1 Cor. 10: 23-24; Rom. 14: 19-20). Love consists in collaborating with God in the work of building or constructing a human existence for human beings. Hence the importance of this *work:* it is—partially and secondarily, to be sure—*the work of God Godself* (14:20) on behalf of humanity, and we are cooperators and joint workers (*sunergoi;* see 1 Cor. 3:9) in it.[63]

In emphasizing the significance of "work" for the definitive validity of love, Segundo relies on "the only New Testament writer to suggest a vision of the divine judgment that takes into account the mixed nature of human action," namely Paul, whom he quotes at length on this subject:

> Let everyone be careful how they build. . .For no one can lay any other foundation than Christ himself. And whether one builds on it with gold or silver or precious stones, or with wood or hay or straw, the work of each one will be made manifest. The day [of divine judgment] will make it manifest, appearing with fire, and fire will test the quality of each person's work. If a persons' work stands the test, the person will receive recompense. But the person whose work is burned up will suffer the loss. Nevertheless that person will be saved, but as one passing through fire (1 Cor. 3: 10-15).[64]

At first glance, no doubt, we are prepared to assert that not everything—or perhaps not much—in our lives is gold and silver and precious stones. Like the ninety year-old heroine of Margaret Laurence's *The Stone Angel,* who in the last few moments of her life is reflecting on what she has done that is truly free, we can recognize—with irony, perhaps—that it was probably what at the time seemed to be some of the most unassuming actions we ever performed that were genuinely free, that were truly the expression of a love that was self-transcending. For Laurence's heroine, there were only two, and they had only just occurred. The first was a lie told to her son during his final visit (by which she created truth for him), and the second was a joke (that she, an old and dying woman, was able to procure a bedpan for the able-bodied but incapacitated young teenager who shared her hospital room).[65]

The Earthly Redundance of God's *Mysterion* and the Heavenly Validity of Love

As was seen in chapter one, the revelation of the values of God's heart that took place in Jesus' kingdom *praxis* is key to the theological understanding of grace. The aim of that chapter was to interpret the religio-theological conception of grace in terms of Jesus' good news about God, the revelation that in an incomplete and tragic universe God has initiated a salvific project creative of a world that will be worthwhile and inhabitable and, thanks to the impassioned love of God and creatures working together at the liberation of the deprived, capable in the end of being pronounced good. To that project Jesus gave the name kingdom of God, manifest secret of God's impassioned love and project dearest to God's heart.

Chapter two attempted to deal with the question of how God's kingdom project can be efficacious in history and nature, how it can be said to be working there at all in the face of negativities as seemingly definitive as Sin and sin. In that chapter, building on the foundation laid in chapter one, it was suggested that, thanks to the evolutionary logic by which Faith is not only subjected to apparent futility by the entropic energies of Sin but is also productive of gratuitous breakthroughs of efficacious change through negentropic energies of self-transcending love, God's project is efficacious not in spite of Sin but by means of it. Even though the determinisms of Sin make it appear that Sin is winning out on earth and may well be carrying the world as a whole to a critically unstable point, God's values continue to be found at work wherever Faith strives to incorporate the energies of Sin into ideologies of self-transcending love.

As was seen in chapter three, thanks to the reciprocal corrective continually taking place between faiths and ideologies at the level of persons' and groups' everyday *praxis*, there is a capacity in anthropological faith itself, even under the ambiguous and negative conditions of Sin, to go on investing itself in ideologies responsive to the needs of the deprived, to go on engaging in ameliorative action as though the building of self-transcending love were ultimately worthwhile. There is a creative dynamism inherent in the sensitive heart (as opposed to the self-deceptive reasonings and enslavement to injustice inhering in the hardened heart) that enables Faith to welcome the gratuitous breakthroughs of neighborly love wherever they occur, to celebrate their arrival in the truth-constructive manner of the unknown woman's daring action of anointing the head of Jesus in face of his impending death.

Not only are such ideological creations gratuitously constructive of truth, but the neighborly response of the sensitive heart to the suffering and deprivation of others is the only reliable truth criterion by which Faith can know it is striving to be constructive of love and can make a new reality. And it can do this with the same degree of efficacy with which God is willing love's definitive creation in heaven.

The argument of the first three chapters thus led to the conclusion that in the context of the logic of action, the good news of revelation has to do with the datum about God's values communicated in Jesus' kingdom *praxis,* namely that God thinks the liberation of the deprived is constructive of new reality, too. According to Jesus' kingdom Faith and its liberative ideologies, the values of God's heart in heaven ratify the values of sensitive hearts on earth, and that makes the good news *good.* This chapter must now turn to the datum of revelation that claims something more exciting and unprecedented, namely, that in generosity, durability and efficacy, God's gratuitous response to the work of Faith definitively surpasses what the human heart could ever hope for or imagine, and that makes the good news *news.*

REVELATION OF GOD'S *MYSTERION* AND THE COSMIC RELEVANCE OF ESCHATOLOGY

In the context of wanting to present a version of God's news that is normed by Jesus' life-story and kingdom *praxis*--in other words, in the context of wanting to make exactly the secularly relevant kind of eschatology referred to in the previous sections—and in light of the meandering hermeneutical course by which: (1) Jesus first translated the values of God into a religio-political kingdom *praxis,* (2) Paul translated the significance of Jesus' life-story into anthropologically decisive categories, (3) Segundo translated both the significance of Jesus and the categories of Paul into an evolutionary liberationist framework, and (4) I am trying to sketch a few lines along which one might begin translating the originality of Segundo's achievement into categories pertinent to the logic of action—in the context of all of that, it appears that essential to linking heaven and earth in terms relevant to the interests of both must be an interpretation of what Jesus called God's kingdom project that connects utopian striving for the liberation of the deprived with the definitive worthwhileness of self-transcending love.

If one asks where it is possible to find a theological category equal to the task, it seems appropriate to turn to the biblical notion *mysterion,* technical term in Paul's vocabulary for the gratuitously revealed "secret" of God's project and promise of definitive salvation.[66] In Jesus' life-story, the promise of a salvation that is "coming down out of heaven from God" has been made definitively manifest as God's gratuitous initiation of, and creatures' free participation in, the creation of a world that is good. Where Jesus called this project the "at-handness" of God's kingdom to "sinners" and the poor, Paul reinterprets it as "a battle, coextensive with humanity itself, against the infrahuman condition of human beings."[67] According to the anthropological connotations given to that project by Paul, the promise inherent in the *mysterion* is God's everlasting commitment to the worthwhileness and validity of self-transcending love, God's pledge to take the destiny of suffering creatures as seriously as God's own, God's impassioned love in the friendship that is grace, God's definitive manifestation of the secret dearest to God's heart.[68]

While use of this almost exclusively Pauline category could initially present a stumbling-block to persons of sensitive heart (because it is susceptible of being co-opted by theological experts in the interests of religious mystification and because, as Segundo admits, Paul's anthropology, to which it is connected, tends to be negative, pessimistic and complicated),[69] pronouncing the word *mysterion* in the context of eschatological hope can serve a theologically useful purpose. It can release eschatology from subservience to exclusively other-worldly religious connotations. It can save it from the theological obscurity of possibly worn-out formulas like "mystery of salvation" or "mystery of faith" by giving God's project a practical foothold in the secular realm. Interpreted in a way directly concerned with the logic of action, i.e., the secular interest in liberation of the deprived and utopian hope in the overcoming of evil, *mysterion* is capable of restoring to the religious notion of salvation the secularly relevant connotations originally given that term by Jesus. And this retrieval of what can be easily lost or forgotten about Jesus' God-revealing kingdom *praxis* can make a difference in the way persons of good will who are disciples of Jesus might engage in a liberative *praxis* of eschatological hope that is grounded in Jesus' revelation of God's values today.

In spite of the fact that over the course of centuries "efforts have been made to set up an opposition between historical importance on the one hand and eschatology on the other," Segundo notes that the categories of Paul's eschatology remain relevant to the complicated problems of society, politics and ecology facing the world today.[70] Paul's categories thus form an essential element of what makes the gospel a piece of good news to the deprived, since in spite of the primarily anthropological significance his categories have, they continue to represent "a revaluation of the historical . . .the only kind of eschatology that can reinforce committed involvement with the problems of causality and effectiveness in time."[71]

Briefly recalled, Segundo's reading of Paul maintains that Sin (including its perversion into sin) is condition for the realization of love in an evolving world.[72] Although the universe is incomplete and has been fraught with the negativities of evil and suffering from the beginning, God wills the creation of a world that is good, a world that is inhabitable and worthwhile for both creatures and God, by creative incorporation of the negative energies of Sin and sin into ideologies of self-transcending love.[73] Chief among these are the huge investments of randomness, entropy and time that are required for the emergence of qualitative change. They create a contrast between what is immediately visible under the obvious conditions of action's subjection to Sin and what is just as real but not so clearly visible from the point of view of Faith's gratuitous capacity to realize efficacious results in ideologies of neighborly love.

What accumulates visibly in history and nature is Sin, with its potential in the human sphere to be distorted into sin. This makes it appear that love can never—or at least seldom—be victorious over the determinisms of Sin on earth. What emerges invisibly, however, is love, which will be made fully manifest only under the definitive conditions of the eschaton, where Jesus' resurrection will finally shed light on, or give a clarifying "setting" to, love in a way that manifests its intrinsic value and brings out its hidden worth.[74] "What accumulates," Segundo writes, "is what is emerging," and he explains what this means in terms of the definitive victory of love over the negativity and inefficacy of Sin:

> Paul makes clear to us that accumulation and emergence *are not on the same plane*. The plane of the definitive accumulates *only* what is free: i.e., love. That which accumulates impersonally and seems to destroy love fails to do so and ends up destroying itself. Our hope is not delusory because a single act of love wins out over the multitude (i.e., totality) of Sin."[75]

What Paul is saying, Segundo believes, is not only that love is strong, not only that it is more powerful than Sin, sin and death. He is saying that, exactly *qua* power to effect the good, love has an ontological value that sin *qua* egotism lacks.[76] For Segundo, the definitive value of love is grounded in what he calls "one of the most important data of the Christian message: the *essential disproportion* between the solidity and efficacy of love and that of egotism."[77] The importance of this datum is that it prohibits theologians' trying to view good and evil, love and egotism, in Manichæan fashion as two opposed and equal forces. Instead, the work of Faith, like reality itself, is profoundly mixed. There is always something of love and something of egotism mixed together in human action that is present in every work.[78] How, then, can Paul be so sure that on the plane of the definitive, love is really emerging? Segundo's answer is that love has an ontological value that qualitatively surpasses the apparent weightiness of egotism.[79] He writes:

> Even though both love and egotism come under our responsibility, they are not on the same plane. Nor do they have the same ontological efficacy, so to speak. They are not situated vis-à-vis the absolute, the definitive, in the same way.[80]

What makes them different from Segundo's point of view is precisely their relation to efficacy, i.e., the power freedom has *qua* Faith has to effect something good and worthwhile:

> If the freedom of the human being *is capable of carrying out what it chooses,* and... chooses the good, one single performance of the good means more than all the "alien" stuff that has accumulated in that human life. Thus *love wins by covering a multitude of sins,* not by magic or the absence of liberty but rather *by the very anthropological makeup of the human being.* [81]

Love is efficacious unto the making of new reality where egotism is not.

As was seen in chapter two, Segundo believes that in every generation, human beings are faced with the task of making their Faith efficacious. They are faced with the challenge of meeting what Paul calls the "sufferings of the present moment" with an eschatological hope in the ultimate value of placing their Faith in constructive service to love, and when they do, they are contributing irreversibly to the emergence of the definitive reality:

> Only a world in which Sin can accumulate and become Law, as meaningless in itself as Death is, can prevent the accomplishments of one generation from diminishing the importance and decisive character of the next generation. If Sin were quantitatively overcome as humanity advanced in history, then human beings would become useless and wander in vain about the world. We need a world in which creation, love, and life triumph qualitatively, transforming reality irreversibly without ever escaping the quantitative victory of Sin. Only such a world can make human existence worthwhile, can put Faith in the human heart as energy concentrated on its committed involvement in history, and all the power of God in its inner creativity as a child of God.[82]

A brief review of Segundo's response to the question of what God has to say about the persistence of evil in a universe of Sin will help to clarify the meaning of this point. In the evolutionary framework of Segundo's eschatology, the cumulative effects of evil in the world and its affrontive consequence in the possibility and actuality of creaturely suffering are signs that in the face of evil, God is engaged with creatures in a salvific project creative of a world that is good. God's interest in the liberation of the deprived is an indication that from God's point of view, the task of creating a world that is good "means inheriting something immensely worthwhile *to do*... something to be done."[83] Given the cumulative power of the negative energies of Sin, action's most properly human *charism* is to place the energies of freedom at the service of creative syntheses of love. In a universe structured not by projectivity alone but also by givenness and chance, a universe in which there not only gratuitously emerge occasional breakthroughs of negentropic change but also visibly accumulate the continual negativity and affrontive effects of entropy, freedom's *raison d'être* is to create. It is to make in a medium of seemingly old and worn-out quantitative energies something qualitative, positive and new, a world that is lasting and good, constructive manifestations of negentropic energy. In face of the "build-up of breakdown" that is Sin, the logic of grace is to allow to be manifested the contrastive results of efficacious freedom which are love.

In a world headed for the definitive manifestation of the absolute value of love but still groaning under the conditions of Sin in the labor of trying to bring love's realization about, the creativity of human freedom is God's only way of realizing the values of the *mysterion*. Evil and suffering are the disconcerting, indeed affrontive yet apparently unavoidable ontological conditions under which the constructive contributions of God's and creatures' conjoint action must ultimately be made. On the creative incorporation of the negativity of Sin into works of self-transcending love depends the definitive worthwhileness of the *mysterion* itself, not only for creatures but for God:

> God Godself would have created a world *in vain*, a world that does not honor God directly, if the human being did not turn this suffering into *the meaning and mainspring of its freedom*, of what can still be called 'creation' in an already created world: the appearance of a new being, the building up of the brother and sister, the 'birth' that gives meaning to labor pains. If human freedom never managed to stamp the seal of its unique, personal intention on its performances, then God Godself would be a failure.[84]

Even more importantly, that last sentence shows, the effecting of neighborly love is the only way creatures can come to have real substance vis-à-vis the intensive reality of God.[85]

As chapter one attempted to show, from the point of view of Segundo's evolutionary ontology, love is ultimately what makes creatures real. Not simply the love of God alone, which is the love God offered first, a love God gives not by necessity but in the gratuitous initiative by which God graces creatures with God's own power and by which they learn to create in an ontological sense and thereby manifest on earth what freedom really is—this is not the only love which makes creatures real. There is also the love that creatures themselves can make, their own proper love, the love that belongs to them as lovers and creators and is properly the achievement of their own relatively efficacious freedom. If God and creatures were unable to befriend one another in such a gratuitous reciprocity of loves, creatures would be charming Pinocchios and God would be a kindly Gepetto but neither would be truly real.

From Segundo's point of view, God's refusal to bring to a premature end the subjection of the universe to Sin means that "God has left creation dependent on human decision. . . .[and] only the glorious manifestation of the freedom of God's children will restore to creation its usefulness."[86] In the end, that usefulness derives for God from the constructive power of Faith, the gratuitous capacity of the sensitive heart to make a neighborly response to the needs of the deprived and thus create in the face of Sin and sin a precious residue of love. What Segundo is saying is that God is unwilling to take the easy way out by sacrificing the definitive manifestation of creative freedom for the sake of ending suffering in the present. For God, the definitive manifestation of creative freedom is worth what it costs in God's and creatures' pain, since there is no other way for either of them to make the value of freedom manifest. Were God to have ended suffering before it began, freedom would never be able to be manifested for what it truly is: the capacity to make a love that is truly creatures' own, the power to impart a tangible substance of reality to the creation of a world that must be made definitively good by creatures' finite love on earth and held fragilely in their hands.

Segundo's reading of Paul is thus original and liberative, for both God and creatures. The evolutionary ontology on which it is based focuses eschatology on a reciprocity of loves and keeps the efficacy of God's and creatures' freedom real.[87] Yet Segundo's preference for interpreting God's project primarily in terms of the "humanization" of the cosmos tends to limit Paul's eschatology to the interests of human liberation. It transposes eschatology into an exclusively anthropological key. Although Segundo points out that it is not only persons but their projects which are saved, i.e., the "work" of Faith understood as the totality of people's historical existence—what Paul calls the "tent" of the body comprising people's relatives, friends, interests and projects[88]—he does not explicitly include in that totality the objective givenness of reality, i.e., nature in the ordinary sense, the rest of the creatures on earth, the cosmos in all its aspects.

In other words, in spite of the constructive role Segundo gives nature as facilitator of the gratuitous accomplishments of freedom in an evolving world, he does not give evolutionary spheres other than the human an explicit—and thus everlasting—value in the eschaton. For example, although he interprets Paul's notion of general resurrection in an earth-affirming way in terms of the biblical doctrine of the new creation,[89] Segundo places heaviest stress on the anthropological relevance of the "new heaven" and "new earth." He makes them the arena of neighborly love rather than situating the definitive relevance of neighborly love in the more inclusive context of the making of a cosmos that will be inhabitable and good for all—a methodological irony, considering the striking originality of both his insistence on the ecological density of freedom in the dialectic between Faith and Sin and his project-centered exegeses of Mt. 25: 31-46 and 1 Cor. 3: 13-15.[90]

I believe a further "transposition" of Segundo's eschatology, a hermeneutical rendition of the Faith-Sin dialectic in the inclusive context of the *mysterion,* can overcome the limits of a predominantly anthropological reading of Paul, expanding the notions of liberation and salvation to include a revaluation of nature or the cosmos as a whole.[91] Doing so would lead, as Segundo's evolutionary categories already suggest but do not explicitly develop, to an ecologically conscientized discourse about eschatology that does not end in a teleology of human action alone but points in the direction of the cosmic link between human destiny and the destiny of all other creatures.

As has been seen, that direction is the God-like one of self-transcending love, the distinctively (although not exclusively) human *charism* of *mysterion* responsibility. This is a creative responsibility shared with God for the building on earth of heaven-like constructions of self-transcending love suited to the creation of a world that meets the needs not only of human beings and their liberation from deprivation but of creatures other than human. Such an approach would make human social persons neighbor to suffering creatures of any species at the level of their most basic and immediate need.

Mysterion responsibility is a human responsibility aimed at making a world that is not only good for human beings, but inhabitable for all creatures, since according to the data of revelation (and this is a case where the ancient Hebrew poet-prophets offer a corrective to the anthropocentric mysticism of the gospels, Acts, letters and Book of Revelation), God has promised the coming of an eschatological reality in which not only will every tear be wiped away, death and grieving will be no more, the deprived will have restored to them more than was taken away and the dead will be brought to new life, but the lion will lie down with the lamb, the little child will play over the adder's lair and the sun and moon will shine not to serve the interests of earth but for the sheer joy of shining. Revelation claims that God has promised (and, in the love that is grace, God and creatures have already begun creating) a cosmos that is a new heaven and a new earth, an earth that will have become a heaven and a heaven that will have come to earth, i.e., an everlastingly inhabitable, all-inclusive world.[92]

The effort to move from Segundo's anthropological reading of Paul toward the making of a cosmocentric eschatology seems justified to the extent that a small difference at the level of theory can contribute to substantial differences at the level of practice. On the one hand, as Segundo's eschatology already does, it can permit the notion of a salvation coming from heaven to be theologically rounded out to incorporate as an essential element any and every instance of secular liberation that comes into view on earth. This restores to the religious content of eschatology an ethical dimension that is appropriately historical, social and political in scope. On the other hand, by a kind of ecologically conscientized evolutionary thinking Segundo describes as analogical,[93] the salvation criterion of liberation of the deprived can be made inclusive enough to comprise the liberation not only of human social persons and their history, but of all creatures. The historical, social and political dimensions can be completed, in other words, by inclusion of the so-called realm of nature. And the taking into account of this cosmic referent gives eschatology a necessary ecological relevance.

The most reliable source of revealed data about the *mysterion* is Jesus' kingdom *praxis,* validated by God in the act of raising Jesus from the dead. The *praxis* of Jesus points to a continuity (which is not a causal connection) between the secrets of God's heart and the hopes and longings of the sensitive human heart.[94] Insofar as what Jesus himself may have called the *"secret"* of the kingdom (Mk. 4: 11) is identical with the truth criterion of self-transcending love accessible to everyone, or, rather, to all who, in the words of Jesus, have "eyes to see" and "ears to hear" the neighbor in distress, the *mysterion* is a truth that is manifest; it is open to observation anywhere and everywhere there is an instance of liberation on earth.[95] But insofar as communication and realization of God's kingdom values are contingent on sensitivity and receptivity, a watchful and ready discipline of anthropological Faith that is the only efficacious means on earth to awaken the heart to truth, the *mysterion* is hidden. As was emphasized particularly in chapter three, appropriation of Jesus' revelation of the values of God's heart is contingent on values already held dear by sensitive hearts on earth.

The fact that the project of God's heart is a *mysterion* thus does not mean it is a secret God has kept, and continues to keep, hidden. On the contrary, God has manifested it from the beginning as both a project and a promise. As a project, it means that love is in labor of being efficaciously realized on earth. As promise, it points to the coming of a "day" on which the ontologically enduring value of love will be definitively manifest in heaven. Each of these dimensions is integral to a Jesus-normed understanding of *mysterion.* Together, they articulate the indispensible eschatological coordinates of the doctrine of creation: its time of creative labor, which is grace, and its time of definitive completion, which is glory. In this stretch of the discussion, emphasis will fall on the revelatory role of Jesus in communicating the *mysterion,* for in his life, death and resurrection—the meaning and value of his kingdom *praxis* apprehended as a whole—occurs God's definitive expression of the news that is being born (and borne) on earth from heaven.

As chapter three pointed out, God's project is being effected on earth where the logic of action is at its best, so to speak. In the tendency of the sensitive heart to establish a reliable truth criterion of love, compatibility is founded between the liberative *praxis* of anthropological faith and the values of God's heart. In the *praxis* of all the prophets, but in a definitive way in the kingdom *praxis* of Jesus, this compatibility is spoken about and given a name: grace. Thanks to grace's being gratuitously expressed in the liberation of the deprived, the ready capacity for hearing an explicit word from God about the values of God's heart—i.e., welcoming revelation of the *mysterion*—is accessible to everyone at the level of action. Yet the welcoming of revelation is not simply present to action in an implicit way in its logic.

If a word from God about the *mysterion* is to be heard on earth, it has first to be revealed. It is not simply already there, just waiting to be uncovered.[96]

Jesus' significance vis-à-vis the *mysterion* is thus that God's project (grace) and its significance for the creation of the cosmos (revelation) are definitively manifest in Jesus' kingdom *praxis* because of the capacity it had during his life to mediate an efficacious salvation from God, and after the events of the resurrection, ascension and sending of the Spirit, to transmit a definitive revelation of God's heart.[97] In Jesus' kingdom *praxis* and resurrection, God has made the *mysterion* known on earth in a definitive way as God's sure and liberative commitment of self-transcending love. To that extent, the *mysterion* is secret only insofar as it is gratuitous. Not only is it not required by the evidence (since, if it were, it would no longer be a secret), but it is not capable of being known at all unless it first would be revealed.

The fact that the *mysterion* is a secret thus has to do more with the gratuitousness of God's initiative than with creatures' longing or capacity for God. History and nature do not need participation in God's *mysterion* in order to have meaning and value in themselves; rather, God's revelation of the *mysterion,* God's gratuitous introduction of action and its intramundane logic into the secret of God's will, is a word from God in heaven. It is God's making plain by God's own impassioned action that efforts made toward liberation of the deprived, utopian strivings that in their own right already have value on earth, make a difference also to the heart of God, have an effect on God in heaven. Since the *mysterion* is nothing other than the impassioned character of God's gratuitous love, God's being moved to involve the logic of creaturely action, already valid and efficacious on earth, in a project that is also definitively creative in heaven, it makes action and its effects on the cosmos matter, and matter definitively, to God.

Theologically speaking, of course, God's having introduced the cosmos to the *mysterion* as a project and promise in grace must also have an effect on creatures. The effect, however, is entirely gratuitous. The *mysterion* brings a piece of good news from God. It communicates a gratuitous yet strikingly redundant[98] datum of revelation that makes a difference to anthropological Faith, shedding new light on human ideologies and manifesting their value as attempts at efficacy that matter not only to the hopes and sufferings of the deprived on earth but also to the heart of God in heaven. The *mysterion*—manifest secret of God's love—is thus hidden insofar as it refers to a gratuitous initiative proceeding from God in heaven; but it is manifest insofar as it refers to the actuality (and not just the abstract possibility) of God's having testified historically and in public, in a testimony of self-revelation mediated by the Faith *praxis* of both Jesus and disciples of Jesus and compatible in Spirit with the already existing secular responses of sensitive hearts to the sufferings of the deprived, to the existence of a gratuitous continuity between the eschatological logic of God's *mysterion* in heaven and the this-worldly logic of utopian striving for secular liberation on earth.

A first conclusion of importance about the this-worldly relevance of God's *mysterion* is thus that it pertains explicitly to the initiative of God. As the project of God's heart, the *mysterion* does not arise from the logic of earth but comes to creatures from outside, from heaven. The continuity between heaven and earth is flexible and gratuitous. It depends on God's free and sovereign commitment, made known as an impassioned and unshakeable love. A second important conclusion, related to the first, is that the *mysterion* can be known on earth only if it is first revealed, at the level of liberative action, as a word from God in heaven about the love of God on earth. We creatures need to be given data of revelation about the *mysterion;* we do not already have access to it by a more or less conscious knowledge of God, however inchoate. A third conclusion, mediated, as has been seen, by hermeneutical transposition of the significance of Jesus' kingdom Faith and resurrection, is that a cosmic interpretation of God's salvific and creative project in grace provides an ecologically conscious means of uniting God's promise of the eschatological worthwhileness of love with the utopian strivings of sensitive hearts. This third conclusion hints that the *mysterion* can be tied to the utopian hope for liberation of the deprived by an eschatological logic at work in action from the start, and so provides a convenient vantage point from which to embark in the remaining sections on a discussion of the definitive efficacy of love over injustice, deprivation, suffering and death.[99]

THE UTOPIAN LOGIC OF FAITH AND IDEOLOGIES AND THE ESCHATOLOGICAL
LOGIC OF THE *MYSTERION*

It seems fitting to make a first theological response to the task of linking heaven and earth with an attempt to fathom how human action, by its own internal logic, must instill into the fabric of earthly existence a capacity for what has traditionally been called glory. I will therefore argue in this section that a solution of continuity between heaven and earth must derive from the fact that, from a theological point of view, the logic of action is inherently eschatological.[100]

It seems that there is no other way to put heaven and earth together, since, in the absence of eschatological significance, both the doctrine of creation and the doctrine of the sovereignty of God risk remaining a cold and purely rational affair. It is the thesis of this section that the logical conclusion of God's impassioned love— a love capable of being documented by data of revelation coming to earth from heaven—is the gratuitous power of self-transcending love to realize God's *mysterion* in glory. And the anthropological fittingness of that capacity (which, exactly *qua* grace, is not a necessity) can be documented by data from earth. In order to clarify the significance of this thesis for an eschatology that wants to be a *praxis* of discipleship of *Jesus*, it is useful to reflect for a moment on the nature of its alternative.

On the basis of a "theological" science that leaves aside essential data about the *mysterion,* i.e., data about the values of God's heart gratuitously available in Jesus' God-revealing kingdom *praxis* and resurrection, a bare doctrine of the sovereignty of God risks reducing continuity between heaven and earth to a calculus of what is due to God by way of obedience from creatures and what is due to creatures by way of just reward or punishment from God.[101] It tends, in other words, to overlook data of good news about the constructive value of human freedom in God's Neighborly project, a project by which God pledges with creatures to create—or creatively to salvage—out of the apparent wasteland of a universe of Sin all earthly constructions remotely resembling love. It tends to leave out of account Jesus' revelation of the eschatological worthwhileness of fragmentary experiences of liberation from deprivation. As a result, it risks being unable to rejoice in the news that God has initiated a *mysterion* in which the truth-creative ideologies of Faith can make a definitive human contribution to the realization of God's project on earth as it is in heaven. Such a "theology" may even become scandalized by Jesus' forthright insistence on the impassioned character of God's love, particularly God's Neighborly attention to the deprived in their situation of historical, social, political and ecological need.[102]

In the context of a universe marked not only by Sin but by the phenomenon of utopian hope, the significance of a doctrine of grace is that it insists without fear of theological scandal that *God* has already taken exactly such a Neighborly initiative with respect to the deprived, an initiative of love gratuitously overflowing from the heart of One who wills to be known not as creator but as friend and companion, kin and participant, impassioned sharer in a *mysterion* that means salvation for the deprived and creation of a world in which Sin will reign no longer.[103] By showing that God has made so radical a commitment to the liberation of the deprived, Jesus manifests that in God's relating to creatures as kin, God is not impressed by creaturely preoccupation with creatorship but is interested instead in responsive participation in a project, the creative *mysterion* of love. At the heart of that project is God's impassioned promise, analogous to the utopian striving of sensitive human hearts, of definitive eschatological victory over evil, deprivation, injustice and death. Essential to the *mysterion* as project, in other words, is its teleological character as promise. It is significative on earth of the definitive completion of grace in glory.

In this sense, God's commitment to the *mysterion* is a 'distraction' to God insofar as it is also an 'irresistible attraction.' God is intent on *loving* us creatures and loving us irrevocably and first, perhaps before the smallest neutrino was released from the primordial mass, perhaps before heaven and earth were initially conceived, but certainly before any of us could deserve or merit such extravagant response from God's heart or raise a single question about the gratuitous fact of our having found ourselves already in possession of a liberty, already faced with the breath of life and longing, already bearing a spark of creativity and kindling of earthly desire, already living a faith and hope that, in the face of incredible sufferings and odds, can still believe in the eschatological eventuality of the definitive worthwhileness of love.

As was seen in chapter one, love can be realized only in the context of a shared and worthwhile project. But the sharing of a project is also the sharing of a destiny. It is the suffering of a risk and the keeping of a promise, the expression of a lasting fidelity. The "secret" of God's exhuberant love is thus that by gratuitously initiating a project, God wills to love creatures definitively and forever, *whether or not God is loved in return.* In earthly mediations of self-transcending love, God is continually engaged in "salvaging" the strivings for liberation effected here on earth and inserting them into the eschatologically definitive new heaven and new earth, the features of which will remain unknown, even to God, until the last contribution of love has been made. This is a project God finds absorbing and worthwhile. Yet God does not force it on creatures. God stands at the door and knocks.[104]

In initiating such a project, God suffers a patient love for creatures. God takes as God's own the destiny of the cosmos, suffering a love that must endure the same laws and determinisms, the same subjection to apparent futility, the same need to rely on randomness and chance, the same dependence on the mechanisms of Sin, the same risk of Sin's being perverted into sin, the same seemingly interminable lengths of intervening time before a single efficacious result can be glimpsed, the same affront of huge quantities of waste and breakdown, the same repulsion at the trampling of the poor, as do human beings of at least now and then, more or less sensitive heart. That suffering is the secret of God's *mysterion,* made known on earth by God's making Godself Neighbor and Friend, Kin and Companion, Beloved Welcomer of the deprived. The secret of this love is not held back but is revealed definitively in Jesus' *praxis* and clarified in the resurrection. Even in the face of failure, abandonment and a violent, unjust death, Jesus' steadfast hope, his refusal to give up faith in this unswerving love that is God's was eschatologically validated: God's raising of Jesus from the dead is the sign that God never fails in this patient love, for it is the gratuitous yet appropriate expression on earth of the definitive eschatological efficacy of God's creative and salvific action, God's impassioned power over evil on earth and manifestation of innermost glory.[105]

A theologian embarrassed by the notion that God finds it attractive to work with creatures at a *mysterion* of such extravagant proportions on the part of God might almost be tempted to say (overlooking the testimony of Jesus to the contrary) that from the point of view of human calculations, God's initiative is blatantly inappropriate: it is entirely out of proportion to creatures' allegedly insignificant status vis-à-vis an utterly transcendent creator. Such an approach, however, appears to be starting from the wrong end of the epistemological spectrum, at the point of the genetic origins of the universe (virtually unknowable) rather than with the concretely observable reality of a *mysterion* made manifest as project and promise in the midst of the universe of here and now, the universe as we know it. Asking why there is evil in the universe—

i.e., how it has come about that evil "as such" exists—is as fruitless as asking why one exists, why God "exists," why one is loved by someone whose gift of self one obviously does not deserve. A more appropriate starting point seems to be in the middle of everything, at the heart of the cosmic drama in which Faith and Sin have already clearly appeared—literally, in other words, "where the action is."

The situation is such that creatures already exist in the midst of a seemingly futile universe, under conditions marked by the cumulative effects of Sin. And that is where, with all the complexity it involves, they must fashion an appropriate response. It is thus the quality of the present response to Sin and not the identification of Sin's "original" cause that is of greatest importance for a doctrine of creation.[106] Theologians can put their energies into developing theoretical explanations of how things got to be the way they are and how, according to a "plan of God," the destinies of creatures must eventually be "worked out" (a descriptive-narrative approach which by focusing subjective consciousness on the phenomenon of origins tries to "uncover" a truth that is presumed to lie hidden in reality from the beginning and thus is thought to be ever present at its depths). Or they can work to create practical, ideological responses of Jesus-normed religious anthropological faith aimed at changing the way things are and making them the way they ought to be (a utopian-hermeneutical approach which by focusing action on a worthwhile eschatological goal tries to realize truth through the creation of a reality that is presumed not as yet to exist). Given the difference between these options, and given the fact that, in the long run, people tend to settle these questions at the level of action rather than theory, it seems appropriate to the logic of action to follow the second approach. Not only does it refuse to let hope in the worthwhileness of love be conquered by the weight of negativity embodied in the facts, but it requires attention to the practial urgency of making a secularly relevant response to Sin which affirms the eschatological value of whatever is being done (and not done) in the present.

By insisting that the link between heaven and earth is a matter of conjoint action centered on realizing an eschatological project and promise, Segundo is taking exactly such a starting point. He is seeking a theological solution by which the realm of history and nature—coextensive with the sphere of action—can escape devaluation at the hands of a doctrine of sovereign creatorship.[107] A continuity of both projects and destinies between the divine and human freedoms liberates history and nature from everything that serves to make them appear lacking in value and meaning. It enables life and experience in this world to be interpreted as valid and worthwhile, the actions and passions which give them shape to be understood as efforts which matter, and matter substantially, whether or not there is posited a creator but which, once the "secret" of God's *mysterion* is introduced as a relevant theological datum, take on the capacity to contribute to the birth of something definitive, everlasting and new, something that comes into history and nature redundantly as grace, that arrives as eschatological breakthrough, that presents itself as unsought-for yet profoundly welcome gift and yet is not discontinuous with the action that went before. Like the anointing of Jesus by the unknown woman in Bethany, such action goes prophetically before the new reality with the truth-making affirmation of self-transcending love. While the laborious dimension of this eschatological creation is called by the name of grace, the new reality it prophetically brings to birth is called glory: the definitive emergence and jubilant celebration of the new heaven and the new earth.

From Segundo's point of view, the notion that creaturely striving is valueless to God has thus been rendered blasphemous once and for all. It has been definitively replaced by the theologically subversive criterion of Jesus' kingdom *praxis*. Here comes Jesus eating and drinking, conceiving of himself and his mission, utterly inseparable, as food and drink, abundant wine, living water overflowing with a thirst-quenching power more refreshing than the waters of a desert well. Here comes Jesus, proclaiming that every hair of the head is cherished by God, that the sabbath is made for human beings and not human beings for the sabbath, that the standard for what is good and evil in heaven is the liberation of the deprived on earth in the context of their most practical immediate need. Here comes Jesus proclaiming, in short, that God is concerned like kin for "sinners" and the poor, that God's project is secular liberation, that more than anything, God wants to be Neighbor to the deprived, restoring to those whose earthly opportunities have been diminished and whose future has been robbed the goods that were taken away. No wonder Jesus' family thought him mad and the authorities looked for means to dismantle his theology and eventually blot him out. No wonder he was regarded as dangerous iconoclast to a "divinely established" order, profaner of sacred protocol and disrupter of religious privilege. With Jesus on the scene, it is the end of secular injustice masked under religious labels like the alleged will of "God."

From Jesus' point of view, to be human in the eyes of God is to be not worthless dust but living salt and savor. To be human means to turn one's action into life-giving food for the life of the deprived. It means to live what some of the letters of the early Jesus-derived communities called *diakonia*—service that is living bread, boldness for the sake of the deprived, singleness of heart like that of a woman who, day after day without giving up, dares to knock at the doors of the importunate judges of this world so as to demand the release from slavery of neighbors held within. To be human is to be both bread and neighbor in one. Depending on the substance each neighborly action provides—a bread-like, utopian substance that exists "nowhere" on earth until it is given a place in reality by this or that action of self-transcending love—others will live or they will die, and that is enough to make God put neighborly action on an equal footing with the earthly significance of food. What human beings attempt in the ambiguous medium of Sin and Faith, even if they do not tangibly succeed, is as essential to the neighbor and as basic to the deprived as food is essential to life. And Jesus is saying it is essential as well to God's *mysterion*.

How do the earthly and heavenly dimensions of one and the same neighborly love come together? In chapters one and two it was observed that action begins in grace as a work of Faith and tends through ideologies toward the completion of projects having objectively fruitful results. *Qua* Faith, action tends by its own inner logic to work toward creative incorporation of determinisms of Sin into ideologies, fragile though they are. Chapter three showed that ideologies of love on behalf of the deprived have a truth-creative value which makes the work of Faith on earth significant to God in heaven. The cumulative effect of these chapters, in other words, is to suggest that Faith tends toward an earthly efficacy or ideological completion that might genuinely be called an anthropological glory.[108] The coining of that unusual phrase is meant to highlight Faith's tendency to want to contribute something substantial to reality, its inherent desire to make neighborly love genuinely efficacious on earth through ideologies. This desire belongs to action by its own utopian logic, which, as has been seen, when normed by the truth criterion of liberation of the deprived, constitutes a substantial contribution to the creation of truth such as the unknown woman of the gospel story gave to Jesus when she anointed him before his death. Insofar as such ideologies create a "difference that makes a difference" to the neighbor in distress, they ring true to victims of injustice and deprivation in their suffering and need. And, as was pointed out earlier, they do so whether they appear in the eyes of observers to have succeeded or to have failed. In the eyes of the disciples, for example, and very likely in the eyes of Jesus himself, the violent and premature death on the cross appeared to be utterly inefficacious vis-à-vis realization of the kingdom project to which Jesus had devoted the energies of his entire life and love.

This means that the new reality love creates in response to the needs of the deprived really matters, and matters substantially, in two equally important ways: to the neighbor and to God. First, it matters to the neighbor who is deprived. Action can make a substantial contribution to the neighbor from the point of view of the neighbor's needs. A cup of cold water is capable of truly relieving the neighbor's thirst. It is capable as well of renewing the neighbor's courage, bolstering the neighbor's faltering strength or hope, giving witness to the possibility of a future in which such evils as the hoarding of water for the few to waste will be replaced by an abundance of water for the many to drink. The results of constructive action that are tangible to the deprived thus matter substantially not only to the neighbor and the neighbor's needs but to the outcome of the neighbor's history and hope. Such results can have repercussions of longer or shorter duration, remaining visible like the rings that chronicle seasons of abundant rainfall inside the trunks of trees. Love makes a difference of longer or shorter duration on earth to neighbors who are deprived.

Second, as chapter three pointed out, the consequences of action make a difference to God in heaven. They matter from the point of view of the values of

God's heart. Insofar as it is not only the needs of the deprived that neighborly love addresses, in however incomplete or fragmentary a fashion (the thirsting neighbor will need to drink again tomorrow; our actions never bring about definitive fulfillments in the realm of history and nature) but also the *mysterion* of God's heart, action on behalf of neighbors' needs is directly relevant to God. Referring to the parable of the final judgment, Segundo observes:

> It is very important that I account for the absolute significance that feeding or not feeding the sister or brother has and that [I recognize that] here is risked [making] a yes or no to God. And that is what is revealed to me under the images of heaven and hell. . . .Practically [speaking], [in feeding the sister and brother] I direct the whole of my being toward God, and to be thus united to God *is* heaven. . . .The sister and brother are not a middle term; in them I have to choose the positive or negative absolute, in them God is asking of me in each instant of my life a yes or a no.[109]

In itself, of course, the difference an action of neighborly love can make to the deprived is always relative and provisional. In terms of its actual content, which under the conditions of Sin can never bring about a change that will be definitive, the difference love makes will last for only a time. Its significance, however, is no less real, since, from the point of view of the deprived, the qualitative change love can elicit in the here and now can mean a difference that makes a difference between situations as serious as that between hunger and fullness, sickness and health, rejection and acceptance, deprivation and abundance, death and life.[110]

Experience thus testifies that by a logic intrinsic to faiths and ideologies, love is set on attaining an end that is valid and worthwhile in itself, whether it actually achieves it to a perceptible degree in the concrete. Love carries an intrinsic worth, an anthropological glory of its own, a validity or meaningfulness that concentrates Faith on the construction of ideologies aimed at making a heaven on earth.[111] And the test of that "glory" is love's capacity to "ring true," to show itself as a difference that makes a difference with respect to observable needs of the deprived. Of course, as discussion in chapter two attempted to show, the results of action, even when they are constitutive of love, always appear ambiguous. Under the entropic conditions of Sin, the large quantities of waste and seeming chaos, the need for taking "time off," the apparent uselessness of periods of seeming passivity and unproductivity like waiting, rest and sleep, the apparent inefficacy of illness, deformation, fatigue, failure, suffering and death, all such forms of apparent interruption, breakdown, randomness and decay that necessarily surround and condition, facilitate and prepare the ground for human achievement—under these conditions it often appears that if love has any efficacy at all it is certainly very short-lived, a drop in the bucket, the flash of an electron across a screen. And certainly it is very expensive, like the prophetic gesture of the unknown woman and the costly nard itself that were extravagantly "wasted" on Jesus who was soon to be executed and buried in a tomb.

Yet in spite of the undeniable fact that the results of action are never permanent and definitive, never efficacious to the absolute degree, love can and does occur. Even though existing generations are killed or die, new children continue to be born; sick persons find surprising ways to turn their illness into constructive love for others; the sufferings of the politically murdered dead germinate in the soil of the politically oppressed living to raise up new witnesses to liberative hope and new protests against the very injustices and sufferings that brought about the deaths of their forebears; Jesus did not lie lifeless in the tomb, bereft of contact with earth and loved ones forever.

In spite of the temptation to which we human social persons more or less frequently succumb, thinking that entropy and disintegration are going to have the final say and failing to trust the eschatological logic at work in our own action, the utopian strivings of self-transcending love are not going to end up degenerating into a meaningless smear of dust but are going to become capable of displaying their inherent worth, their absolute value or definitive glory in the day of the eschaton. On that day there is going to spring to life before the eyes of creatures the surprising way the fruits of their projects appear before the eyes of God in heaven, without the customary trappings of entropy and minus the dimension of Sin by the disconcerting contours of which we are used to seeing love obscured from sight on earth.[112]

On that day God is going to make manifest in plain view of everyone those aspects of our projects which were efficacious to however large or small a degree vis-à-vis liberation of neighbors from deprivation and distress. At the same time, those aspects which were not normed by the liberation of the deprived will be burned away like dross. On that day will be left behind for all to see only the enduring substance, of whatever weight or mass, of each one's positive contribution to the project of trying to release the neighbor from suffering, deprivation, injustice and death. On that day, in other words, there are going to be manifest the eschatological features of self-transcending love, what Paul was probably the first theologian to call "the manifestation of the glorious liberty of the children of God" (Rom. 8:21).

Precisely as kin of God, as more or less mature sharers in God's *mysterion* and its work, human social persons are thus already in possession of a liberty that by its own internal logic has the capacity to be eschatologically valid. For this reason, it is the manifestation of the efficacious realization of that capacity and not the capacity itself that is gratuitous. It is the manifestation of love's absolute value in glory and not the substance of love itself that God gives freely in the love that is grace. As the preceding discussion attempted to show, the eschatological validity of action has more to do with the utopian striving to overcome actual situations of deprivation and injustice on earth—concrete efforts at the realization of a down-to-earth liberation that Jesus did not hesitate to describe as the "at-handness" of God's kingdom and as salvation coming from God—than with a doctrine of a remote and distant future in a next life or in another world. Eschatology has to do with the absolute value residing in love, the dimension of transcendence at work through Faiths and ideologies in the relative sphere of action in the present. It does not pertain to an absolute future reserved to God in heaven. Human action has absolute value not because it will be given value "later on" by a god "standing by" in heaven but because love in response to neighbors' needs has an eschatological logic of its own, a truth-making logic of utopian hope by which it tries to create a heaven on earth for those who are deprived. The eschatological promise that love will live with God forever is the logical conclusion of the project by which Faith works to attain neighbors' release from the apparent futility of life on an earth that at times can seem to be less like an earth than a hell.

The transcendent referent Segundo identifies in love implies that heaven and its opposite, hell, pertain not to the future but to the absolute significance of the present, what Segundo regards as the definitive seriousness of freedom.[113] He writes:

> That hell forms part of the good news, although it seems to belie it, is to say that *the seriousness of my freedom is so great that God is put before me in each one of my sisters and brothers.*[114]

Freedom is not an existential test but the capacity to create heaven on earth by removing the hell of suffering from the neighbor. And in this it has reference to the manifest interest of God's heart:

> Faith, which is the radical loss of the fear of freedom, totally changes the notion that human freedom is a test [set up] between heaven and hell, [and it does this] in order to relocate both [heaven and hell], not in the future, but in each decision of human freedom referring to the sister or brother who is suffering the hell of sorrow on this earth and to God who is suffering it with and in them. We make the decision to say yes or no to the God who is in our sisters and brothers, the ones who are near us and whom we are trying to love.[115]

According to Segundo, the *praxis* of Jesus showed that the love of God in heaven is powerless vis-à-vis the sufferings and destinies of needy creatures unless and until it is effected on earth as a concrete instance of neighborly liberation in the (relatively efficacious) form of self-transcending love:

> On us depend things that are fundamental for God. And the main one is the hell that is precisely the immense suffering that each one of us can prevent for the other. This depends on us, therefore we are important. We do not live in a perfect world where, if we were not present, everything would continue

running the same. If we do not act with our freedom, there is no way for God to prevent suffering. Thanks to us, God can prevent it, so we are of extreme necessity, [and] thus our freedom has immense value for God, because it can free our sisters and brothers from earthly hells, from suffering. And that is the plan of God: that all together, God and we (God as primary creator, we, as God's children, also creators) should make this world useful, so that it might serve love, so that it might help others.[116]

In this sense, heaven and hell represent neither other-worldly places of repose and torment nor goals of a distant future but rather poles of the eschatological logic built into action from the start. The logic of action is eschatological because out of something as apparently futile and intractible as Sin, human Faith, the anthropological faith of ordinary people of sensitive heart, can respond to the deprived with ideologies normed by the need for liberation, ideologies that aim to make earth not an ugly and terrifying descent into hell but a constructive (which is to say laborious yet worthwhile) project of turning history and nature *loveward,* toward the making of earth a heaven. As has been seen, it is exactly the loveward orientation of action's logic that impresses God who wills that the values of heaven be realized on earth. Insofar as that orientation is put into practice in ideologies normed by liberation of the deprived, it moves God to respond with characteristic extravagance, a lavish generosity such as God displayed to Jesus in raising him from the dead.

Central to Segundo's eschatology is thus the assertion that in neighborly love, action is not merely coextensive with the sphere of the relative. Understood in its complexity, love is the place of a decisive meeting between the absolute and the relative.[117] The reference to transcendence put into play in every action of self-transcending love is a function of love's intrinsic connection with the doing and making of truth. As the realm creative of meaning and truth, love is the realm of immanence through which transcendence directly passes, the realm where values from heaven impinge on earth as a present and active dimension.[118]

The reference to transcendence thus conditions history, and the whole of nature as well, with a seriousness not merely transient and temporary but permanent and eternal. This means that history and nature are thoroughly temporal but not simply temporary, relatively absolute but not absolutely relative. They are susceptible of amounting to something meaningful not just for a time but forever. They are capable of attaining significance as an arena of import and value not only in an intramundane way, in themselves, but in an extramundane way, vis-à-vis Someone outside them Who is God. The relative accomplishments of neighborly love can make a difference both to striving for the liberation of the deprived on earth and to the *mysterion* of God who promises to validate such love in heaven. This gives history and nature a more than just temporal destiny. It gives them an ontological density of such magnitude that in the intensive atmosphere of self-transcending love they condense into a new and definitive reality: glory—the eschatological solidity of a world that is good. This suggests that into the structure of hiatory and nature is built not only a capacity to receive an eschatological destiny from God but a tendency actually to achieve it. The latter shows up as utopian hope, the ethical struggle to work in Faith for the making of a heaven on earth. It is the stubborn resilience in the sensitive heart that keeps it positive. It turns Faith toward the needs of the deprived and makes it responsive enough to strive for their liberation in the face of apparent defeat.

As the text of Mt. 25: 31-46 makes plain, the cup of water given in love will have the same eschatological validity as the death of Jesus on the cross. Of course the two actions are not the same, but insofar as each is a work of Faith that embodies a neighborly, self-transcending love, each will find its way into the new heaven and new earth in the eschaton. There, the value of the work of Faith will consist not in quantitative factors like size or weight but in its substantial quality, much as the distinctive ring of crystal can be recognized regardless of the sizes and shapes of individual pieces. In the eschaton, God will manifest the lasting value and definitive meaning of ideologies of self-transcending love. There, the value of each—which is absolute—will be made visible not by the light of the sun or moon but by the light of the glory of God.

Looked at from this perspective, eschatology pertains not to a remote and transcendent future effected by God alone but to the causality of action in the present. The latter is measured by the making of truth which accompanies neighborly love. As was pointed out earlier, this view of hope sees eschatology as an ethical as much as a religious category, for it embodies a utopian interest in the overcoming of earthly evils, which in turn gives rise to the truth-critical dimension in the structure of neighborly love. What joins the ethical dimension to the religious one is the pertinence of utopian striving to definitive realization of the *mysterion*. In other words, when one looks at eschatology from the "earthly" point of view of neighborly response to the deprived, the ethical dimension comes to the fore; but when one looks at eschatology from the "heavenly" point of view of what the data of revelation have to say about the project and promise that are the *mysterion* of God, the religious dimension does. And the link that is capable of making this connection visible is the earthly realization of self-transcending love.

Such a view of eschatology means that what will make the freedom of God's earthly "kin" manifest in glory is the capacity anthropological Faith possesses now, in the provisional realm of history and nature, to participate in the release of neighbors from deprivation on earth, to join with God in fashioning in face of random determinisms of Sin and sin the substance of a new creation. The manifestation of freedom is synonymous with completing the creative project initiated in grace and contributing something of lasting quality to its definitive realization, transforming the shape of its earthly features with a touch of distinctively human love. The project of making a new heaven and a new earth is something that must be done laboriously by hand. It is a work of art that is to be as earthly in features and content as it is heavenly in durability and value.

That the eschaton is a heavenly reality means not that the fullness of time will take place in a remote and distant future but that the time for salvation is ripe on earth right now. Salvation is appropriate and opportune wherever people have ears to hear and eyes to see, wherever Faith is participating in the struggle to liberate the deprived, wherever there is self-transcending love. For where the struggle for liberation is, there is the earthly face of love, and where love is, there is the eschatological seed of the new heaven and new earth promised in the *mysterion* by God.

As was seen in the previous chapters, action's most properly human *charism* is to mediate God's love in a universe of Sin. Chapter one pointed out that a *charism* is a gift that is a task. It alters neither the identity nor value of recipients but qualifies their inherent capabilities. It is a recapitulation, in what Paul calls Spirit, of the efficacy and worth of their own intrinsic power. In this sense, the notion of *charism,* and thus the work of God's Spirit, is inseparable from the notion of *mysterion. Mysterion* points to the glorious realization of the task on which the *charism* focuses, and, as has been seen, that task is nothing other than Faith's creating in the medium of Sin the work of neighborly love. As the characteristic work of Faith, such work is the achievement equally of God's Spirit and of human Faith, and its value is everlasting.

The *charism* of God's love is thus another name for grace. Grace is love's revealed name, the name given to the earthly face of self-transcending love in the context of God's *mysterion* in heaven. It functions within the essential structure of faiths and ideologies themselves, eliciting a gratuitous new Spirit-inspired efficacy but simultaneously continuing to function as action's properly anthropological capability. In this way, the link between the making of the new heaven on earth and the making of the new earth in heaven is forged by a causality and power that are proper to action as action. "We must reunite eternal life and the construction of history," Segundo writes, and he elaborates on this notion as follows:

> Eternal life is *the new earth.* . . .Hence it is the *earth* that we are looking forward to and that is identical with eternal life. It is our earth and our history and our effort transformed by the gift of God's grace. . . .[The connection between] the manifestation of grace and the manifestation of glory. . .means that we must work out two indivisible realities: our construction of human history in Christ and our concrete, joyous acceptance of his gratuitous gift. *Work and gift are two facets of the same reality.*[119]

The complementary dimensions of gift and task thus point to the teleological connection in Christian eschatology between grace and glory.[120] According to Segundo, however, a problem develops when one views eschatological glory solely from what he regards as a "history of salvation" point of view. Although the latter focuses on the necessity of love as a human cooperation with grace in the work of salvation, it risks centering salvation more on the acceptance or rejection of God's self-donation in grace than on the meaning of action for the construction of something lasting and new in the eschaton. While the history of salvation view succeeds in making eschatology an integral dimension of human freedom, giving it definitive meaning vis-à-vis the existential question of individuals' eternal destinies, it does not provide a strong enough link between individual eschatological salvation and the destiny of the world or the meaning of history as a whole.[121]

By contrast, it is precisely the social, historical and ecological relevance of salvation, its significance for the construction of God's *mysterion* values on earth, which takes a new turn in the eschatology of Segundo. For him, grace effects salvation by validating not just existential experience but also the accomplishments of action. It does this by recognizing God's dependence on the work of human Faith. It highlights the need for there to be a project at work that is of interest equally to human social persons of sensitive heart and to God if the values of God's heart in heaven are to be of interest and relevance on earth and if history and nature are to be of significance and value to God.[122] From Segundo's point of view, grace is concerned less with the history of salvation than with the salvation of history.[123] The difference between the two is fundamental. It shows that the problem of the meaningfulness not only of human action but of the cosmos as a whole can be solved theologically only at the level of eschatology.[124]

As something directed toward the quality of history and nature as a whole and not only toward the final outcome of creatures' existential decisions for or against God, the *mysterion* as *charism* of action ceases being a process created and directed by God in heaven and becomes instead a co-creative project conjointly directed by God and creatures on earth.[125] Because that project is nothing other than God's gratuitous introduction of the *mysterion* as an effective and meaningful dimension of action, it implies a shift of focus in traditional ways of thinking about salvation.[126] If, as Segundo suggests, God is in process of creating the world every day in a cooperative project of shared love, then the universe does not exist for the sake of God's filling it with grace and then fulfilling grace in glory. Rather, the action of God's originality (as distinct from God's originating action, about which nothing is known)—i.e., the action on which everything else depends, including creation, is that God has graced the universe. God has introduced the universe to self-transcendent love. In other words, God has done this "new thing" (Is. 43:19), and God has done it for the sake of working as companion with creatures at the creation of a new reality, a "new creation" in which heaven and earth can be equal participants in a glory that is not only everlasting but has also been conjointly fashioned and will be able to be mutually enjoyed. Creation does not exist for the sake of grace but grace for the sake of creation. More accurately expressed, God's initiative of love, the "new thing" that God is doing and promising in grace, is an initiative made with a view to inviting the participation of creatures in a gratuitous yet appropriate eschatological project that is also a celebration: conjoint enjoyment of a definitively good and glorious world in which God and creatures will be able to dwell.

According to the history of salvation view, it is ultimately God who is the subject and goal of history. Although human subjectivity and the creative capacity of love and freedom are by no means excluded, they are understood with reference to each human being's eternal salvation or damnation. In that schema, salvation takes place through a logical series of events that risks being interpreted chronologically as part of a divine design. God first creates the world, in order to communicate the divine self in grace to what is not God. Then, respecting our right to say no, God approaches us with the offer of salvation, gradually releasing it in its fullness until its definitive advent and irreversible acceptance take place in Jesus. The salvation Jesus brings is understood as a matter of an "already" and a "not yet."[127] Both mystery and promise, it is the beginning of an eschatological salvation already present and operative but not yet completely fulfilled. Although history as a whole has been definitively saved by the death and resurrection of Jesus, historical existence as it progresses in the lives of individuals and groups is in need of the appropriation of salvation by means of existential decision-making for or against God. According to this view, salvation is a divinely engineered process: it is a plan the outcome of which is determined by the goal set at its origins and into which each human being must ultimately fit or be excluded. This eschatological goal, which refers more to the meaning of human subjectivity and the existential decisiveness of personal freedom than to a love-constructive project in which human freedom participates with the freedom of God for the sake of creating a *world*, harkens back to the initial creation, to the original intention of God to communicate Godself in grace to what is not God.[128]

Thanks to grace, God's plan is capable, in the history of salvation schema, of overcoming the two main obstacles to its fulfillment: creaturely finitude on the one hand and freedom's resistance, or sin, on the other. This double final victory of grace, already assured by the death and resurrection of Jesus but not yet completed under the conditions of finitude and sin in history, will realize itself definitively in the eschaton. There, God will install an absolute future which transcends both the finite limitations of the original creation and, within it, the sinful decisions of human freedom while validating the genuine acts of acceptance of God which freedom, in grace, has succeeded in making. When all is said and done, glory in this view is a result of God's having succeeded in "filling" created history with "uncreated grace." History and nature exist for the purpose of human communion in the being of God, for the sake of human *being's* (and individual human beings') becoming the definitive eschatological receptacle of the fullness of God's freely communicated being.

By contrast, Segundo's schema posits human social persons as definitive subjects of history equally along with God and makes the intramundane achievements of human freedom (and not just the historical act of disposition of it) the eschatological goal of grace. Through action, which, in the face of Sin, opens human freedom to the gratuitous but appropriate *charism* of the *mysterion,* history and nature are saved from meaninglessness. They take on a meaning which they otherwise would lack, even for God.[129] So far as Segundo is concerned, the *mysterion* gives history and nature an eschatological weight and meaning precisely in and by means of the causality of action. This means that vis-à-vis salvation, creation is not the *locus* of grace but its eschatologically enduring product, its final and definitive result. Sin (even in the case of its perversion into sin) is the medium, simultaneously existing along with Faith, of creative love, and both Sin and Faith contribute in distinctive ways to the making of a world that will become meaningful to God and creatures only as a result of constructive conjoint action.[130] Human destiny, like the destiny of the cosmos as a whole, is a matter of Faith's turning a universe of Sin into a world of love through self-transcending ideologies, a matter of action's making a world that is good out of humanly mediated neighborly liberations that in substance are equivalent to the creative love of God. Thanks to the love that is grace, human social persons together with God become conjoint subjects of history, and the accomplishments of God's and humans' conjoint action are its goal. The earth itself has something of value to contribute to the *mysterion,* for out of its substance will be constructed the glorious features of the eschaton.

For Segundo, eschatology has less to do with the definitive culmination of a 'history of salvation' than with the definitive manifestation of the salvation of history. It is the building on earth of the glorious content of what Jesus called God's kingdom. In discussing this content, Segundo points out that the glory of God is not safeguarded by theological efforts to make the realization of the *eschaton* a function of God alone.[131] If the message and work of Jesus are not a mere 'announcement' of the irruption of God's kingdom on earth but a call to cooperate historically in the effective beginning of the *eschaton,* then God does not receive more glory when human beings contribute less, but when they act to cooperate in historical efforts to realize on earth what Jesus called God's kingdom.[132]

The creation of the new heaven and new earth thus depends on the capacity of human Faith to create ideologies that ring true to the values of God's project, the criterion of which is Jesus' kingdom criterion, the needs of the deprived. While the historical features of these ideologies are normed on earth by liberation from deprivation, the eschatological features of their constructive results are recognizable in heaven as love, everlastingly valid human contributions to the transcendent glory of God.

So far as Segundo is concerned, liberation of the deprived must remain the truth criterion for whether any given action is a realization of neighborly love. But liberation of the deprived does not exhaust everything that can be said about action's constructive *mysterion charism*. The latter is directed toward the outburst of the truly new on earth as it is in heaven. Creation of the new is the goal of God's *mysterion* love, a love toward which the liberation of the deprived on earth spontaneously already tends. The actual liberation of the neighbor in need is that from which the creation of the new is inseparable and that in which human social persons of sensitive heart can occasionally catch sight of an entirely gratuitous definitive liberation efficaciously at work in the realm of Sin. At such moments action is not incapable of welcoming the redundant—because utterly gratuitous and yet strangely appropriate—word of revelation which speaks of an eschatological liberation still to be hoped for, the definitive manifestation of earthly liberation as the human face of the glory of God in heaven.

The response of the sensitive heart to the needs of the deprived is God's only means of mediating love. The sensitivity of the human heart, the creativity of love in Faith, is God's only means of liberating creatures from deprivation and injustice in history and nature. The causality of God's liberative and salvific love in grace depends for its efficacy on the causality of the freedom of creatures, circuitous, indirect, and imperfect as it is in light of the inevitable working of Sin and the possibility and actuality of sin. The fragmentary causality of creatures like us is the only causality by which the freedom of God can act for the realization of love. Insofar as it is the only way God can act on earth to overcome deprivation, injustice and death, it is the only way God can create.

Like God, we human social persons can neither love nor create in a vacuum.[133] We must be sensitive to, and continually take account of, the sufferings and needs of neighbors who are deprived; otherwise, our ideologies and cultural creations, our scientific theories and works of art, our constructions of truth themselves, however rationally coherent, however laden with elegance and flair, however seemingly magnificent in scope, end up full of sound and fury, signifying nothing. They are sounding brass and tinkling cymbal. On the day of the eschaton works of "liberation," "science" and "art" lacking in sensitivity to the deprived and having no constructive bearing on the alleviation of injustice, will be the first of a painfully embarrassing set of eschatologically irrelevant "anthropological glories" to go up in smoke.[134]

Yet the truth criterion of action tells only whether love is true or not, whether it is real. It does not have anything to say about the shape that is given to love by ideologies, love's laboriously constructed content. The latter can vary, depending on the creativity of the Faith or Faiths that are seeking to solve the problems of history and nature. Since that search is always historically conditioned, ideologies are humanly devised responses of a Spirit-guided Faith and thus are capable of endless variations on the common theme of love. The tension between the truth criterion of action and its historically variable content constitutes an ethical problem for freedom: it has to learn by experience what shape to give to love. Some ideologies are better, more effective at meeting neighbors' needs, than others, depending on how well they meet the truth criterion of liberation of the deprived.[135]

The Absolute Value of Human Action and the Manifestation of God's Glory

As was seen in chapter one, to understand God's *mysterion* as *charism* of human action is to give anthropological faith a vocation to maturity. God places responsibility for the heavenly success of the *mysterion* on earthly shoulders. If the *charism* is to be efficacious, the world that it participates in creating must be substantially different from what it would have been without the "welcome intrusion" of the *charism*. Because of Faith's capability to mediate friendship with God, a friendship that is utterly gratuitous and yet highly appropriate to the secular bent of action's logic, ideologies are given a meaning and value from the point of view both of the sensitive heart on earth and the heart of God in heaven. Made capable of significance from a "heavenly" point of view, ideologies are understood in the light of Faith as earthly mediations of a love that will not die and pass into oblivion, as earthly projects, including love, appear to do, but that, even if they die, will be brought again to life and made to last with God forever.

In a universe in which the purpose of freedom is the creation of truth and the manifestation in the eschaton of its absolute value as self-transcending love, what is lasting can appear only in the shape of ideologies. Because they give objective substance not only to anthropological faith but to the Faith that brings salvation, they are the only reliable means by which God can "tell" that actual traces and markings of grace have been made extant in the universe and have showed up there as constituent elements of the definitive reality. With the notion of ideologies Segundo thus creates a basis for the meaningfulness of history and nature vis-à-vis the eschaton. He shows that the work of Faith—always the accomplishment of ideological embodiments or *praxes*—is going to last forever. To the extent that the Faith that determines them embodies love for the deprived, ideologies are going to be inserted into the definitive reality of the new heaven and the new earth. Incomplete and fragile though they be, they are not just provisional realities pertaining solely to this world.

For this reason, it is the thesis of this concluding section that love contributes definitive weight and substance not only to the new reality of the eschaton, but to the glory of God strictly speaking. It thus remains in the following paragraphs to say an intelligible word only about what love as link of continuity between the liberation of the deprived on earth and the glory of God in heaven actually can mean, not only with regard to disciples and, through the effects of their *praxis*, with regard to persons and groups of sensitive heart of other anthropological faiths, but also with regard to God. I will attempt to do this from the point of view of the promise built into the *mysterion* from the start, and I will try to conduct the argument in a style of theological discourse that wants to be both meek and bold, like the prayer of Jesus which dared to address God with the intimate vernacular of human experience and succeeded in acknowledging God's transcendence in heaven with categories supplied by a language of action on earth.

THE DEFINITIVE EFFICACY OF IDEOLOGIES AND THE ABSOLUTE VALUE OF SELF-TRANSCENDING LOVE

One way to appreciate the boldness of Segundo's eschatology is to consider it in light of an alternative, a particularly striking example of which occurs in the work of Frederick Gogarten.[136] For Gogarten, the sphere of human action is utterly discontinuous with the eschaton. The task of secular problem-solving has been handed over to reason in such a way that what human beings do in their existence on earth depends entirely and utterly on them. They are stewards of the world and heirs of the universe to whom everything on earth has been given but for whom everything in heaven is reserved for the action of God. When God chooses to inaugurate the eschaton, it will be the start of a reign that comes entirely from above. For Gogarten, heaven and earth are like parallel lines in a Euclidian universe: at the concrete level of experience and action the two will never meet. Intramundane existence remains the work of reason while the eschaton remains the work of God. In this view of things, God's transcendence requires that the eschaton be realized by the freedom of God alone.[137]

In spite of striking similarities, Segundo's eschatology is utterly opposed to that of Gogarten. Because Segundo utilizes the categories of an evolutionary and ecological science, his cosmology prohibits what he criticizes as the "di-planar" conception of the God-world relation which characterizes Reformation theology.[138] For Segundo, heaven and earth are radically continuous and the source of their continuity is eschatological. As was seen in chapter one, it results from the gratuitous yet appropriate cooperation of the divine and human freedoms in a common project and destiny, the eschatological significance of which Segundo illustrates by making what he calls a mature theological interpretation of the doctrines of heaven and hell.[139] Of course most people agree that these are not eschatological neighborhoods. Even less are they final rewards. Yet if theologians are to come up with a secularly relevant concept of eschatology capable of taking into account the problems not only of history and society but of ecology and nature as well, then heaven and hell can not be understood (as they have been traditionally) as other-worldly, ahistorical, non-ecological realities pertaining to the end of chronological time. On the contrary, they must be made as they were in Jesus' kingdom *praxis* to pertain to the end of evil, injustice and death. They must be understood as representing the transcendent referents of the structure of human freedom which signal the definitive victory of meaning and value over the high visibility of seemingly definitive futility.[140]

As theological symbols of the definitive significance of freedom, heaven and hell represent for Segundo what might be called the eschatological consistency of utopian striving, the reference to the transcendent in any and every *praxis* of love that is creative of truth on earth. In religious terms, heaven and hell articulate the eschatological import of a love that can exercise creative power in the face of Sin and death with an efficacy that is as definitive on earth as God's efficacy is in heaven. Between heaven and hell is ranged the definitive value—the ethically decisive meaning—of every human action. Yet there is more to their significance than that. Speaking not in spatial terms but by analogy, Segundo understands that action pertains not only to the horizontal referent of liberation of the deprived on earth but to the vertical, or transcendent, referent of God's *mysterion* in heaven. Theologians may therefore speak of heaven and hell as symbols of the manifest datum of revelation that the *mysterion* places the already existing (and intrinsically valid) utopian strivings of faiths and ideologies in a new and redundant transcendent context. This new context does not give ideologies a value that they otherwise would lack; on the contrary, it sheds a clarifying light on the seriousness and decisiveness they already have.

As was seen in chapter one, what Segundo understands by the categories of "heaven" and "hell" is ultimately that, in the concrete, action is always "mixed."[141] It never pertains exclusively to either love or evil in an absolute sense but, on the contrary, always represents a complex tangle of both. Insofar as faith's intentions are never totally efficacious unto good or unto evil, no human action is ever either completely loving or completely egotistical. Although it belongs not to disciples but to the judgment of God to sort out that tangle at a level of finality and definitiveness, nevertheless the fact of the tangle itself faces human freedom with a gravity and seriousness that can not be denied. It shows that in every human action one is dealing with a constitutively absolute responsibility. And from the point of view of a *mysterion* in which God has taken on the destiny of the cosmos gratuitously as God's own, this means that action is dealing not merely with projects of interest and value for the creation of a world that is good but with options and values of utter significance to the happiness and heart of God.

Like Gogarten, Segundo thus believes that human beings must take radical responsibility for the creation of more just and loving ideological structures in history and nature. Like Gogarten, Segundo refers to the texts from Paul which state that everything that is God's has been given to disciples, that they are "heirs" of the universe and "daughters and sons" of God whom Jesus called "Father." Unlike Gogarten, however, Segundo interprets the secular referent of these texts in a radically eschatological way. He incorporates them into a Jesus-normed affirmation, reinterpreted in terms of the eschatological vision of Paul, that heaven and earth are not only radically continuous, but also reciprocally related and absolutely interdependent. Grace does not make divine *use* of human action, drawing good out of evil in the mysterious way in which Augustine thought. Rather, grace *needs* human action and God *depends* on the accomplishments of love on earth if the *mysterion* dimensions of both project and promise are to be made definitively efficacious.[142] Where so far as Augustine is concerned, God's ways are far above the earth and infinitely unlike those of creatures, from Segundo's point of view God's ways could not be more manifest. That is because, for Segundo, God's ways are above all eschatological: they are concerned with the elimination of evil. They are the utopian "ways" of neighborly love which is normed by the liberation of the deprived, ways which pertain to the eschatological realization here on earth of the values of what Jesus called the coming of God's kingdom from heaven.[143] As chapter three was intent on showing, God's "ways" are obvious and accessible in Jesus' kingdom *praxis* as well as visible to the sensitive heart in the objective results and earthly consequences of liberative action, i.e., action aimed at making oneself neighbor to the deprived.

Such results and consequences show up in history and nature as ideological concretions of love. They represent the earthly mediations in which the *mysterion* is brought to definitive realization in the eschaton. As has been seen, of course, Segundo is not at all unaware that ideologies are frail and limited. He emphasizes that like all historical-ecological mediations, ideologies are ambiguous, even when they embody self-transcending love. The problem is not only that they are bound by the conditions of historical and ecological relativity.[144] Far more problematic, they are weighed down by egotism and guilt, the pull of the pole of hell in every human action. That means that they can never represent perfect expressions of love or convey the fullness of eschatological liberation. Neither can they accomplish the kingdom of God once and for all on earth. The continual thriving and even increasingly staggering dimensions of moral evil in the universe is a basic argument against that. As has been seen in chapter two, so far as Segundo is concerned, Sin, which implicates ideologies in sin, is a basic ontological datum. It is intrinsic to the human condition, where it shows up in experience as the apparent futility of action which Paul designates by the theological category *Flesh*. Not even the ideologies of Jesus, whose *praxes* of love in word and deed definitively placed what he called the kingdom of God at hand, were able to achieve an eschatological efficacy of such decisive proportions as to wipe out evil from the face of the earth. Why not? From Segundo's point of view the answer is that for God to have used the divine freedom to wipe out the ongoing actuality of evil would have been for God to erase the transcendent referent of freedom. At the same time, this would have been for God to have obliterated the absolute value of action: it would have been equivalent to God's having made the interest of Faith in neighborly love impotent in the face of Sin: the ultimate trivialization.

On the cross, Jesus was not an abstract instrument of the divine freedom but a fully human being, a human social person like each of us. Precisely as something human, the action which was Jesus' death—the culmination of a life of ideological choices vis-à-vis Jesus' human faith in what he called the kingdom of God— displayed a human and intramundane efficacy which was finite and limited. Only in the new context provided by the resurrection was Jesus' life and death as a whole capable of mediating a salvation that is definitive. That is because only in that eschatological setting was Jesus' self-transcending love able at last to be viewed in a context capable of revealing the truth of Jesus' concrete ideologies or works (the inner meaning and decisive value of which were "hidden with Christ in God"), a truth that embodied and clarified the creative efficacy of his neighborly love and liberative kingdom *praxis* on earth as it is in heaven.

The story of Jesus' life in its entirety, the manifestation of the definitive eschatological value of his *praxis,* death and resurrection, shows that at one and the same time love is what human action is all about and what the gospel is all about. The logic of love, that life is worthwhile for creatures only if they can participate through faiths and ideologies in a project of creative efficacy on earth as it is in heaven, is the logic of human existence itself. As the kingdom *praxis* of Jesus showed, love, participation in a project that is worthwhile, is the logic of God's promise in the *mysterion.* Jesus' kingdom *praxis* revealed the gratuitous yet able-to-be-welcomed news that God loves the logic of Faith and ideologies and wants it to be productive on earth as it is in heaven.

THE ESCHATOLOGICAL COMPLEXITY OF LOVE

It could be said that action's *mysterion charism* to contribute to the creation of a world that is good is the point not merely of this final chapter but of these reflections as a whole. Yet precisely insofar as these reflections are on the subject of eschatology, the task dimension of that *charism* can not be the end of the story. There is more to Jesus' revelation of the *mysterion* than the creation of a world that is good because there is more to the story of God's gratuitous love than the labor and suffering of bringing to birth the manifestation of the new creation.[145] What exactly is this "more?" It is the celebration of creation's definitive completion, the day of communal blessing and jubilant *berakah* on which the goodness of a world finally "come of age" is "baptized" and confirmed in glory. On that day, which will be the dawning of the eschaton in the Sin-shrouded horizon of the universe, a world will rise more brilliant than the sun. Its beauty will be dazzling to the point of its being almost unrecognizable as the same world made painstakingly by hand on earth, and yet both God and creatures will be able to recognize it at once as a unique and pleasing work of art created from the patient fidelity of love. This strange yet familiar definitive reality will be given the name every creature of good will, and God along with them, have been longing a lifetime to hear: Inhabitable, world that can be lived in, world capable of being pronounced good because measurable by a criterion that is the same on earth and in heaven, world capable at last of being rejoiced in and enjoyed, world that is a new creation. In the love that is not task alone but also promise of unending glory, there is not only the labor of a *mysterion* which presents itself in the impassioned project of a conjoint work and suffering, but love's consummate pleasure, the gratuitous ecstacy of shared companionship and play, the celebration of the bringing to life of a world, with all its inhabitants, that will live with God forever.

From the point of view of disciples' having heard a word from God about the *mysterion*—a word that is unsolicited and gratuitous, namely, God's unprecedented action of validating Jesus' life and *praxis* by raising from the dead not only Jesus but also the intramundane causality of his kingdom project—it is clear that in action that is graced, action that is not shrouded in religious "mystery" but lived experientially as a *praxis* of truth, God's project is capable of being brought to definitive eschatological completion (just as it was in the case of Jesus), simply and straightforwardly as ordinary human love. Out of the everyday struggle to make oneself neighbor to the deprived, a work of Faith which forms a costly circuit between action and passion, achievement and failure, joy and suffering, life and death, creatures can make everlasting contributions to the glory of God, indestructible mediations of a love that is not only theirs but God's.

It is also clear that this positive affirmation can continue to be made even in face of the question which casts persistent doubt, at least in modern times, on the ultimate meaningfulness of God's love: is the suffering involved in the realization of the *mysterion* worth it? Is the agony of apparent defeat, experienced as something real and eventually deadly, something fraught with absurdity, frustration, failure, deprivation and pain, too high a price to pay for full participation in the eschatological enjoyment of love? In the context of a Jesus-normed religious anthropological faith, the answer that can be given appears as a story of gratuitous love and eschatological hope. It tells of a continuity of destinies between God and creatures that grounds the affirmation of the ultimate worthwhileness of love both theologically and anthropologically. Theologically, it grounds it in God's preoccupation with making Godself Neighbor of Neighbors in heaven to suffering creatures on earth, and anthropologically, it grounds it in people's utopian preoccupation with a liberative *praxis* aimed at making a heaven for the deprived on earth, admittedly a task inevitably minoritarian in the face of Sin and seemingly inefficacious. Hope in the face of Sin and death, the human *yes,* however half-hearted, to the question of the definitive worthwhileness of love, can not be accounted for by the digital arguments of reason.[146] It is not susceptible of proof. It is a wager of anthropological faith.[147]

As an eschatological logic built into Faith from the start, hope affirms that love is capable of making a substantial contribution not only to the creation of a new earth but to the celebration of a new heaven. Yet insofar as the category of heaven pertains to what is proper to God, and insofar as revelation has made it manifest that in the *mysterion,* the destiny of God is inseparably bound with that of creatures to the extent that God's ability to rejoice in heaven depends on the liberation of the deprived on earth, the notion of a creaturely contribution to the making of a new heaven means that so long as the needs of even the smallest of creatures go unattended on earth, so long as their deprivations go unrecognized and unrelieved, God is deprived of the glory that is proper to God (not "God" in the abstract but precisely God whom Jesus reveals, who reveals as well the *mysterion*). If what Jesus indicates about God is true, if God's love for the deprived is Neighborly and real, then God can have no glory in heaven if suffering is not relieved on earth. That is the jarring yet undeniable consequence of acknowledging Faith's gratuitous capability, made plain in revelation, to construct on earth the values of God's heart in heaven, to mediate in a universe of Sin a love by which God makes Godself not creator but Neighbor.

NOTES

[1] Similarly, with words like "Yours is the kingdom and the power and the glory forever," they are acknowledging the creative efficacy of God's love, God's definitive power over evil, suffering and death.

[2] As earlier discussion has shown, Segundo makes no effort to place those who are not disciples of Jesus, whether atheists or theists, in a relationship of religious faith with Jesus.

[3] To speak of God's sharing a destiny with creatures is not to speak of God's having a "fate" imposed from outside. God's gratuitous decision to tie to the action of creatures the definitive realization of what Jesus called God's kingdom is the result of God's freedom and love. It is God's manifest will, communicated in revelation, that the salvific and creative project begun in grace be brought to completion in glory.

[4] As has been emphasized from the start, the word *heaven* is a technical eschatological term. It refers to neither an afterlife nor a place, even less to a future reward. Rather, it is a theological category for talking about the transcendence of God. It points to what is proper to God *qua* God, namely, God's uniqueness or "Godliness," which is not derivable from earthly experience but is gratuitously communicated on earth wherever there is self-transcending love.

[5] For Segundo, such hope consists in "the assertion that *loving is worthwhile, whatever it may cost in self-giving and even death*" (*HCP*, p. 152; italics Segundo's).

[6] The utopian logic of human action and its connection with the meaning of history have been explored from a critical Marxist point of view by Ernst Bloch, *A Philosophy of the Future* (New York: Herder and Herder, 1970), who views history as structured by utopian hope. Although Segundo does not utilize utopia as a category (in spite of the fact that in *FI*, p. 73, he links to anthropological faith's acceptance of transcendent data the human tendency to have a "store of utopias"), a careful look at his eschatology shows that he employs a logic in the general spirit of (but not, strictly speaking, similar to) Bloch's. According to Segundo, anthropological faith strives through ideologies to realize efficacious change, and the nature of faith's epistemological premises is to ground action in a "hope against all hope" that "love's projects and works" *qua* ideologies of "true self-giving, no matter how imperfect [they] may be," have intrinsic value and worth (*HCP*, p. 152).

[7] This question was the subject of a debate spanning several issues of *Christianity and Crisis* [vol. 33 (1973), numbers 15, 17 and 20]. In the lead article, "The Theology of Liberation: Christian Utopianism," (September 17), pp. 167-173, Thomas Sanders faults liberation theologies for a "soft utopianism." Basing his position on Reinhold Niebuhr's well-known objection to the "utopian moralism" of dividing the world naively into oppressors and oppressed, Sanders advocates as corrective a (Niebuhrian) "Christian Realism." In the accompanying response, "Christian Realism: Ideology of the Establishment," pp. 173-176, Rubem Alves argues that utopia represents a faith-filled recognition that historical realities stand under the relativizing effects of God's eschatological promise, which generates a need for continual critical revision, thus giving utopia a historical and sociopolitical foothold in reality. The issues surrounding this early conflict are picked up and treated at length in Dennis P. McCann, *Christian Realism and Liberation Theology* (Maryknoll, N.Y.: Orbis, 1981).

[8] For a brief but pertinent analysis presenting utopia in exactly such a light, see *Concilium* General Secretariat, "Utopia," in E. Schillebeeckx and J.B. Metz, eds., *The Problem of Eschatology, Concilium* 41 (New York: Paulist, 1969), pp. 149-165.

[9] This does not imply that sensitivity to the deprived is simply automatic, an inevitable response to others' pain. Although utopian hope derives from the logic of action, it is neither an automatic nor necessary component of it. The fact that the heart can be hardened rather than sensitive to the cries of the deprived means that anthropological faith is not always and necessarily "good faith". On the contrary, it can be a good faith that is operating out of a mistaken criterion of truth and thus expressing itself in ideologies more or less wittingly inattentive to the needs of the deprived, or it can be an anthropological faith that, virtually insensitive to the needs of the deprived, either already is bad faith or else is gradually degenerating into it. See *FI*, p. 46 ff. and *HCP*, p. 57, p. 120, pp. 147-148 and p. 151.

[10] See *Concilium* General Secretariat, "Utopia," pp. 162-165.

[11] See n. 7 above.

[12] Chapter three showed that, according to Jesus, what constitutes the truth criterion of action is not an extrinsic and arbitrary mandate from heaven but the cry of the deprived on earth. Such a criterion does not need to be deduced from a religious law, since it presents itself to the sensibilities of the sensitive heart as a demand for secular liberation.

[13] *EAJN*, p. 112 (inclusive language substituted concerning God). As was pointed out in chapter one, Segundo believes that the only meaningful significance of freedom is to create, which for Segundo means to create love; see *OIG*, pp. 107-111 and pp. 136-139 and *HCP*, p. 136; see also *Infierno*, p. 31.

[14] *HCP*, p. 136 (italics Segundo's). As Segundo suggests, this seems to be an anthropologically intelligible way of understanding the biblical notion of image and likeness. "What reality of the human being," he asks, "can somehow be likened to

the idea of 'creation' [as it pertains to God]? The reality of *freedom* as Paul understands and stresses it throughout his christology" (*ibid.*; italics Segundo's). For Paul, Segundo points out, freedom is "an eschatological reality"; it strives to "turn. . . suffering into the meaning and mainspring. . .of what can be called 'creation' in an already-created world: the appearance of a new being, the building up of brother and sister, the 'birth' that gives meaning to labor pains" (*ibid.*, p. 137). The significance of freedom is that creatures are "like" God not in the capacity to create but in the capacity to create *good*. In other words, we are like God not in the abstract but in the concrete. Insofar as in the givenness of the universe, creation involves the apparent futility of loving in the face of Sin, God and creatures are conjoined in a labor of suffering. They are working to suffer the eventual creation of a world that is going to be good. As will be seen, this does not mean they are creating abstractly "out of nothing" but in the face of all the actual suffering, injustice, sin and death that subjection to Sin can entail.

     15 Although I do not wish to deny the possibility of theology's being made meaningful from an æsthetic point of view, e.g., by theologians who "exegete" the link between grace and glory with reference to the transcendent value of beauty, I believe that unless an æsthetic approach is willing to measure its truth against the criterion of anthropological faith—a criterion the deprived themselves actually constitute—the æsthetic commitment does not embody what theology calls the eschatological validity of love. In other words, the condition for meaningful *theological* conversation and *praxis* is concern for victims, a caring consciousness and practice vis-à-vis the needs of the deprived. In liberationist terminology, such consciousness and practice express themselves as an option for the poor. For Segundo, the immense majority of the poor, oppressed and marginalized constitutes a new theological locus, and the option on their behalf is grounded in the fact that God whom Jesus revealed has always made that option (*RC,* p. 125).

     16 Realism about utopian striving rules out the sinful deformations of action discussed in chapter two: (1) unrealistic day-dreaming about recapturing the lost perfection of a golden age of the past or, what is worse, timid reliance on a purely divine efficacy "from heaven," a bypassing of intramundane causality by attributing efficacy to God alone or relying on God for some type of apocalyptic reversal; and, (2) the tendency of the hardened or overly pessimistic heart to trust in sheer force, i.e., efficacies pursued "by ideologies alone" and purchased at the expense of long-term gain for the sake of immediate—and death-dealing—profit. Examples of the latter, Segundo believes, are totalitarian repression and terrorism (*FI,* pp. 290-303 and p. 302, n. 6). Segundo observes about his own work that he moves from the overriding optimism of Teilhard's evolutionary categories to the more realistic ones of Gregory Bateson precisely through a biblical—which, for Segundo, means Pauline—appropriation of the complexity of relations between Faith and Sin (see *RC,* pp. 273-274, n. 15).

[17] Juan Luis Segundo, "Fundamental Theology and Dialogue," in J.B. Metz, ed., *The Development of Fundamental Theology, Concilium* 46 (New York: Paulist, 1969), p. 74.

[18] For Segundo, what is "new" about Jesus' resurrection is not that it provides new data, and thus new premises, for anthropological faith but that it serves to clarify (with a gratuitously revealed yet appropriate word from God) data and premises *already available* to anthropological faith (*HJS*, p. 170 and pp. 175-177; *HCP*, p. 69, pp. 152-154 and p. 220, n. 228). On this important point, Segundo writes, "A transcendent datum *already present* in humanity is...made explicit in Christ" (*HCP*, p. 154; italics mine). It is "accessible to all humans from the very start but...[is] spelled out in terms of the message, life, death and resurrection of Jesus of Nazareth" (*ibid.*, pp. 152-153). As was seen in chapter three, the datum in question is available in the logic of action itself, in the sensitive heart's reading of the signs of the times in a neighborly way responsive to the needs of the deprived. Insofar as such a datum is both gratuitous and appropriate, i.e., both new to action and yet already available to its logic, it is "redundant" (*HJS*, p. 177).

[19] On the reasons for this, which have to do with the nature of revelation, see chapter three, section two. Here it is necessary only to note that making theology is not the same as "making converts." In fact, the latter is neither desirable nor feasible in a context like Segundo's where acceptance of transcendent data grounding religious faith is no different from acceptance of transcendent data grounding any other type of faith (see previous note). Evangelization is not proselyzing or indoctrination. Justifying the hope that is in disciples is not something disciples do in order to make sure "God gets God's due" but in order that, having themselves experienced the gratuitousness of God's love—God's apparent lack of concern about getting God's due and God's impassioned concern about giving to creatures what is precisely not due but is simply given out of love—they might learn to let it fund their own and others' neighborly responses to the deprived and sharpen the quality of their own and others' participation in the common struggle to find appropriate solutions to secular problems. For Segundo's interpretation of this dynamic, which involves an unconventional minoritarian ecclesiology, see *CCC, RC* and *TC*. In these works, he describes the (Christian) church(es) as minoritarian. Their purpose is not to keep members and accumulate more but to contribute to the common struggle to solve secular problems. The practical issues involved in the pastoral *praxis* of such a church are treated in *HMPA* and "On a Missionary Awareness of One's Own Culture," *Jesuit Missions Newsletter,* May, 1974, pp. 1-6.

[20] "Fundamental Theology and Dialogue," p. 75 (brackets my addition).

[21] *Ibid.*, p. 69. Segundo believes that fundamental, or foundational, theology is in process of disappearing because it makes what used to be called "dogmatic theology" a specialized language not available for conversation with persons and groups outside the portals of dogma. As Segundo sees it, "Vatican Council II clarified

THE GLORIOUS DESTINY OF ACTION   253

an essential point which completely destroys th[at] foregoing schema: dialogue with non-believers is realized with what properly constitutes dogmatic theology. . . . Dialogue is not carried on up to the portals of dogma, but from the very center of dogma itself" (pp. 73 and 75). According to Segundo, that is because by its very nature, "revealed truth is. . .a message destined to form part of, and be possessed in, *a dialogue"* (p. 74; italics mine).

[22] This need was discussed in the introductory remarks of chapter two.

[23] Of course Segundo admits that transcendence is accessible on earth only at the level of the heart; but far from being a purely interior, "spiritual" affair, the heart is an intrinsically social consciousness inseparable from the public and secular dimensions of action. This does not negate the fact that the heart has a genuinely individual dimension of personal interiority which may be distinguished from, but not permitted to subsume, its social and secular orientation. As the preceding chapters have shown, the *praxis* of the sensitive heart is normed by the needs of the deprived and conditioned by the signs of the times. The structure of the heart is thus inseparable from the *charism* of Faith, with its secular task of social, political and ecological liberation. This was the message of a lecture, "Is Liberation Theology a Bad Word?" (Regis College, Toronto, March 14, 1985), which subsequently was incorporated into *TC.* There, Segundo states: "Where, then, is transcendence? It is not a shortcut from the individual heart to God; it passes through history, where the love of neighbor, made real, is *already* initiated transcendence" (p. 72; italics Segundo's). For Segundo, this means affirming that the heart is a matter of earthly commitment and passion (*TC,* p. 71). He argues that the heart is not really in touch with transcendence at all unless it is directed earthward as well as heavenward, toward the implementation of ideologies responsive to the down-to-earth needs of the poor and the oppressed (*Masas y minorías,* p. 93).

[24] Theological statements are always fraught with danger, but in the case of this one the risk of misunderstanding is particularly grave. What I am getting at is that secular liberation is constitutive of salvation but not exhaustive of its eschatological significance. Liberation of the deprived is salvation's truth criterion and is constitutive of salvation's content, which is self-transcending love. But the validity and reality of neighborly love are "multiplied" in the eschaton, which gives the love of human beings a gratuitous yet appropriate (redundant) setting in the glorious context of the death-defeating power of God's love. The latter is capable of being welcomed with joy by an already operative utopian hope, yet on earth it remains no more than a gratuitous invitation. God does not force utopian striving to become anything more than it already is. Grace does not intrude on creaturely integrity but manifests God's infinite respect. God stands at the door and knocks. God never barges in.

[25] *EAJN,* p. 113 and *HCP,* pp. 135-142.

[26] Carried to logical conclusions, what is at issue here is whether religion ought to be collapsed into ethics. This question is at the heart of objections to liberal

theology [see Karl Rahner and Herbert Vorgrimler, *Concise Theological Dictionary*, second edition (London: Burns and Oats, 1983), p. 276] and central to the more recent objections to liberationist theologies raised by advocates of "Christian Realism" like Dennis P. McCann (see note 7 above). Like earlier objections to liberalism, objections to liberationist theologies concern an alleged "failure to clarify the theological relationship between 'liberation' and 'salvation'" and a lack of "theoretical resources for distinguishing religious transcendence from political enthusiasm" (McCann, pp. 1-4). On the basis of the data presented here, I believe it is fair to argue that Segundo retains the distinction between religion and ethics while demonstrating their inseparability, grounding their unity-in-distinction in a theologically developed—and secularly relevant—eschatology.

27 As will be seen, Segundo utilizes the new heaven and the new earth as a major interpretive key to unlock the meaning of salvation and to emphasize the significance of the fact that "in the New Testament we come across four main terms that are used to describe the final reality: resurrection, regeneration, restoration and recapitulation" (*EAJN*, p. 102).

28 *HCP*, p. 134. As Segundo shows, "what has to undergo resurrection, according to Paul, [is] the corruption or death of human projects" (*ibid.*, p. 75).

29 In connection with the doctrine of the resurrection of the body and clearly suggesting such a cosmic understanding of salvation, Segundo points out that "'body' has the meaning of 'flesh' and takes in the whole human being and what surrounds it" (*HCP*, p. 214, n. 191). See also pp. 207-208, n. 153, where Segundo links 'body' with "the 'circumstance' of the human being: everything that surrounds the human being and forms an integral part of its life." As will be seen, however, the salvation of the cosmos remains for Segundo a function of its anthropological relevance.

30 *HCP*, pp. 129-131.

31 *EAJN*, p. 136, n. 161. See also *HCP*, pp. 115-116.

32 *HCP*, p. 122, pp. 128-132 and pp. 145-160, especially pp. 159-160.

33 *HCP*, p. 132; inclusive language added. As was seen in chapter two, what is most significant about the "law of the members," or Sin, is precisely its *secular* relevance, its capacity to undercut utopian hope and make the struggle for liberation powerless: "The central problem of our human condition today [is] the creation and maintenance of structures and power-centers that are bound to block all effective forms of loving our neighbors and our fellow human beings in either the public or the private sector. The crucial issue is not the existence of individual *sins* of frailty, even those involving conscious exploitation, which will ultimately be forgiven and forgotten. The crucial problem is the idol that has been erected against everything human, the global power that has been set up to endure, to enslave human beings, to strip them of their freedom to create, to make them useless and kill them. Sometimes it does actually kill them physically. Most of the time it kills their projects that are designed to offer hope and meaningfulness" (*HCP*, p. 175; italics Segundo's).

[34] Segundo regards self-transcending love as having a homeostatic function vis-à-vis the creation of the new reality. Love acts like a "thermostat" set at a point at which persons *qua* diverse centers of meaning and value can be integrated into "a rich circuit," a "synthesis of centers" or "circuit of circuits" made possible by the free and reciprocal "losing" of the self for the sake of the coming to light of the other: "We must take the initiative of *gratuitousness* as our approach," he writes (*EAJN*, p. 64; italics Segundo's), and, for him, gratuitousness involves the Jesus-like logic of self-transcendence, since love is the only efficacious way by which to integrate the marginalized, exploited and peripheralized members of society into richer, fuller syntheses of love (*ibid.*, p. 62). Injustice—the opposite of self-transcending love—is an unintegrated or poorly integrated circuit, a fact reflected in the meaning of the term *marginalization* (*ibid.*).

[35] This willingness is the best definition of freedom I can think of. It is unlike that found in pessimistic worldviews. In fact, it reflects Segundo's optimistic conviction that "the only Christian significance of liberty has to be that of *creation*" (*OIG*, p. 108; italics Segundo's). On this point I take exception to what, from one perspective, could be read as the nihilism of Timothy Findley's previously mentioned novel, *Not Wanted on the Voyage*. In the voice of Mrs. Noyes, Noah's wife, Findley declares that to start the world all over again (in the aftermath of the Great Flood) is simply not worth the trouble. It is not worth what it will cost in suffering, pain and sin, symbolized in this book by the tyrannical and destructive Noah and his feeble accomplice, "Yaweh," both of whom are insensitive in the extreme. It would be depressing if Findley's book were to lead to the conclusion that ultimately love is powerless. If he is saying it would be better not to risk having a world at all than to have one in which Sin, with its disturbing potential to be co-opted into sin, makes it necessary for people to try loving and creating over and over again, then he is saying that we human beings are ultimately more scandalized by evil than is God (not the "God" in Findley's novel, but God revealed in the kingdom *praxis* of Jesus). But perhaps Findley is making an ironic statement; perhaps he is issuing a prophetic warning to a superficial, overly purposive culture which, like Findley's Noah, goes on being enchanted by the "magic tricks" of technology, even when they involve the destruction of something as beautiful and complex as a planet.

[36] Nevertheless, for optimists like Segundo, there is a problem involved in holding such a positive view of freedom. What about human ideologies and "creations"—products of freedom that are really "anti-creations"—that are not the triviality of sounding brass and tinkling cymbal but heavy millstones around the necks of the poor? What about the crushing weight on victims' backs of deliberate human wickedness? A beginning of an answer to this difficult question occurs in the preceding note. (On this topic, see also chapter one, n. 33.) The rest of an answer would have to speak, as Segundo begins to do, about something as senseless and out of proportion as Jesus' being put to a violent death on a cross, due precisely to a logic

of self-transcending love that he himself had set in motion by the disruptive effects of his kingdom *praxis*. In other words, as Segundo frequently points out, creative and constructive freedom, i.e., self-transcending love, is tremendously expensive. Its price tag carries the outrageous sum of seemingly endless amounts of entropy in the form of violence, hatred and sin. This apparently uncalled-for price is the "bad news" about existence in a universe in which Sin plays a constitutive and not merely accidental part. The good news is that Someone Who Wants to be Neighbor (even when everyone else has failed to do so and perhaps is failing even to try) will come along in the end who will pay the exhorbitant price. By binding the wounds of the injured at God's own expense, this Neighbor of Neighbors will put the sufferings of the deprived, the utter negativities of which are ontologically significant in themselves, in a setting of eschatological justice that will make their true value shine forth for all to see, who will cherish them as a glory that is not only the sufferer's but God's.

[37] *GHC*, pp. 80-81.

[38] *EAJN*, pp. 110-121.

[39] *FI*, pp. 134-136, pp. 155-159 and p. 163.

[40] Segundo observes that the biblical adjective *kainos* (new) "designates that which is new in quality," and, emphasizing the continuity between what has gone before and what emerges as new in relation to it, he adds, "Hence it is the *earth* that we are looking forward to and that is identical with eternal life" (*GHC*, p. 73).

[41] For Segundo, love's eschatological power to create a reality that is truly new is identical with Faith's gratuitous capacity to be definitively efficacious in the face of Sin: "Newness is an historical category which expresses the complex experience of love. . . .It. . .transforms our 'stiff-necked' sinfulness and our 'hearts of stone' (Ezek. 36: 25-29) into an openness to grace. . . . Newness is the category which expresses the transcendence of love" (*GHC*, p. 122).

[42] *RC*, p. 266. See also *OIG*, p. 46; *ST*, p. 83; *HCP*, p. 152; *GHC*, p. 45.

[43] That is because, for Segundo, the nature of newness derives from the structure of freedom, which is marked by a creative tension between what is laboriously achieved and what is gratuitously given as gift. The structure of freedom is that it is "at the same time breakthrough and continuity, crisis and incarnation, life in the world and eschatology" (*HCP*, p. 81; see also *RC*, p. 262, n. 8).

[44] An early expression of this occurs in *EG*, especially pp. 108-110, p. 122 and pp. 126-131. A more nuanced and clarified later expression is presented in *EAJN*, pp. 69-70: "Manichæism. . .shows up as soon as we start to conceive entropy and negentropy as *two lines between which we must choose*" (italics Segundo's; see also *ibid.*, pp. 74-75 and pp. 113-114). In a sentence that immediately follows in the original Spanish text but which does not appear in John Drury's translation, Segundo goes on to argue that we place ourselves in a basically Manichæan position every time we tend—in simplistic fashion—to identify negentropy with God (or love) and entropy with sin (see *HHJN* II/2, p. 899).

45 For Segundo, the solution to Manichæan dualism is an ecological logic which incorporates into the dialectical relations between entropy and negentropy a time-consuming circuitousness which conditions our action and helps it to be efficacious (see *EAJN*, pp. 69-74).

46 *EAJN*, p. 74 (italics Segundo's).

47 *HCP*, p. 122.

48 *Ibid.* As Segundo points out, "Here, then, [in the Faith-Sin dialectic] we have a key point for our hypothesis: the final antithesis. . .is not between *wanting-in-principle* and *serving-in-reality*, but between *two real services*" (*ibid.;* italics Segundo's).

49 *EAJN*, p. 64 (italics Segundo's).

50 *Ibid.*, p. 104.

51 *Ibid.*, p. 35; *GHC*, p. 118.

52 *EAJN*, p. 103.

53 *Ibid.*, p. 104 .

54 A notable although brief exception occurs in Edward Schillebeeckx's *On Christian Faith* (New York: Crossroad, 1987), pp. 29-30.

55 For Segundo, reliance on immediacy and facility represents an abuse of entropy, the attempt to make quantity more powerful than quality by leaving quality out of account. This is the point of his discussion of means and ends in relation to the ecological scale of political ideologies in industrially developed countries (*FI*, pp. 257-270). It is also the point of his observations on the destruction of the social ecology in Latin American countries (*ibid.*, pp. 282-291). Finally, it is the point of his warnings to those liberation theologians who would attribute creative power over sociopolitical evil *solely* to the factor of powerlessness, e.g., "the people" or "the poor" alone (*HCP*, pp. 179-182 and p. 224, nn. 254 and 257).

56 For Segundo, the lack of appreciation for the givenness of reality constitutes a failure of ecological wisdom. It reflects a lack of trust, which is basically a lack of gratitude to the logic of gratuitousness. He sees this lack as the root of a pessimistic over-purposiveness that is ultimately destructive: "*Systematic pessimism exacerbates the use of rationality* in one's search for means, for solutions to a crisis. And this is done at the expense of ecological wisdom, of course" (*FI*, p. 290; italics Segundo's). "But," he adds, using this remark to condemn what he sees as a repressive shift toward fascism in Latin American countries, "as Chesterton pointed out, fools do not lack the use of reason; they *lack a sense of reality*" (*ibid.*, p. 291; italics mine).

57 In the words of Iris Murdoch, *The Sovereignty of Good* (London: Routledge & Kegan Paul, 1970), p. 95, "Humility . . .is selfless respect for reality."

58 As Segundo shows, religious faith is not a matter of human beings' being able to determine whether or not God "exists" but affirming whether God's values have anything to do with the values of anthropological faith. Similarly, theology must

not begin with the theoretical problem of God's existence (and its stress on the vertical relation between creator and creature), but with the existential problem of determining, in the face of one's neighbors and their needs, the *values* God upholds (see *RC*, p. 282 ff., especially pp. 294-295).

[59] *RC*, p. 325. Later in this same work, Segundo points out that contemplation is a matter of being ever more interested in the plan of God, learning how to participate in and celebrate all the realizations of the kingdom of God that happen on earth, knowing that, provisional though they appear, they depend on God who has wagered on that project and the values it entails (p. 327).

[60] To account for this reciprocity, Segundo does not employ the categories of process philosophy. Instead, as all of these chapters have shown, he utilizes a combination of evolutionary and ecological categories taken from the biological and physical sciences, placing them at the service of practical, politically realistic cultural analyses deriving not from the social sciences *per se*, but from an awareness of the complexity and urgency of sociopolitical change on the one hand and a critical correlation of that data with Jesus' revelation of God's values on the other. Chief among these are categories like efficacious change, intramundane causality and the priority of future over past, all of which contribute to a theologically realistic understanding of eschatology that is relevant to secular concerns and capable of validating the logic of action.

[61] This is the fault for which Segundo criticizes the theological presuppositions and content of the Vatican "Instruction on Certain Aspects of the Theology of Liberation" (*TC*, pp. 46-66).

[62] Of course, there is a paradox here. On the one hand, the quality of love is measured not by its degree of actual success but by the truth of its criterion, yet on the other, it is structured by a logic that tends intrinsically toward efficacy. Love is thus the capacity to continue trying, but even more, the capacity to incorporate the data of inefficacy and failure into epistemological premises that continue to have faith in eschatological success, that continue to hope in the definitive worthwhileness of love, in spite of appearances to the contrary.

[63] *HCP*, pp. 130-131 (first italics Segundo's; second italics mine; inclusive language for God substituted).

[64] Quoted in *HCP*, p. 130 (John Drury's translation of Segundo's own Spanish text).

[65] Margaret Laurence, *The Stone Angel* (Toronto: McClelland and Stewart, Ltd., 1964), p. 307.

[66] The biblical concept *mysterion* does not mean something beyond human ken. On the contrary, it refers to the secrets of God's heart which are not hidden but made known in the *praxis* of prophets, especially the kingdom *praxis* of Jesus. In the liberation of the deprived, the secrets of the *mysterion* are manifest at the center of action. They are capable of being put into practice by any and every human being

whose *praxis* is self-transcending love. Precisely as a member of a community of exactly such prophets, a disciple of Jesus is one who not only practices love but knows that it is the realization on earth of God's *mysterion* in heaven. In this sense, the disciple is one who knows a secret of the heart of God. And, in the context of Segundo's theology, the secrets of God's heart are always historical projects deriving from the fact that God comes to the aid of the poor, the marginalized, the dehumanized and the oppressed (*RC*, p. 109).

[67] *HCP*, p. 96.

[68] Although Segundo explicitly refers to *mysterion* as God's "plan of love" (*CCC*, pp. 27-32 and pp. 163-165), to my knowledge, he has not elaborated on it apart from its traditional connection with the efficacy and sign-value of sacramental realities (*CCC*, p. 32); except for the reference in n. 66, he does not seem inclined to link *mysterion* explicitly with what Jesus called the "secrets" of the kingdom (*HJS*, p. 138 and p. 159). I think that is because in interpreting Paul, Segundo focuses on the anthropological implications of Rom. 1-8 rather than on the cosmic dimensions of a Jesus-revealed project. Where according to Jesus, "the kingdom or reign of God meant that God was coming to Israel to combat the infrahuman situation affecting the lives of the poor, the helpless and the marginalized," according to Paul, the emphasis falls on the liberation of human beings for "maturity, the freedom of faith that propels human beings towards untrammeled and unreserved creative activity out of love for their brother and sister humans" (*HCP*, p. 96).

[69] See *HCP*, p. 54 and pp. 161 ff., and *RC*, p. 272.

[70] *HCP*, p. 137.

[71] *Ibid.*, p. 138. Segundo points out that, for Paul, "eschatology is not the suppression of human freedom or a replacement for it, but rather the manifestation ot it."

[72] This was the underlying point of *GHC* and *EG* taken together, and while the conception of grace presented in *GHC* has been substantially developed (see *RC*, pp. 219-276, especially pp. 238-239), Segundo has not changed his basic insight about the complexity of its relations with Sin. See, for example, *RC*, p. 271 and p. 334.

[73] Segundo's most concise statement of this appears in a summary of ten points about grace in which are condensed what he considers to be the originality of Paul in contrast to the largely unbiblical (Catholic) reflection on grace (e.g., by P. Fransen, T. Rast and K. Rahner) carried out as part of the theological renewal pre-dating the Second Vatican Council. See *RC*, pp. 265-268, For Segundo's discussion of these theologians see *ibid.*, pp. 254-265.

[74] *HJS*, pp. 176-177; *HCP*, pp. 142-144 and p. 216, n. 212.

[75] *HCP*, p. 160 (italics Segundo's).

[76] As will be seen, Segundo bases this understanding not only on Paul's eschatology but on the early tradition which relied, e.g., on Prov. 10: 12— "'Above

all, keep your love for one another at full strength, because love cancels innumerable sins' (1 Pet. 4: 8)" (*GHC*, p. 148). See also *RC*, p. 201 and p. 262.

[77] *GHC*, p. 148 (italics Segundo's).

[78] *GHC*, pp. 146-147; *HCP*, p. 130. See also *Infierno*, p. 53.

[79] *HCP*, p. 160. In the pages of *Infierno*, the unpublished transcript of a course on the doctrine of hell that Segundo gave in 1983 at a local parish, there is an illuminating explanation of the qualitative difference between love and egotism which deserves to be quoted here: "There is a qualitative difference between love and egotism. Egotism does not destroy love, but simply does not construct it. Egotism does not stop the intention of love—it simply makes love less efficacious. It lowers the quality of love. . . .It is not a matter of two things which annul one another. It is a matter of egotism's diminishing the quality of love but not turning it into hate" [*Infierno*, pp. 53-54; translation mine (version not edited by the author)]. Because this is the case, Segundo notes that egotism does not consist in making a decision of freedom but rather in losing it (*ibid.*, p. 53).

[80] *GHC*, p. 149.

[81] *HCP*, p. 204, n. 127 (italics mine).

[82] *HCP*, p. 160.

[83] *Ibid.*, p. 137.

[84] *Ibid.* (first italics Segundo's; second italics mine; inclusive language concerning God substituted).

[85] This was the point of the reference in chapter one to Blondel's notion of God's patience before the action and passion of creatures. See chapter one, final section.

[86] *HCP*, p. 215, n. 203.

[87] As was observed in chapter one, however, one sees in Segundo's language a concurrent thread of ambiguity about the role of God as creator, a stress on the pre-established and deliberate character of God's decision about what kind of world to create, i.e., precisely one fraught with Sin (*RC*, p. 265). While Segundo's use of such language is never in isolation from the eschatological context of the love that God offers in grace, it risks contributing to the impression that the doctrine of creation can be accounted for as a presupposition for the doctrine of grace, and thus can be considered in relative isolation from it. Segundo is of course aware of the epistemological limitations of the creator-creature schema as a source of theological knowledge about—and effective relationship with—God. He considers such a schema overly reliant on the ahistorical categories of abstract reason and philosophical speculation (see *OIG*, especially pp. 98-115 and p. 136), and he explicitly critiques it in exactly that light (*CIE*, pp. 42 and 46 and *RC*, p. 195). Consistent with the down-to-earth orientation of his eschatology, he observes that a too-deep awareness of the creaturely condition, described as "a profound terror and total adoration. . . toward the transcendent. . .signifies that the creature is afraid to confront

God with criteria (ontological and epistemological premises) deriving from the human being" (*HCP*, p. 26). He also points out that Paul depreciates relations with God based on a conception of the human being as Flesh or creature alone, i.e., without reference to the reciprocity of loves being effected gratuitously in Faith (*HCP*, p. 108).

88 *HCP*, p. 134. See also nn. 28 and 29 above.

89 *EAJN*, p. 105.

90 For Segundo, both of these passages are concerned less with the judgment of persons and more with the definitive value and ontological durability of their projects, i.e., the work of Faith which, in self-transcending love, includes action's observable results in the sphere of objective reality. See *HCP*, p. 119 and pp. 129-131, *GHC*, p. 150 and *Infierno*, p. 24 and p. 54.

91 I believe such reinterpretation remains faithful to the liberative spirit of Segundo's theology while carrying his interest in Faith's relations with the objective givenness of reality a step forward.

92 It is worth recalling that in the biblical idiom, grammatical constructions comprising pairs of apparent opposites (e.g., good and evil, male and female, heaven and earth) point to the inclusiveness of reality, to a wholeness or completeness in which nothing is forgotten or left out.

93 *EAJN*, pp. 36-38.

94 The fact that continuity does not have to involve a causal connection is important here because in disciples' conversation with persons of different anthropological faiths, it is necessary to show not only that God's purposes are not incompatible with secular efforts to liberate the deprived but that God is not needed to supply an extrinsic reason for the value of utopian striving. In other words, the relation between heaven and earth is gratuitous rather than necessary.

95 See notes 66 and 68 above.

96 In this respect, the concept of *mysterion* may not be identified with Rahner's conception of 'absolute mystery.' *Mysterion* refers to a secret of God's heart that can not be inductively arrived at from the nature of experience on earth. Insofar as it pertains to the transcendent values of God, i.e., the absolute, unconditioned character of God's sovereign will, knowledge of the *mysterion* does not derive from a human consciousness, more or less explicit, of transcendent mystery as horizon or ground of historical contingency. Rather, *mysterion* represents a brand new project in which action is invited to participate, yet a project which is neither extrinsic to the logic of action nor incompatible with the liberative orientation of secular utopian hope.

97 For discussion of Jesus' mediation on two inseparable levels (salvation and revelation) of one and the same grace, see chapter three, third section.

98 God's *mysterion* is redundant because it strikes the "ready" soil of the sensitive heart like a happy summer shower: it comes as a gift "from heaven"—understood as a synonym for the transcendence of God—to soak the hopeful and

neighborly heart on earth with a refreshment that is not required of necessity but, once it is experienced, is able to be welcomed as appropriate.

99 I am using the word *convenient* here in a strictly theological sense to refer to something that is both appropriate to the requirements of human experience and demanded by the task of trying to communicate the data of God's revelation.

100 Segundo suggests this when he observes that "hope. . .is incorporated into our activity as a fundamental, transcendent datum" (*EAJN*, p. 115), and, again, when he states that "eschatology [is] an essential and integral component of every human life" (*HJS*, p. 173). As he points out, the transcendent datum on which hope is based is both "unverifiable and verified" with respect to human experience: it can not be verified by one's own experience itself but is verified through the medium of a witness or witnesses (*ibid.*, p. 172).

101 A purely scientific sort of "theological" reflection, which is really a theory of retributive justice in the absence of a doctrine of gratuitous love, is placed in quotation marks here because, strictly speaking, it is not theology at all. Rather, it is philosophical speculation (which, *qua* philosophy, can be either good or bad). The point is that in order for a human science to regard itself as theology, it must grapple with the problem of a revelation coming from *God*. But in order to regard itself as Christian, it must account for the revelation of God's values accessible in the kingdom *praxis* and resurrection of *Jesus*. Obviously, the point is not to suggest that because theology relies on a datum which philosophy does not require, i.e., revelation, theology is "better." It is the character of theology and not philosophy that is here being called into question. As Segundo observes, "A 'natural theology' that judges and even goes so far as to 'abridge' the theology of faith [i.e., revelation] is not Christian" (*OIG*, p. 119, n. 17).

102 Segundo regards as false any "Christian theology" that is scandalized by Jesus' revelation of God's (conflictual) option for the deprived, no matter how orthodox, from a rationally coherent point of view, it may be proved to be. It is false because it conveys a false image of God. A true image of God is available only through the truth criterion provided by revelation, which is why Jesus' revelation of God's values must be normative for a theology that calls itself Christian. According to Jesus' criterion, any theology that contributes to the oppression of the poor, i.e., that works against the liberation of the deprived from observable evils and ills, is not a true theology. For a discussion of Segundo's views on this topic and an account of how he derives the criterion of truth from the kingdom *praxis* of Jesus, see chapter three, section three.

103 One could argue that part of the significance of a Christian doctrine of grace is precisely that it affirms not that God's power is absolute and sovereign (to which a doctrine of creation attests) but rather that God's heart is gracious and impassioned, overflowing with Neighborly love. A doctrine of creation devoid of grace leads to a hard and oppressive piety in which personal relations with God and communal

relations with neighbors must be subsumed under the relentless order of universal harmony and subjection to Law.

[104] *HJS*, p. 35.

[105] For Segundo, the glory of God is most clearly manifested in Jesus' washing of the disciples' feet (*CIE*, p. 37 and p. 129, n. 30; *OIG*, p. 111). Thus glory is most characteristically revealed in human actions of self-transcending love. So true is this, Segundo argues, that in the eschaton, the substantial content of neighborly love (normed by the needs of the deprived) will replace the need for a "temple" in which to "locate" the glory of God. God's glory will not be a product of God alone but will consist in the myriad embodiments of neighborly human love that will comprise the new heaven and new earth themselves (*ST*, p. 150). This understanding of glory is reaffirmed in *RC*, pp. 55-56, where Segundo observes that the glory of God consists in human beings' being incorporated as co-workers in God's eschatological project, to which they make decisive historical contributions which are the effective beginning of what Jesus called God's kingdom.

[106] This seems to me to be one of the most significant conclusions Segundo reaches in *EG*, that what is "original" about Sin does not pertain to its cause (conceived of chronologically) but to its essential character, along with Faith, as an ontologically creative vector of efficacious evolutionary change.

[107] This is borne out by the fact that, for Segundo, religion exists for the sake of the world, not the world for the sake of religion. Commenting on a discourse of Pope Paul VI, Segundo observes: "The religious has often been identified only with the transcendent dimension of the individual. The Pontiff. . .returns to the religious its instrumental character: religion, rightly understood, humanizes the person. . . . '[It is] completely at the service of [human] good'" (*TC*, p. 71; italics mine; inclusive language substituted).

[108] As Segundo points out in his discussion of the "wages" of the work of Faith (which are not rewards), "glory [i.e., seeking incorruption]. . .is characteristic of all *authentic* projects, where truth is not shackled by injustice and bad faith is not the underlying attitude" (*HCP*, p. 74; italics Segundo's). In the biblical sense, glory refers to the weight or substance of something, that which makes it what it truly is and causes its inmost identity to be revealed. The term *anthropological glory* can thus be justified by pointing to the capacity of ideologies to realize truth. This is different from what Luther calls "glorying" in "works," which is counter to the logic of Faith (*HCP*, pp. 64-65 and p. 149). Yet a Reformation stress on faith alone runs counter to the notion that the "wages" of Faith is glory: "The glory of God and the defense of the Absolute do not entail relativizing historical reality in order to make room for the irruption of God alone" (*HCP*, p. 157). Instead, glory is the result of self-transcending love: "To comprehend and appreciate the divine quality that gives solidity and consistency to human beings' creative building. . .we must understand what exactly goes to make up the glory of God, . . .[which is] the tangible manifestation of the

divine presence [encountered]....in every human being who needs our love" (*ST*, p. 150; inclusive language substituted). See also *HCP*, p. 131; p. 213, n. 184; p. 157; p. 221, n. 233.

[109] *Infierno*, p. 23 (translation and inclusive language mine; italics Segundo's; version not edited by the author). In relying here and in the following pages on quotations from this unpublished transcript, I am relying on the word of Segundo himself about the relative weight of this work; for when, in a conversation with him at Regis College, Toronto, March 7, 1985, I discussed my intention to write about the absolute value of human action, he handed me the *Infierno* manuscript as an illuminating presentation of his theological position. Even though the transcript is a locally produced mimeographed version that has not been edited by Segundo, its significance is borne out by the fact that its central ideas appear consistently, although in random fashion, throughout Segundo's published works, notably *GHC*, pp. 162-167; *RC*, pp. 265 ff.; *HCP*, p. 137 and *passim;* and *EAJN*, p. 24 and *passim.* The benefit of quoting from *Infierno* is that it presents a focused, extended and in-depth discussion of what elsewhere shares space with other issues and concerns. Of additional interest is the conversational tone of the work, which reflects the informal character of its pastoral setting.

[110] As was seen in chapter two, however, not all action is so "lucky." Seemingly more often than not, especially when one leaves the sphere of interpersonal relations to consider action in its more complex political and ecological dimensions, action is in fact disconcertingly inefficacious.

[111] To speak of anthropological glory is of course to speak of action at its best, action functioning as a *praxis* of truth that is constructive in the way described in the story of the anointing. The action of the unknown woman is a display of anthropological glory insofar as it is capable of illumining the content of history and nature—in the case of her action, the outcome and meaning of Jesus' life—with a clarifying truth that brings out its intrinsic meaning and worth. And this is true even though, thanks to entropic effects of Sin in the gospel transmission, we do not even know her name.

[112] *EAJN*, p. 118.

[113] *RC*, p. 262 and p. 266. Segundo takes this notion from Rahner, whom he credits with its theological explication, but whom he criticizes for maintaining what he regards as an unbiblical dichotomy between the individual and universal levels of God's gratuitous will to save (see also *Infierno*, p. 51). On this subject elsewhere, in the context of a discussion about the existential notion of a fundamental option, Segundo argues that the historical Jesus replaces the decisive option with a historical project, i.e., the kingdom of God (*Infierno*, p. 30).

[114] *Infierno*, p. 24 (translation, inclusive language and italics mine). Preceding this statement, Segundo observes: "Each decision of mine is made before the absolute; there are no 'relative' decisions in which God is not implicated or in which I could give a yes or a no to a reality which is less than God. I am always deciding

a yes or a no to God, although in reduced form, because I am incapable of being absolutely logical in my acting, since I am the human being that I am. Knowing that logic leads me to understand the immensity of each one of my decisions, and I can not avoid speaking of heaven and hell because it is the central point of my Christian faith that in all my actions I am affecting God" (translation mine). Following this, he states: "We have to understand [hell] as a present dimension in all our options, since all of them, by placing us in face of the sister and brother who are in need, place us face to face with God and with the possibility of saying yes or no to God" (p. 25; translation and inclusive language mine).

115 *Infierno,* p. 57 (translation and inclusive language mine).

116 *Ibid.,* p. 56 (translation and inclusive language mine).

117 As will be pointed out in the next section in connection with the alternative eschatology of Frederich Gogarten, Segundo's eschatology is a way of addressing the problem of the relation between the absolute and the relative. This question was raised at the beginning of the twentieth century most notably by Ernst Troeltsch. For optimistic nineteenth-century categories of progress, however, Segundo substitutes the more realistic evolutionary categories of entropy and negentropy, represented in the anthropological sphere by the dialectic of Faith and Sin. On Segundo's awareness of the realism of his evolutionary categories, see *RC,* pp. 273-274, n. 15; *EAJN,* p. 22; *HCP,* p. 114.

118 *TC,* p. 72.

119 *GHC,* pp. 72-73 (first italics Segundo's; latter italics mine).

120 In 1939 Karl Rahner wrote an important essay entitled "Some Implications of the Scholastic Concept of Uncreated Grace," *Theological Investigations* I (Baltimore: Helicon, 1961), pp. 319-346, in which he stressed the principle—not at all foreign to the scholastic theology of grace as "inchoate" glory—that "the inner nature of grace as a whole in this life must allow of being more closely determined in terms of the nature of the ontological presuppositions of the immediate vision of God" (Rahner, p. 326). What Rahner solves by means of transcendental Thomistic categories, Segundo solves with biblical ones, with the notion of gift and task.

121 See *RC,* p. 251.

122 See *RC,* pp. 191-195. Segundo argues that an existential view sees freedom essentially as a test, a deciding for or against God. Such a view does not pertain to the decisiveness of the realization of a project (p. 195). While the notion of life after death—a strictly eternal eschatological destiny—thus restores the existential decisiveness of freedom vis-à-vis "eternal life," by itself it does little to support the importance of constructive action in history and nature.

123 *OIG,* pp. 37-42, pp. 46-49 and p. 53, n. 10.

124 As Segundo observes, only a complex eschatology can give meaning and value to history without obliterating the gratuitousness of grace as a project initiated by God (*HCP,* p. 151).

[125] See *RC*, p. 259. Segundo shows that God values human freedom by associating it with the intrinsically social project of the construction of history. In the validity of that project alone resides the hope of salvation not only for human social persons but for the cosmos.

[126] Segundo states this point clearly in "Intellecto y salvación," pp. 87-91, where he shows how such a shift is really a return to biblical ways of thinking (e.g., he shows how Paul always links salvation with concrete goods or evils, giving it a significance that is intramundane).

[127] Segundo explicitly distances his eschatology from the "already-not yet" schema of Oscar Cullman: "His 'already but not yet' does not show up as an anthropological dimension of action in history. It tells us that Christ has already triumphed but we cannot yet see the consequences of his victory. Those consequences are hidden in the mystery of God, as it were, and have no connection with, or impact on, human involvement in history. Indeed, they seem wholly to dispense with it. If human beings nevertheless *ought* to get involved, it is a *moral* duty deriving indirectly from justification....It is not that *the victory has need of our human involvement and commitment" (HCP*, pp. 180-181, n. 187; latter italics mine).

[128] From Rahner's perspective, for example, the resurrection of Jesus reveals that God's future is "already present and definitive in a hidden way" which orients history toward "realization of the possibility established by God in the beginning" ["Eschatology," in *Sacramentum Mundi* 2 (Montreal: Palm Publishers, 1968), p. 244 (italics Rahner's)].

[129] *HCP*, p. 137. This notion was already at the heart of Segundo's early work, where the meaning and value of history for God are dependent on the capacity of human freedom to give ontological content to a creation left incomplete by God (*Berdiaeff*, pp. 112-128). In later works, the significance of the historical Jesus and his kingdom *praxis* come increasingly to the fore until they become the center of an explicitly eschatological divine-human project centered on definitive realization of the kingdom of God (*HJS*, pp. 86-103; *RC*, pp. 35-128). An increasing reliance on biblical categories, especially the innovative ones of Paul, together with a refinement of Segundo's evolutionary teleology, eventually makes realization of the kingdom of God the *telos* of God's *mysterion* and a ruling datum of Segundo's eschatology. See *HCP*, pp. 137-138 and p. 215, notes 202 and 203; *RC*, pp. 265-268; and *EAJN*, p. 24, pp. 110-111 and pp. 114-116.

[130] See *RC*, p. 265 and *HCP*, pp. 136-137.

[131] *RC*, p. 55. See also *GHC*, p.72.

[132] *RC*, pp. 55-56.

[133] Perhaps in light of the traditional doctrine of creation *ex nihilo*, this formulation will appear unorthodox. However, why should it be the case that in creating a world, God is related to no one and nothing else? Given the data of revelation about the *mysterion*, it seems more fitting that *ex nihilo* refer to the impassioned character

of God's love than to the unlimitedness of God's power. God's love, which is creative power not in the abstract but in relation to the sufferings of creatures in the concrete, is neither threatened nor diminished by the gratuitous decision to embrace creatures in such a way that the efficacy of creation depends causally upon their own creative freedom.

[134] Of course, there is no such thing as a work's having *no* neighborly consciousness at all, since every work of human hands participates to however minute a degree in *some* vague awareness that there are other beings in the world. However, only those aspects of each human creation which embody neighborly sensitivity will last. The remainder of each project will be burned away as irrelevant, i.e., lacking in significance to the project of the *mysterion*, which is normed on earth as it is in heaven by the needs of the deprived.

[135] This is the reason, as was seen in chapter three, for Segundo's recurring insistence on an ethics of appropriateness—an ethics based not on the law or an absolute norm but on creativity, maturity and what is liberating of the neighbor.

[136] *Despair and Hope for Our Time* (Philadelphia: Pilgrim Press, 1970).

[137] Gogarten is in the Reformation tradition of *sola gratia* here. Segundo objects to that tradition on the grounds that, like Jesus' *praxis*, human action has a genuine anthropological causality vis-à-vis the kingdom of God and thus an eschatologically creative power (see *HJS*, p. 198, n. 17). With reference to the *sola Dei gloria* view of Reinhold Niebuhr on this point, for example, Segundo asks, "Is it possible to exercise *agape*. . .[self-transcending love] without exercising power over the causes of evil, be it physical or social in origin?" (*ibid.,* p. 64). For Segundo, there can be no eschatology of "God alone" because God is powerless over evil unless human beings act to alleviate suffering by making themselves neighbor to the deprived: "Unless we act with our freedom, there is no way for God to prevent suffering. . . .Our freedom has an immense value for God, because it can free our sisters and brothers from earthly hells, from sorrow" (*Infierno,* p. 56; translation and inclusive language mine). See also *RC,* p. 266; and *HCP,* p. 213, note 184 and p. 221, n. 233.

[138] In strong opposition to the notion of an "eschatological reserve" pertaining to God alone, this theme surfaces repeatedly in Segundo's work. In *GHC,* he writes: "The absolute eschatological dimension of salvation is present, not as something opposed to the present 'age,' but as its gratuitous and actual, even though still invisible absolutization" (p. 156). Similar statements occur in *LT,* p. 144, *HCP,* p. 157 and *RC,* p 23, n. 9. In addition, Segundo points out that it remains a considerable temptation for Christian theologians to lapse into a competitive mode, implying, for example, that the spheres of religion and politics, conceived of as representing the absolute sphere of transcendence on the one hand and the relative realm of earthly action on the other, have been ordained by "God" never to be "mixed." See *TC,* pp. 21-43 and 70-72.

[139] *GHC*, pp. 162-167. This is also the point of the entire text of *Infierno*.
[140] *RC*, p. 266 and p. 268. See also *GHC*, p. 147 and pp. 165-167.
[141] *HCP*, pp. 129-130.
[142] Here Segundo creatively rehabilitates the Tridentine notion of "merit." See *LT*, pp. 138-151.
[143] I think it is significant that Segundo criticizes Augustine for failing to give enough credence to the complexity of freedom (*HCP*, p. 221, n. 232). He believes that Luther achieved a wiser assessment of that complexity in his stress on the existential ambiguity of the *simul justus et peccator*. As has been seen, however, Segundo does not follow Luther's *sola Dei gloria* in the analysis of that complexity.
[144] The problem of historical relativity is a legacy of Enlightenment. One could ask whether, even when subjected to the critique represented by critical theory and, subsequently, political theology, an Enlightenment preoccupation with relativity takes sufficient account of the affrontive face of evil in a contextually determined way. The notion of context makes evil visible in the features of *specific* poor and oppressed persons. It makes evil audible in the radically distinctive voices of the many marginalized and deprived and makes apparent the utter helplessness and deprivation of the "disappeared," the erased and the dead. Among theologians, who are by no means the only people to be concerned about these issues, the problem of context is not only being taken into account by liberationists but is a central element of their theologies (*TC*, pp. 86-90).
[145] This "more" is of course precisely the heaven-sided dimension of grace, what from one point of view Edward Schillebeeckx, in the context of a doctrine of cooperative grace, calls the mystical element of Faith complementary to its political relevance (*On Christian Faith*, pp. 65-84), and from another point of view Reinhold Niebuhr, in the context of a Reformation stress on God alone, calls the culmination of justice in love (*The Nature and Destiny of Man*, Vol. II, pp. 246-247). With characteristic emphasis on the intramundane causality of human action, Segundo, relying on the categories of Paul, calls this "heaven-sided" dimension of the *mysterion* by a directly eschatological name: "the manifestation of the glorious liberty of the children of God" (*HCP*, p. 157 and pp. 153-154). Its significance for the making of a theologically intelligible account of the continuity between heaven and earth is crucial: "'Manifestation' should not be taken to mean that we are going to exchange historical reality for another, non-historical reality. Instead, it means that we are going to see how suprahistorical life is ultimately injected into what has been accomplished *in history*. . . .The glory of God. . .[does] not entail relativizing historical reality to make room for the irruption of God alone. The glory of God means seriously making human beings sharers in a joint construction project and giving them all they need to offer this cooperation, without which God alone will do nothing. The personal, creative stamp of each one of these human cooperators (*synergoi* in Greek) with God will be tested and verified in love, in 'mutual service.' Then it will

be inserted into the definitive reality, . . .[i.e.,] turned into God's new heaven and humanity's new earth, the new creation as the joint work of [God and human social persons]" (*HCP,* p. 157; italics Segundo's; the phrase in the latter brackets originally read "Father and children").

146Perhaps this is the meaning of the Pauline notion that disciples of Jesus are "fools for Christ's sake" (1 Cor. 4: 10). The logic of eschatological hope is ultimately the logic of the cross, which in the eyes of the deprived and those in solidarity with them, religious or not, comes across not only as "foolishness" and a "stumbling block" but as a terrible injustice—a "double-cross"—insofar as the countless crosses weighing down the world make it look as though in the face of evil God is powerless to save. Yet in the eyes of an anthropological faith that is normed by the life-story of Jesus in its entirety, i.e., the story as a whole of his life, *praxis,* death and resurrection, the cross is a door hewn out of a rock and the rock itself has flown open to reveal a power over Sin and death that is unprecedented in history and nature: the power to bring to life what is dead.

147See *HCP,* 152-153 and *HJS,* pp. 172-173.

KEY TO ABBREVIATIONS

Berdiaeff	*Berdiaeff: Une réflexion chrétienne sur la personne*
CCC	*The Community Called Church*
CIE	*The Christ of the Ignatian Exercises*
EAJN	*An Evolutionary Approach to Jesus of Nazareth*
EG	*Evolution and Guilt*
Etapas	*Etapas precristianas de la fe: Evolución de la idea de Dios en la Antiguo Testamento*
FI	*Faith and Ideologies*
GHC	*Grace and the Human Condition*
HCP	*The Humanist Christology of Paul*
HHJN	*El hombre de hoy ante Jesús de Nazaret*
HJS	*The Historical Jesus of the Synoptics*
HMPA	*The Hidden Motives of Pastoral Action*
Infierno	*Infierno: ¿Futuro o presente?*
JNYT	*Jesus of Nazareth Yesterday and Today*
LT	*The Liberation of Theology*
OIG	*Our Idea of God*
RC	*Reflexiones críticas*
ST	*The Sacraments Today*
TC	*Theology and the Church: A Response to Cardinal Ratzinger and a Warning to the Whole Church*
¿Utopia?	*La cristiandad, ¿una utopia? I. Los hechos. II. Los principios*

BIBLIOGRAPHY

I. Primary Sources

A. Books by Juan Luis Segundo

Existencialismo, filosofía y poesía: Ensayo de síntesis. Buenos Aires: Espaca-Calpe, 1948.

Función de la Iglesia en la realidad rioplatense. Montevideo: Barreiro y Ramos, 1962.

Etapas precristianas de la fe: Evolución de la idea de Dios en la Antiguo Testamento. Montevideo: Cursos de Complementación Cristiana, 1962.

Berdiaeff: Une réflexion chrétienne sur la personne. Paris: Montaigne, 1963.

Concepción cristiana del hombre. Montevideo: Mimeográfica "Luz," 1964.

La cristiandad, ¿una utopia? I. Los hechos. Montevideo: Mimeográfica "Luz," 1964.

La cristiandad, ¿una utopia? II. Los principios. Montevideo: Mimeográfica "Luz," 1964.

Esa comunidad llamada Iglesia. Buenos Aires: Carlos Lohlé, 1968. (*The Community Called Church.* Trans. John Drury. Maryknoll, N.Y.: Orbis Books, 1973).

Gracia y condición humana. Buenos Aires: Carlos Lohlé, 1968. (*Grace and the Human Condition.* Trans. John Drury. Maryknoll, N.Y.: Orbis Books, 1973).

De la sociedad a la teología. Buenos Aires: Carlos Lohlé, 1970.

Nuestra idea de Dios. Buenos Aires: Carlos Lohlé, 1970. (*Our Idea of God.* Trans. John Drury. Maryknoll, N.Y.: Orbis Books, 1973).

¿Que es un cristiano? Montevideo: Mosca Hermanos/S.A. Editores, 1971.

Los sacramentos hoy. Buenos Aires: Carlos Lohlé, 1971. (*The Sacraments Today.* Trans. John Drury. Maryknoll, N.Y.: Orbis Books, 1974).

Evolución y culpa. Montevideo: Carlos Lohlé, 1972. (*Evolution and Guilt.* Trans. John Drury. Maryknoll, N.Y.: Orbis Books, 1974).

Acción pastoral latinoamericana: Sus motivos ocultos. Buenos Aires: Búsqueda, 1972. (*The Hidden Motives of Pastoral Action: Latin American Reflections.* Trans. John Drury. Maryknoll, N.Y.: Orbis Books, 1978).

Masas y minorías en la dialéctica divina de la liberación. Buenos Aires: La Aurora, 1973.

Liberación de la teología. Buenos Aires: Carlos Lohlé, 1975. (*The Liberation of Theology.* Trans. John Drury. Maryknoll, N.Y.: Orbis Books, 1976).

El hombre de hoy ante Jesús de Nazaret. 3 Volumes. Madrid: Ediciones Cristiandad, 1982. {Vol. I: *Fe e ideología.* [*Faith and Ideologies.* Trans. John Drury. Maryknoll, N.Y.: Orbis Books/London: Sheed and Ward/Melbourne: CollinsDove*Publishers,* 1984.] Vol. II/1: *Historía y actualidad: Sinópticos y Pablo.* [*The Historical Jesus of the Synoptics.* Trans. John Drury. Maryknoll, N.Y.: Orbis Books/London: Sheed and Ward/Melbourne: CollinsDove*Publishers,* 1985 and *The Humanist Christology of Paul.* Trans. John Drury. Maryknoll, N.Y.: Orbis Books/London: Sheed and Ward, 1986.] Vol. II/2: *Historia y actualidad: Las cristologías en la espiritualidad.* [*The Christ of the Ignatian Exercises.* Trans. John Drury. Maryknoll, N.Y.: Orbis Books, 1987 and *An Evolutionary Approach to Jesus of Nazareth.* Trans. John Drury. Maryknoll, N.Y.: Orbis Books, 1988.]}

Teología abierta. 3 Volumes. Madrid: Ediciones Cristiandad, 1983-1984. [Second Spanish edition of *Teología abierta para el laico adulto* (Buenos Aires and Montevideo: Carlos Lohlé, 1968-1972), but with a new additional volume of critical reflections on the first edition: Vol. I: *Iglesia-Gracia;* Vol. II: *Dios/ Sacramentos/Culpa;* Vol. III: *Reflexiones críticas.*]

Infierno: ¿Futuro o presente? Pocitos: unpublished mimeographed transcript, Parish of San Juan Bautisto, 1983.

Theology and the Church: A Response to Cardinal Ratzinger and a Warning to the Whole Church. Trans. John W. Diercksmeier. London: Geoffrey Chapman and Minneapolis: Winston Press, 1985.

B. Articles by Juan Luis Segundo

"Transformación latinoamericana y conducta moral." *Cuadernos latinoamericanos de economía humana.* (Montevideo) No. 9 (1960), pp. 252-267.

"El circulo vicioso de la miseria: El universitario latinoamericana." *Mensaje* 2 (1962), pp. 478-483.

"Diagnostico politico de América Latina." *Mensaje* 2 (1962), pp. 656-661.

"Los caminos del desarrollo politico latinoamericano." *Mensaje* 2 (1962), pp. 701-707.

"La variable politica." *Revista Interamericana de ciencias sociales* 2 (Bogatá, 1963), pp. 239-293.

"Síntesis de la tipología socioeconomica." *Revista Interamericana de ciencias sociales* 2 (Bogatá, 1963), pp. 1-32.
"The Future of Christianity in Latin America." *Cross Currents* 12 (1963), pp. 273-281.
"Pastoral latinoamericana: Hora de decisión." *Mensaje* 4 (March-April, 1964), pp. 74-82.
"La función de la Iglesia." *Diálogo* 1:1 (December, 1965), pp. 4-7; I:2 (February, 1966), pp. 5-10, and I:3 (April, 1966), pp. 3-10.
"El diálogo Iglesia-mundo: reflexión." *Diálogo* 1:6 (October, 1966), pp. 3-7.
"¿La Iglesia, es necessaria?" *Diálogo* 1:7 (September, 1966), pp. 3-8.
"El diálogo Iglesia-mundo." *Diálogo* 1:9 (November, 1966), pp. 5-22.
"Lo que el concilio dice." *Diálogo* 1:10 (December, 1966), pp. 3-13.
"¿Qué nombre dar a la existencia cristiana?" *Perspectivas de Diálogo* 2:11 (January-February, 1967), pp. 3-9.
"The Church: A New Direction in Latin America." *Catholic Mind* 65 (March, 1967), pp. 43-47.
"La condición humana." *Perspectivas de Diálogo* 2:12 (March-April, 1967), pp. 30-35.
"Camilo Torres, sacerdocio y violencia." *Vispera* 1:1 (May, 1967), pp. 71-75.
"La vida eterna." *Perspectivas de Diálogo* 2:14 (June, 1967), pp. 83-89 and 2:15 (July, 1967), pp. 109-118.
"La dialectica del miedo." *Perspectivas de Diálogo* 2:17 (September, 1967), pp. 168-177.
"Un nuevo comienzo." *Vispera* 1:2 (August, 1967), pp. 39-43.
"Intellecto y salvación." In *Salvación y construcción del mundo*. Barcelona: Editores Nova Terra, 1967.
"America hoy." *Vispera* 1:2 (October, 1967), pp. 53-57.
"Profundidad de la gracia." *Perspectivas de Diálogo* 2:19 (November, 1967), pp. 235-240 and II:20 (December, 1967), pp. 249-255.
"Hacía un exegesis dinámica." *Vispera* 1:3 (October, 1967), pp. 77-84.
"¿Dios nos interesa o no?" *Perspectivas de Diálogo* 3:21 (March, 1968), pp. 13-16.
"Christianity and Violence in Latin America." *Christianity and Crisis* 28 (March 4, 1968), pp. 31-34.
"Del ateismo a la fe." *Perspectivas de Diálogo* 3:22 (April, 1968), pp. 44-47.
"Social Justice and Revolution." *America* 118 (April 27, 1968), pp. 574-577.
"El poder del habito." *Perspectivas de Diálogo* 3:23 (July, 1968), pp. 90-92.
"Padre, Hijo, Espiritu: Una historia." *Perspectivas de Diálogo* 3:23 (July, 1968), pp. 71-76.
"Padre, Hijo, Espiritu: Una sociedad." *Perspectivas de Diálogo* 3:24 (July, 1968), pp. 103-109.

"Padre, Hijo, Espiritu: Una libertad I." *Perspectivas de Diálogo* 3:25 (July, 1968), pp. 142-148.

"Padre, Hijo, Espiritu: Una libertad II." *Perspectivas de Diálogo* 3:25 (August, 1968), pp. 183-186.

"Has Latin America a Choice?" *America* 120 (February 22, 1969), pp. 213-216.

"¿Un Dios a nuestra imagen?" *Perspectivas de Diálogo* 4:32 (March, 1969), pp. 35-39.

"Fundamental Theology and Dialogue." In J.B. Metz, ed. *The development of Fundamental Theology. Concilium* 46. New York: Paulist Press, 1969, pp. 69-80.

"¿Hacía una Iglesia de izquierda?" *Perspectivas de Diálogo* 4:32 (April, 1969), pp. 35-39.

"Riqueza y probreza como obstáculos al desarrollo." *Perspectivas de Diálogo* 4:32 (April, 1969), pp. 54-56.

"Ritmos de cambio y pastoral de conjunto." *Perspectivas de Diálogo* 4:35 (July, 1969), pp. 131-137.

"¿Autoridad o qué?" *Perspectivas de Diálogo* 4:39-40 (December, 1969), pp. 270-272.

"Introduction." In *Iglesia latinoamericana ¿protesta o profecía?* Buenos Aires: Búsqueda, 1969. Pp. 8-17.

"Evangelización y humanización: Progreso del reino y progreso temporal." *Perspectivas de Diálogo* 5:41 (March, 1970), pp. 9-17.

"Confrontation over Latin America, Borderland of Despair." *Christian Order* (1970), pp. 458-466.

"Desarrollo y subdesarrollo: Polos teologicos." *Perspectivas de Diálogo* 5:43 (May, 1970), pp. 76-80.

"La ideología de un diario católico." *Perspectivas de Diálogo* 5:44-45 (June-July, 1970), pp. 136-144.

"El posible aporte de la teología protestante para el cristianismo latinoamericano en el futuro." *Cristianismo y sociedad* 8:22 (1970), pp. 41-49. ["Possible Contribution of Protestant Theology to Latin American Christianity in the Future." *Lutheran Quarterly* 22 (Fall, 1970), pp. 60-68.]

"Wealth and Poverty as Obstacles to Development." In *Human Rights and the Liberation of Man in the Americas.* Ed. Louis Colonnesse, pp. 23-31. Notre Dame: University of Notre Dame Press, 1971.

"La Iglesia chilena ante el socialismo I." *Marcha* No. 1558 (August 27, 1971).

"La Iglesia chilena ante el socialismo II." *Marcha* No. 1559 (September 4, 1971).

"La Iglesia chilena ante el socialismo III." *Marcha* No. 1560 (September 11, 1971).

"Education, Communication and Liberation: A Christian Vision." *IDOC International: North American Edition* (November 13, 1971), pp. 63-96.

"Liberación: Fe e ideología." *Mensaje* (July, 1972), pp. 248-254.

"Las elitas latinoamericanas: Problematica humana y cristiana ante el cambio social." In *Fe cristiana y cambio social en América Latina: Encuentro de El Escorial.* Salamanca: Sigueme, 1973, pp. 203-212.

"Teología y ciencias sociales." In *Fe cristiana y cambio social en América Latina: Encuentro de El Escorial.* Salamanca: Sigueme, 1973, pp. 285-295.

"On a Missionary Awareness of One's Own Culture." *Studies in the International Apostolate of Jesuits* 1 (1974), pp. 33-47.

"Reconciliación y conflicto." *Perspectivas de Diálogo* 9:86 (September, 1974), pp. 172-178.

"Fe e ideología." *Perspectivas de Diálogo* 9:89-90 (December, 1974), pp. 227-233.

"Theological Response to a Talk on Evangelization and Development." *Studies in the International Apostolate of Jesuits* (November, 1974), pp 79-82.

"Teología: Mensaje y proceso." *Perspectivas de Diálogo* 9:89-90 (December, 1974), pp. 259-270.

"Capitalism—Socialism: Theological Crux." In *The Mystical and Political Dimensions of the Christian Faith.* Ed. Claude Geffré and Gustavo Gutiérriez, pp. 105-123. *Concilium* 96. New York: Herder and Herder, 1974.

"Conversión y reconciliación en la perspectiva de la moderna teología de la liberación." *Cristianismo y sociedad* 13 (1975), pp. 17-25.

"Condicionamientos actuales de la reflexión teologica en Latinoamérica." In *Liberación y cautiverio: Debates en torno al método de la teología en América Latina.* Ed. Enrique Ruiz Maldonado, pp. 99-101. Mexico City: Comité Organizador, 1975.

"Statement by Juan Luis Segundo." In *Theology in the Americas.* Ed. Sergio Torres and John Eagleson, pp. 280-283. Maryknoll, N.Y.: Orbis Books, 1976.

"Liberation et évangile." *Relations* (Montreal) 36 (1976), pp. 151-155.

"Perspectivas para una teología latinoamericana." *Perspectivas de Diálogo* 9:17 (1977), pp. 9-25.

"Derechos humanos, evangelización e ideología." *Christus* (November, 1978), pp. 29-35.

"Faith and Ideologies in Biblical Revelation." In *The Bible and Liberation: Political and Social Hermeneutics.* Ed. Norman K. Gottwald, pp. 482-496. Maryknoll, N.Y.: Orbis Books, 1983.

"The Shift within Latin American Theology." Public lecture, Regis College, Toronto. March 22, 1983. Toronto: Regis College Press, 1983.

"Les deux théologies de la libération en Amérique latine." *Études* 361 (September, 1984), pp. 149-161.

"Les deux tendances actuelles de la théologie de la libération." *La documentation catholique* 81 (October 7, 1984), pp. 912-917.

"Two Theologies of Liberation." *Month* 17 (October, 1984), pp. 321-327.

"Is Liberation Theology a Bad Word? The Relevance of the Vatican Instruction for Theology." Unpublished lecture text, public lecture, Regis College, Toronto. March 14, 1985.
"Challenge to Rome: Two Theologies of Church and World—Excerpts from *Theology and The Church.*" *National Catholic Reporter* 21 (August 16, 1985).
"The Shift within Latin American Theology." *Journal of Theology for Southern Africa* 52 (September, 1985), pp. 17-29.
"Christ and the Human Being." *Cross Currents* 37 (Spring, 1986), pp. 39-67.

II. Secondary Sources

A. Selected books and articles dealing with the theology of Juan Luis Segundo

Baum, Gregory. "The Theological Method of Segundo's *The Liberation of Theology.*" *CTSA Proceedings* 32 (1977), pp. 120-124.
Buckley, Mary. "Feminist Perspectives on a Faith that Liberates." *Chicago Studies* 19 (Summer, 1980), pp. 129-143.
Cabestrero, Teófilo, ed. "A Conversation with Juan Luis Segundo, S.J." In *Faith: Conversations with Contemporary Theologians.* Maryknoll, N.Y.: Orbis Books, 1980, pp. 172-180.
Cook, Michael L. "Jesus from the Other Side of History: Christology in Latin America." *Theological Studies* 44 (June, 1983), pp. 258-287.
DeMuth, J. "Segundo: Latin American Church Irreversibly Altered." *National Catholic Reporter* 15 (February 16, 1979), p. 5.
"Editorial: God in a Changing World." *Studies* 76 (Spring, 1987), pp. 5-8.
Ferm, Dean W. "South American Liberation Theology." *Religion and Life* 48 (Winter, 1978), pp. 474-491.
Goizueta, Roberto S. "Review of *Faith and Ideologies.*" *Horizons* 12 (Fall, 1985), pp. 395-396.
Haight, Roger. "Book Reviews ... Juan Luis Segundo's *Liberation of Theology.*" *Emmanuel* 83 (1984), pp. 605-610.
_____. "Review of *Faith and Ideologies.*" *America* 145 (September 29, 1984), p. 173.
_____. "Review of *Faith and Ideologies.*" *Cross Currents* 34 (Spring, 1984), pp. 106-109.
_____. "A Political Interpretation of Jesus." *Cross Currents* 36 (Spring, 1986), pp. 85-90.
_____. "Segundo's Pauline Anthropology." *Cross Currents* 37 (Spring, 1987), pp. 99-104.

Hebblethwaite, Peter. "Liberation Thinker Rebuts: New Book Takes on Ratzinger Statement." *National Catholic Reporter* (August 16, 1985), pp. 1, 29.

Hennelly, Alfred T. "The Challenge of Juan Luis Segundo." *Theological Studies* 38 (March, 1977), pp. 125-135.

_____. "Review of *The Hidden Motives of Pastoral Action.*" *Theological Studies* 39 (December, 1978), pp. 807-808.

_____. "Review of *The Liberation of Theology.*" *Theological Studies* 38 (December, 1977), pp. 709-736.

_____. "Theological Method: The Southern Exposure." *Theological Studies* 38 (December, 1977), pp. 709-735.

_____. *Theologies in Conflict: The Challenge of Juan Luis Segundo.* Maryknoll, N.Y.: Orbis Books, 1979.

Jiménez Limón, Javier, S.J. "Sobre la cristología de Juan Luis Segundo." *Christus* 49 (August, 1984), pp. 57-61.

Kress, Robert. "Review of *The Liberation of Theology.*" *Horizons* 4 (Spring, 1977), p. 132.

Kroger, Joseph. "Prophetic-Critical and Practical-Strategic Tasks of Theology: Habermas and Liberation Theology." *Theological Studies* 46 (March, 1985), pp. 3-20.

Lakeland, Paul. "Responding to Liberation Theology: Interaction of Faith and Social Commitment." *Month* 13 (January, 1980), pp. 12-15.

_____. "Theological Trends: Political and Liberation Theology II: Liberation Theology." *The Way* 26 (April, 1986), pp. 145-154.

Leech, Kenneth. "Liberating Theology: The Thought of Juan Luis Segundo." *Theology* 84 (July, 1981), pp. 258-266.

Lowe Ching, Theresa. *Efficacious Love: Its Meaning and Function in the Theology of Juan Luis Segundo.* Lanham, Md.: University Press of America, 1989.

McCann, Dennis P. *Christian Realism and Liberation Theology: Practical Theologies in Creative Conflict.* Maryknoll, N.Y.: Orbis Books, 1981.

_____. "Political Ideologies and Practical Theology: Is There a Difference?" *Union Seminary Quarterly Review* 36 (Summer, 1981), pp. 243-257.

_____. "Review of *The Liberation of Theology.*" *Religious Studies Review* 3 (April, 1977), pp. 98-105.

Nevin, Michael. "The Historical Jesus." *The Month* 19 (March, 1986), p. 106.

Niemeyer, Gerhart. "Structure, Revolution and Christianity." *Center Journal* I (Winter, 1981), pp. 79-99.

O"Donnell, James G. "The Influence of Freud's Hermeneutic of Suspicion on the Writings of Juan Segundo." *Journal of Psychology and Theology* 10 (Spring, 1982), pp. 28-34.

Peel, David. "Juan Luis Segundo's *A Theology for Artisans of a New Humanity:* A Latin American Contribution to Contemporary Theological Understanding." *The Perkins School of Theology Journal* 30 (Spring, 1977), pp. 1-9.

Persha, Gerald J. *Juan Luis Segundo: A Study Concerning the Relationship between the Particularity of the Church and the Universality of Her Mission (1963-1977).* Maryknoll, N.Y.: Orbis Probe Editions, 1980.

Riddell, Roger. "Part I: The Liberation of Theology." *Month* 238 (May, 1977), pp. 149-153.

Roach, Richard R. "A New Sense of Faith." *Journal of Religious Ethics* 5 (Spring, 1977), pp. 135-154.

Sanks, T. Howland and B. Smith. "Liberation Ecclesiology: Praxis, Theory, Praxis." *Theological Studies* 38 (March, 1977), pp. 3-38.

_____. "Seminar on Theology and Social Sciences." *CTSA Proceedings* 32 (1977), p. 120.

Shields, David L. *Growing beyond Prejudices: Overcoming Hierarchical Dualisms.* Mystic, Connecticut: Twenty-Third Publications, 1986.

_____. "Liberation Anthropology: Segundo's Use of Teilhard de Chardin." *Studia Biblica et Theologica* 9 (1979), pp. 61-80.

Strain, Charles R. "Review of *Christian Realism and Liberation Theology*." *Religious Studies Review* 8 (1982), pp. 239-244.

Sweeney, John. "For the Builders of a New Ireland: The Theology of Juan Luis Segundo." *Furrow* 31 (December, 1980), pp. 738-739.

Tambasco, Anthony J. *The Bible for Ethics: Juan Luis Segundo and First World Ethics.* Washington, D.C.: University Press of America, 1981.

Tripole, Martin Ralph, S.J. "Segundo's Liberation Theology vs. an Eschatological Ecclesiology of the Kingdom." *Thomist* 45 (January, 1981), pp. 1-25.

Weir, J. Emmette. "The Bible and Marx: A Discussion of the Hermeneutics of Liberation Theology." *Scottish Journal of Theology* 35 (1982), pp. 337-350.

Wells, Harold. "Segundo's Hermeneutic Circle." *Journal of Theology of Southern Africa* 34 (March, 1981), pp. 25-31.

West, C. "Review of *Faith and Ideologies*." *Commonweal* 111 (Jan. 27, 1984), p. 53.

Williams, T. "Review of *Faith and Ideologies*." *New Blackfriars* 66 (May, 1985), p. 252.

B. Selected books and articles related to this study

Alves, Rubem A. *A Theology of Human Hope.* Washington, D.C.: Corpus Books, 1969.

Aquinas, Thomas. *Summa Theologiae.* Blackfriars Edition: Latin text and English translation. London: Eyre and Spottiswoode, 1963-1966.

Assmann, Hugo. *Practical Theology of Liberation.* Trans. Paul Burns. London: Search Press, 1975.

Augustine of Hippo. *Basic Writings of St. Augustine.* Vol. I. Whitney Oates, ed. New York: Random House, 1948.

Bateson, Gregory. *Mind and Nature: A Necessary Unity.* New York: Bantam Books, 1979.

_____. *Steps to an Ecology of Mind.* New York: Ballantine Books, 1972.

_____. "Conscious Purpose Versus Nature" in *The Dialectics of Liberation.* Ed. David Cooper. Middlesex, England: Penguin Books Ltd., 1968, pp. 34-49.

Baum, Gregory. "The Impact of Sociology on Catholic Theology." *CTSA Proceedings* 30 (1975), pp. 1-29.

_____. "Debate over Utopia." *Ecumenist* 18 (May-June, 1980), pp. 60-64.

_____. "The Meaning of Ideology." *CTSA Proceedings* 34 (1979), pp. 171-175.

_____. *Religion and Alienation: A Theological Reading of Sociology.* New York: Paulist Press, 1975.

_____., ed. *Sociology and Human Destiny.* New York: Seabury, 1980.

_____. "Theology and Ideology." *Ecumenist* 8 (Jan.-Feb., 1970), pp. 25-31.

Berdyaev, Nicholas. *The Destiny of Man.* Trans. Natalie Duddington. London: G. Bles/The Centenary Press, 1937.

_____. *Freedom and the Spirit.* Trans. Oliver F. Clarke. New York: Charles Scribner's Sons, 1935.

_____. *The Meaning of History.* Trans. George Reavey. Cleveland: Meridian Books, 1962 and 1936.

_____. *Solitude and Society.* Trans. George Reavey. London: G. Bles, The Centenary Press, 1938.

Berger, Peter L. and Thomas Luckmann. *The Social Construction of Reality: A Treatise on the Sociology of Knowledge.* New York: Doubleday Anchor Books, 1967.

Berryman, Phillip. "Latin American Liberation Theology." *Theological Studies* 34 (September, 1973), pp. 375-395.

_____. *Liberation Theology.* New York: Pantheon, 1987.

_____. *The Religious Roots of Rebellion: Christians in Central American Revolutions.* Maryknoll, N.Y.: Orbis Books, 1984.

Birch, Charles and John B. Cobb, Jr. *The Liberation of Life from the Cell to the Community.* Cambridge: Cambridge University Press, 1981 and 1984.

Bloch, Ernst. *Atheism in Christianity: the Religion of the Exodus and the Kingdom.* Trans. J.T. Swann. New York: Herder and Herder, 1972.

_____. *Man on His Own: Essays in the Philosophy of Religion.* Trans. E.B. Ashton. New York: Herder and Herder, 1970.

_____. *On Karl Marx.* New York: Herder and Herder, 1971.

_____. *A Philosophy of the Future.* Trans. John Cumming. New York: Herder and Herder, 1970.

Blondel, Maurice. *L'Action. Essai d'une critique de la vie et d'une science de la practique.* Paris: Alcan, 1893. [English translation: *Action: Essay on a Critique of Life and a Science of Practice.* Trans. Oliva Blanchette. Notre Dame: University of Notre Dame Press, 1984.]

_____. *The Letter on Apologetics and History and Dogma.* Trans. Alexander Dru and Illtyd Trethowan. London: Harvill Press, 1964.

Boff, Leonardo. *Liberating Grace.* Trans. John Drury. Maryknoll, N.Y.: Orbis Books, 1979.

Brown, Robert McAfee. *Theology in a New Key: Responding to Liberation Themes.* Philadelphia: Westminster, 1978.

Cabestrero, Teófilo, ed. *Faith: Conversations with Contemporary Theologians.* Trans. Donald D. Walsh. Maryknoll, N.Y.: Orbis, 1980.

CELAM (Second General Conference of Latin American Bishops). *The Church in the Present-Day Transformation of Latin America in the Light of the Council. Part II: Conclusions.* Third edition. Washington, D.C.: NCCB, 1979.

Coleman, John. A. *An American Strategic Theology.* New York: Paulist Press, 1982.

_____. "Vision and Praxis in American Theology." *Theological Studies* 37 (March, 1976), pp. 3-40.

Comblin, José. *The Church and the National Security State.* Maryknoll, N.Y.: Orbis, 1979.

_____. "Freedom and Liberation as Theological Concepts" in *The Mystical and Political Dimension of the Christian Faith.* C. Geffré and G. Gutiérrez, eds. *Concilium* 96. New York: Herder and Herder, 1974, pp. 92-104.

_____. "Humanity and the Liberation of the Oppressed." in *Is Being Human a Criterion of Being Christian?* C. Geffré and J.P. Jossua, eds. *Concilium* 155. New York: Seabury, 1982, pp. 74-80.

Concilium General Secretariat. "Utopia" in *The Problem of Eschatology.* Edward Schillebeeckx and Boniface Willems, eds. *Concilium* 41. New York: Paulist Press, 1969.

Cone, James H. *God of the Oppressed.* New York: Seabury, 1975.

Cormie, Lee. "The Hermeneutical Privilege of the Oppressed: Liberation Theology, Biblical Faith, and Marxist Sociology of Knowledge." *CTSA Proceedings* 33 (1978), pp. 155-181.

Daly, Gabriel. *Transcendence and Immanence: A Study in Catholic Modernism and Integralism.* Oxford: Clarendon Press, 1980.

Darlap, Adolph. "Time." *Sacramentum Mundi* 6. Montreal: Palm Publishers, 1970, pp. 257-262.

Davis, Charles. "From Inwardness to Social Action." *New Blackfriars* 67 (March, 1986), pp. 114-125.

_____. "Theology and Praxis." *Cross Currents* 23 (1973), pp. 154-168.

de Finance, Joseph. "Value." *Sacramentum Mundi* 6. Montreal: Palm Publishers, 1970, pp. 331-333.

Dussell, Enrique. *History and the Theology of Liberation: A Latin American Perspective.* Trans. John Drury. Maryknoll, N.Y.: Orbis, 1976.

_____. *A History of the Church in Latin America.* Trans. Alan Neely. Grand Rapids: Eerdmans, 1981.

Elizondo, Virgil and Norbert Greinacher, eds. *Tensions between the Churches of the First World and the Third World. Concilium* 144. New York: Seabury, 1981.

Enrigues Cardoso, Fernando and Enzo Faletto. *Dependency and Development in Latin America.* Trans. Marjorie Mattingly Urquidi. Berkeley: University of California Press, 1979.

Fabella, Virginia and Sergio Torres, eds. *Irruption of the Third World: Challenge to Theology.* Maryknoll, N.Y.: Orbis, 1983.

Falk, Harvey. *Jesus the Pharisee: A New Look at the Jewishness of Jesus.* Mahweh, N.J.: Paulist, 1985.

Ferm, Dean William. *Third World Liberation Theologies: An Introductory Survey.* Maryknoll, N.Y.: Orbis, 1986.

Fiorenza, Elizabeth Schüssler. *In Memory of Her: A Feminist Theological Reconstruction of Christian Origins.* New York: Crossroad, 1983.

Fiorenza, Francis Schüssler. "Latin American Liberation Theology." *Interpretation* 28 (October, 1974), pp. 441-457.

_____. "Political Theology and Liberation Theology." In *Liberation, Revolution and Freedom: Theological Perspectives.* Ed. T. McFadden. New York: Seabury, 1975, pp. 3-29.

_____. "Political Theology as Foundational Theology." *CTSA Proceedings* 32 (1977), pp. 142-177.

Flannery, Austen, ed. *Documents of Vatican II.* Grand Rapids: Eerdmans, 1975.

Freud, Sigmund. *Civilization and Its Discontents.* Trans. and ed. James Strachey. New York: W.W. Norton, 1961.

Freire, Paulo. *Pedagogy of the Oppressed.* Trans. Myra B. Ramos. Middlesex, England: Penguin Books Ltd., 1972.

Fromm, Erich. *Escape from Freedom.* New York: Avon Books, 1965 and 1972.

Gadamer, Hans-Georg. *Truth and Method.* Eng. trans. by Sheed and Ward Ltd., 1975. New York: Crossroad, 1982.

Geffré, Claude. *A New Age in Theology.* Trans. R. Shillenn *et al.* New York: Paulist Press, 1972.

Gogarten, Frederick. *Despair and Hope for Our Time*. Philadelphia: Pilgrim Press, 1970.

Gottwald, Norman K, ed. *The Bible and Liberation: Political and Social Hermeneutics*. Maryknoll, N.Y.: Orbis, 1983.

Gustafson, James. *Ethics from a Theocentric Perspective*. Chicago: University of Chicago Press, 1981.

Gutiérrez, Gustavo. "Liberation Praxis and Christian Faith." In R. Gibellini, ed. *Frontiers of Theology in Latin America*. Maryknoll, N.Y.: Orbis, 1979, pp. 1-33.

_____. "Liberation, Theology and Proclamation." In *The Mystical and Political Dimension of the Christian Faith*. C. Geffré and G. Gutiérrez, eds. *Concilium* 96. New York: Herder and Herder, 1974, pp. 57-77.

_____. *The Power of the Poor in History*. Trans. Robert R. Barr. Maryknoll, N.Y.: Orbis, 1983.

_____. *A Theology of Liberation: History, Politics and Salvation*. Trans. and ed. Sister Caridad Inga and John Eagleson. Maryknoll, N.Y.: Orbis, 1973.

Gutiérrez, Gustavo *et al*. *Salvación y Construcción del Mundo*. Ed. Dilapsa-Nova Terra. Santiago, Barcelona, 1968.

Haight, Roger. *An Alternative Vision: An Interpretation of Liberation Theology*. New York: Paulist Press, 1985.

_____. *The Experience and Language of Grace*. New York: Paulist Press, 1979.

_____. "Grace and Liberation: An Interpretation of History." *Thomist* 42 (October, 1978), pp. 539-581.

_____. "The Suppositions of Liberation Theology." *Thought* 58 (June, 1983), pp. 158-169.

_____. "Spirituality and Social Justice: A Christological Perspective." *Spirituality Today* 34 (Winter, 1982), pp. 312-325.

Halder, Alois. "Technology." *Sacramentum Mundi* 6. Montreal: Palm Publishers, 1970, pp. 205-210.

Harrison, Beverly W. "Challenging the Western Paradigm: *Theology in the Americas* Conference." *Christianity and Crisis* 35 (October 27, 1975), pp. 251-254.

Heidegger, Martin. *Being and Time*. Trans. John Maquarrie and Edward Robinson. New York: Harper and Row, 1962.

Heisenberg, Werner. *Tradition in Science*. New York: Seabury, 1983.

Herzog, Frederick. *Liberation Theology*. New York: Seabury, 1972.

Hertzog, J.A. "Liberation: Hermeneutics as Ideology Critique?" *Interpretation* 28 (October, 1974), pp. 387-403.

Hick, John. *Evil and the God of Love*. New York: Harper and Row, 1966.

"Instruction on Certain Aspects of the 'Theology of Liberation.'" Congregation for
the Doctrine of the Faith. *Origins* 14 (September 13, 1984), pp. 195-204.

Jay, Martin. *The Dialectical Imagination: A History of the Frankfurt School and the
Institute of Social Research,1923-1950.* Boston: Little, Brown and Company, 1973.

Kaiser, Edwin G. "Cosmic Evolution: The Contemporary Setting of Theology."
CTSA Proceedings 28 (1973), pp. 31-46.

Kant, Immanuel. *Religion within the Limits of Reason Alone.* New York: Harper
Torchbooks, 1960.

_____. "What Is Enlightenment?" In *Foundations of the Metaphysics of
Morals and What Is Enlightenment?* Indianapolis: Bobbs-Merrill, 1959.

Kaufman, Gordon D. *The Theological Imagination: Constructing the Concept of
God.* Philadelphia: Westminster, 1981.

Kerr, Fergus, O.P. "The Need for Philosophy in Theology Today." *New Blackfriars*
6 (June, 1984), pp. 248-260.

Kerstiens, Ferdinand. "Hope." *Sacramentum Mundi* 3. Montreal: Palm Publishers,
1969.

Kittel, Gerhard, and Gerhard Friedrich, eds. *Theological Dictionary of the New
Testament.* Volume IX. Trans. and ed. Geoffrey W. Bromily. Grand Rapids:
Eerdmanns, 1974.

_____. *Theological Dictionary of the New Testament.* Abridged in One
Volume. Eerdmanns: Grand Rapids, 1985.

Lalande, André, ed. *Vocabulaire technique et critique de la philosophie.* Fifth edition.
Paris: Presses Universitaires de France, 1947. Also fourth edition, vols. I and
III. Paris: Librarie Félix Alcan, 1932.

Lamb, Matthew L. *Solidarity with Victims: Toward a Theology of Social Transformation.* New York: Crossroad, 1982.

_____. "The Theory-Praxis Relationship in Contemporary Christian The-
ologies." *CTSA Proceedings* 31 (1976), pp. 149-178.

Langan, John. "Liberation Theology in a Northern Context." *America* 140 (January
27, 1979), pp. 46-49.

Lobkowics, Nicholas. *Theory and Practice: History of a Concept from Aristotle to
Marx.* Notre Dame and London: University of Notre Dame Press, 1967.

Lonergan, Bernard. "Theology and Praxis." *CTSA Proceedings* 32 (1977), pp. 1-
16.

Luther, Martin. *Christian Liberty.* Harold Grimm, ed. Philadelphia: Fortress, 1957.

Machovec, Milan. *A Marxist Looks at Jesus.* London: Darton, Longman & Todd,
1976.

Mahan, Brian and L. Dale Richesin, eds. *The Challenge of Liberation Theology: A
First World Response.* Maryknoll, N.Y.: Orbis Books, 1981.

Mannheim, Karl. *Ideology and Utopia: An Introduction to the Sociology of Knowledge.* Trans. L. Wirth and E. Shils. New York: Harcourt, Brace Johanovich, 1936.

Marx, Karl and Frederick Engels. *The German Ideology: Part One with Selections from Parts Two and Three and Supplementary Texts.* Ed. C.J. Arthur. New York: International Publishers, 1981.

McDermott, Brian O. *What Are They Saying about the Grace of Christ?* New York: Paulist, 1984.

Metz, Johann Baptist. "Creative Hope." In *New Theology No. 5.* Martin E. Marty and Dean G. Peerman, eds. Toronto: Macmillan, 1969, pp. 130-141.

_____, ed. *The Evolving World and Theology. Concilium* 26. New York: Paulist Press, 1967.

_____. *Faith in History and Society: Toward a Practical Fundamental Theology.* Trans. David Smith. New York : Crossroad, 1980.

_____. *Theology of the World.* Trans. William Glen-Doepel. New York: Seabury, 1973.

Midgley, Mary. *Beast and Man: The Roots of Human Nature.* New York: New American Library, 1978.

Miguez Bonino, José. *Doing Theology in a Revolutionary Situation.* Philadelphia: Fortress, 1975.

Min, Anselm K. "The Vatican, Marxism, and Liberation Theology." *Cross Currents* 34 (Winter, 1984-85), pp. 439-455.

Moltmann, Jürgen. *God in Creation: A New Theology of Creation and the Spirit of God.* Trans. Margaret Kohl. San Francisco: Harper and Row, 1985.

_____. *Theology of Hope: On the Ground and the Implications of a Christian Eschatology.* New York: Harper and Row, 1967.

Monod, Jacques. *Chance and Necessity: An Essay on the Natural Philosophy of Modern Biology.* London: Fontana/Collins, 1974.

Murdoch, Iris. *The Sovereignty of Good.* London: Routledge & Kegan Paul, 1970.

Murray, John Courtney. *The Problem of God Yesterday and Today.* New Haven and London: Yale University Press, 1964.

Niebuhr, Reinhold. *The Nature and Destiny of Man.* Volumes I and II. New York: Charles Scribner's Sons, 1943.

Ogden, Schubert. *Faith and Freedom: Toward a Theology of Liberation.* Nashville: Abingdon, 1979.

_____. "The Faith We Hold in Common—or Do We?" Unpublished manuscript. Paper delivered at the Faith and Order Conference of the Texas Conference of Churches. Presbyterian Mo-Ranch (October 19-21, 1973).

_____. *The Reality of God and Other Essays.* New York: Harper and Row, 1977.

Ortega y Gasset, José. *The Revolt of the Masses.* New York: W.W. Norton, 1932.

Pesch, Otto H. "Existential and Sapiential Theology—The Theological Confrontation between Luther and Thomas Aquinas" in *Catholic Scholars Dialogue with Luther*. Jared Wicks, ed. Chicago: Loyola University Press, 1970, pp. 61-81.

Post, Werner. "Theory and Practice." *Sacramentum Mundi* 6. Montreal: Palm Publishers, 1970, pp. 246-249.

Rahner, Karl. "Christology within an Evolutionary View of the World." *Theological Investigations* 5. Baltimore: Helicon Press, 1966, pp. 157-192.

_____. "Concerning the Relationship between Nature and Grace." *Theological Investigations* 1. Baltimore: Helicon Press, 1961, pp. 297-346.

_____. "Current Problems in Christology." *Theological Investigations* 1. Baltimore: Helicon Press, 1961, pp. 149-200.

_____. "Eschatology." *Sacramentum Mundi* 2. Montreal: Palm Publishers, 1968.

_____. *Foundations of the Christian Faith: An Introduction to the Idea of Christianity*. Trans. William V. Dych. New York: Crossroad, 1978.

_____. "The Hermeneutics of Eschatological Assertions." *Theological Investigations* 4. New York: Seabury, 1974, pp. 323-346.

_____. "History of the World and Salvation History." *Theological Investigations* 5. Baltimore: Helicon Press, 1966, pp. 97-114.

_____. "Nature and Grace." *Theological Investigations* 4. New York: Seabury, 1974, pp. 165-188.

_____. "Reflections on the Unity of the Love of Neighbor and the Love of God." *Theological Investigations* 6. Baltimore: Helicon Press, 1966, pp. 231-249.

_____. "Salvation." *Sacramentum Mundi* 6. Montreal: Palm Publishers, 1970.

_____. "The Theological Concept of *Concupiscentia*." *Theological Investigations* 1. Baltimore: Helicon Press, 1961, pp. 347-382.

_____. "Theology of Freedom." *Theological Investigations* 6. Baltimore: Helicon Press, 1969, pp. 178-196.

_____. "Utopia and Reality." *Theology Digest* 32 (Summer, 1985), pp. 139-144.

_____. "Works." *Sacramentum Mundi* 6. Montreal: Palm Publishers, 1970, pp. 373-375.

Rahner, Karl and Herbert Vorgrimler. *Concise Theological Dictionary*. Trans. R. Strachan *et al.* Second edition. London: Burns & Oates, 1983.

Rauschenbusch, Walter. *A Theology for the Social Gospel*. Nashville: Abingdon, 1917, 1961, 1978, 1981.

Ricoeur, Paul. *The Conflict of Interpretations: Essays in Hermeneutics*. Evanston: Northwestern University Press, 1974.

_____. *Hermeneutics and the Human Sciences: Essays on Language, Action and Interpretation.* John B. Thompson, ed. Cambridge: Cambridge University Press, 1981.

_____. "Philosophical Hermeneutics and Theological Hermeneutics: Ideology, Utopia and Faith." In *The Center for Hermeneutical Studies in Hellenistic and Modern Culture, Protocol of the Seventeenth Colloquy.* Vol. 17. Berkeley: University of California Center for Hermeneutical Studies, November, 1975.

_____. *Political and Social Essays.* David Stewart and Joseph Bien, eds. Athens: Ohio University Press, 1974.

Rohner, Peter. "Will." *Sacramentum Mundi* 6. Montreal: Palm Publishers, 1970, pp. 356-359.

Rondet, Henri. *The Grace of Christ: A Brief History of the Theology of Grace.* Trans. and ed. Tad Guzie. Westminster, Md.: Newman Press, 1967.

Ruether, Rosemary Radford. *Liberation Theology: Human Hope Confronts Christian History and American Power.* New York: Paulist Press, 1972.

_____. *Sexism and God-Talk: Toward a Feminist Theology.* Boston: Beacon Press, 1983.

Scannone, Juan Carlos. "La relación teoria-praxis en la teología de la liberación." *Christus* 40 (June, 1977), pp. 10-16.

_____. "The Theology of Liberation—Evangelical or Ideological?" *Concilium* 93 (1974), pp. 147-156.

Schillebeeckx, Edward. *Jesus: An Experiment in Christology.* Trans. Hubert Hoskins. New York: Crossroad, 1979.

_____. *Christ: The Experience of Jesus as Lord.* Trans. John Bowden. New York: Crossroad, 1980.

_____. "Liberation Theology between Medellín and Puebla." *Theology Digest* 28 (Spring, 1980), pp. 3-7.

_____. *On Christian Faith: The Spiritual, Ethical, and Political Dimensions.* New York: Crossroad, 1987.

_____ and Boniface Willems, eds. *The Problem of Eschatology. Concilium* 41. New York: Paulist, 1969.

Sobrino, Jon. *Christology at the Crossroads: A Latin American Approach.* Trans. John Drury. Maryknoll, N.Y.: Orbis, 1978.

_____. *Jesus in Latin America.* Maryknoll, N.Y.: Orbis, 1987.

Sœlle, Dorothy. *Political Theology.* Trans. John Shelley. Philadelphia: Fortress Press, 1974.

Splett, Jörg. "Symbol." *Sacramentum Mundi* 6. Montreal: Palm Publishers, 1970, pp. 199-201.

Swidler, Leonard. "The Pharisees in Recent Catholic Writing." *Horizons* 10 (Fall, 1983), pp. 267-287.

Teilhard de Chardin, Pierre. *The Phenomenon of Man*. New York: Collins, Fontana Books, 1959.

TeSelle, Eugene. "The Problem of Nature and Grace." *The Journal of Religion* 45 (July, 1965), pp. 238-241.

Thomas, Lewis. "Things Unflattened by Science" in *Late Night Thoughts on Listening to Mahler's Ninth Symphony*. New York: Bantum Books, 1984, pp. 68-80.

Tillich, Paul. *Dynamics of Faith*. New York: Harper Torchbooks, 1957.

_____. *Systematic Theology*. Three volumes. Chicago: University of Chicago Press, 1951-1963.

Torres, Sergio and John Eagleson, eds. *Theology in the Americas*. Maryknoll, N.Y.: Orbis, 1976.

Toulmin, Stephen. *The Return to Cosmology: Postmodern Science and the Theology of Nature*. Berkeley and Los Angeles: University of California Press, 1982.

Tracy, David. *Blessed Rage for Order: The New Pluralism in Theology*. New York: Crossroad, 1975.

Tracy, David and Nicholas Lash, eds. *Cosmology and Theology*. *Concilium* 166. New York: Seabury, 1983.

Troeltsch, Ernst. *The Absoluteness of Christianity and the History of Religions*. Richmond: John Knox Press, 1971.

Vermes, Geza. *Jesus the Jew*. London: SCM, 1973, 1983.

Vidales, Raul. "Methodological Issues in Liberation Theology." In R. Gibellini, ed. *Frontiers of Theology in Latin America*. Trans. John Drury. Maryknoll, N.Y.: Orbis, 1979, pp. 34-57.

Vidler, A.R. *The Church in an Age of Revolution*. New York: Penguin Books, 1971.

von Balthasar, Hans Urs. *The Glory of the Lord*. Vol. I. Trans. Erasmus Leiva-Merikakis and ed. Joseph Fessio and John Riches. New York: Crossroad, 1982.

Walsh, Jerome. "Despair as a Theological Virtue in the Spirituality of *Ecclesiastes*." *Biblical Theology Bulletin* 12 (1982), pp. 46-49.

Wildiers, N. Max. *The Theologian and His Universe: Theology and Cosmology from the Middle Ages to the Present*. Trans. Paul Dunphy. New York: Seabury, 1982.

Woschitz, Karl. "Utopia." *Sacramentum Mundi* 6. Montreal: Palm Publishers, 1970.

GENERAL INDEX

Action: absolute responsibility of, 244; definition of, xix; deriving criteria for, 137-138; eschatological causality of, 237, 240; eschatological logic of, 226, 233-235; eschatological worthwhileness of, 18-19, 233; freedom and, 2-10, 10-14; logic of, xvi-xvii, 10, 17-18, 231, 237; logic of in relation to truth, 129-134; mixed nature of, 62n.136, 105n.18, 219, 244; of God, 9, 33-34; relevance of Jesus to, 18; structure of in grace, 19; value to God, 48n.41, 232, 245

Analogy: and difference, 109n.36; and meaning of Sin, 80; theory of evolution and, 43n.12

Anthropocentrism: contrasted with cosmocentrism, xxx-xxxi n.51; of Christian scriptures, 223; and evolutionary theory, 42n.10; of Segundo's eschatology, 222-224

Anthropological faith (*see also* Faith): and conflicting truth claims, 130; definition of, 11; and efficacy, 50n.53, 51n.59; and ideologies, 13-14, 150, 163-165, 176n.15; as knowledge, 12; and logic of action, 11-13, 50n.58; and objec-

tive reality, 14-16; and self-validating premises, 131; as source of *praxis*, 130-131, 159; and truth, 14, 51n.61, 130; and values, 11; vocation of in grace, 25-26

Anthropomorphism, 115n.78

Atheism: contribution of to theism, 26-27; as critique of God-language, 60n.120

Augustine: derogatory connotations of sinful freedom in, 113-114n.68; grace and freedom in, 107n.25

Bateson, Gregory: ecological categories of, 4, 42n.11, 44n.22, 77, 207; digital and iconic language in, 114n.71; Segundo's use of categories of, 251n.16

Bloch, Ernst: on utopia, 249n.6

Blondel, Maurice: influence of, xxviii-xxix n.45; on the logic of action, 49n.50; on the nature of the action of God, 34, 179n.35; on revelation, 179n.33

Causality (*see also* Historical causality): nature of in grace, xviii, 55n.90, 181n.45, 241; and realization of kingdom of God, xxix n.47

Chance: manifestation of freedom and, 5; and newness, 43-44n.15;

and project-mindedness of evolution, 45n.26
Charism: eschatological orientation
of, 62n.131; grace as, 28-32; as
learning to learn, 4; and love, 31;
and *mysterion*, 237-238, 242
Christology: as "antichristology",
174-175n.3, 175n.6; as project-
christology, 60n.122; as Spirit-
christology, 60n.122, 181-182n.47
Concupiscence: and ideologies,
102n.2, 206; as synonym for
entropy, 83
Context: North American experience
and, xii-xiv, xxiii n.20; impact of
Latin American on Segundo's
theology, 94-95; revelation and,
103nn.4, 5; and liberation of
theology from fear of political
involvement, 118n.99; and visibility of evil, 268n.144
Cosmogony, 7
Creation: completion of in glory, 246-
247; criticism of Segundo's
doctrine of, 47-48n.40, 260-
261n.87; and doctrine of grace, 8,
42n.7, 209, 238-239, 240;
eschatological character of, 209,
229-230, 238-239; *ex nihilo*, 39,
65nn.161, 162, 266-267n.133;
incompleteness of, xviii, 2, 7-8,
27, 41-42n.6; Sin as medium of,
99; slowness of, 42n.9, 45n.23; of
a world that is good, 7-10
Cross: efficacy of, 28-29; logic of,
269n.146
Cullman, Oscar: Segundo's criticism
of "already-not yet" schema in,
266n.127
Death: ecological logic of, 113n.66,
157-158, 188nn.106, 107; and

entropy, 45n.29, 61-62n.129;
injustice and, 158-159; of Jesus,
28-29, 46n.32, 246; Jesus' view
of, 187-188n.105
Difference that makes a difference, a:
definition of, 44n.22; and manifestation of freedom, 4-5
Discipleship: definition of, 174n.1; as
spirituality, 171-172; task of, xxi
n.2, 61n.126, 170, 172
Ecological density of reality: characteristics of, 79; and efficacy of
Faith, 84-86; explained, 71,
104n.12; faiths and ideologies
and, 14-16; and gratuitousness of
results, 16; and Sin, 79
Ecology: effects on evolutionary
categories, 77, 44n.18; effects on
theology, xiii-xiv, 78-79, 96; lack
of interest of liberation theologies
in, xiii; mentality of, 52n.66;
Segundo's criticism about, xxv-
xxvi n.27
Egotism, 116n.84; mixed with love,
219, 62n.136; ontological disvalue
of, 219-220, 260n.79
Entropy (*see also* Sin): abuse of,
257n.55; and efficacy, 82; and
grace, 5, 82; gratuitousness of, 5;
and love, 232-233; and manifestation of freedom, 4-6; and
negentropy, 82, 208, 256n.44; and
quantitative dimension of reality,
44n.18; as *raison d'être* of creation, 221; sleep as example of,
119n.104; and suffering, 6; and
tolerance for error, 206
Eschatology: anthropological character of Segundo's, 222-224; characteristics of, 175n.4, 233-234;
distinctiveness of Segundo's, 243-

God, 122n.116; and knowledge of
God, 58-59n.111; of the saints,
48n.41; and theory, 50n.57, 58-
59n.111, 131
Prayer: for the coming of the kingdom, 173, 193n.148, 195; and
God's values, 213, 258n.59
Rahner, Karl: causality in, 181n.45;
and doctrine of concupiscence,
83; doctrine of cooperative grace
in, xiv; doctrine of salvation in,
59n.112, 63n.151; contrasted with
Metz, 59n.116; optimism of
compared with Segundo's, 116-
117n.89; on resurrection of Jesus,
266n.128; Segundo's criticisms
of, 64n.154, 112n.58, 264n.113
Rauschenbusch, Walter, xi, xxii n.15,
51n.64
Religion: function of, 263n.107
Resurrection (in general): of projects,
254nn.28, 29
Resurrection of Jesus: as clarifying
datum, 54n.79, 252n.18; as
eschatological "setting",
191n.137, 219; and Faith,
57n.100; as inseparable from his
praxis, 61n.125, 144, 143-144,
180-181n.43; redundancy of,
191nn. 139, 140; and truth, 169
Revelation: appropriation of as an
ethical task, 135; and
christological categories, 192-
193n.147; criterion of, 179n.32;
distinguished from grace, 144-
145; as educative process, 164;
hermeneutical interpretation and,
126; nature of, 137-141, 175n.8,
179n.34; relevance of, 180n.37;
and "signs from heaven", 135-
137, 149-150; stages of,

192n.146; and task of theology,
142-146, 252-253n.21,
262nn.101, 102; and validity of
love, 168
Salvation: eschatological, 203-204; as
historical project, 57n.103; and
the intellect, 57n.102; as *kairos*,
207; and liberation, xiv, 204-206,
211, 237, 253n.24; liberation of
freedom and, 19-21; logic of
action and, 18-19; and *praxis* of
Jesus, 142, 148; and resurrection,
205; Segundo's shift in concept
of, 238-240
Sartre, Jean Paul: view of freedom of,
26-27
Schillebeeckx, Edward: on evil as
demand for creative action,
108n.27; Jesus' *Abba*-experience
in work of, x; on mystical dimension of faith, 268-269n.145;
negative contrast experience in
work of, xxiii n.17; scandal of
suffering in work of, 46n.33
Sensitive heart: and bad faith, 250n.9;
characteristics of, 133-134,
177nn.18, 23, 253n.23; relation to
faiths and ideologies, 216-217
Sin (*see also* Guilt): as capacity to
undercut hope, 254n.33; characteristics of, 80-86; as
concupiscence, 83; as condition
for working of Faith, 81-82,
113n.67, 208, 219-220, 263n.106;
as condition for realization of
love, 218-219, 221; as distinguished from sin, 76-77, 103n.8,
113-114n.68, 120n.108; and
God's project, 84; and grace, 96-
97, 118n.98; and the logic of
action, 51n.61, 83-84, 97; as